WOMEN
◆ AND MEN ◆
IN SOCIETY

WOMEN
◆ AND MEN ◆
IN SOCIETY

Cross-Cultural Perspectives
on Gender Stratification

Second Edition

Charlotte G. O'Kelly
Providence College

Larry S. Carney
Rhode Island College

Wadsworth Publishing Company
Belmont, California
A Division of Wadsworth, Inc.

Cover: Thailand hill tribe couple.
Photo by J. Brignola / © The Image Bank West.

Sociology and Anthropology Editor: Sheryl Fullerton
Production Editor: Hal Humphrey
Cover Designer: Paula Shuhert
Print Buyer: Karen Hunt
Copy Editor: Elaine Linden
Composition: Omegatype Typography, Inc.

Printed in the United States of America

2 3 4 5 6 7 8 9 10—90 89 88 87 86

ISBN 0-534-06144-3

Library of Congress Cataloging-in-Publication Data

O'Kelly, Charlotte G.
    Women and men in society.

    Includes index.
    1. Sex role—Cross-cultural studies.   2. Sexism—
Cross-cultural studies.   3. Sexual division of
labor—Cross-cultural studies.   I. Carney, Larry S.
II. Title.
HQ1075.037 1986   305.3   85-15391
ISBN 0-534-06144-3

To Seth, Adam, and Robin

◆ PREFACE ◆

The treatment of case studies in this edition of *Women and Men in Society: Cross-Cultural Perspectives on Gender Stratification* has been considerably revised and expanded in light of new scholarly contributions to the study of gender stratification as well as world and national events which have had important impact on the relations between women and men in contemporary societies.

Larry Carney has joined Charlotte O'Kelly in carrying out this revision. The result represents not only our efforts at collaboration on this project, but also our exchange of ideas, criticism, and support through a number of years of mutual preoccupation with the comparative study of gender relations.

In addition to the revisions and expansion of materials contained in the first edition of this text, new case studies on Sweden, Japan, Ghana, Iran, China, and Cuba have been added. A visit to Cuba in 1978, a brief visit to Hong Kong and China in 1983, and a nine-month stay in Japan in 1983 were helpful in adding some first-hand impressions to our consideration of available research on three of these cases. We also carried out research on women and social change while in Japan, and the section in Chapter 7 on that country reflects our preliminary efforts in analyzing some of our findings.

We have eliminated chapters on sexism in social scientific views and theoretical perspectives on gender relations in this edition.

Considerations of space were involved in the first deletion, but so was our belief that the gender biases characteristic of much research on gender relations are more widely known and condemned than they were a few years ago. (Although recent developments—such as the persistent onslaught against the legitimacy of gender studies and the failure to incorporate gender perspectives in standard history texts—have somewhat tempered our optimism in this regard.) The second deletion is our response to the suggestion of some reviewers of the first edition that information concerning theories of gender relations would probably be more useful in a book of this kind if it were incorporated at relevant places throughout our analyses of the case studies. This suggestion seemed a good one to us, and we have rearranged our theoretical materials—and added some new ones—using this approach.

We would like to acknowledge the help and support of the following persons and organizations in the preparation of this revision: the Fulbright Program, Providence College and its Fund for Aid to Faculty Research, Kyushu University, and Seinan Gakuin University for their support of our research on Japan; Kyoko Katsuki for her generous help in interviewing Japanese women, translating materials, reviewing the chapter on Japan, and helping us understand what we were reading and hearing about men and women in Japan; the Agora women's group in Fukuoka for reviewing the chapter on Japan; Professor Hiroko Hayashi of Fukuoka University; Professor Yoko Sakaoka of Kumamoto Business University; Minako Nakahara; the National Endowment for the Humanities for its fellowship to participate in Dr. Mary Lefkowitz's Summer Seminar on "Women in Antiquity" at Wellesley College which helped us in revising the chapter on agrarian societies; Professor Lefkowitz for her invaluable help in reading and commenting on several revisions of Chapter 5 and for the insights and guidance provided by her seminar; Rhoda Halperin of the University of Cincinnati, Jennie McIntyre of the University of Maryland, Margaret L. Signorella of Pennsylvania State University, and Jane C. Hood of the University of New Mexico, who reviewed earlier drafts of this manuscript; to the Rockefeller Library at Brown University, Phillips Memorial Library of Providence College, and the James P. Adams Library of Rhode Island College; Barbara Farrell, interlibrary loan librarian at Providence College, for her help in locating dozens of obscure books and articles; and to our editors Sheryl Fullerton and Hal Humphrey and the staff of Wadsworth Publishing Company, who have helped us bring this second edition to completion.

Finally, we would like to acknowledge an intellectual debt to Arthur J. Vidich. Arthur was not associated with the writing of this book and is, therefore, in no way responsible for its viewpoints, possible errors, or shortcomings. Nevertheless, throughout a distinguished career, his work has exemplified the best of what can happen when the critical traditions of anthropology and sociology find common ground in the attempt to broaden our understanding of where we have come from, where we are, and where we may be going as women and men in the modern world. Our conviction as to the continuing relevance of these traditions to the understanding of the human condition has shaped our own efforts to produce this text on comparative gender stratification.

◆ CONTENTS ◆

WOMEN
◆ AND MEN ◆
IN SOCIETY

CHAPTER 1

Gender Stratification in Cross-Cultural Perspective

The general topic of this book is what social scientists call *gender stratification:* To what degree and in what ways do men and women enjoy different access to and control over the scarce economic, political, social, and cultural resources in a particular society?

Gender stratification was largely ignored as a theoretical and empirical research problem until the revival of feminism in the late sixties and seventies drew both public and academic attention to "the woman problem." The few social scientists who had puzzled over the origins, maintenance, and evolution of gender stratification before the sixties tended to accept male dominance and female subordination as either biologically or socially necessary or both. It seemed only "natural." Evidence of gender equality was overlooked, denied, or explained away, and the actual range and diversity in gender roles and the degree of gender stratification in human society was accorded little significance. The *androcentric*, male-centered, focus of science blinded practitioners from the various branches of science to the need to explain gender stratification.[1]

The past two decades have seen a burgeoning of interest in this area. Sociologists, anthropologists, psychologists, political scientists, economists, and even biologists have pursued empirical and theoretical studies of gender stratification. The issues have not all been clarified, of course; disagreement is rife. But important steps have been taken to ask the appropriate questions and to begin to suggest answers.[2]

It is important to note that gender stratification, male dominance, and female subordination are not constants. They vary from society to society. They also vary within a society. Different social classes and racial and ethnic groups in the same society can differ in the relative advantage they accord to males versus females.

In this book we analyse the nature and degree of gender stratification in different types of human societies and subgroups within societies. We also try to trace out the linkages between different gender stratification systems and practices and the wider social, economic, cultural, political, and environmental contexts. What factors promote equality between men and women? What factors promote inequality, and what forms does the inequality take?

We attempt to integrate and synthesize data on a wide range of contemporary and historical studies to ascertain the structural, cultural, psychological, and biological processes leading to and flowing from various gender roles and gender stratification systems. Dialectical processes seem to be at work in the development and evolution of gender stratification systems. Certain environmental, economic, political, and social circumstances encourage people to devise certain relationships and practices to solve the problems they face. But once a set of practices and relationships has been established, this will influence the possible future choices that the people will be able to make when faced by new circumstances and new problems.

Primarily, we analyse the dialectical forces that encourage or hinder the development of different types of gender stratification by peoples involved in different modes of economic production and organization. Here we follow a method of presentation and analysis with a long social scientific tradition.[3] We begin by considering societies with the lowest degree of gender stratification, *forager or hunter-gatherers*. They are also, not coincidentally, the simplest, technologically least advanced, and smallest types of human societies. Among the societies for which we have both historical and contemporary data, they also probably most closely resemble the earliest forms of human society. The social practices of foragers may not constitute the irreducible bedrock of human existence; but with their simplicity and equality, they can be used to help us understand the possible origins of gender stratification and the evolutionary paths societies have followed in developing more elaborate, advanced technology and more highly stratified inegalitarian social structures.

The second type of society studied is *horticultural societies*. These peoples are more technologically advanced than foragers.

They produce food rather than simply gathering or hunting what nature provides. In facing problems of food production and resource exploitation in different ecological and social niches, some groups remain fairly egalitarian; others do not. Some horticulturalists have extremely hierarchical relationships between men and women; others are quite equal.

The low productivity techniques of horticulture, like those of foragers, are insufficient to the demands of increasing population pressure and resource scarcity. Some may turn to nomadic animal husbandry or *pastoralism* in rugged ecological settings that cannot be farmed to any great extent. These pastoralists face different problems than foragers or horticulturalists and devise significantly different cultures and social structures to meet their survival needs.

Another developmental path horticulturalists can take, and that pastoralists may adopt also, is that of settled agriculture. *Agrarian societies* practice more intensive cultivation techniques, have much larger production surpluses, more advanced technology, much larger and much denser populations. Agrarian peoples also have much more complex cultures and social structures including highly hierarchical class and gender stratification systems. Inequality is pronounced in this type of society. We look at the preindustrial, historical examples of agrarian societies found in ancient Greece and Rome and in Europe during the Middle Ages.

Industrial capitalism arose gradually within the feudal preindustrial setting and eventually came to be the dominant economic form in Europe and much of the rest of the world. The early, more competitive forms of capitalist society produced social, economic, and political relationships quite distinct from those of agrarian society. The position of women and men in turn developed in new directions as capitalism spread, deepened, and became transformed into *advanced capitalist society.*

We look at the impact of early industrial capitalism on gender stratification in the United States and then to the effects of the rise of advanced industrial society in the capitalistic and welfare state contexts of the United States, Japan, and Sweden. We then examine the *socialist* response to the rise and spread of the capitalist world system by examining gender relations in the Soviet Union, the Israeli kibbutz, China, and Cuba.

We also consider contemporary societies that are still undergoing the capitalist transformation of their previous agrarian/horticultural bases of production and that occupy an essentially dependent and subordinate position within a world market system dominated by the advanced capitalist nations. The circumstances of these *capitalist societies of the Third World* are markedly different from those of preindustrial agrarianism and of advanced industrialism.

The categorization, or typology, of different human societies that we use is partly heuristic (a convenient device for organizing our materials to explore relationships) and partly theoretical (a reflection of our perception of how human societies have evolved over time and the importance of economic organization and technology in the structuring of social relations). We draw upon a variety of theoretical perspectives in specific analyses. Our principle aim is to present the reader with a sense of the variety and, at the same time, the continuities in gender relations and gender stratification in the development of human societies. At the end of our survey, we briefly note some of the implications of our analysis for the future of gender relations in a world which, in many important respects, has become a global international society that includes all existing "types" of societies and their combinations in one, single world system.

For those unfamiliar with the conceptual terminology used by social scientists who are concerned with the subject matter of this book, we want to clarify the term *gender* as we use it in the following chapters. Gender is a social, not a biological, construction; that is, it is the result of social definitions rather than the fact that females have two X chromosomes while males have an X and a Y chromosome. Biological differences may inform the social definitions: The fact that women give birth can provide the basis for the development of a range of social beliefs about the nurturing, maternal behaviors and attitudes appropriate to females; the fact that males are on the average larger than females may be used to define males as "naturally" strong, brave, or aggressive. But the basic biological structures of maleness and femaleness can give rise to a diversity of such social definitions of *masculinity* and *femininity.* The differences may be emphasized or deemphasized. We use the term *gender* to refer to the social rather than the biological component of what it means to be a male and a female.* *Gender stratification* then refers to the unequal and persistent distribution of resources such as income, political power, or prestige on the basis of gender—to males being, in a particular society or subgroup, the advantaged gender and females the disadvantaged gender, generation after generation.

Sex role was one of the earliest terms for these phenomena. The term has come under criticism because it focuses too much attention on the aspect of sexuality in male/female relations. Therefore, we use concepts such as *sexual relationships* or *sexual bargaining* only when they are referring directly to sexuality.

Notes

1. See, for example, Herbert Schwendinger and Julia Schwendinger, *Sociologists of the Chair* (New York: Basic Books, 1974); Pauline Bart, "Sexism in Social Science," *Journal of Marriage and the Family* 33 (November 1971): 734–746; Helen Longino and Ruth Doell, "Body, Bias, and Behavior: A Comparative Analysis of Reasoning in Two Areas of Biological Science," *Signs* 9, no. 2 (1983):206–327; Stephanie Shields, "Functionalism, Darwinism, and the Psychology of Women: A Study in Social Myth," *American Psychologist* 30 (July 1975):739–754; Marcia Millman and Rosabeth Moss Kanter, eds., *Another Voice* (Garden City, N.Y.: Doubleday/Anchor, 1975); James Gregory, "The Myth of the Male Ethnographer and the Woman's World," *American Anthropologist* 86 (1984), 313–327; Kay Milton, "Male Bias in Anthropology," *Man* 14, no. 1 (1979): 40–54; Joan Aker, "Women and Social Stratification: A Case of Intellectual Sexism," *American Journal of Sociology* 78 (January 1973); Cynthia Fuchs Epstein, "A Different Angle of Vision: Notes on the Selective Eye of Sociology," *Social Science Quarterly* 55 (December 1974); Carol Ehrlich, "The Male Sociologist's Burden: The Place of Women in Marriage and Family Texts," *Journal of Marriage and the Family* 33 (August 1971); Ann Fischer and Peggy Golde, "The Position of Women in Anthropology," *American Anthropologist* 70 (1968); 337–343; Ruby Rohrlich-Leavitt, ed., *Women Cross-Culturally: Change and Challenge* (The Hague: Mouton, 1976); Rayna Reiter, *Toward an Anthropology of Women* (New York: Monthly Review Press, 1975); Eleanor Leacock, "Introduction," in Frederick Engels, *The Origin of the Family, Private Property and the State* (New York: International Publishers, 1972); Bernice Carroll, *Liberating Women's History* (Urbana, Ill.: University of Illinois Press, 1976); Mary Hartman and Lois Banner, eds., *Clio's Consciousness Raised: New Perspectives on the History of Women* (New York: Harper & Row, 1974); Elise Boulding, *The Underside of History: A View of Women Through Time* (Boulder, Colo.: Westview Press, 1976).

2. See, for example, Janet Chafetz, *Sex and Advantage: A Comparative, Macro-Structural Theory of Sex Stratification* (Totowa, N.J.: Rowman & Allanheld, 1984) and Rae Lesser Blumberg, "A General Theory of Gender Stratification" in Randall Collins, ed., *Sociological Theory 1984* (San Francisco: Jossey-Bass, 1984): 23–101.

3. See, for example, Gerhard Lenski, *Power and Privilege: A Theory of Social Stratification* (New York: McGraw-Hill, 1966); Gerhard Lenski and Jean Lenski, *Human Societies: An Introduction to Macrosociology,* 4th ed. (New York: McGraw-Hill, 1982); Marvin Harris, *Culture, People, Nature: An Introduction to General Anthropology,* 3rd ed. (New York: Harper & Row, 1980); M. Kay Martin and Barbara Voorhies, *Female of the Species* (New York: Columbia University Press, 1975); Ernestine Friedl, *Women and Men* (New York: Holt, Rinehart & Winston, 1975); Chafetz, 1984; Blumberg, 1984.

CHAPTER 2

Forager Societies

One of the most important variables for understanding the different positions that women and men occupy in various societies is the type of economic system found in the society. Certain important patterns in the data on gender roles and gender stratification systems become apparent once we compare societies and gender roles on the basis of type of economy.

When dealing with small-scale societies with premodern technologies and relatively simple divisions of labor, this type of economic analysis usually takes the form of *ecological analysis*, which deals with the interaction between social and cultural behavior and environmental phenomena. Andrew P. Vayda notes that such analyses usually take one of two forms,

either showing that items of cultural behavior function as parts of systems that also include environmental phenomena or else showing that the environmental phenomena are responsible in some manner for the origin or development of the cultural behavior under investigation.[1]

Occasionally, we find a social or cultural practice that does not appear to be adaptive to the existing environment. However, closer examination may reveal that such a practice evolved under conditions that no longer exist or that the practice does fulfill functions that

are not easily discernible. (An example is Marvin Harris's analysis of the warfare complex discussed in Chapter 3.)

Ecological analysis is perhaps more easily applied to low-technology societies than to advanced technology societies because the advanced technology can be used to reduce the impact of environmental phenomena on social and cultural behavior. But the economic systems associated with advanced technological societies interact with nature in ways that also exert an important impact on the social and cultural patterns of these societies. In this chapter we use ecological analysis in considering societies with the simplest technology: *hunting and gathering* or *foraging societies*.

Economy and Technology

As the term hunting and gathering suggests, people in these societies support themselves by hunting game, fishing, and gathering wild plant foods. Their technology is simple but effective.[2] They have various types of bows, arrows, spears, knives, poisons, nets, axes, and clubs for bringing down game and a variety of digging sticks, knives, axes, and containers for gathering and transporting wild berries, grains, and roots. They are of necessity *nomadic,* moving their camps regularly in response to fluctuating supplies of game, edible vegetation, and potable water.

Foragers produce only at the subsistence level. Foragers usually have an adequate diet, simple shelters, and clothing appropriate to the climate but they have little in the way of material possessions beyond the necessities. Hence, little private property exists in these societies. Even though they could produce more goods, they could not keep them. The demands of their nomadic life force them to travel light. Any urges to build bigger and better homes or to accumulate more goods are checked by the regular need to abandon or transport these goods on foot to new areas.

Production is geared almost exclusively to *use values,** that is, food is gathered for people to eat it, not because it can be sold or exchanged for some other product. Foragers do not have a market economy. What little production for *exchange value* they do is with other peoples and typically does not constitute a significant part of their economy. Pygmies, for example, establish trade partnerships with neighboring Bantu horticulturists and exchange meat for bananas and metal arrowheads.[3]

Exchange within foraging groups does not involve market relationships as we know them or even the formality of trade partnerships. Sharing, or *reciprocity,* is the norm among hunters and gatherers. Bushmen returning to camp after a day of foraging share all they have found even with those who have done little or no work that day. Each family's evening meal is made up of contributions from the other family groups. "There is a constant flow of nuts, berries, roots, and melons from one family fireplace to another until each person resident has received an equitable portion. The following morning a different combination of foragers moves out of camp and when they return late in the day, the distribution of foodstuffs is repeated."[4]

Food sharing is highly adaptive for foragers. It serves as a form of insurance. The product of foraging can be unpredictable.[5] If you give generously when you are successful, you can expect others to provide for you during those times when you do not forage or when you are unsuccessful. In these societies giving also confers prestige and the recipient incurs a debt although it is never stated as such. No one says, "I'll share with you this time if you'll share with me next time." It is simply accepted that the recipient of food feels obliged to reciprocate some time in the future. This serves to encourage those who owe gifts to work harder to even the balance or to tip it in their own favor and gain prestige themselves. Reciprocity thus encourages subsistence level productivity without the use of coercive mechanisms to force people to work.

Aspects of foraging technology are often physically demanding. Gatherers may walk many miles carrying heavy loads of roots, nuts, and berries, and hunters may run for hours without a rest through thick jungle undergrowth in pursuit of game. However, the Westerners' image of primitive peoples and particularly of primitive women as overworked, undernourished, and always living on the edge of starvation is inaccurate. Most

*The same product or labor can have either use value or exchange value. For example, a parent preparing a meal for his or her family is usually not paid for labor or for the food served. She or he prepares the meal because the family needs to eat a meal—because of its *use value.* A cook in a restaurant, however, may prepare the same food but is paid for the work, and the product of the labor—the food—is sold to customers. The customers buy it because they need to eat, but the product is produced not so much for its use value as for its *exchange value,* the price it can command in the marketplace.

hunters and gatherers have a great deal of leisure time. They rarely work a forty-hour week: an average work day of two or three hours is usually sufficient. Famine is not a recurring problem among most foragers. Their knowledge of nature's resources combined with their nomadism usually can see them through times of shortage. In fact, more advanced agricultural peoples who live near foragers often turn to the foragers for help during droughts and other times of crop failure. The diets of foragers are also usually more varied and often more nutritious than the diets of farming peoples.

Social Organization

Camp Size and Composition

Foraging technology requires that the communities be small and flexible. The camps of foragers living and working together range in size from twenty-five to two hundred people. Membership in the camps is flexible and based on a wide network of kinship ties. People can change from one camp to another quite readily. There is a continuous process of new kin arriving, others departing, and of visiting relatives in other camps for varying periods of time. Furthermore, the camps themselves periodically break up into smaller units to fan out over a larger foraging territory. They then regroup later when it is no longer advantageous or necessary to disperse.

Leadership

There is little inequality of any kind in these societies. Since private property is minimal, there are no social classes; no one is rich and no one is poor. There are no rulers and there is no specialized institutional form of government. Leadership is gained through the force of one's personality, skill, and intelligence. A leader has no powers of coercion. He or she can only persuade, cajole, or shame people into obeying. The leader, furthermore, usually has to set the best example by working the hardest and sharing the most. Leadership does not confer privilege among foragers. Decision making is dispersed in these societies. Even recognized leaders cannot make decisions alone or enforce decisions on anyone who does not agree with the decision.

In general, the person who engages in a particular activity, male or female, is the one who makes the decisions concerning it. When group decisions are required, however, those who have demonstrated skills necessary to the topic being discussed (such as skilled hunters when the decision is when and where to have a collective hunt) will be more likely to have their opinions deferred to than those who do not excel in the relevant task. But even the respected skilled hunter or gatherer will usually not impose his or her opinions on others. Cooperativeness and nonassertiveness are highly valued traits. Eskimos, for example, often find it excruciatingly embarassing to express a direct opinion on a debated issue. Sensitivity to other people's desires and willingness to compromise are norms for participation in the decision-making processes. Aggression and dominance are usually frowned on in these societies. Foragers tend to be peaceful, nonviolent peoples.[6]

Aggression and Territoriality

Although many popular writers have argued that human beings are innately aggressive, hierarchical, and territorial because of the evolutionary impact of the hunting technology on our ancestors, current hunting and gathering societies do not confirm this view.[7] Use of hunting technology has not rendered these peoples aggressive, hierarchical, or territorial. Aggression and dominance are not encouraged and are rarely displayed in these societies. Furthermore, partly because of their geographic mobility, they are not highly territorial. The common response to encroachments or threats by other peoples is to withdraw to an undisputed area. Violence and warfare are relatively rare among hunters and gatherers.[8]

Family and Kinship

Kinship is extremely important among foragers. Almost all of their social, economic, and political relationships are embedded in kinship relations. Collective work is organized, food is shared, camps are organized, and disputes are settled through the use of kinship ties. Because of the importance of reciprocity and the open flexibility of camp organization, it is adaptive for hunters and gatherers to recognize as wide a range of kin as possible.[9] Foragers therefore tend to have *bilateral descent systems;* that is, they recognize kinship ties on both the mother's side and the father's side. One of the characteristics of bilateral descent systems is that they have no logical stopping points. A person can theoretically establish ties to second, third, and fourth cousins. For foragers this is again a form of insurance. In time of need or difficulty, a wide kinship network means there is a large number of people one can turn to for help. If a third cousin is an excellent hunter, for example, it can be advantageous to recognize that kinship tie and move in with his camp.

Foragers also tend to be at least serially *monogamous* (to have only one spouse at a time) and to live in *nuclear family* structures of mother, father, and dependent children. Although they tend to be monogamous in practice, there are usually no rules prohib-

iting multiple marriages and *polygyny* (a man having more than one wife) is not uncommon. *Polyandry* (a woman having more than one husband) is, however, almost unheard-of among foragers. Hunting and gathering people have little motivation for polygamy of any type. Productivity is usually not high enough for one worker to produce in excess of his or her own subsistence needs consistently. Taking multiple wives, then, does not free a man from productive labor or provide him with greater wealth (common motivations for polygyny). But he does have to deal with the problems associated with polygyny—jealousy and disputes among cowives. Colin Turnbull describes one polygynous family group among the Pygmies he studied.[10] The man did not receive prestige from having multiple wives. He did not have greater leisure time. In fact, he probably had to work harder than other husbands to provide as much for each of his three wives as most Pygmy husbands provide for their one wife. Furthermore, the internal disputes among his wives made him the object of ridicule and gossip.

The nuclear family form is widespread among foragers because it is well suited to their highly mobile way of life, their flexibility of camp membership and organization, and their gender division of labor. Marvin Harris describes the changes typical in camp membership and their relationship to the nuclear family structure.

On a daily basis, smaller task groups leave the camp to carry out specialized subsistence activities such as collecting fruits or berries, grubbing, or hunting of large game. Sometimes task groups split off for longer periods—weeks or months—in which case they will usually consist of several genealogically related nuclear families. From time to time—days or weeks—depending on the regional ecology, the local band will break camp and move as a group to another site within a range generally comprising about fifty to seventy-five square miles. Before, during, and after such moves, genealogically linked nuclear families may migrate independently from one band to another. During periods of environmental stress, the bands may break up entirely into several groups of nuclear families. Under extreme duress the band may even break up further into single nuclear families. Such families, however, will not survive long on their own. Wherever food and water are sufficiently abundant, nuclear families reaggregate into local bands. Similarly, several local bands, related by a criss-cross of marriage and descent, tend to aggregate into larger camps whenever local conditions permit.[11]

This continual shifting or nomadism is also related to the fact that foragers tend to be *bilocal* in residence patterns. That is, the married couple sometimes lives with the wife's relatives and at other times with the husband's kin, depending on such factors as abundance of food in one camp's area, friendship patterns among kin, and even whim. Again, however, it reflects the importance of having widespread kinship ties as a means of knitting these shifting, often amorphous groups of people together without any real governmental apparatus.

Family Size

Family size is small among foragers. The women of hunting and gathering societies typically space their children about four years apart. They achieve this without modern contraceptive technology, although most groups have knowledge of various abortion techniques and some infanticide is practiced.[12] The low birthrate is achieved partly through placing a taboo on having sexual intercourse for a few weeks or months after childbirth. But such taboos are not firmly enforced and do not usually last for years. A causal relationship has been observed between lactation, body fat, and the cessation of ovulation. Research indicates that for every woman there is a critical body weight below which she ceases to menstruate or to

ovulate and is therefore infertile until her weight increases. Although foragers often have a nutritious diet, it is typically a low-fat diet, which results in low body fat. Lactation burns up approximately 1,000 calories per day. (Women usually breast-feed their children for about four years in these societies.) For most forager women, lactation may push them below their critical weight and render them temporarily infertile.[13] An alternative perspective has been offered by Richard Lee, on the basis of research charting !Kung foragers' body weights. Their weights did not vary much with lactation; Lee argues rather that it is the vigorous, twenty-four hour, on-demand nursing that stimulates hormonal secretions that suppress ovulation.[14] Both processes may operate to reduce fertility among foragers.

Whatever its source, the wide spacing of births is highly adaptive for the forager way of life. It serves to control population growth and it keeps pregnancy and child rearing from interfering with the females' essential role in production. A woman can continue most of her food-producing activities throughout pregnancy. Although gathering is demanding work, it does not require spurts of great energy expenditure that would endanger the pregnant woman. The woman can also return to productive labor soon after the birth of her child. She can usually manage to carry one child with her on her foraging expeditions and breast-feed it without unduly disrupting her work. However, she could not manage her productive tasks with two or more infants or toddlers. By the time a child is four years old, he or she can be weaned and can easily be left in camp under the supervision of others whenever the mother must leave camp, or the child can sometimes accompany the mother without being carried constantly. Thus pregnancy and child rearing with wide birth spacing do not render women the economic dependents of men. The vision of the woman weighted down by the burdens of childbearing and child care, awaiting a food supply from the unhampered male breadwinner, does not seem to be the case for existing foragers.

Gender Division of Labor

The demands of different aspects of foraging technology do, however, usually result in an important gender division of labor. Hunting, in particular the hunting of large game and dangerous deep-sea fishing, are male specialties, while gathering, hunting small game, some fishing, and the bulk of child care, home building, and cooking are done primarily, but not exclusively, by women.

It appears that pregnancy and child care can be combined with the gathering technology; but it is often difficult, although not impossible, to combine pregnancy, child care, and gathering with the hunting technology. Hunting under primitive technologies can require arduous long-distance tracking of animals both before and after they are wounded. It can also require a great deal of physical strength. These activities could be especially difficult for a pregnant woman or for someone carrying a nursing child. Great skill and precision are often required in spearing animals, reptiles, and fish or bringing down birds and animals by means of a throwing stick. Such precision is difficult to maintain for a person carrying a burden. Pregnancy and lactation burden women with limitations on their speed and endurance in tracking and the chase and inhibit their precision in spearing and throwing.

Furthermore, the presence of an infant or young child can be a disruptive factor in the hunt, because a child is likely to be noisy and frighten away the prey and because of the problem of protecting the child from the

potential hazards of the hunting situation. Since females in foraging societies spend most of their late adolescent and adult lives either pregnant or nursing, they may not constitute a ready and efficient labor force for hunting large, dangerous game. It would therefore be a waste of resources for societies dependent on this type of hunting to expend time and energy training females to hunt. In addition, gathering and hunting require specialized skills and these skills cannot always be combined on the same expedition. Carrying large quantities of vegetable foods limits one's ability to pursue large game, just as pregnancy and child care interfere with some hunting. (Men will often gather after a day's hunt is over.) It is also possible that body odors resulting from menstruation or lactation might warn some types of game away and thus interfere with hunting.[15] For all these reasons it may be functional to practice a division of labor that allows females to concentrate on gathering and males on hunting.[16]

This type of division of labor is common in forager societies, but it is not universal, nor is it rigid where it is practiced.[17] Foragers are pragmatic about their division of labor. It is not considered demeaning to do the tasks usually performed by the other gender. So men are often involved in gathering and child care, and women sometimes participate in hunting. The G/Wi Bushmen, for example, place little emphasis on masculinity and femininity and have few strongly contrasted gender roles.

Among subsistence activities, the only generally valid distinction is that women do not hunt or work with bows, arrows, or spears. Most gathering and preparation of plant foods for household consumption is done by women, but men collect their own plant food while out hunting and also help in providing for the household in early summer. In most households women build the shelters and huts at each new campsite, but many husbands habitually help their wives without there being any regularity in the range of tasks for each partner. Similarly, the allocation of the chores of collecting firewood and setting pit-oven fires is a matter settled by each couple.[18]

Even the distinction between male and female participation in hunting does not always hold. Among some peoples, described later in this chapter, hunting is also done by women.[19]

Food Sharing and Gender Inequality

Foragers regularly share food among camp residents. This food sharing can have a differential impact on the sexes. The products of gathering expeditions are typically more reliable sources of food than the wild game from the hunt. Furthermore, game cannot usually be stored and large animals provide too much for an individual or one family to consume immediately. Meat is sometimes shared more widely than vegetable foods. Even when they have the technology for drying and preserving meat, foragers do not necessarily do so. If a family went to the trouble of preserving their kill for future use, they would have to eat it in full view of other camp members. This would create jealousies and disrupt camp cooperativeness and harmony. It would also undermine the "insurance system" built into reciprocity and generosity. In addition, since foragers often prefer meat to vegetable foods (perhaps because of its more unpredictable and scarce nature in most environments), it would be more disruptive not to share meat than it would be to withhold more common vegetables.

Both men and women participate in formal and informal exchange networks, which establish important social ties within the wider society. Because the meat from large game can usually be more widely distributed and is highly valued, the sharing of meat may involve men in wider networks than are available for women in some societies. In the hunting and gathering context, these links do not result in large power differentials between men and women. But they do provide an organizational basis for the exercise of power in case a surplus is ever produced on a regular basis or if the society turns to planting instead of foraging. Even in the foraging context, meat-sharing networks may mean greater prestige and influence for the male hunters than for the female gatherers. But hunting is not the only source of prestige and respect. Individuals are ranked according to their skills in performing different tasks. So one person may be known as an excellent hunter or as a particularly skilled gatherer or as a ritual specialist. Respect is given to individuals, male or female, who acquire exceptional skills.

Ernestine Friedl argues that the sharing of meat is the basis for whatever gender inequality exists in hunting and gathering societies and that there is a direct relationship between the extent of male dominance and the proportion of meat supplied by men.

The opinions of hunters play an important part in decisions to move the village; good hunters attract the most desirable women; people in other groups join camps with good hunters; and hunters, because they already participate in an internal system of exchange, control exchange with other groups for flint, salt, and steel axes. The male monopoly on hunting unites men in a system of exchange and gives them power, gathering vegetable food does not give women equal power even among foragers who live in the tropics, where the food collected by women provides more than half the hunter-gather diet.[20]

Friedl has probably overstated the case for male hunting; males do not monopolize hunting in all foraging societies. Among the desert-dwelling Aboriginals of Australia, Diane Bell points out, women gather and hunt, and women distribute meat and control camp movements by deciding when the area has been depleted of food sources. Furthermore, Bell notes that the emphasis placed on high-quality animal protein by some researchers often overlooks other non-hunt sources of this protein such as eggs, grubs, fish, reptiles, and the small game often supplied on a regular basis from female food gathering. The experience of "meat hunger," which some argue leads people to value meat more highly than other foods, may also be overstated. Aboriginal men are required to go through ritual periods during which they can eat only meat; they complain of "vegetable hunger" and desire vegetable foods during these times.[21]

Patterns in the Gender Division of Labor

Rhoda Halperin criticizes Friedl for placing too much emphasis on the distinction between hunting and gathering.[22] Halperin proposes an "optimal foraging model," which holds that foragers adjust their food-gathering and -processing activities according to what is likely to produce the most benefit for the least cost. Food-processing activities are just as vital as food-procuring activities and therefore should be included in any assessment of the relative contributions of men and women to the group's diet. The often time-consuming and arduous work associated with food processing is, of course, vital to a group's existence, and Halperin is correct in pointing out a tendency to over look this work. But even when we include these contributions, women's status still seems to vary somewhat according to the patterns in the food-gathering division of labor. While recognizing Friedl's over-emphasis on the male monopoly in providing animal protein, we consider below the applicability of the four patterns of gender division of labor that she has found among

foragers and add two more patterns that include females as hunters. Although all foraging societies are highly egalitarian in gender roles compared to other types of societies, there are important differences among foragers, some being less egalitarian than others.

Men and Women Gather, Men Hunt. In pattern one both men and women gather, largely individually, and men do a little hunting, but the contribution to food supply from hunting is not great. In this situation each individual has ready access to food resources and can support himself or herself independently of others. The Hadza of Tanzania are an example of this pattern.[23] Although the land occupied by the Hadza appears to Western eyes to be barren, it is actually rich in wild foods and abundant in game. An abundant supply of edible vegetation is probably a prerequisite for this pattern. The desert dwelling G/Wi Bushmen, for example, must make maximum use of all the available food resources and cannot so often afford to pass up opportunities to hunt.[24] The Hadza can afford the luxury of individual independence in food gathering. Furthermore, this example may indicate that hunting, in particular collective hunting, may be an adaptation to a poor natural habitat. Scarcity may require the concerted efforts of several hunters. Hence collective hunts may not have developed until fairly late in the evolution of human species.[25]

Among the Hadza, women and children leave camp every day in groups for the leisurely task of food gathering. Most of what they gather is eaten on the spot to satisfy their immediate hunger. Some is brought back to camp to be eaten later by the women and children, and some is shared with the men in camp. However, men do not rely on the foods the women gather. The men for the most part do their own gathering individually. Unlike the women, they do not bring vegetable foods back to camp to share. They do share meat whenever they are successful in hunting, after they have cooked and eaten their fill at the scene of the kill, but this is rare. Meat and honey gathered primarily by men constitute only 20 percent of the diet of the Hadza. The men are not avid hunters despite their love of meat, the abundance of game, and their self-image as hunters. Woodburn notes that

although vegetable foods form the bulk of their diet, the Hadza attach very little value to them. They think of themselves and describe themselves as hunters. From informants' assertions, one would gather that little but meat is eaten. In addition to being the preferred food, meat is also intimately connected with rituals to which Hadza men attach great importance.[26]

Subsistence activities do not consume a great deal of the Hadza's time or energy. Woodburn estimates that they average less than two hours per day obtaining food.

The genders are highly independent of each other for food among the Hadza, but women still depend upon men for whatever meat they eat. Women also depend on men for items obtained through trade with other peoples. The Hadza do not rely on trade except for luxuries such as tobacco, but males control this trade network through their control over the key item of trade—honey. However, to obtain and keep wives, men must supply their wives and mothers-in-law with meat, tobacco, beads, and cloth. These obligations create interdependencies of the genders. Within the Hadza economic system, males and females are independent of each other in gathering food and males control meat and trade goods. Friedl concludes that the Hadza represent a situation of minimal gender stratification, made possible because of the economic independence of the genders.[27] But male control over trade can easily lead to inequality.[28]

Men and Women Communally Hunt and Gather. Pattern two is characterized by male and female participation in collective hunting, fishing, and gathering expeditions. The Pygmies of the Zaire rain forest are examples of this pattern. Like pattern one, this division of labor gives rise to highly egalitarian gender roles. The collective nature of the division of labor creates an important interdependency of the genders in subsistence activities.

The Mbuti Pygmies inhabit the dense Ituri rain forest. They live in an environment of relative abundance in wild vegetation and game. But unlike pattern one societies, instead of individuals hunting and gathering alone, the Pygmies organize their subsistence tasks, as well as most other work, communally. This cooperative interdependence is associated with highly egalitarian gender roles. As Turnbull describes it:

The woman is not discriminated against in BaMbuti society. . . . She has a full and important role to play. There is relatively little specialization according to sex. Even the hunt is a joint effort. A man is not ashamed to pick mushrooms and nuts if he finds them, or to wash and clean a baby. A woman is free to take part in the discussions of men if she has something relevant to say.[29]

The woman is an essential partner in the economy. Without a wife a man cannot hunt, he has no hearth, he has nobody to build his house, gather fruits and vegetables, and cook for him.[30]

Hunting among the Pygmies requires the organization of several family groups and the cooperation of the genders. The men arrange their nets in a large semicircle and wait with their spears for the women to beat the game toward the nets. The animals caught in the nets are speared by the men and then carried away by the women. The animal "belongs" to the man in whose net it was caught. However, the meat is always

shared according to rules and past obligations. Women do most of the cooking and
food processing, but an unmarried male
does not find it demeaning to cook for himself and other bachelors. "Between men and
women there was . . . a certain degree of
specialization, but little that could be called
exclusive."[31] Friedl argues that pattern two
results in minimal gender stratification and
gender inequalities because of the economic
interdependence of the genders.[32]

Men Hunt, Women Gather. In pattern
three men hunt and women gather. There
is a complementary division of labor, but the
greater value foragers attach to meat gives
men an advantage (although not a major
one) over women. The Washo Indians of the
Great Basin in California and Nevada were
perhaps intermediate between pattern two
and pattern three.* Friedl classifies the
Washo as pattern two primarily on the basis
of the participation of men, women, and
children in fishing during the spring runs
and the pine nut harvest in the fall. However,
these were not the only sources of subsistence for the Washo. Furthermore, these
were the most predictable but least skilled
of their subsistence activities.

The other two equally important sources
of food were more firmly divided according
to gender—males hunted and females gathered. Gathering for immediate consumption
was done individually, primarily by women.
In the summer, "while the men fished the
lake and streams, the women spent more
and more of their days wandering in the
mountain meadows in the foothills gathering

plant food,"[33] and "except for the pine nuts
and those foods taken in small amounts and
eaten on the spot, all gathering was done by
the women."[34] Women did most of the food
processing and wove the baskets necessary
for gathering and as cooking utensils. Moreover, although gathering required great skill,
it was not a focus of ritual and magical powers as hunting was. "All in all, gathering
was a much more mundane and rational activity than either hunting or fishing."[35]

In the fall, men continued to hunt as
women began the very important pine nut
gathering. Pine nuts were the basic staple of
the Washo diet throughout the barren winter
months. Without an adequate supply of pine
nuts, they would starve before the spring
fish runs and vegetation appeared. Men co-
operated with women in the pine nut harvests. Husbands and wives and their households worked furiously to gather as many as
possible during the short harvest season.
The heavy loads of pine nuts were then
transported by the men and women to their
winter camp.

Hunting was the exclusive activity of
males and was taboo to women except under
exceptional circumstances. Men were expected to hunt throughout their lives. Hunting required great skill in stalking as well as
accuracy with the bow and arrow. The
hunter had to know in detail the hunting
grounds and the habits of his various prey.
But even a skilled, knowledgeable hunter
could not be certain of success. Therefore,
he turned to magic and ritual. "In addition
to physical and weapon-using skills and a
knowledge of animal lore, a hunter had to
learn the ritual and magic that were part of
hunting. It was a long apprenticeship and a
demanding one that was not complete until
a youth was a young man."[36] A man was
eligible for marriage when he killed a deer
with antlers large enough for him to crawl
through when set on their points.

---

*Discussion of the Washo is in the past tense because
the traditional culture of this people was destroyed by
the expansion of white settlements into the western
United States.

To socialize the apprentice hunter into the importance of sharing the catch, he was never allowed to eat any animal he killed. "Usually he gave the game away to neighbors or relatives, displaying at once the Washo virtue of generosity and learning the important lesson of mutual dependence and . . . building up a number of small debts which he might someday call in if he needed food or assistance."[37] Thus hunting allows males to create important food-sharing networks and reciprocity arrangements from which females were excluded by virtue of the gender division of labor.

Unlike the Hadza, a great deal of pressure was put on the Washo male to hunt. In the environment of scarcity, the Washo could not afford to waste hunting opportunities. "Hunting virtually dominated the Washo's image of himself. Even today to suggest that a man had no taste for hunting and preferred to remain in camp with the women is an oblique way of attacking his entire character. The ritual of hunting, preserving the usefulness of his weapons, the respect shown to the hunted animal all combined in a pattern of behavior which influenced most of the day-to-day routine of a Washo man."[38] Thus hunting created important cultural, life-style, and perhaps personality differences between men and women.

The Washo as well as the Pygmies (pattern two) differ from the Hadza in their high degree of economic interdependence between the genders. Survival requires a partnership between a man and a woman among the Washo and the Pygmies. Marriage is desirable among the Hadza, but the relative economic independence of the genders does not elevate it to an issue of survival.

The Washo differ from the other hunters and gatherers considered here in that they had greater problems with scarcity, they were more territorial or property oriented, and they had more severe defense problems.

The Washo probably worked much harder in their subsistence activities than the Hadza or Pygmies. They had to be much more diligent in food gathering to store enough surplus from warm months to see them through the winter. Such surpluses are not necessary for Pygmy or Hadza survival. Furthermore, the Washo subsistence techniques did not require the group efforts characteristic of the Pygmies. The Washo work group was the *household* consisting of a husband and wife, their children, and sometimes young unmarried relatives or elderly relatives. This work group was large enough for the communal fishing and pine nut gathering and large enough for the gender division of labor between gathering and hunting. These household groups had firm property rights over specific winter camp sites, fishing areas, and pine nut groves. Downs notes that "if a man found a stranger trespassing on his pine nut plot, he seized his equipment, broke it and confiscated the nuts," and "men might come to blows over the use of a fishing platform, but here again custom established who had prior rights."[39]

Friedl argues that food sharing outside the household was not significant among the Washo and therefore "only a limited difference in opportunities for distribution were [available] to each sex."[40] But food-sharing networks did exist among the Washo, and sharing meat from the hunt was probably more important than other types of food sharing, again because of the unpredictability of the hunt.

The defense problems of the Washo were also different from those of the Hadza and the Pygmies. Washo territory was bounded by that of other Indian groups who often encroached upon Washo food sources. Downs describes the Washo as essentially peaceful, but they could not afford to lose any of their food supplies. They would attack only those trespassers who took valuable foodstuffs. Washo warfare was primarily defensive in nature, but even defensive warfare creates another male specialty in primitive society. Furthermore, households traveling outside the center of Washo territory had to be vigilant against attack, limiting the women's freedom to gather alone over a wide area. It was important for the males to be available to defend their households under such circumstances.

A clearer example of the pattern three gender division of labor is found in the various groups of Bushmen who live in the Kalihari Desert of southern Africa. The G/Wi and the !Kung Bushmen do not suffer the seasonal scarcity problems of the Washo despite the fact that they live in a harsh desert environment. They follow fluctuating supplies of water, but food is always available. Hence there is no attempt among the Bushmen to build up a surplus. During the harsh dry season they merely turn to less desirable edible vegetation. Thus the Bushmen are not characterized by periods of intense subsistence activity like the Washo during their fish runs and pine nut harvests. They lead a much more leisurely life and like the Hadza and Pygmies devote only an average of few hours a day to subsistence work.*

Like the Washo, Bushmen males specialize in hunting, but they do some gathering to satisfy their own immediate hunger while away from camp. They also gather some vegetable foods to bring back to camp if they are unsuccessful on a hunting expedition. Women specialize in gathering and typically do not take part in the hunt. Game is scarce in the Kalihari, and the Pygmy style of collective hunting using game beaters would not be effective here. Both hunting and gathering take the Bushmen many miles from camp, and the hunter typically ranges farther than the gatherer.

Vegetable foods again constitute the bulk of the diet (60 to 70 percent), but meat is preferred. The successful hunter gains prestige, builds up obligations from others, and attracts kinsmen to his camp. However, among the Bushmen the vegetable foods are also shared throughout the camp, and the skilled gatherer can also gain prestige and incur obligations. Still, these are probably less significant than "meat debts" because the gathering is predictable once a person has learned the necessary skills.

As with the Pygmies and the Washo, Bushmen men and women are economically interdependent. The hunting and gathering is more gender-segregated than among the other two groups, but it is *complementary*. In general, these first three patterns in the gender division of labor result in situations of separate but fairly equal gender roles. In the fourth pattern, however, males are almost the sole providers of the group's food supply, and this appears to result in less egalitarian gender roles.

Men Hunt, Women Process the Catch. In pattern four men hunt large game and do dangerous deep-sea fishing while women process the product from these male activities. Gathering is an insignificant source of food. The various Eskimo societies use this pattern. The frozen tundra provides little in the way of edible vegetation, and game, sea animals, and fish are the staple foods. This pattern carries with it the least egalitarian gender roles of any type of hunting and gathering societies. Women are economically dependent on men to a degree that does not occur in the other patterns. This results in a power advantage for males and more sub-

---

*Recent policies of the South African government confining these peoples on reservations have severely disrupted their way of life. The patterns described here would not be found unchanged under such severe conditions.

ordinate roles for females in other areas of the society and culture. For example, at meals men and boys are served first, then the girls, and the mother last.[41] There is an important degree of gender segregation in village life, and even in her own home the woman remains passive in predominantly male gatherings.[42] The most influential individuals are the male hunting-group leaders, who are important community leaders, and the *shamans* (religious specialists). Many hunting-group leaders increase their influence through practicing shamanism themselves. The group leaders earn their influence through the power of their personality, hunting skill, and possession of sufficient wealth to outfit and support a boat crew. The hunting boat leader "owns" the largest share of the kill, which he distributes to gain prestige and obligations from others or sells for profit. Only males participate in trade with non-Eskimos. Females cannot obtain this kind of prestige, leadership, or control of resources. However, women can become shamans if they demonstrate the appropriate skills of spirit possession. Leadership within the extended family is another source of influence in Eskimo society. It usually goes to the eldest male. Younger men, but not females, can gain influence through hunting skills, physical strength, and good judgment. But older women can act as influential advisers even in matters of politics and warfare.[43]

Despite a greater degree of inequality than is characteristic of other foraging societies, Eskimo gender roles and gender division of labor remain quite flexible. "In theory there are domains which are predominantly male such as sea mammal and caribou hunting, running boats, and doing the heaviest household chores; female domains include doing indoor housework, caring for children, butchering meat, and sewing skins. Nevertheless, members of each sex know the oth-

er's skills and can perform these roles when necessary."[44] Eskimo women are more housebound than women in other forager societies. Since there is little gathering for them to do, they usually remain in camp to do their work—processing the skins and meat from the male hunt. The severity of the northern winters also requires great vigilance in attending to children to prevent their wandering out into the cold unprotected. In conjunction with the frequent need to break up into small units that sometimes consist of only one nuclear family, this means that women are often tied down with the sole care of small children and have little freedom of movement. But in the village setting the mother does share responsibility for infant care with older children and other female relatives. Fathers have traditionally been the dominant, more distant parent, leaving most child-care activities to the females.[45] Thus there is a greater *domestic/public split** among Eskimos than is found among other foragers.

There is a complementarity in the tasks of men and women in Eskimo societies. Women make the essential protective clothing and much of the equipment necessary for hunting and fishing and also provide some gathered foods and raw materials. This allows women as well as men to be active in the reciprocal exchange networks.[46] But men provide most of the food and reap more prestige, benefits, and debts from food sharing. Hunting dominates the Eskimo male's image of himself. Courage and daring are highly valued traits in males. A large body of traditional magical practices and taboos is associated with hunting, especially the difficult and dangerous whale hunt.[47]

---

*A separation of the domestic realm dealing with household tasks and child care from the nondomestic or public arena of politics and nonhousehold work. Most foragers merge the domestic and public arenas.

Both men and women view the male life as more glamorous and exciting than the female life and the hunter role as more important. But males and females both recognize that women's skills are also indispensable to survival. Males often consider female skills so important that they see it as necessary to have a female accompany a male on long trips.[48] Furthermore, a woman has the personal autonomy "to make many decisions such as whether or not she will accompany her husband on a long hunting trip or visit relatives in another village."[49] Individualism is culturally valued for females as well as for males. However, Jean Briggs argues that among the Utku Eskimos she studied, a wife must ask her husband's permission to accompany him or to visit relatives. Decision making is male dominated, although wives may be able to influence or manipulate the husband's decision. Among the Utku Eskimos, "men also direct domestic affairs. . . . In general, an Utku woman decides for herself how she is going to spend the day. . . . However, her husband may veto her plan if he sees fit, whereas the reverse is not true. . . . Moreover, an Utku wife tends to serve her husband in small ways more than he serves her."[50]

Friedl notes that there is more sexual aggression against women among Eskimos than among hunters and gatherers of the first three patterns. Rape of unmarried girls is often an acceptable practice. "Physical and verbal aggression among men is frowned on, but sexual aggression against women in the form of abduction or sexual violence is common."[51] Friedl also goes so far as to describe Eskimo women as "objects to be used, abused, and traded by men."[52] But anthropologists who have studied Eskimo peoples extensively, such as Briggs and Leacock, disagree with such a characterization and emphasize the egalitarian aspects of Eskimo

gender roles as compared with more technologically advanced societies.[53]

Women Hunt and Gather, Men Hunt and Fish. In addition to the four patterns outlined by Friedl, there is a fifth pattern in which men fish and hunt some animal species and women hunt other animals and gather. The Tiwi, an Aboriginal people on islands off the coast of Australia, exemplify this division of labor. Their division of labor is not on the basis of hunting versus gathering, but rather females are responsible for land resources, which include vegetable foods and land animals, while males are responsible for food resources in the water and air, which include birds, aquatic reptiles, and mammals. Friedl places the Tiwi in pattern two, but they differ significantly from the division of labor of the Pygmies and the Washo. Of particular importance is the way many men are freed from subsistence activities.

The Tiwi woman hunts with the aid of her highly trained dog which is considered as important as a family member. The female hunter uses a stone ax which she makes and maintains herself. Men use different tools and techniques in hunting birds, reptiles, and turtles. Women also collect plants and shellfish. This division of labor is probably related to the differences in strength required and the danger involved in hunting the different types of prey. The land animals on the islands are not as likely to be large and dangerous as the crocodiles and other reptiles pursued by the men. Males do usually hunt the few large game animals available such as the wallaby. Jane Goodale concludes:

The outstanding characteristic of Tiwi hunting is related both to the abundance and to the nature of the fauna of the islands. There is no land animal, with the possible exception of the wallaby, that cannot be killed with a minimum of physical strength, skill and equipment. Thus, the women not only could but did provide the major daily supply of a variety of foods to members of their camp. Children too could learn the necessary techniques at an early age, and since strength and energy were minor requirements, they began early to contribute to the larder. Men's hunting required considerable skill and strength, but the birds, bats, fish, crocodiles, dugongs, and turtles they contributed to the household were luxury items rather than staples.[54]

Single males and husbands with only one or two wives participate in the daily hunting parties, but a man with many wives can depend on them to provide food for him and his small children. As with the other foragers considered here, the Tiwi's gender division of labor seems sharply defined. In reality, however, it is flexible and at many points deviates from the model. Males sometimes hunt "female" game and collect vegetables and women sometimes accompany the men on turtle or goose hunts. The Tiwi do not consider these deviations to be "wrong" and do not believe that bad luck or any other evil result from such cross-gender behaviors.[55]

Both males and females participate in elaborate food-sharing networks. Among the females the hunter relinquishes her catch to the "cook" (also female). The cook receives her share of the catch. The cook and the hunter then further share their portions among their kin in a set order of priority. In the case of a large catch, portions will be shared with all those present in the camp. Males first distribute the product of a turtle or crocodile hunt according to their positions in the canoe. Then each man's share is distributed along the same kinship priorities and camp residents as the women's distribution.[56]

Although monogamy is the primary form of marriage in most hunting and gathering societies, among the Tiwi polygyny is the rule for males and *serial marriage* is the rule for females.* This is probably related to the high productivity of Tiwi females in the collection of both vegetable and meat foods. Polygyny in this situation does not require a man to work harder to keep two or more wives in meat as would be the case among the Eskimos, Bushmen, Washo, Pygmies, and Hadza. Rather, the extra wives free the husband to stay in camp. This is especially important since a man with several wives is likely to be advanced in age and therefore in need of food from others.

The Tiwi marriage system is incredibly complex and has been the subject of considerable scholarly debate. Some writers have viewed their marriage structure as clear evidence of sexism and gender inequality. C. W. Hart and Arnold Pilling, for example, characterize women as little more than currency in a male system of competition and exchange.[57] Goodale's research on the same people balance this point of view with a female perspective on the marriage structure.

Among the Tiwi, females are always married. They are betrothed by their fathers before their birth in a system of reciprocity among males. Males gain prestige through the number of marriage contracts they make. Marriage contracts are highly valued, even if the wife is not yet born or not yet old enough to join the husband's household. Since the husband has to be at least a young adult before the infant girl can be married to him, a female's first husband is much older than she. For this reason, she is likely

Serial marriage: having several different spouses in one's lifetime, but never more than one at a time.

to be widowed at an early age. Her father (or her brothers if her father is dead) then has the right to make a new marriage contract for her on the death of her husband. Given the male prestige system based on marriage contracts, all women are valuable as wives, even the aged. There is no such thing as an unmarried female among the Tiwi.

The young girl joins her husband's household before puberty and is gradually initiated into sexual activity by her older husband. She works in his household along with her cowives and is under the authority of the older cowives and her husband. But her husband is required to keep his household in the same camp as the young wife's mother, so she continues to be under the protection of her own kin, who have the right to intervene if she is mistreated.

Since her husband is elderly, the young wife is likely to engage in extramarital affairs with the young unmarried men of the tribe. The wife's full adult status is achieved with the birth of her first child. And unlike highly patriarchal societies, female children are preferred. Female babies enable the father to provide wives for other males in exchange for marriage contracts from these prospective husbands. They also, of course, represent important productive labor.

An important aspect of the Tiwi marriage system is that women are not simply passive objects of exchange. They are active participants in the system. The marriage contracts do not simply represent exchange relationships between the father and husband. They also involve an important exchange relationship between the mother-in-law and the son-in-law—the *ambruina* relationship. When the young wife has her first female child, she becomes the ambruina to the child's husband, her son-in-law. The son-in-law is obligated to supply the mother-in-law with all that she demands in food and trade goods.

As Goodale describes it, "It would seem that although in the marriage 'game' men thought of women as so much capital wealth to manipulate as they wished, in reality, it was through the relationship that women gained a balance of power over a male. A man might lose his temper at his mother-in-law's husband but he usually maintained his control with his mother-in-law, no matter how hard-pressed he might be to fulfill her demands."[58] This relationship lasts until death.

Polygyny, although a source of power and prestige for males, also serves as an avenue of power and prestige for females. The eldest cowife, the *taramaguti*, is an important figure among the Tiwi. Like her husband, she does not have to go out on the daily foraging parties; she can direct the activities of her household and remain relaxing in camp. Thus the system allows the elderly of both genders to withdraw from subsistence activities. The taramaguti directs the education of the young wives and gives respected advice on the rearing of the other wives' children. She is influential over her own and her cowives' adult children. However, the taramaguti's position is never as elevated as that of some of the elder males. "Women are not considered to be 'big bosses' or leaders in a funeral ceremony—this is a man's role—but the men do consult members of the patrilineage that is in charge of the ceremony and the women voice their opinions freely. The nominal male leaders consider these opinions to be important."[59]

While it is true that females can gain the position of taramaguti only in old age it is also true that males can become "big men" only in old age. Becoming a "big man" requires the acquisition of many marital contracts and this is impossible to accomplish at a young age. Most young men are unmarried. It is particularly difficult to obtain an infant bride because fathers prefer to give them to men who have daughters to give in return. So young men often take an elderly widow as their first wife, again resulting in a large age difference between the spouses.

This system of polygyny for men also results in multiple husbands for women. But instead of having several husbands simultaneously, the Tiwi woman has a series of husbands over her lifetime, usually beginning with a husband much older than herself and often ending with one much younger. Moreover, Frederick Rose asserts that women want to be part of these polygynous units because they ease the burdens of child-rearing and household tasks.[60]

Culturally similar desert-dwelling Aborigines studied by Bell have corresponding marriage practices. Past researchers have described these women as highly subordinated, but this is far from accurate. Aboriginal peoples are highly gender segregated, but women are not subordinated. They are "owners" of land just as men are; they participate in the political and legal decision making; they provide meat and animal protein as well as vegetable foods. A high degree of female solidarity exists among Aboriginal women. Women participate actively and vigorously in the politicking associated with marriage alliances—marriage is not just a system of contracts among men—and women have as extensive and important ritual lives as men do.[61]

The economic contribution by Tiwi women of meat as well as vegetable foods does not result in a female status equal to the males' or to that of the hunter in other forager societies. According to Goodale, males still have more avenues for prestige and influence, but women are not highly subordinated to men. Bell did not see as much inequality among the desert dwellers as Goodale did among the island Aborigines, perhaps because large game is rare in the desert and women's economic role is not offset by much male hunting or fishing for dangerous game.

Men and Women Independently Hunt, Fish, and Gather. The Agta of the Philippines furnish another example of women as hunters.[62] This people has only a modest division of labor by gender. Most of the Agta diet is animal protein, and women and men both provide this through hunting and fishing. Women withdraw from hunting only in late pregnancy. Gathering is less important, but both genders participate in this too. As with the Australian Aboriginal peoples, the game hunted by the Agta—wild pig, deer, and monkeys—are not especially dangerous. Fishing done by swimming under water and spearing the fish, does require both skill and endurance. Griffin and Griffin found the Agta to be highly egalitarian. In general, the pattern of female participation in hunting and fishing seems to result in a high degree of gender equality.

Economy, Environmental Risk, and Gender

Peggy Sanday's research on preindustrial societies provides us with a somewhat different but complementary perspective on the relationship between the economy, environment, and gender relations. This perspective has implications for the differences among the foraging societies we have described.[63] According to Sanday, people who operate within dangerous environmental contexts, hunting large game or regularly facing attack by human or animal predators, are more likely to exhibit higher degrees of male dominance than peoples who perceive the environment in benign terms. Where the environment is lush in resources and nonthreatening, gender equality is more pronounced. Thus the Eskimos with their need to hunt large game and sea mammals and their more threatening climatic environment exhibit higher degrees of gender segregation in work, male control of economic and political decision making, and aggression against females than the pygmies who see the forest as the generous mother, father, and lover who protects rather than harms them.

Marriage, Sex, and Children

Marriage in Foraging Societies

Almost everyone marries in foraging societies because the complementarity of the gender division of labor makes it difficult for single adults to take care of all their needs for food, shelter, and clothing and reciprocal obligations. Marriage usually entails little ceremony. The couple may merely begin living together and come to regard themselves and be regarded by others as married. Marriage alliances between different families are important in general for establishing and maintaining ties within and among the different camps. Marriage functions to keep resources more evenly distributed, rather than to maintain unequal concentration in a few elite families.

First marriages are often arranged by parents, especially for girls. But the girls often resist, and divorce is common. Later marriages are usually made on the basis of the mutual attraction of the two people involved. Any one person may go through several unsuccessful marriages before settling into a stable union. There is little or no sexual double standard and virginity is not a concern.

Marriages may involve some gift exchange typical of any social occasion in foraging society, but there is no elaborate property exchange in the form of dowries or brideprices. But *brideservice* is common. The groom may be expected to regularly give gifts of food to the girl's parents in exchange for the right to marry her.

In the first two patterns we described, where the division of labor is minimal and where men and women hunt together collectively, lack of male control over food supplies may be reflected in lack of male control over women. Marriages are made quite freely by the couples involved. In pattern three, where men hunt and women gather, a skilled hunter makes a more desirable husband and son-in-law than an unskilled or lazy hunter. Friedl says meat can be exchanged for women in this pattern and brideservice is likely.[64] The skilled hunter may also have a marriage advantage even in pattern one. Woodburn notes that among the Hadza, there is little pressure put on men by other men to hunt, and a few do not hunt at all. Although poor hunters or nonhunters do not suffer a loss of status among males, they do have difficulty obtaining and keeping wives, who generally prefer marriage to good hunters.[65] However, since gathering is likely to produce a more predictable product, a particularly skilled gatherer may not be as advantaged in the marriage market. Girls also often marry before they have demonstrated any real gathering skills.

In pattern four where men hunt and gathering is insignificant, the skilled hunter is definitely a desirable husband, but a woman skilled in processing the catch may also be a more desirable wife. In pattern five, among the Tiwi, men desire any female as a wife. With child betrothal, females have no choice in first marriage partners, but they do have a choice of lovers and later husbands. Because marriage contracts are a source of prestige for males and mothers-in-law, the mutual attraction of the partners is not an important consideration. Fathers and mothers betrothing their daughters and women agreeing to later husbands prefer more prestigious and influential men and therefore are likely to give preference to skilled hunters. The desert-dwelling Aborigines have little large game available so distinctions among hunting abilities of men are less important, while ties to male and female relatives who hold prestigious ritual knowledge or have "ownership" of desirable foraging grounds are important considerations in marriage alliances. The elaborate marriage practices of Australian Aborigines are not found among the Agta. Most marriages are arranged through discussions, meetings, and gift exchanges between the two families, but some couples elope without permission.[66] Skills of both Agta males and females may influence their desirability as mates.

Divorce is easy for all but the Tiwi. A marriage ends whenever the couple decides the relationship is over. Women as well as men can initiate the separation. Children usually remain with their mother, but there is little or no property to divide. This reflects the general pattern of a high degree of personal autonomy and individualism among foragers.

Relations between the Genders

The relations between the genders are highly egalitarian in hunting and gathering societies. But arguments and physical fights between males and females occur, especially between spouses. Fighting is generally disapproved of in foraging societies, but this does not prevent it. Other camp members will usually interrupt the battle, however, and force the participants to quiet down before they become dangerous. There is always a fear that such disputes will get out of control and endanger the solidarity and well-being of the entire band. The lack of privacy allows for public control over private disputes.

But wife beating is uncommon among most foragers. Bell notes a great deal of wife beating among contemporary Aboriginals, but this was probably not so common in the precolonial setting. Turnbull witnessed physical attacks by women on men as well as by men on women among the pygmies.[67] Also, wife beating is not an uncommon method of controlling wives among the Eskimos, reflecting again the greater gender inequality among Eskimos than among other foragers.[68] Friedl notes that the chief cleavage among the Hadza is between the genders.[69] Females, for example, ridicule husbands who cannot keep them supplied with meat or desirable trade goods. But despite these occurrences, foragers exhibit more relaxed, easygoing relations between males and females than are found in many horticultural, agricultural, or industrial societies.

Sexuality

Foraging societies tend to be sexually permissive. However, foragers with patrilineal descent systems and patrilocal residence place greater importance on premarital virginity and exert greater control over the young girl's sexual behavior than do foragers with bilateral or matrilineal descent systems.[70] Adultery is not strongly tabooed among most foragers whatever their descent systems. Among the Tiwi, extramarital affairs are fairly common, although the husband and sometimes the wife's kin express disapproval. The husband cannot physically abuse his wife for infidelity, but he is allowed to attack her lover.[71]

Among the Bushmen, jealousy and accusations of adultery are common and may end in divorce.[72] But little comes of such liaisons unless the husband or wife is forced to publicly recognize the partner's infidelity. Even if a wife returns pregnant from a long visit to another camp, there is little concern unless the wife or her lover publicly boast of the relationship.

Extramarital sexuality is a source of great jealousy among the Eskimo, and both wives and husbands are quick to suspect their spouses. However, this jealousy exists alongside the practice of sharing or swapping spouses, which requires the mutual approval of all participating parties and serves to establish close kinshiplike ties among the nonkin involved. As Leacock points out, it is highly ethnocentric to view this as evidence of a low status for women in Eskimo society. Such a view "presumes that a woman does not (since she should not) enjoy sex play with any but her 'real' husband and . . . refuses to recognize that variety in sex relations is entertaining to women (where not circumscribed by all manner of taboos) as well as to men."[73]

Sexual permissiveness is also usually extended to children and adolescents. Among the !Kung, for example, sexual awareness begins at a very early age. Sex is the favorite conversational topic. The lack of privacy in foraging society often means that children are exposed to adult sexual behavior throughout childhood. Childhood sex play is common and may even include intercourse. "Parents say they do not approve of this among young and adolescent children. . . . But the parents played this way when they were children and, although they usually deny it, they know their children are playing the same way. As long as it is done away from adults, children are not prevented from participating in experimental sexual play."[74]

Child Rearing

Child-rearing practices among foragers reflect the egalitarian social structures. Children are reared to be cooperative, generous, peaceful, and unassuming, but independent and self-reliant adults. The noncoercive, nonauthoritarian social structure is supported by noncoercive, nonauthoritarian adult-child relations. Adults seem to have infinite patience in dealing with the children of the camp. Patricia Draper describes one example of this patience among the !Kung Bushmen:

One afternoon I watched for 2 hours while a father hammered and shaped the metal for several arrow points. During this period his son and grandson (both under 4 years old) jostled him, sat on his legs, and attempted to pull the arrowheads from under the hammer. When the boys' fingers came close to the point of impact, he merely waited until the small hands were a little farther away before he resumed hammering. Although the man remonstrated with the boys (about once every 3 minutes), he did not become cross or chase the boys off; and they did not heed his warnings to quit interfering. Eventually, perhaps 50 minutes later, the boys moved off a few steps to join some teenagers lying in the shade.[75]

Eskimos are well known for their indulgence of children: "I have seen children being allowed to leave and enter a snowhouse four or five times in the course of an hour even though closing and opening the door has a considerable cooling effect in the house. The mother patiently dresses and undresses the child as often as he wishes in these cases."[76]

Obedience is not stressed by forager parents.[77] Westerners are often shocked by the lack of respect shown parents and other adults by these children. Self-reliance, rather than obedience to authority, is stressed for both girls and boys. The independence allowed even young children is almost unimaginable to Westerners. Among the !Kung Bushmen children learn early to assert themselves against the authority of their parents and other adults: "Individualism is encouraged and strict obedience of parental authority is considered neither necessary nor desirable."[78]

Goodale's description of childhood among the Tiwi is vivid on the issue of child independence. Goodale observed two- and three-year-old girls building fires without eliciting any parental concern. Parents do not even tell the children to be careful. The basic principle informing their child-rearing practices is that *experience* is the best teacher. Children's activities are interrupted by adults only if they endanger a younger child who cannot protect itself. The following incident illustrates parental aceptance of childhood independence: While a group of Tiwi adults were playing cards, two young girls, Althea and Dennis, and Dennis' younger brother, played around the adults.

They repeatedly got into fights, but only when the wrangle became serious were they separated. The children received no words of reproach, nor was a hand laid on them, even when they eventually became "cheeky" and rolled about on their mother's laps, kicking sand in the cardplayers' faces and grabbing cards. Then Dennis "borrowed" a large hunting knife and began swinging it around jabbing at her much younger brother. One of the men took the knife away, whereupon Dennis went into a minor tantrum and the knife was given back to her. She then began to hit herself on the head with the knife and went into a long verbal tirade that sent the adults into roars of laughter. After quite some time the knife was again taken from her and thrown into some dense bushes where she was unable to find it.[79]

The techniques most often employed by hunting and gathering parents to deal with dangerous aggressive behavior in their children is to interrupt the behavior and divert the child's attention elsewhere.

Goodale also describes the remarkable skills as well as independence of two seven- or eight-year-old girls who built a large paperbark raft from bark they cut from trees themselves. Goodale and the two girls spent the day cruising the swamp near the camp. The girls dove into the swamp for plant foods, eggs, and flowers. "Many days later someone mentioned that large crocodiles are quite apt to sleep in [that swamp] . . . and I marveled at the extent of the parents' belief in experience being the best teacher. I asked the girls if they had known about the crocodiles. 'Oh yes,' they said, 'that's why we get on canoe. When no more sun, can't see crocodiles.'"[80]

Along with independence, generosity is another important value stressed in foragers' child-rearing practices. "!Kung children are encouraged to share things from infancy, because exchanging food and possessions is so basic to adult social interactions. Among the first words a child learns is 'na' ('give it to me') and 'i' ('here, take this'). This type of socialization is hard for children, especially when they are expected to share with someone they resent or dislike.[81]

Males as well as females care for children even if the stereotypic ideal of the society is that females care for the children. Among Naskapi Eskimos child care is considered woman's work but their practices are actually flexible.

For the greater part of one day a man sat patiently, lovingly crooning over his sickly and fretful infant of but a few weeks old. His wife was busy. Though worried for the baby's health, he appeared in no way inept or harassed by his responsibility, nor did he call on another woman around the camp for help. . . . This was his task while his wife tanned a caribou skin, a skilled and arduous job that demanded her complete attention. The men knew how to cook and tend the babies when called upon to do so, but did not really know how to tan leather.[82]

Silberbauer also found that among the G/Wi Bushmen both males and females aid in infant and child care and that "men and boys show the same fondness for babies as do women and girls."[83] Whoever is left in camp, male or female, cares for the children.

The entire G/Wi camp shares the economic and socialization responsibilities for the children. Any adult is expected to instruct children in toilet training if the occasion arises and to correct them if they misbehave.

Infants receive a great deal of attention and physical contact among the !Kung Bushmen. Not only do !Kung mothers spend significantly more time in physical contact with their infants than do English or American mothers, but !Kung infants also have more social contact with other people.[84] Among hunters and gatherers, infants are nursed on demand and are rarely allowed to cry unattended.

Forager children spend little time with children their own age. Since camps are always small, it is unlikely that there will be many children of the same age in camp. Play groups, therefore, are made up of children of varying ages. This limits the possibility for competitive games and team sports: "The players are at such different levels of motor skill, motivation, and cognitive development that it is difficult and unrewarding to play a game involving intense competition, rules, and fairly complex strategy."[85] The games hunting and gathering children play therefore do not encourage aggressive competition, but rather they encourage individual development and the acceptance of individual differences in skill and motivation.

Not only are children not age segregated among themselves, but they are not segregated from adults either. Among the !Kung,

the relationship between children and adults is easygoing and unselfconscious. Adults do not believe that children should keep to themselves. . . . The organization of work, leisure, and living space is such that there is no reason for confining children, or excluding them from certain activities. Everyone lives on the flat surface of the ground; hence there is no need to protect children from falls or from becoming entrapped behind doors. With the exception of spears and poisoned arrows, adult tools do not constitute a hazard to children. Those weapons

are simply kept hanging in trees or wedged on top of a hut, safely out of reach.[86]

!Kung children observe adult work activities but they do not actively participate in them. Girls do not begin regular food-gathering activities until they are about fourteen years old and boys do not begin serious hunting until they are about sixteen. Because the !Kung can feed themselves easily without child labor, they do not train or expect their children to be economically self-sufficient.[87]

Gender Role Distinctions

Although there is little gender segregation among hunting and gathering children, gender role distinctions are recognized and encouraged. A great many unisex activities take place in childhood, but girls do come to excel in the society's "female activities" and boys focus more of their attention on mastering "male activities." Among the Eskimos

Regardless of sex, it is important for a child to know how to perform a wide variety of tasks and give help when needed. Both sexes collect and chop wood, get water, help carry meat and other supplies, oversee younger siblings, run errands for adults, feed the dogs, and burn trash.

As a child grows older, more specific responsibilities are allocated to him, according to his sex. Boys as young as seven may be given an opportunity to shoot a .22 rifle and at least a few boys in every village have killed their first caribou by the time they are ten.[88]

Chance further emphasizes the flexibility of Eskimo gender role socialization into gender division of labor:

Although there is a recognized division of labor by sex it is far from rigid at any age level. Boys, and even men occasionally sweep the house and cook. Girls and their mothers go on fishing or bird-hunting trips. Members of each sex can usually assume the responsibilities of the other when the need arises, albeit in an auxiliary capacity.[89]

Among the Bushmen, girls learn the skills of gathering by accompanying their mothers on foraging expeditions and further their socialization into adult womanhood by listening to the uninhibited gossip of the women in the foraging group. Boys learn hunting skills largely through games and listening to the hunters talk of the day's activities. Since youngsters are more likely to be disruptive of a hunt than a foraging party, boys are usually older than girls before they can begin taking part in the adult food getting activities.[90] Friedl argues that child-rearing patterns tend to vary according to the work women perform in a particular social group.[91] Instead of viewing the problem from the standpoint that women's work is adjusted to the requirements of child care as Judith Brown does,[92] Friedl argues that child-care requirements are adjusted to the work women do. From Friedl's perspective, then, foraging activities of women in most hunting and gathering societies require such institutions as multiple-child caretakers and campwide sharing of some child-care responsibilities.

Sanday found that the distinction between hostile and positive environments was also related to child-rearing practices.[93] In societies with dangerous environments, where men devoted much of their attention to killing animals or enemies, fathers were distant authoritarian figures who spent little time with babies and young children. Few foragers fit this pattern. Foragers are more likely to view the environment positively, and this is associated with fathers helping in the rearing of children.

Religion and Ritual

Sanday's research is particularly relevant in analyzing the relationship between religion and gender relations among foragers. All societies embody a *sex role plan* in their religious symbols and their myths of creation, which explain where people came from and how the world began.[94] These sex role plans tell men and women what their proper place is in society. They can take an *inner orientation*, focusing on the importance of female fertility and reproductive powers, or they can take an *outer orientation*, focusing on power, domination, and killing. The first type tends to afford women a relatively high place in society, the second tends to see men as more important than women. Sex role plans can also take a *dual orientation*, which combines elements of both the inner and outer orientation.

Creation myths follow a similar pattern. The creator can create from within his/her/its own body. This type of creator may come from within the earth or the sea. This is again associated with important roles and respect for women. The more masculine creator found in outer-oriented religions usually creates through magical means. He usually comes from a high place—the sky, a mountaintop—and has great powers.* Other times the outer-orientation creator is a *culture hero* cast in more human but heroic terms. Dual orientations are associated with an *original couple* who created the first people through natural means of sexual intercourse.

Societies that derive their livelihood primarily from plants and small animals will tend toward the inner orientation and a more feminine or original couple creator. These societies are likely to see their environment as benevolent, they tend to be peaceful, and males are more involved with the care of infants and young children. Outer-oriented societies usually hunt or herd large animals,

---

*The Judeo-Christian creation story fits this pattern. A male God from Heaven creates Adam from dust and Eve from Adam's rib.

the environment is dangerous and threatening, and fathers are distant from their infants and young children. Dual-oriented societies are intermediate, sharing aspects of both.

Forager religions reflect the basic egalitarianism of these societies. They tend to be animistic, believing that spirits live in nature, in animals, plants, land, and water holes. They have an inner orientation (except among hunters of large game) and perhaps no creation myth, only the forest as both father and mother as among the Pygmies. Other forager religions emphasize original ancestors of both sexes. The gods or spirits are usually male and female. The Hadza and Aborigines with their high degrees of gender segregation have a dual orientation combining both masculine and feminine orientations in what Sanday calls a "relationship of balanced complementarity."[95]

Pattern-three-type foragers in the southernmost regions of South America have myths that support ideological male dominance. Their myths hold that there was once a time when women ruled; but women were immoral and ruled badly, so men wrenched power from them. Joan Bamberger found that women represent "chaos and misrule through trickery and unbridled sexuality."[96] The men in these tribes hunt large game or sea mammals such as sea lions. Peoples in pattern four, dependent on male hunting of dangerous game, also focus more on the masculine or outer orientation. The Chipewyan caribou hunters of Northwest Canada fit this pattern, and their symbols (more than their actual social relations) emphasize male superiority. Their myths depict men and women as opposites. They symbolically associate men with the wolf, an honored and skilled predator, and women with the dog, a depreciated beast of burden and scavenger. Men are seen as the holders of ritual knowledge and power necessary in the unpre-

dictable and often fearful world of subarctic hunting.[97] Chipewyan, Eskimo, and the South American foragers exemplify Sanday's *mythical male dominance*. Men are aggressive against women, but women hold important economic and political power. The violence against women makes it appear that men are powerful and more in control than they actually are. But foragers without dangerous hunting or severe environmental stress exhibit gender equality in their practices and their religions.

Most foragers have rituals associated with maleness and femaleness and are particularly likely to celebrate firsts such as the first kill for a boy and menarche (first menstruation) for a girl. Males and females typically participate fairly equally in religion and ritual, but there may be gender segregation with males excluded from female rites almost as often as females are excluded from male rites.

Collier and Rosaldo point out that hunting and gathering societies tend to stress marriage bonds in their rituals, rather than other kinship bonds.[98] Little ritual attention is given to childbirth, not because children are unimportant, but because lineages and generational links are not the bases for significant conflict and problems.

Men are ritually celebrated as hunters because this is often the necessary skill for obtaining a wife. Protein needs and male strength do not account for the ritual importance of hunting. Rather it is the political problems faced by foragers that are important. "People celebrate those very self-images that they use when creating relationships, promoting cooperation or conflict, articulating desires and claims."[99] In foraging societies the heterosexual bonds in marriage are crucial for the economic, political, and social organization of the bands.

In these societies boys are not dependent on their own mothers and fathers for wives.

Parents cannot accumulate a surplus to allow them to "purchase" a bride for their son. Usually, the son must obtain a wife largely through his own efforts, convince her and her parents to accept him through providing them with gifts of food. Such contracts are inherently unstable in foraging societies, however, because no one has sufficient power to enforce an agreement if the other parties decide they no longer want to abide by the agreement. So marital bonds can be unstable. This is why conflicts so often focus on loss of wives. "Theirs is a politics of sex. . . . Men compete and fight for the attainment of a secure marital status."[100] This is the problem being addressed in ritual.

Although it provides considerable theoretical insight, Collier and Rosaldo's theory probably overemphasizes the function of meat-sharing networks among men in creating male prestige and forging marriage alliances. They argue that women merely provide food for their families while men share with the wider community. It appears, however, that women are not just feeders of families but are active participants in food- and craft-sharing networks along with men. Collier and Rosaldo also argue that marriage represents a loss in autonomy and status for women and cite as evidence the reluctance and resistance of young girls to marriage. Girls do often resist marriage, but this probably represents a resistance to the responsibilities of adulthood in general, rather than a resistance to marriage in itself. Men typically marry later than women; they have already been pressured to relinquish the freedom and leisure of adolescence. Boys' resistance to take on the full responsibilities of foraging for food is not seen as resistance to marriage because it precedes marriage for boys, but girls face a similar transition in their own lives after marriage.

Circumcision rites provide evidence that the father is a loyal and trustworthy member of the group, willing to risk the loss of his son's reproductive powers to demonstrate his commitment to the group.[101] This practice is not as widespread among foragers as it is among groups with strong corporate kin groups, but it is very important among the Australian Aborigines. Aborigines are unusual also in the degree of gender segregation practices and the strength of both male and female solidarity groups. Male and female initiation rites are likely to be one of the ritual means of trying to maintain group solidarity within groups having few political or economic resources for generating and maintaining solidarity. Other foragers have painful or exhausting initiation rituals for males, which may serve a similar purpose of promoting solidarity among men or commitment to the society in general.

Menarche is a more common focus of ritual among foragers. Unlike male initiations, this does not usually involve danger or pain for the girl. Rituals celebrating menarche furnish the occasion for the girl's father to solicit social support for his right to make marriage contracts with prospective sons-in-law willing to give bride service, that is, willing to live in the girl's parents' camp and provide food for them.[102] (We would include mothers as beneficiaries as well, since they are often eager to obtain the advantages of having a son-in-law.) The exchange relationship between the son-in-law and the girl's parents is important. But no one can force another to comply with such a contract (and these first marriages are very unstable). So sons-in-law have to be encouraged to wait for the girl to become sexually mature and capable of childbearing. (There is often enough of a shortage of females to make it worth the man's time and effort to try to please the girl and her parents in the hopes of keeping her as his wife.)

Ritual and religion do not typically emphasize fear of women or female pollution, and the menstrual and childbirth taboos associated with such beliefs are rare among foragers. Paige and Paige suggest that foragers exhibit a *ritual disinterest* in both childbirth and menstruation so as not to call attention to the superior resources of couples who have several children and through menstruation exhibit the continuing possibility of having more children. Such a resource cannot be easily shared, but to boast about it through public *ritual displays** would introduce potentially disruptive elements into societies that depend on cooperation rather than competition.[103]

Ortner and Whitehead have also found a widespread relationship between beliefs in female pollution and cultural emphases on male honor as a function of female behavior.[104] Foragers do not emphasize invidious comparisons and focus little attention on "honor" compared with other societies. Individuals usually obtain respect or honor through their own skills as healers, hunters, or "owners" of land resources. A man typically does not depend on his wife's assistance or behavior to obtain such honor, although having a wife is important to his social standing. Beliefs about female pollution are largely absent among such peoples.

In general, the religions of foragers show few similarities with the major religions that developed in patriarchal agricultural or pastoral societies, such as Christianity, Judaism, Islam, or Confucianism. They reflect and promote the basic equality of the foraging way of life and emphasize people's relationship to, dependence on, and respect for nature.

Ritual displays: large feasts or parties accompanying ceremonies celebrating a significant event. Examples in our society are elaborate weddings and bar mitzvahs.

Forces for Change

Hunting and gathering societies are remarkably stable. Because of their egalitarian, non-acquisitive, non-property-oriented natures, there are few forces for change within these societies. Their noncoercive mechanisms of conflict resolution (gossip, ridicule, group intervention in private disputes, and simply moving to another camp when disputes arise) prevent the formation of important cleavages and militate against the concentration of power in the hands of any individual or group. Their technology affords the people subsistence without disruption of the environment. Hunters and gatherers generally find their life-style satisfying and are usually unwilling to abandon it permanently unless forced to do so by external circumstances. For example, Pygmies regularly move into the Bantu horticulturalists' villages and partake of the luxuries available there. But they soon return to their life in the forest.[105]

The foraging way of life is, however, rapidly disappearing in the contemporary world, not because it is not a viable way of life, but because of the encroachments of more technologically advanced peoples onto the lands occupied by the foragers. National governmental policies in countries containing hunters and gatherers are often aimed at destroying the foraging way of life and at incorporating these peoples into modern society. The results are usually disastrous for the foragers. Their death rates often soar when they are forced into permanent settlements, and the culture and social structure of those who survive cannot be maintained in a sedentary way of life.[106] Bell provides a moving account of the personal and social problems that followed in the wake of military conquest and European colonization of Australia. Forced into welfare dependency on settlements, Aboriginal males turned to alcoholism, rape, and wife beating. Alienation from their land and male control of the new governmental machinery, have seriously undermined the traditional autonomy and independence of Aboriginal women.[107]

The environmental scarcity and danger accompanying outside encroachment encourage an increase in gender inequality and the physical abuse of women. This is particularly likely to accompany the transition to a settled life. Draper's comparison of a traditional nomadic foraging camp of !Kung with a group of !Kung living in a permanent village setting is sobering in its implications.[108] A high degree of gender egalitarianism and personal autonomy of women still prevails among the foraging !Kung. However, in the sedentary group women lost a good deal of their autonomy and their influence over group affairs. In the village a more rigid division of labor developed and the socialization of boys and girls became more dissimilar. There was a decrease in the mobility of women compared with men and an increase in male control over important economic resources such as domestic animals. Males but not females entered into public politics. Households became more private, resulting in a decrease in public control over private disputes, which allowed an increase in wife beating. As Frederick Engels suggested long ago, the shift to animal husbandry and crop planting required by life in permanent settlements appears to undermine gender egalitarianism.*

---

*Frederick Engels in his book *The Origins of the Family, Private Property and the State*, written in 1884, attempted to apply the Marxist perspective to an analysis of gender stratification. He argued that more primitive peoples, thought to be inferior by most Westerners of his time, were actually more "civilized" in their treatment of women. Technological advance and the processes of civilization had only increased the inequality suffered by women.

Some foragers are now taking advantage of the legal mechanisms offered by some central governments to fight for protection of their lands and their ways of life.[109] But the predominant trend is the disappearance of foraging. As such peoples become extinct, these examples of male-female relations will probably disappear also.[110]

Conclusion

Foraging societies provide examples of social organization and cultural patterns that place a high premium on social stability, cooperation, egalitarianism, flexibility in human relationships, and recognition of individual integrity and freedom irrespective of age, gender, or personal achievement. Gender and other socially significant distinctions and divisions exist among foragers, and social inequalities—including gender inequalities—are certainly not unknown. Yet, by and large, these societies have developed institutional arrangements in which the interdependence of the genders and the generations is not conditioned by economic and political repression; the social order depends on neither the fact nor theory of male dominance.

Such institutional arrangements have characterized most of the life of the human species on this planet, yet these arrangements in their "primitive" form will probably be extinct by the end of this century. Perhaps one of the most intriguing and urgent questions facing our species in its quest for survival is whether or not "civilized" equivalents of these primitive forms of egalitarianism and nonrepressive social organization can be discovered and maintained in modern societies. Relationships between the genders are among the most problematic historical realities addressed by this question.

To shed further light on these realities, we now turn to an examination of more technologically advanced societies—societies that allow more productive use of the earth's resources but have made the peculiar combination of personal autonomy, equality, and social cooperation characteristic of most foraging societies a utopian dream rather than a common design for human relationships.

Notes

1. Andrew P. Vayda, "Introduction," in Andrew P. Vayda, ed., *Environment and Cultural Behavior* (Garden City, N.Y.: Natural History Press, 1969): xi–xvii. For an excellent example of this type of analysis see C. Daryll Forde, *Habitat, Economy, and Society* (New York: E. P. Dutton, 1963).

2. For good descriptions of this societal type see Gerhard Lenski and Jean Lenski, *Human Societies: An Introduction to Macrosociology*, 4th ed. (New York: McGraw-Hill, 1982): 82–133 and Marvin Harris, *Culture, People, and Nature: An Introduction to General Anthropology*, 2nd ed. (New York: Thomas Y. Crowell, 1975): 230–371.

3. Colin Turnbull, *The Forest People* (New York: Simon & Schuster, 1962): 23.

4. Richard Lee, "!Kung Bushman Subsistence: An Input-Output Analysis," in Vayda, 58.

5. See, for example, Polly Wiessner, "Risk, Reciprocity and Social Influences on !Kung San Economics," in Eleanor Burke Leacock and Richard Lee, eds., *Politics and History in Band Societies* (Cambridge: Cambridge University Press, 1982): 61–84.

6. See George Silberbauer, "Political Process in G/Wi Bands," in Leacock and Lee, 23–35; Richard Lee, "Politics, Sexual and Non-Sexual in an Egalitarian Society." in Leacock and Lee, 37–59, for discussions of the continuing struggle required to maintain peace and harmony among the Bushmen. It is not simply part of the nature of foragers to eschew arrogance and selfishness.

7. Such popular writers include Robert Ardrey, *African Genesis* (London: William Collins, 1966); Konrad Lorenz, *On Aggression* (New York: Oxford University Press, 1966); Lionel Tiger, *Men in Groups* (New York: Vintage Books, 1970); Lionel Tiger and Robin Fox, *The Imperial Animal* (New York: Holt, Rinehart & Winston, 1971). Evidence from the archeological record of early human beings and evidence from the study of chimpanzees refutes many of these views. See, for example, Frances Dahlberg, "Introduction," in Frances Dahlberg,

ed., *Woman the Gatherer* (New Haven, Conn.: Yale University Press, 1981): 1033; W. C. McGrew, "The Female Chimpanzee as a Human Evolutionary Prototype," in Dahlberg, 35–73; Adrienne L. Zihlman, "Women as Shapers of the Human Adaptation," in Dahlberg, 75–120; Nancy Tanner and Adrienne Zihlman, "Women in Evolution. Part I: Innovation and Selection in Human Origins," *Signs: Journal of Women in Culture and Society* 1, no. 3, pt. 1 (1976): 585–608; and Adrienne Zihlman, "Women in Evolution, Part II: Subsistence and Social Organization among Early Hominids," *Signs: Journal of Women in Culture and Society* 4, no. 1 (1978): 4–20.

8. Harris, 1975, 260; Jean L. Briggs, "Living Dangerously: The Contradictory Foundations of Value in Canadian Inuit Society," in Leacock and Lee, 109–131, discusses how the Eskimo group combines through the psychological mechanisms of rationalization and comparmentalization a high value on killing animals with a horror and fear of any kind of aggression against human beings; and Colin Turnbull, "The Ritualization of Potential Conflict among the Mbuti," in Leacock and Lee, 133–155, describes the way Mbuti pygmies are socialized from birth away from violence and aggressivity and how social rituals serve to dissipate or control tendencies toward conflict.

9. Harris, 339.

10. Turnbull, *The Forest People*, 25–26, 120–126.

11. Marvin Harris, *Culture, Man, and Nature* (New York: Thomas Y. Crowell, 1971): 300.

12. See, for example, June Helm, "Female Infanticide, European Diseases, and Population Levels among the Mackenzie Dene," *American Ethnologist* 7 (1980): 259–285; Marjorie Shostak, *Nisa: The Life and Words of a !Kung Woman* (Cambridge, Mass.: Harvard University Press, 1981): 54–56, 66–67, 76–77, 238; Don Dumond, "The Limitations of Human Population: A Natural History," *Science* 187 (February 28, 1975): 715.

13. Paula Weideger, *Menstruation and Menopause* (New York: Delta, 1977): 4–41; Rose E. Frisch, "Demographic Implications of the Biological Determinants of Female Fecundity," *Social Biology* 22, no. 1 (1975): 17–22; Rose E. Frisch, "Critical Weights, a Critical Body Composition, Menarche, and the Maintenance of Menstrual Cycles," in Elizabeth S. Watts, Francis E. Johnston, and Gabriel W. Lasker, eds., *Bio-social Interrelations in Population Adaptation* (The Hague: Mouton, 1975): 319–355; Rose E. Frisch, "Nutrition, Fatness, and Fertility: The Effect of Food Intake on Reproductive Ability," in W. H. Mosley, ed., *Nutrition and Human Reproduction* (New York: Plenum Press, 1978); Rose E. Frisch and Janet W. MacArthur, "Menstrual Cycles: Fatness as a Determinant of Minimum Weight for Height Necessary for Their Maintenance or Onset," *Science* 185 (1974): 949–

951; Lewis R. Binford and William J. Hasko, Jr., "Nunamiut Demographic History: A Provocative Case," in Ezra B. W. Zubrow, ed., *Demographic Anthropology: Quantitative Approaches* (Albuquerque: University of New Mexico Press, 1976):63–143; and Edwin N. Wilmsen, "Interaction, Spacing Behavior, and the Organization of Hunting Bands," *Journal of Anthropological Research* 29, no. 1 (1973): 1–31; Gini Bara Kolata, "!Kung Hunter-Gatherers: Feminism, Diet and Birth Control," *Science* 185 (September 13, 1974): 934.

14. Richard Lee, *The !Kung San: Men, Women, and Work in a Foraging Society* (Cambridge: Cambridge University Press, 1979): 325–330; see J. E. Tyson and A. Perez, "The Maintenance of Infecundity in Postpartum Women," in Mosley, 11–27 for a review of this research.

15. Marlene Dobkin De Rios, "Why Women Don't Hunt: An Anthropologist Looks at the Origin of the Sexual Division of Labor in Society," *Women's Studies* 5 (1978): 241–247.

16. Ernestine Friedl, *Women and Men* (New York: Holt, Rinehart & Winston, 1975): 16–18; and Ernestine Friedl, "Society and Sex Roles," *Human Nature* 1 (April 1978): 68–75.

17. Frances Dahlberg, "Introduction," in Frances Dahlberg, ed., *Woman the Gatherer* (New Haven, Conn.: Yale University Press, 1981): 1–33.

18. George Silberbauer, "The G/Wi Bushmen," in M. G. Bicchieri, ed., *Hunters and Gatherers Today* (New York: Holt, Rinehart & Winston, 1972): 304.

19. Agnes Estioko-Griffin and P. Gion Griffin, "Woman the Hunter: The Agta," in Dahlberg, 121–151; Catherine H. Berndt, "Interpretations and 'Facts' in Aboriginal Australia," in Dahlberg, 153–200; Jane Goodale, *Tiwi Wives* (Seattle: University of Washington Press, 1971); Diane Bell, *Daughters of the Dreaming* (Sydney: McPhee Gribble/George Allen & Unwin, 1983).

20. Friedl, 1978, 71.

21. Bell, 1983, 54–56.

22. Rhoda H. Halperin, "Ecology and Mode of Production: Seasonal Variation and the Division of Labor by Sex among Hunter-Gatherers," *Journal of Anthropological Research* 36 (1980): 379–399.

23. James Woodburn, "An Introduction to Hadza Ecology" and "Stability and Flexibility in Hadza Residential Groupings," in Richard Lee and Irven DeVore, eds., *Man the Hunter* (Chicago: Aldine, 1968): 49–55, 103–111.

24. Elizabeth Marshall Thomas, *The Harmless People* (New York: Vintage Books, 1959).

25. Theorists such as Tiger and Fox, who place tremendous revolutionary importance on the development of male/male bonding in the collective hunt, exaggerate its importance among early human beings. They base

their observations on current hunter-gatherers' adaptations to life in poor habitats. We can probably assume that paleolithic foragers would have had access to the more fertile areas now under the control of more complex societies who have destroyed their usefulness to foragers.

26. Woodburn, 52. See also Woodburn, "Hunters and Gatherers Today and Reconstruction of the Past," in Ernest Gellner, ed., *Soviet and Western Anthropology* (New York: Columbia University Press, 1980): 102–103.

27. Friedl, 1978, 73.

28. Mona Etienne and Eleanor Leacock, "Introduction: Women and Anthropology: Conceptual Problems," in Mona Etienne and Eleanor Leacock, eds., *Women and Colonization: Anthropological Perspectives* (New York: Praeger, 1980): 12–14.

29. Turnbull, 1962, 154.

30. Turnbull, 206.

31. Turnbull, 110.

32. Friedl, 1978, 73.

33. James F. Downs, *The Two Worlds of the Washo* (New York: Holt, Rinehart & Winston, 1966): 48.

34. Downs, 21.

35. Downs, 22.

36. Downs, 26.

37. Downs, 36.

38. Downs, 36.

39. Downs, 51.

40. Friedl, 1975, 36.

41. Norman Chance, *The Eskimo of North Alaska* (New York: Holt, Rinehart & Winston, 1966): 48.

42. Chance, 52.

43. Lynn Price Ager, "The Economic Role of Women in Alaskan Eskimo Society," in Erika Bourguingnon, ed., *A World of Women: Anthropological Studies of Women in the Societies of the World* (New York: Praeger, 1981): 311–312.

44. Chance, 51.

45. Jean Briggs, "Eskimo Women: Makers of Men," in Carolyn J. Matthiasson, ed., *Many Sisters: Women in Cross-Cultural Perspective* (New York: Free Press, 1974): 262–265.

46. Ager, 310–311.

47. Chance, 37, 40.

48. Ager, 317.

49. Chance, 73.

50. Briggs, 276.

51. Friedl, 1975, 42.

52. Friedl, 1978, 74.

53. Briggs, 299–300; Eleanor Leacock, "Introduction," in Frederick Engels, *The Origin of the Family, Private Property and the State* (New York: International Publishers, 1972).

54. Goodale, 169.

55. Goodale, 154.

56. Goodale, 170–171.

57. C. W. Hart and Arnold Pilling, *The Tiwi of North Australia* (New York: Holt, Rinehart & Winston, 1964).

58. Goodale, 126–127.

59. Goodale, 228–229.

60. Frederick G. B. Rose, "Australian Marriage, Land-Owning Groups, and Initiations," in Lee and DeVore, 206.

61. Diane Bell, "Desert Politics: Choices in the Marriage Market" in Etienne and Leacock, 239–269; and Bell, 1983; Phyllis M. Kaberry, *Aboriginal Woman: Sacred and Profane* (London: Routledge & Kegan Paul, 1970; orig. 1939).

62. Griffin and Griffin.

63. Peggy Sanday, *Female Power and Male Dominance: On the Origins of Sexual Inequality* (Cambridge: Cambridge University Press, 1981).

64. Friedl, 1975, 24.

65. Woodburn, 54.

66. Griffin and Griffin, 137–139.

67. Turnbull, 120–125.

68. Peter Fruechen, *Peter Fruechen's Book of the Eskimos* (New York: World, 1961): 171.

69. Friedl, 1975, 34.

70. M. Kay Martin and Barbara Voorhies, *Female of the Species* (New York: Columbia University Press, 1975): 188.

71. Goodale, 131.

72. George B. Silberbauer, *Hunter and Habitat in the Central Kalahari Desert* (Cambridge: Cambridge University Press, 1981): 157, Shostak, 1981.

73. Leacock, 1972, 21.

74. Marjorie Shostak, "A !Kung Woman's Memories of Childhood," in Lee and Irven DeVore, eds., *Kalahari Hunter-Gatherers* (Cambridge, Mass.: Harvard University Press, 1976): 266–267; see also Shostak, 1981, 105–125.

75. Patricia Draper, "Social and Economic Constraints on Child Life among the !Kung," in Lee and DeVore, 1976, 206.

76. David Damas, "The Copper Eskimo," in Bicchieri, 41.

77. See also Herbert Barry III, Irving L. Child, and Margaret K. Bacon, "Relation of Child Training to Subsistence Economy," *American Anthropologist*, 61 (1959): 263; and Michael R. Welch, *Subsistence Economy and Sociological Patterns: An Examination of Selected Aspects of Child-Training Processes in Preindustrial Societies* (unpublished Ph.D. dissertation, University of North Carolina, 1980).

78. Shostak, 1976, 276.

79. Goodale, 36.

80. Goodale, 40.

81. Shostak, 1976, 256; and in Shostak, 1981, Nisa recalls in detail the pains of learning to share as a child.

82. Leacock, 39.

83. Silberbauer, 1972, 314.

84. Melvin Konner, "Maternal Care, Infant Behavior and Development among the !Kung," in Lee and DeVore, 1976, 2287.

85. Draper, 203.

86. Draper, 205.

87. Draper, 210; Shostak, 1981, notes that even after marriage girls do not begin regular food gathering; children are given a long carefree adolescence.

88. Chance, 25.

89. Chance, 26.

90. Silberbauer, 1972, 315–316.

91. Friedl, 1975, 8.

92. Judith Brown, "A Note on the Division of Labor by Sex," *American Anthropologist* 5 (September–October 1970): 1073–1078.

93. Peggy Reeves Sanday, *Female Power and Male Dominance: On the Origins of Sexual Inequality* (Cambridge: Cambridge University Press, 1981), 66–68.

94. Sanday, 3–5.

95. Sanday, 89.

96. Joan Bamberger, "The Myth of Matriarchy: Why Men Rule in Primitive Society," in Michelle Zimbalist Rosaldo and Louise Lamphere, eds., *Woman, Culture, and Society* (Stanford, Calif.: Stanford University Press, 1974): 208.

97. Henry S. Sharp, "The Null Case: The Chipewyan," in Dahlberg, 221–244; and Henry S. Sharp, "Man: Wolf: Woman: Dog," *Arctic Anthropology* 13 (1976): 25–43.

98. Jane F. Collier and Michelle Z. Rosaldo, "Politics and Gender in Simple Societies," in Sherry B. Ortner and Harriet Whitehead, eds., *Sexual Meanings: The Cultural Construction of Gender and Sexuality* (Cambridge: Cambridge University Press, 1981): 275–329.

99. Collier and Rosaldo, 276.

100. Collier and Rosaldo, 290.

101. Karen Erickson Paige and Jeffrey M. Paige, *The Politics of Reproductive Ritual* (Berkeley: University of California Press, 1981): 124–166. See also Turnbull, "Initiation among the BaMbuti of the Central Ituri," in Simon Ottenberg and Phoebe Ottenberg, eds., *Cultures and Societies of Africa* (New York: Random House, 1960): 421–442 for a description of initiation rites for boys and girls. Turnbull describes the circumcision rites for boys, but notes that the practice is borrowed from and performed on the boys by neighboring horticulturalists who have trade relationships with the pygmies.

102. Paige and Paige, 87.

103. Paige and Paige, 49–50.

104. Sherry B. Ortner and Harriet Whitehead, "Introduction," in Ortner and Whitehead, 21.

105. Turnbull, 1962, 26; see also Heiga I. D. Vierich, "Adaptive Flexibility in a Multi-Ethnic Setting: The Basarwa of the Southern Kalahari," in Leacock and Lee, 213–222, and Robert K. Hitchcock, "Patterns of Sedentism among the Basarwa of Eastern Botswana," in Leacock and Lee, 223–267.

106. Lee, 1979, 401–431.

107. Bell, 1980, 1981. The impact of colonization on a number of foragers is dealt with in Etienne and Leacock and in Leacock and Lee.

108. Patricia Draper, "!Kung Women: Contrasts in Sexual Egalitarianism in Foraging and Sedentary Contexts," in Rayna Reiter, ed., *Toward an Anthropology of Women* (New York: Monthly Review Press, 1975): 77–109.

109. But see John S. Matthiasson, "Northern Baffin Island Women in Three Cultural Periods," in Ann McElroy and Carolyn Matthiasson, eds., Special Issue on "Sex-Roles in Changing Cultures," *Occasional Papers in Anthropology* 1 (April 1979): 61–71, and Ann McElroy, "The Negotiation of Sex-Role Identity in Eastern Arctic Culture Change," in McElroy and Matthiasson, 49–60. Both find evidence that these women are finding bases for maintaining the traditional female assertiveness and participation in the public sphere even in the context of sedentary village life.

110. Eleanor Leacock, "Relations of Production in Band Society," in Leacock and Lee, 159–170; Brian Morris, "The Family, Group Structuring and Trade among South Indian Hunter-Gatherers," in Leacock and Lee, 171–187; Serge Bahuchet and Henri Guillaume, "Aka-Farmer Relations in the Northwest Congo Basin," Sheila M. Van Wyck, trans., in Leacock and Lee, 189–211.

CHAPTER 3

Horticultural Societies

Chapter 2 described the positions of women and men in simple hunting and gathering societies. In the evolution of human societies, one of the patterns that developed out of the hunting and gathering way of life was *horticulture*, or simple digging-stick and hoe agriculture. Early human beings in different parts of the world discovered that plants and animals could be domesticated. That is, they learned to produce their own food instead of depending on nature to provide it to the diligent and skilled forager. These technological advances, although gradual in development and effects, eventually resulted in the evolution of very different types of social structures and cultures. These changes, of course, included significant changes in gender roles and the development of gender stratification systems.

Economy and Social Organization

First and foremost, horticulture requires knowledge of the principles of plant cultivation.[1] Simple horticultural societies practice the *slash-and-burn* or *swidden* method of cultivation. This involves felling the trees, cutting away the underbrush of forest lands, and then burning the dried plant growth.

The ashes from the burning process provide necessary fertilizer. The gardens are then planted with the aid of simple wooden digging sticks which do not allow the soil to be turned to any depth. Depending on the original fertility of the soil, the land can be used for only a few years at most. It is then abandoned for many years, allowing the forest to retake the land and restore its fertility for future slash-and-burn use. Horticulture may be combined with hunting, gathering, fishing, or herding to increase the overall productivity of the group.

In horticultural society, uncleared land is usually available to anyone who wants to clear it, and cleared land is usually held communally by extended family groups. Land is a vital resource among horticulturalists, but it usually does not constitute individually owned private property. However, both cleared and uncleared land can represent a scarce resource to be exchanged, stolen, or attacked.

Perhaps the most significant result of horticultural technology as compared with foraging technology is that it allows for the production of a surplus. Horticulturalists have exchangeable forms of wealth in the form of productive garden land, stored food, and domesticated animals. Since they are less mobile than hunters and gatherers, they can also accumulate more and bulkier household goods and personal possessions. Production continues to be primarily for use value. Exchange within kinship groups, villages, and neighborhoods tends to remain reciprocity based and not market oriented. However, the surplus does allow for the development of trade networks and market relationships between different groups.

In advanced horticultural societies productivity is often vastly increased through the knowledge of metallurgy and the development of metal-tipped hoes. These permit the farmers to turn the soil to greater depths and thereby increase its productivity and extend its period of fertility. This same technological advance also allows for the production of better weapons and a resulting increase in both the amount and potential effectiveness of warfare. The surpluses in advanced horticultural societies have sometimes been vast, both because of the societies' increased productivity and because of the spoils of war in the form of booty and slave labor.

Community Size and Social Structure

Horticultural technology allows for more permanent, larger, denser populations and for more complex social and political structures than are found among foragers. The production of crops requires a more sedentary life-style. Simple horticulturalists may move every several years, more advanced horticulturalists may move only once a generation. Some become productive enough to establish permanent towns and urban settlements. While the median size of communities among hunting and gathering societies is 40 persons, it is 95 among simple horticulturalists and 280 among advanced horticulturalists.[2]

The society size among hunters and gatherers and simple horticulturalists is the same as their community size because they do not usually have extracommunity political organization of any significance. However, advanced horticultural societies often have complex political structures that tie different communities into a wider society network. This gives rise to a median society size of 5,800 persons with some having populations of 20,000 or more.[3]

Leadership and Social Inequality

Simple horticultural societies tend to be highly egalitarian. Their leaders typically have no coercive powers over others. Like headmen among foragers, they can only attempt to cajole, persuade, or embarrass others to do their will. Class inequality does not exist among simple horticulturists. Access to food, land, and other material resources is egalitarian, and the actual distribution of the products of the society is fairly equal. Significant differences in wealth and power do not occur. But in comparison with foraging societies, considerable competition exists and results in great differences in prestige. Prestige is gained much as it is among hunters and gatherers, through generosity—the ability to give to others and thereby to incur their debt. However, unlike among foragers, boastfulness and overt competition accompany the gift-giving process among horticulturalists. Givers of feasts, for example, openly praise the abundance and quality of the food they offer and denigrate past feasts given by others. The ability to organize kin to produce food for a large feast confers prestige and the status of "big man" on the organizer. This is often a highly coveted status for men. It does not translate into greater consumption rights or differences in economic power for the big man. He gains prestige and influence but not coercive economic or political power. Such a position is also not hereditary; it must be achieved by each individual who aspires to "big man" status.

Advanced horticultural societies often exhibit hereditary class inequality, slavery, and hereditary leadership positions. A noble class of warriors can often exempt itself from productive labor and exact tribute from the commoner (nonnoble) and slave classes. Some advanced horticulturalists such as the Incans and Mayans of South and Central America controlled vast empires of conquered peoples. This requires, of course, a large and complex, multilayered political and military structure. These peoples are much less likely to practice village autonomy than simple horticulturalists. Furthermore, those that do develop multicommunity governmental structures tend to develop absolutist monarchies with powerful kings, queens, and court members. Upper-class women exercise power over common males by virtue of their class position, although they do not have power over males of equal or higher rank.

Gender Division of Labor

There are three main patterns in the gender division of labor among horticulturalists. Among all horticulturalists the task of clearing the land is assigned to men. This is probably due to the strenuous nature of the work of felling trees and clearing underbrush, which is highly incompatible with pregnancy and the care of small children. Ernestine Friedl argues, however, that it probably originated in needs for defense and fighting to obtain new land and in the opportunities for hunting provided by the uncleared territory.[4] After garden areas have been cleared, Friedl states, there are no consistent adaptive advantages to having either males or females perform the planting, weeding, and harvesting tasks. Pregnancy and child tending do not significantly hinder women in this work except (as among the Yanamamö discussed later) where there is

danger of attack. This is uncommon, however, and the pattern of men clearing and cultivating is relatively rare among horticulturalists. Friedl notes that the Hopi as well as the Yanamamö practice this pattern.[5] Hopi cultivation entails an easy clearing process but strenuous irrigation projects. Hopi women tend small vegetable gardens instead of assisting in the production of the staple crops.

Predominantly male cultivation patterns are associated with increasing population density and scarcity of land.[6] If a group cannot easily abandon a used garden plot for a new one, the land will require more work to maintain its fertility. The increased labor input necessary may force men to help with cultivation tasks previously left only to women. Increased population density also increases the danger of raiding and makes it more difficult for women to tend the gardens without male protection.

The intensification of crop production leads to greater male participation in horticulture, especially if seasonality—a long dry season and a short wet season—creates intense short-term labor demands incompatible with pregnancy and the continual performance of necessary daily domestic labor.[7] Tree crops are associated with increased male contribution to crop production. Male monopoly of tree crop production is probably due to the danger of climbing trees for harvesting and of the danger of attack. Planted trees represent a sizable investment in labor; they also attract theft. Furthermore, if horticultural peoples have to keep shifting their residences, the trees may eventually be a long distance from the residences, making it difficult and dangerous for the women to attend to them and simultaneously attend to their domestic tasks.

Two other patterns are more common among horticulturalists: *men clear and women cultivate*, and *men clear and both genders cultivate*. The Iroquois Indians practiced the "men clear, women cultivate" pattern and, as we discuss later, this was associated with high status and important economic control by women. "Men clear and both genders cultivate" is a very common pattern. Sometimes it involves women cultivating "women's crops" and men cultivating "men's crops." This is particularly true in areas such as highland New Guinea where men raise prestige crops for exchange value while women raise the staple crops for domestic use value. This, of course, gives men the advantage of participating in reciprocity networks and offers them opportunity of gaining power and prestige through these exchanges. Among other peoples both men and women raise the same crops. In West Africa it is common for both men and women to cultivate staples for use value and prestige crops for exchange value. Female trading has been an important phenomenon in Africa for raising the status of women and giving them the economic basis to exercise power and personal autonomy.

Female Trading

In advanced horticultural societies in West Africa with well-developed market systems, females handled a large share of the trading.[8] This probably results from female farming systems that gave women control over the products they produce. Thus when markets arose women had products to exchange. Boserup finds that in Africa, in regions of female farming women dominate market trade, whereas in regions of male farming men dominate trade. This even overrides the influence of the Moslem religion, which often forbids women taking public roles in the marketplace as either buyers or sellers. This religious teaching is not obeyed by Moslem female farmers in countries such as Senegal and the Sudan.

Women rarely become wealthy or powerful as traders in advanced horticultural so-

cieties, but trading does give them a basis for greater power in their marital relationship and greater personal autonomy. Since the husband usually benefits economically from his wife's trading, he is not as likely to interfere with her use of her profits as he would be with a working wife's salary. He fears hurting her profits in the long run by interfering in the short run.[9]

Women's trading often allows them to travel widely, to hire others to care for their children and households, and even to use their profits to aid their husbands in obtaining a second wife to assume much of the domestic work load. These women traders are not isolated in the domestic sphere; they are active participants in the public economic spheres of their societies. The extent of their commitment to and participation in their public economic roles was apparent in the Women's Riot of 1929–1930 in Nigeria. The colonial government of Britain successfully levied a tax on men in 1926. When they attempted to extend the tax to women in 1929, however, women spread the news through their marketplace connections and "rose like an army in massive protest against this injustice, looting European trading stores and banks, breaking into prisons to release prisoners, and beating chiefs and court messengers.[10] The men did not react in such an organized political manner in defense of their interests.

Gender Segregation and the Division of Labor

Extreme gender segregation is a striking characteristic of the division of labor in many horticultural societies and is often reflected in the entire life of the society. It is not uncommon for women and men to lead almost separate lives. We see an example of this in the Mundurucu of Brazil.[11] Men work continuously in collective groups clearing new land for gardens. They also hunt in large groups. Women work communally in the gardens as the primary cultivators, as gatherers, and in the onerous, time-consuming task of processing the manioc roots into flour. The work and the worlds of men and women are largely separate. The men live in the men's house where they eat, sleep, and practice male rituals. Women and children live in separate houses. Husbands and wives do not sleep together in this society.

Institutionalized Homosexuality and the Division of Labor

Some horticultural societies recognize intermediate gender categories in addition to male and female. Harriet Whitehead analyzes the role of the *berdache* and institutionalized homosexuality common among North American Indians. Individuals taking the cross-gender or *berdache* role were not denigrated or considered deviant.[12]* Both males and females could adopt the role of the other sex, but it was easier and more common for males than for females to gender-cross, largely because taking on the female role constituted downward mobility, whereas the male role required the more difficult upward mobility. Once a person adopted the clothing and occupation appropriate to the other gender, he or she could then participate fully in that status, including the marriage appropriate to the new gender status.

North American Indian gender hierarchies relied heavily on the gender division of labor, in particular, occupation, as the

defining characteristic for gender. Furthermore, women could control their own economic labor and its products and sometimes become wealthy and gain considerable prestige in their own right. This made it attractive for some men and possible for some women to gender-cross. Male *berdache* often adopted the most lucrative of the female curing specialties or crafts. Thus a man who was not successful in the male warrior role could gain wealth and some prestige in the female role. Similarly, the females who gained sufficient wealth were "masculinized" and could head ceremonies usually reserved for male sponsorship. They could also dominate their husbands and cowives when they gained the economic upper hand. A few girls also crossed gender and took on the full male warrior role.

Occupation was more important than physiological differences for gender differentiation. These societies were highly stratified on the basis of gender, ranking the male warrior/big game hunter superior to the female farmer or craft or curing specialist. Yet some of the female occupations could accrue wealth and prestige inconsistent with the gender stratification system. Whitehead believes that had not colonization intervened to disrupt these cultures, their gender stratification was on the verge of collapse. Gender crossing was a transitional stage between a high degree of gender statification linked to occupation and a low degree of gender stratification with occupational stratification.

Kinship Patterns and Gender Roles

Because the technology of horticulture usually requires some collective work effort and often collective defense efforts as well, horticultural societies have tended to develop

---

*Similar institutionalized transvestites/homosexuals among the Samoans and Tahitians are denigrated and serve as negative role models for males.[13] But among all three of these groups—North American Indians, Samoans and Tahitians—the nontransvestite men who have sexual relations with these men are not defined as either homosexual or deviant.

kinship systems to help them organize to solve these problems. Therefore, horticultural peoples are more likely to have *unilineal descent groups,* which jointly hold interests in property and people. As we noted in Chapter 2, foragers are likely to be *bilateral* in their descent reckoning; that is, they recognize kinship ties evenly and symmetrically through both the father's and mother's line. This is functional for hunters and gatherers because it allows them to draw upon the widest possible kin network during times of need. However, it is not a useful system for developing and maintaining corporate ownership of land and other resources. A bilateral system has no logical stopping point, and each person has a unique *kindred* or set of kinsmen. For example, a daughter includes all her father's and mother's kindred in her kindred. However, her kindred differs from her mother's, which does not include descent lines through the father's kindred (although they are tied by *affinity* or marriage). Also, it differs from her father's kindred, which does not include her mother's descent line. Thus, a bilateral system does not produce a definite non-ego-centered group of people who could live, work, and own property together.[14]

One way a people can define kinship to produce a series of such definite, nonoverlapping, corporate kinship groups is to exclude systematically at each generation either the mother's or the father's line. A system that excludes female generational links is called *patrilineal.* In patrilineal systems descent is traced solely through the male line. Systems that exclude male generational lines are called *matrilineal* and trace descent solely through the female line.

The Matrilineality Puzzle

Patrilineality is more common, but the mere existence of matrilineal descent systems was considered a puzzle by early Western social scientists. Western kinship systems, although primarily bilateral, still exhibit strong strains of patrilineality in naming, inheritance, and forming one's identity. In the nineteenth century Western societies were even more strongly patrilineal than they are today. Thus patrilineality seemed only "natural" to early social scientists; they saw no need for explaining its existence. But they considered the existence of *matrilineality* to be a perplexing question. One of their incorrect assumptions about matrilineality was that it indicated that such societies were also *matriarchies;* that is, they assumed that matrilineal peoples would be ruled by women and practice male subordination. This is not the case, however. Although matrilineality has important consequences for women and can afford them greater power, influence, and personal autonomy than patrilineality, it has not given rise in any known societies to matriarchy. Patrilineality is, however, sometimes associated with patriarchy. Furthermore, from the standpoint of scientific theory, both matrilineality and patrilineality need explaining. We cannot assume that one is "natural."

In searching for the causes of these different descent systems, it has been noted that matrilineality is more common among horticulturalists than among any other types of societies. Only 10 percent of hunting and gathering societies practice matrilineality, along with only 4 percent of agrarian societies and virtually no industrial societies. However, 26 percent of simple horticultural societies and 27 percent of advanced horticultural societies have matrilineal kin groups.[15]

Attempts to explain why some societies, especially horticultural societies, exhibit matrilineality, have often focused on the female economic contribution to the society. There is some connection between this factor and matrilineality, but it does not appear to be the important causal variable. Matrilineality is not likely to develop in societies where males make the primary economic contributions. But where females are the primary producers, or at least equal contributors with males, both patrilineality and matrilineality are found.[16]

Marvin Harris argues convincingly that it is not female economic contribution that is important so much as it is the existence of factors requiring males to be absent from the community for long periods of time such as for long-distance trade, work, or external warfare. Patrilineality and *patrilocality* (the new couple resides with the husband's father's household) keep men from the same kinship group together and bring in wives from other patrilineages. These women have not been reared together and are not accustomed to working together in collective enterprises. They often compete with one another for resources from their husbands' patrilineage. They may not develop strong allegiance to the husbands' group. This creates a problem of who will look after the kin group's property and interests while the males are away.

Matrilocality solves this problem because it structures the domestic unit around a permanent core of resident mothers, daughters and sisters who are trained in cooperative labor patterns from birth and who identify the "minding of the store" with their own material and sentimental interests.[17]

Matrilocality refers to the new couple residing with the wife's mother's household. If male absence encourages matrilocality, in the long run matrilocality is likely to give rise to matrilineality, because descent systems usually reflect, legitimate, and regulate actual kinship-related practices.[18]

Furthermore, matrilineality appears to be undermined by *population pressure* and *internal warfare*, which give the adaptive advan-

tage to groups that concentrate male fighting strength (the effects of the warfare complex are discussed later in this chapter). Elaborating on this, M. Kay Martin and Barbara Voorhies point out that

matrilineal horticultural societies . . . seem to be adaptive in habitats that allow considerable stability in human organization. . . . Matriliny is ideally an *open* system, this disperses rather than consolidates its potential sources of power—its men. Such an adaptation seems to arise where resources are equal to or exceed those required to accommodate the needs of extant populations, and where competition between communities in the same niche is absent or infrequent.[19]

Matrilineal societies therefore tend to be internally peaceful. If this internal peace is regularly disrupted by defense needs generated by increased local competition over scarce resources, the society may eventually transform its descent system to patrilineality or bilaterality. But such change is not inevitable.[20] A transitional form which retains matrilineal descent but concentrates the male power of the matrilineage involves *avunculocal* residence. That is, the new couple moves in, not with the wife's mother, but with the wife's maternal uncle. The maternal uncle or mother's brother occupies a position similar to that of the father in a patrilineal system.

Effects of Matrilineality on Gender Roles

Apart from their origins or causes, matrilineality and matrilocality are important here because of the effects they have on the positions of women and men who practice such *matricentric* (matrilineal and/or matrilocal) kinship and residence systems. First, since they divide the male fighting force, they promote peace and stability instead of competition and feuding. They are not likely to be associated with the *warfare complex* and the denigration of women that that involves. Second, since they often facilitate female collective work, ownership, and residence patterns, they promote *female solidarity,* which can increase female power in a society. With matrilocality, mothers, daughters, and sisters stay together throughout their lives. They can maintain close ties and joint interests and provide support for each other. Husbands enter as strangers and suffer the anxiety and isolation that the structural position of outsider in a close-knit group entails. This serves to strengthen female power and weaken male power. It does not necessarily mean that women will dominate in such structures, but it does lessen the possibility of harsh, authoritarian dominance of wives by husbands. The wife's close kin are readily available to aid her; the husband may be separated from his kin.

Patrilineality and Patrilocality

Patrilineality is often associated with patrilocality, which, of course, places the adjustment burden on females. The wife must leave her natal kin group and move, often as a stranger, into the household and lineage of the husband. Patrilineal societies are also more likely to practice *village exogamy* (marriage partners come from different villages), while matrilineal societies are more likely to practice *village endogamy* (marriage partners come from the same village). Where village exogamy is practiced, the female is separated from her own kin and has little opportunity to call upon them for help. Isolation from her kin makes her vulnerable and dependent on her husband and his kin. Thus, while patrilineality is likely to remove the wife from her kin, matrilineality is not likely to isolate the husband from his kin group. In this respect, matrilineality does not disadvantage males as much as patrilineality disadvantages females.

Female solidarity can be inhibited by patrilocality. The women of the household come from different villages. They lose much of the protection of their own lineage and have little basis for developing close ties. Furthermore, they must often compete with cowives (where polygyny is practiced) and with the wives of their husband's brothers. Often, each woman is given a separate hut and separate gardens to tend and does her work individually rather than communally. This does not create ties of interdependence and reciprocity among the women. To the degree that women are isolated from one another by competition, jealousy, and individualistic work and consumption patterns, they are not likely to develop the "safety in numbers" associated with strong female solidarity and therefore are likely to be more vulnerable and dependent on men.

Competition and Warfare. Patrilineality is more adaptive to a competitive environment than matrilineality. Where conditions arise requiring the accumulation of greater surpluses, competition is usually necessary to motivate people to expend the extra effort to produce more. And where conditions (such as population pressure) arise that require the group to defend or aggrandize its holdings, patrilocality and patrilineality are adaptive responses because they concentrate the male fighting power of the group. Matrilineality encourages peace, stability, and low competitiveness. Matrilineal cultivation does not, however, produce the same levels of competitive productivity as patrilineal cultivation does:

Typically, matrilineal groups are concerned with the production of adequate food for their respective lineage and clan members, rather than with the maximization of resources through coercion or increased exploitation.

Patrilineal subsistence farmers, in contrast, are found in much less favorable habitats, where considerably more effort must be expended to attain similar rewards.[21]

Sanday's distinction between inner-oriented cultures of peoples living in nonthreatening environments versus the outer-oriented cultures of peoples in hostile circumstances applies to many horticultural societies. Matrilineal peoples tend to be more inner or feminine oriented than patrilineal peoples.

Sisters versus Wives. Karen Sacks's research on preclass- and prestate-level societies (societies without social classes or strong central governments) in Africa illuminates the significance of the sister versus wife status within patrilineages and the importance of women's participation in communal or kin-based corporate production groups.[22] As struggles for power among competing groups in society led to the emergence of ruling classes and central governments, the communal production relations of foragers were abandoned and the kin-based productive units of simple horticulturalist were destroyed. In the kin-based corporate groups, women held important positions as sisters, and women as well as men participated in collective work groups rather than as isolated individuals. Production was primarily for use value. With the development of class society and an increased importance for male production of exchange values, women's status as wives emerged as the defining social position for women, and work for both men and women became more individualized, resulting in losses in power and autonomy for both men and women of the nonruling classes and for women relative to men in both nonruling and ruling classes.

Forager production, as we saw in the preceding chapter, is organized communally with important divisions made largely on the basis of age and gender, but all adults labor in support of the group as a whole. Every person becomes an adult, assumes the responsibilities of adults, and shares in the "ownership" of resources equally as an individual irrespective of kinship ties to a particular lineage. Corporate kin groups are of little importance. Women's positions as wives and sisters and men's positions as husbands and brothers are of no great significance in the organization of work or decision making.

Horticulturalists, however, rely heavily on corporate kin groups, especially patrilineages, to organize production and decision making. Property, production, and decision making are located within the separate lineages. But females are not necessarily excluded from any of these spheres. As sisters they often share with their brothers important roles in their lineages.

Among the Lovedu horticulturalists of Africa, for example, Sacks found that sisters and brothers both retain their positions in the patrilineages throughout their lives despite the fact that women must marry out of the lineage. Sisters marry their *cross-cousins* (children of parental siblings of the opposite sex who therefore always fall into different lineages), usually the sons of their fathers' sisters. Their marriages link the different patrilineages together through affinity (marriage ties). A young wife is subordinate to her mother-in-law (her aunt) and to her husband's patrilineage. But as a sister gets older she becomes a mother-in-law and gains authority over her daughters-in-law, who are the daughters of her brother and provided by her patrilineage. Brothers similarly gain authority with age over their sons. With cross-cousin marriage, the female does not have to move far away from her lineage. She can continue to work for and exercise authority in her own lineage. The husband/

wife roles are much less significant than the sister/brother roles. Gender relations are relatively egalitarian, since women can exercise both economic and political power and are not subject to much aggression from men. They do not lose the protection of their own kin group or of the women with whom they share collective work.

In contrast to the Lovedu, among the Mpondo women's positions as sisters are not important in the exercise of political and economic power, and Mpondo women are more subordinate to the men of their society. The Mpondo are horticulturalists and cattle herders in a very hostile environment of endemic warfare and cattle raiding. Sacks's, Harris's (discussed in the next section), and Sanday's theories all point to the negative impact such situations have for gender equality.

Kin-based corporate ownership prevails among the Mpondo as among the Lovedu, but there is greater concentration of power under Mpondo chiefs than with the relatively powerless Lovedu chiefs and queen. The Mpondo, then, represent a society with some class inequality, and this is associated with a loss of power, autonomy, and respect for women within the lineages. Mpondo women are producers for their husbands' patrilineage, but they do not share in the ownership of that patrilineage's property. As sisters they link the patrilineages through marriage and hold some ownership rights in their brothers' patrilineage, but they do not produce for it. Brothers, however, are both producers and owners within the same patrilineage. This separation of ownership rights and productive contributions of women prevents them from exercising much power within either their brothers' or their husbands' lineages. Mpondo women do work in collective work groups with other women of the lineages, and this provides

some basis for resisting the forces of subordination.

However, Mpondo women do not suffer the same degree of subordination as Sacks found among the more fully developed class society with a strong central government of the Buganda. With the emergence of a full-scale ruling class and central government to enforce the interests of that class, kin-based corporate productive units are suppressed in favor of transforming the lower class males into dependent clients producing on land owned by the ruling class. Brother/sister relations lose their economic and political significance in all but the ruling class lineages. Women as wives are the wards of men who continue to produce use values within the domestic sphere while men produce exchange values in the public sphere. The domestic/public dichotomy arises within advanced horticultural societies with high degrees of class inequality and, as we shall see in Chapter 5, is a prevailing characteristic of settled agrarian societies.

Warfare and Gender Inequality

Marvin Harris also analyzes the significance of patrilineages in gender inequality and finds that under certain circumstances, especially in hostile environments, strong tendencies toward male dominance may be encouraged.[23] He explains the origins and variability of male supremacy in prestate level band and village peoples as a result of the need to limit population growth. In brief, he argues that reproductive pressure leads to primitive warfare and primitive warfare results in the male supremacy complex.

Primitive societies lack safe and effective birth control and abortion techniques. Yet unrestrained population growth would in most cases expand their numbers beyond the capacity of their ecological system. The one effective population control technique available to them is *infanticide*, in particular female infanticide. Female infanticide is far more effective than male infanticide in limiting population growth, because, as Harris puts it, males are "reproductively superfluous." One male can keep dozens of females pregnant. The fertility of a group is determined by the number of women, not the number of men. Killing males then has no long-term effect on population growth, but killing females does.

However, it would require a powerful force to motivate people to kill their daughters or to allow them to die. Women make important contributions in primitive societies and daughters are important as a labor force and as sex objects. Yet the often drastically imbalanced sex ratios in primitive societies with severe population pressure, defense, and warfare problems indicates that female infanticide is widely practiced among these peoples.

It is the *warfare complex* that motivates parents to kill their daughters. Under primitive conditions males make the best warriors, not because they are innately aggressive, but because they are in general taller, heavier, stronger, and better runners than females. Females could be socialized to be fierce warriors, but societies using male warriors would have the advantage and would probably overrun the female war parties. But Harris adds that this does not explain why the strongest, fastest females are not trained as warriors instead of the weaker male members. Why not have mixed-gender war parties comprised of the strongest regardless of gender? Harris replies that this does not occur because of the need to motivate humans to become fierce warriors willing to withstand pain and to risk their lives in battle.

Two kinds of rewards are possible to induce people to be fierce. One kind of reward is to allow them access to more and better food and other creature comforts. However, the corollary to this would be to deprive the less brave and less successful warriors of food and comforts. This would weaken the overall strength of the fighting force and would be counterproductive to the goal of maximizing fighting strength. Hence this form of reward and punishment is not a primary one among primitive warriors. Rather, they rely on the second kind of motivator. Successful warriors are rewarded with the services and subordination of women. Women are turned into the sexual and menial servants of men as part of a system to motivate men to be brave warriors. Poor warriors are not given access to women, and this deprivation does not weaken them for battle as food deprivation would.

It would be equally possible to train women to be warriors and to motivate them with males' services as the reward. There is nothing inherent in the nature of either gender to make one the natural warrior gender and the other the natural subordinate. And in fact the female control over young children deriving from women's ability to give birth and nurse children would make it especially easy for women to render men the subordinate gender. Boys could be selectively allowed to die in favor of girls. Boys could be punished for displays of aggression and rewarded for passivity and carefully trained as servants for their mothers, sisters, and wives. Yet this does not happen because the female fighting force would be less effective than a male fighting force.

If all societies used female warriors, there would be no disadvantage in rearing males to be subordinate and passive. But as long as one group uses male warriors, other groups must protect themselves by using male warriors as well. Since the motivation system requires one gender to be the rewards of the warrior gender, this subordinate gender is always the females. Even the potentially effective females are denied access to training for warfare because the inclusion of females in the fighting force would upset the gender hierarchy and ruin the motivation system and ideology necessary to make anyone want to be a warrior. Warfare therefore leads to female subordination.

Thus Harris notes a strong correlation between population pressure and warfare and the following other phenomena: patrilineality (kinship traced through the father's line), patrilocality (residence with the husband's kin), bride price (goods provided to the bride's family by the groom or his kin), male control of political institutions, cultural imagery of women as unclean, including pregnancy and menstrual taboos, and female assignment to the tedious, menial, drudge work in the division of labor:

My argument is that all of these sexually asymmetric institutions originated as a by-product of warfare and the male monopoly over military weaponry. Warfare required the organization of communities around a resident core of fathers, brothers and their sons. This led to the control over resources by paternal-fraternal interest groups and the exchange of sisters and daughters between such groups (patrilineality, patrilocality and bride-price) to the allotment of women as a reward for male aggressiveness and hence to polygyny. The assignment of drudge work to women and their ritual subordination and devaluation follows from the need to reward males at the expense of females and to provide supernatural justifications for the whole male supremacist complex.[24]

It is, furthermore, adaptively advantageous for primitive peoples to practice warfare because this provides the motivation necessary for female infanticide. The group that maximizes its male muscle power is the group that is likely to prevail in the constant feuding and fighting. Therefore, given the fact of limited resources to rear children, male children are given preference in survival. Women need the male warriors for defense against other groups' males as much

as the men do. These warfare-generated problems serve as the motivation to kill off daughters. This then limits population because it also eliminates all the children the daughters would have had if they had been allowed to live. (Male deaths in warfare do serve to limit the population in the short run but are not important in limiting overall population increase.)

A vicious cycle comes into operation with the warfare complex. Female infanticide aids in maximizing the fighting strength of a group in its competition with other groups for scarce resources in land and game. But female infanticide also increases the need to fight. The shortages of women induced by female infanticide and by the monopolization of numbers of women by the most successful warriors increase the motivation of the males without women to raid other groups for women. Hence disputes over women provide an important basis for going to war. Having to fight in wars, in turn, induces the groups involved to keep killing off their daughters which makes the female shortage problem chronic. Once a population is involved in the warfare complex, it is very difficult to break out of the cycles it creates.

Harris cautions us to remember that it is not war as such that causes female subordination but the population pressure that gives rise to war in the primitive (but not the modern) context. When game or land become scarce owing to population growth and overexploitation of the environment, people are likely to fight over these resources. Warfare serves to distribute them more widely and sometimes to leave disputed areas fallow, which allows them to regain their fertility. But most important for purposes of population control, it results in female infanticide.

Thus female subordination is likely to be greatest among primitive peoples with population pressure problems and the resulting warfare complex. However, not all warrior groups follow this pattern. It is necessary to distinguish between *internal* and *external warfare*. The pattern of warfare leading to male supremacy is associated with internal warfare in which geographically close and culturally similar peoples are involved in chronic intermittent warfare over local resources.

External warfare creates a different pattern of female status. In fact, external warfare often results in an improved social position for women instead of degradation and subordination. The Iroquois Indians of upstate New York are often cited as a near matriarchy (a society ruled by women) because of their matrilineal descent system and the important political and economic power their women held. Yet they were an extremely vicious warlike people. However, their wars were fought against distant, culturally different peoples and involved the consolidation of local groups into large federations. Furthermore, this type of war is not the result of local population pressure and does not involve disputes over women. Males of the local groups are not encouraged to feud with each other. This type of warfare takes the men away from the home base, often for long periods of time. Women are left in charge of the family economic holdings and exercise a great deal of control over decision making and a high degree of personal autonomy. Absent males cannot exert much control over their women. Thus *male absence* for long-distance war and for other purposes such as for work or trade allows for higher female status and power.

Although Harris's perspective on the warfare complex has special relevance to the understanding of environmental determinism among horticultural peoples, his extensions of the perspective to the analysis of other types of societies is also of interest.

What appears to be external war among *nomadic pastoral peoples* (people who make their living by herding livestock from one grazing area to another; see Chapter 4) results in the same high degree of female subordination as the pattern associated with internal war. Athough these nomadic herding peoples move great distances in their war and attack culturally dissimilar peoples, it is really a form of internal war because they have no permanent home base. Their wide-ranging warfare does not require them to leave their property, women, and children behind. "Home" is taken with them as they attempt to conquer new grazing lands and water holes. It is another variation on the population pressure, warfare, male supremacy complex with the element of wide-ranging nomadism added.

Foragers may develop analogous situations. Hunters and gatherers such as the Eskimos usually do not get involved in the warfare and male supremacy complexes and in general exhibit highly egalitarian gender roles. The Eskimos are, however, the most inegalitarian of hunters and gatherers and they practice female infanticide. But maximizing male muscle power and motivating males for the difficult and hazardous arctic hunt is similar to the need for male muscles and motivation in the warfare complex. The Eskimos do not have a problem of overpopulation and the consequent danger of "eating up" the environment. They simply have to find enough to eat to sustain themselves. Furthermore, female gathering is practically nonexistent in the arctic environment because of lack of vegetation. Male hunting and deep-sea fishing are the almost exclusive sources of food. This makes sons more valuable than daughters and motivates female infanticide and the devaluation of women in the absence of war.

The impact of internal warfare and of dangerous hunting in a scarce environment on gender stratification and gender roles holds only for preindustrial band and village level peoples. Male dominance has a different basis in industrial societies. Male muscle power is of little importance under industrialization. Neither the females' weaker musculature nor their physiological processes associated with childbirth, lactation, and menstruation can explain male dominance in modern societies. None of the aspects of gender *dimorphism* (physical differences between the gender) have much causal influence on the division of labor, gender hierarchies, or gender roles. Harris argues that male dominance continues because males control the key institutions. Industrialization makes gender equality possible but not inevitable:

The fact that warfare and sexism have played and continue to play such prominent roles in human affairs does not mean that they must continue to do so for all future time. War and sexism will cease to be practiced when their productive, reproductive, and ecological functions are fulfilled by less costly alternatives. Such alternatives now lie within our grasp for the first time in history. If we fail to make use of them, it will be the fault not of our natures but of our intelligence and will.[25]

Three Cases

The Iroquois, the Truk, and the Yanamomö furnish a range of examples of gender roles in different kinship patterns.

The Iroquois. If matrilineality and matrilocality are combined with female economic control, women may be in a particularly advantageous position for exercising power in the society. The Iroquois Indians of upstate New York during the eighteenth and nineteenth centuries are a fascinating example of such a society.[26] The Iroquois were a matrilineal, matrilocal, simple horticultural people whose women exercised significant legitimate economic and political power. As Judith Brown points out, the high status of women among the Iroquois is evidenced not in deferential, "placed on a pedestal" treatment, but rather can be seen in the real power and personal autonomy accorded women. Males devoted their primary energies to the organization and execution of large-scale external wars involving the federation of different Iroquois villages against far distant non-Iroquois peoples. These wars took the men away from the local communities for long periods, leaving the women in effective control. It was, therefore, adaptive to organize the kinship, residence, and collective work systems around the matrilineal core of mothers, daughters, and sisters.

The longhouse was the symbol of the matrilineage and of the Iroquois people as a whole. Each lineage lived and worked communally as an extended family in its own longhouse. The chief *matron* of the lineage held authority over the longhouse; this authority was not exercised by either her husband or brother. The men of the lineage cleared the land for planting, but groups of women took care of most of the other horticultural production activities. Men also contributed some meat to the food supply through hunting. The crucial factor in explaining the high status and power of Iroquois women is not so much their productive work as the control they exercised over the food supply. Land was cleared by men and owned communally, but use rights were held by women. The food supply and the distribution of food both within and among the households was controlled entirely by women. Even the food from the men's hunt was distributed by the women, not the hunters. Through their control of stored food they could veto the war expeditions by not providing the necessary dried provisions for the long treks. They could also prevent certain meetings of the Council of Elders from being held by withholding the necessary supplies for the accompanying feasts.

This economic power of women, which originated in their economic control, was institutionalized in their political power. The Council of Elders, which was the highly egalitarian governing body of the village, was all male. But eligibility for office was passed through the female line and members could be nominated only by females. In addition, females could institute impeachment proceedings against officeholders who did not perform adequately. The matrons were also consulted on the important decisions made by the Council, including decisions related to the conduct of war and the making of treaties.

Women also participated in the selection of religious leaders and in the ceremonial and ritual life of the tribe. Women's activities were celebrated as well as men's. Marriages were arranged by the mothers. Divorce was easily available to men and women.

We should note, however, that matrilineality does not always confer power and status upon women. Alice Schlegel, for example, has found that under matrilineality women are still usually subject to the authority of males. It may be the brother rather than the husband who dominates, but in 78 percent of the sixty-four matrilineal societies Schlegel examined, females were dominated by males.[27] Matrilineal or matrilocal females often have more control over property than women in other types of societies, but Martin Whyte has noted only a weak statistical association between female domestic authority (matrilineality and matrilocality) and important indicators of high female status (ritualized female solidarity, a high value for female life, and equal sexual restrictions between men and women).[28]

The Truk. The Truk of the Caroline Islands in the Western Pacific Ocean provide an example of a matrilineal society with high male dominance.[29] An important difference between the Truk and the Iroquois is that males control the food supply among the Truk, whereas females have control among the Iroquois. The staple food of the Truk is the breadfruit and men control its entire production and distribution. They plant the trees, care for them, harvest the fruit, peel it, and cook it. Access to trees and land may come through the wife's lineage, but the husband has the economic control. He even controls and distributes the fish his wife catches. This food sharing is very important for creating reciprocity ties between the Truk males.

Truk matrilineages live and work together and exercise collective ownership of the land. However, the eldest male of the lineage administers the lineage's resources and organizes and directs the labor of the other members. The Senior Male has power over the entire lineage, but the females are governed more directly by the Senior Woman. The Senior Woman is not the equal of the Senior Man, however, as she must report to and defer to the wishes of the Senior Man. The females must defer to any of the lineage's males past the age of puberty. Husbands dominate their wives and have the support of the wives' lineages in controlling them.

A man has exclusive sexual rights in his wife and has the support of her lineage in punishing any infractions which may be discovered. He expects his wife to treat him with deference, to take care of his clothes, and to fish and cook snacks for him. If she fails in any of these respects he may beat her, and—unless he is entirely unjustified or carries the beatings to extremes—her lineage will not interfere.

Although a man finds it easy to leave in divorce, merely using the pretext of adultery, the wife finds it considerably more difficult to terminate a marriage unless her husband consistently fails in his obligations, when her brother may tell him to leave.[30]

In addition to male economic control, male dominance in this matrilineal, matrilocal society also appears to be encouraged by practices that develop male solidarity but not female solidarity. Females work together under the direction of the Senior Woman, but these communal efforts do not encourage the same degree of interdependence as the collective work of the males. Women depend more on their brothers than they do on the other women of the lineage. Men, however, depend on the other men of their wives' lineages for support in times of need, communal work, and for companionship.

The outsider status of males in matrilocal societies does, however, take its toll on Truk males. Despite their superordinate position in the Truk gender stratification system, psychological tests indicate that females are more secure while the males are more anxious and insecure. This derives perhaps from the fact that females have stable, secure homes where they are always accepted, but males do not. They are secure members of neither their sisters' nor their wives' households. Matrilocality, therefore, appears to cause females few adjustment problems while it may force men to face dislocations as they move from their mothers' households to their wives' homes.

The Yanamamö. The Yanamamö Indians practice simple horticulture supplemented by hunting in the tropical forest areas of the Brazil and Venezuela border.[31] They are regarded as one of the most male-dominated societies in the world. The important variables for explaining this extreme of male dominance and brutalization of women appear to be the intensity of the population pressure and protein shortage, which results in the warfare complex, patrilineality, patrilocality, male solidarity, and in the male economic control of the productive process and the food supply. The particular intensity and combination of these variables among many Yanamamö villages produces extremes of situations found to lesser degrees among other peoples.

The Yanamamö suffer from a chronic protein shortage. Although they can produce all the vegetable foods they need, they rely on hunted game for protein, and game is in short supply. Constant feuding and warring help keep the villages dispersed over the widest possible hunting area, keep them from hunting the game to extinction, and help control population growth through deaths in battle and encouraging female infanticide. Janet Siskind explains that the Yanamamö are involved in intense competition over protein, but this source of competition is masked by the conventionally accepted view among the Yanamamö that they are competing over women as sexual property. If they openly acknowledged the competition over game, this would increase hunting efforts and permanently deplete the area's animal resources. Women serve as the overt goal instead of game for both hunting and fighting. Their economy involves what Siskind describes as the exchange of meat for sex. For such an economy of sex to operate effectively, the resource involved—women—must be scarce. The scarcity of women is artificially produced through the practices of female infanticide, polygyny, and strict sexual mores for women, creating a situation where many men do not have access to women. This encourages them to raid other groups for women and keeps the internal warfare complex operating.

The warfare complex, in turn, encourages the devaluation and degradation of women and the exaltation of fierce aggression and *machismo* for men. The Yanamamö male's life is devoted to fighting; his body is covered with battle scars and wounds. Men commonly engage in brutal duels which test both strength and endurance. Such duels may involve each man in turn dealing out severe blows with fists, rocks, or clubs to the other man's chest, side, or head. The receiver of a blow will be knocked down, knocked unconscious, deeply bruised, and may suffer broken bones. The point is to prove that "he can take it." For each blow received and endured one can be given in return. Such duels may also erupt into pitched battles between the different groups of males watching the duel. A male must maintain a public image of fierce aggressive bravery.

This aggressiveness is directed toward women as well as men. Yanamamö women are among the most brutalized and victimized women in the world. Their bodies are covered with wounds and scars inflicted on them by their husbands. A man may stab his wife on the slightest or even no provocation. As Marvin Harris puts it, "It help's a man's 'image' if he publicly beats his wife with a club."[32] There are no recognized limits for wife abuse among the Yanamamö. Murder of wives is even acceptable. The women expect to be beaten, degraded, and humiliated. Adultery on the part of wives is viciously punished.

Marriage is definitely viewed as the exchange of women by men. The Yanamamö words for marriage can be translated as "dragging something away" and divorce translates as "throwing something away." Females are given to their husbands as young children and are expected to serve and obey them and to submit to intercourse as young as the age of eight. Men often exchange sisters, and brothers-in-law are often the closest of friends. This type of male solidarity ends any possibility of the female turning to her kinsmen for protection. Her brother is often more interested in her husband's welfare and interests than in hers.

Wives are also obtained through raiding. The captured women are gang raped by the successful warriors and then distributed with much haggling to the fiercest, most successful fighters. Polygyny (having more than one wife) is highly valued as a source of prestige for males. This both maintains an artificial shortage of women and helps motivate men to be brave raiders.

Women are expected to provide menial labor for their husbands, but unlike many horticultural societies, women are not primary economic producers. In addition to the extremely demanding nature of banana and plantain cultivation, the constant threat of attack makes it impractical for the Yanamamö to allocate gardening to women. Men are also the exclusive hunters. This gives the males almost total control over the economy as well as the military might. The combination seems disastrous for the position of women in this society.

Marriage, Gender Relations, and Child Rearing

Polygyny

Polygyny is widely practiced among horticulturalists, especially in patrilineal societies. This is related to the productivity of women as well as to the warfare complex. A man can expand the amount of land under cultivation and the overall productivity of his household by adding more wives.[33] In addition to the increased labor force that multiple wives represent, they also often entitle the husband to land belonging to each of his wives' kin groups. In one region of Uganda, for example, there is a direct relationship between number of wives and the amount of land cultivated by men.

Among advanced horticultural societies with class inequality polygyny may be one of many forms of conspicuous consumption practiced by the noble class. In this case, women are desired as sexual property, for display purposes, and often for their reproductive powers, but not so much for their labor.

Polygyny is less common among matrilocal peoples except for *sororal polygyny* (a man marries two or more sisters). If a man took wives from more than one matrilineage, unless they lived in the same village, it would be very difficult for him to perform his role as husband in each matrilocal household.

Polygyny may facilitate or inhibit female solidarity. Where polygyny involves communal work and consumption patterns among the cowives, it can lead to the development of close ties and mutual support. However, polygyny often involves the separation of women into individual huts with separate gardens. If each wife competes for access to the husband's resources for herself and her children, polygyny does not facilitate female solidarity.

Competitiveness and disunity among women is also encouraged by jealousy. Many societies require the husband of multiple wives to share his time, attentions, and resources equally among wives. But even these rules do not prevent invidious comparisons and hostility among wives.

Junior wives often do not have an enviable status in patrilineal societies whether polygynous or monogamous. In the polygynous situation, junior wives are often sought by senior wives to ease the domestic labor burden. The junior wife often functions as little more than a servant in the household. Where the new wife is the man's first wife, she may still be treated as a servant to a harsh and demanding mother-in-law. Her status in the household and her treatment by her mother-in-law often improve considerably with the birth of her first child, es-

pecially if it is a boy. This ties the wife more firmly to the patrilineage and also proves she was worthy of the brideprice paid for her.

Relations between the Genders

Patterns of work organization have an important impact on the relations between the genders. Where women work individually they may be isolated and vulnerable. The Yanamamö, for example, combine collective male labor with the forced individualization of female labor and only occasional cooperative labor between husband and wife. This combination, structured within an over-determined version of the warfare complex, results in extremely high levels of male dominance, female isolation, hostility between the genders, and female victimization. On the other hand, as Orna and Allen Johnson have pointed out, "where men and women engage in complementary and reciprocal labor, the husband/wife bond is reinforced through cooperation and interdependency, resulting in mutuality and respect between the sexes."[34] The Machiguenga, the Cubeo, and the Mekranoti of South America represent this pattern.

In general, however, the social positions of women and men in horticultural societies tend to give rise to a high degree of tension and hostility between the genders. The hostility may remain below the surface in groups that emphasize internal peace, stability, and harmony, or it may be openly displayed among internally disruptive, feuding groups. Horticultural societies are not likely to emphasize close, loving, trusting relations between men and women as groups or as individual couples.

Where there is a high degree of gender segregation, conflicting interests on the basis of gender and solidarity groups of either or both genders, the relations between the genders are likely to be particularly hostile rather than close and loving. The Mundurucu exemplify this situation:

Each sex is a social entity, each has its own internal organization, and each has its sense of solidarity and a consciousness of its own unity and its opposition to the other. The battle of the sexes is not carried on by individual gladiators, as in our society, but by armies.[35]

Male dominance is the cultural ideal among the Mundurucu, and male informants will assure researchers that men are superior, dominant, and in control. Female informants, however, disagree. Mundurucu women do not accept the male standards and evaluations. They openly ridicule men as a group and as individuals. Intersexual hostility and antagonism are openly expressed in words and ritual, yet women do not openly challenge their secondary social position:

They recognize it, and they actively resent it, but they cope with it as a fact of life. One way of coping is through the minor etiquette of female demeanor. . . . Women guard their emotions before men, communicate as little as possible of their subjective states, set themselves off with reserve.[36]

This is an example of a *mythical male dominant* society, according to Sanday's typology. Men are very aggressive against women, making it appear they are in complete control, but in fact women hold some economic and political power.

Within marriage Mundurucu women and men also remain relatively aloof. Marital partners may develop a degree of affection and intimacy over the years, but the general isolation of the genders and the creation of solidarity within each gender rather than between individual men and women militate against such closeness. Similarly, Alice Smedley found that among the Udu of Ni-geria, compatibility between husband and wife is almost irrelevant to domestic and family life. It is considered good for spouses to be friendly, but being "in love" in the Western sense can be disruptive of household harmony. As among the Mundurucu, Udu "men and women spend most of their lives in the company of their own sex. . . . Conjugal companionship is generally considered inconsistent with the work conditions of husbands and wives."[37]

Women may also cope with their secondary status through the manipulation of males. Again this does not indicate close, affectionate, trusting relationships between the genders. Women's success at manipulating men may also lead them to denigrate men and view them as childlike and foolish. This manipulation, along with the potential threat of withholding domestic duties, sex, or even food, creates a fear of women in men. Men often develop close trusting relationships only with women who are not sexually available to them, such as their mothers and sisters, whereas women develop such ties only with males sexually unavailable to them—their sons, fathers, and brothers.[38] Hostilities and tensions are too great for such ties to be forged between husbands and wives and other potential sexual partners.

It is not uncommon for these tensions and hostilities between the genders to be manifested in cultural beliefs attributing great danger and uncleanliness to sexual intercourse and to women. The Hagen of New Guinea, for example, regard sex and the genitals, especially female genitals and menstruation, as polluting and weakening.[39] The men fear the hidden powers of their supposedly inferior women. They live in almost constant fear that their wives will poison them with menstrual blood. Women, in turn, may use these fears to manipulate and sometimes to coerce males. This fear of women is also manifested in the fear of witchcraft by women.

Control is sometimes exercised over horticultural women through rape, and particularly serious offenses by women may be punished by gang rape. Mundurucu women who are flagrantly promiscuous are subjected to painful and humiliating gang rapes. Mundurucu women who leave the village alone, even if it is just to fetch firewood or water, are subject to legitimate rape by any male who encounters them. These practices, of course, increase the hostility and ill-will between the genders.

The men are thus seen as potentially threatening in a very real, direct, and physical way. They force the women together, make them travel in bands, and actually increase their dependence on each other. The men do enforce the propriety of the women, but they do so at the expense of heightening female antagonism toward them and strengthening female cohesion.[40]

Where horticultural women have little power to defend themselves in disputes with husbands or kin, their ultimate act of revenge may be suicide.[41] By committing or attempting suicide, they can gain sympathy, force their kin to support their interests, humiliate their tormentors, and force their tormentors to pay significant fines and face the possibility of blood revenge. Among the Kaliai of New Guinea, the wife is in a particularly difficult situation as an in-marrying outsider with few kin nearby. Marital tension and antagonism with in-laws are high. Suicide can be a wife's only escape.[42]

Jealousy between the genders is also a common problem. Husbands and wives argue often over real or imagined acts of adultery. In polygynous households a husband often has to contend with constant jealousy and bickering over his real or imagined inequitable treatment of cowives or their children. Wife beating is often legitimized in

horticultural societies but is less common or less extreme where the wife can rely upon the aid of her kin.

Gender antagonism exists even in gender-egalitarian horticultural societies such as the Hopi.[43] Both the sister-brother and husband-wife dyads are important elements of Hopi social structure. The sister-brother dyad is important for the organization of the matrilineal clan and the community. Antagonism here is kept under control, yet given free play in ritual. When it gets out of hand, the result is the very serious accusation that the brother practices witchcraft against his sister and her daughter. The husband-wife dyad is less important to the wider clan or community but is important to the household unit. The wife has authority, yet the husband has heavy responsibilities to support the household. Marriages are unstable. Adultery is morally condemned but is widespread. The husband expresses aggression against his wife by initiating adultery with another woman.

Among horticulturalists there is a wide range of sexual mores. Some are very permissive for men and women. Among the matrilineal Truk, for example, extramarital affairs are universal. However, husbands, but not wives, may demand a divorce on the basis of adultery. Furthermore, a Truk man may sleep with the wives of any of his brothers-in-law and a woman may sleep with her sisters' husbands. Martin and Voorhies found that in general matrilineal societies are permissive concerning premarital sex for women but that patrilineal societies are more likely to be strict. Among the patrilineal Hagen of New Guinea, for example, virginity is highly valued in brides and chastity in wives. But sex is considered unclean and dangerous for both sexes and males are expected to abstain almost as strictly as females are, although violations are considered less blameworthy in males.[44]

Postmarital sexual freedom for women is allowed in some matrilineal societies and some patrilineal societies and prohibited by others. However, where competition over women is part of the economy and ecology of a people, as among the Yanamamö, strict control over the sexual activities of wives is an important part of maintaining the necessary shortage of women.

Child Rearing

Child-rearing practices among horticulturalists vary in relationship to other aspects of the societies' cultures and social structures. Clear divisions in gender roles are found, however, in the child-rearing modes of all these societies. As would be expected, among the Yanamamö fierce aggressiveness is encouraged in young boys and the personality of the passive, submissive, victim is produced in young girls.

When a girl's little brother hits her, she gets punished if she hits back. Little boys, however, are never punished for hitting anybody. Yanamamö fathers howl with delight when their angry four-year-old sons strike them in the face.[45]

The fierce Mekranoti Indians of Brazil, also living in a hostile environment, encourage cruel aggressive behavior in children of both sexes. Children will gang up on a pet dog and beat it to death. Parents do not discourage this behavior; they merely dispose of the carcass. In the past, in addition to dogs, children would be given a sickly child, who was likely to die anyway, to kill to accustom them to warfare.[46]

The Hopi, on the other hand, do not have a hostile environment with pressing defense needs or a warfare complex. They do not therefore emphasize aggressive machismo for young boys and men. Instead, they socialize both boys and girls to be peaceable,

noncompetitive, cooperative, and humble.[47] But females are not expected to control their aggressive impulses as much as males. This is perhaps because male aggression is potentially more harmful and disruptive of the communities' stability and solidarity than female aggression owing to greater potential male fighting strength. The Hopi also prefer daughters over sons and seem to treat daughters somewhat better.[48]

Gender role socialization into the division of labor begins early among horticulturists, especially for girls. Young girls are often given the job of child-nurse which involves caring for younger siblings or cousins while the mother is busy with other tasks. It is not uncommon to see a small eight-year-old girl carrying a heavy two-year-old for hours. Among the Udu, girls of four and five take care of babies and learn to carry them on their backs.[49]

The gender division of labor is often quite rigidly enforced by horticultural adults. The Udu rarely strike their children. In the one instance witnessed by Smedley, a four-year-old boy was chastised for repeatedly copying the female task of carrying a head pan. Children are clearly impressed with the idea that certain tasks are appropriate only to females, others to males.

Religion and Ritual

Opposition and hostility between the genders often pervade the religious and ritual life of horticulturalists. Since religion and ritual are largely under the control of males, they usually emphasize the male point of view and legitimate and rationalize male dominance and female submission. Women are not always impressed by such rituals, however.

Mundurucu myth and symbols, for instance, give males a symbolic importance they do not have in real life. This is common in mythical male-dominant societies.[50] The creator role of males is emphasized in myth to offset the importance of females as current producers of life. Nadelson argues that they exalt hunting and the value of meat, but not manioc, precisely because women do not hunt.[51] Mundurucu religion is controlled by males who possess the ritual flutes and keep them hidden from women. The symbolism exalts the power of the penis and portrays women as inferior to men. The Mundurucu myth of origin is similar to myths of origin among other horticulturalists. It postulates a time when females had control of the ritual flutes and dominated males. However, males eventually outwitted the females and stole the flutes and the power they conferred. Such myths may indicate a real fear of women by men. They are not likely, however, to be remnants of a time in which such matriarchies actually existed.[52] Sanday argues that such myths are found where females exert considerable informal power; they mirror actual gender relations. "Myths of former female power provide men with a rationale for segregating themselves from women and a reason for dominating 'tyrannical' women."[53]

The gender symbolism of the Mundurucu myths also depicts women as triggering dangerous and destructive impulses in men. Religion and ritual also often emphasize female uncleaness and attribute dangerous, polluting properties to women and sex. Menstrual taboos and the seclusion of menstruating women and women after childbirth are common. This may also arise out of situations of real hostility between the genders and male fears of the imperfectly subordinated female.

Collier and Rosaldo find an important distinction between *brideservice* and *bridewealth* (or *brideprice*) societies that has implications for horticultural societies. They argue that the types of marriages a people make and the accompanying rituals they practice correspond to their economic and political organization.[54] In foragers' and simple horticulturalists' low-surplus societies without social rank or class inequality, marriage tends to be legitimized through brideservice.[55] A groom maintains an ongoing relationship with his in-laws in the same manner as all adult relationships are maintained, through the continual offer of gifts and services. Horticultural societies that produce greater surplus, however, tend to require elaborate payments on important occasions and to legitimize relationships and exchanges. Payments of bridewealth, usually in stages, for the right to marry a girl characterize horticultural marriage exchanges and represent significant financial investments by the groom's lineage.

In bridewealth societies, rituals and symbols focus on reproductive capacities; women are defined not so much as sexual partners as they are as mothers. Rituals show respect for women as mothers but simultaneously demonstrate male fears of pollution from females, especially through contact with menstruation and childbirth.[56] Young men and poor men are dependent on their better-off elders to provide them with the necessary brideprice for wives. But once married, a man controls both the wealth produced by his wife's labor in the gardens and the wealth brought in through the marriages of the daughters she produces and the labor of both sons and daughters.[57] Horticultural men are dependent on their wives' productivity to attain high status. Wives can, therefore, "make or break" their husbands. (Forager men, by contrast, need wives to achieve an equal status in society as independent adults, but not to compete for high status. Forager rituals show neither respect nor fear of women, nor do they focus on female productivity or reproductive powers. Rather, the focus is on female sexual prowess and on male productivity and sexual virility as means of attracting and keeping a wife; the heterosexual bond is celebrated.)[58]

The Bimin-Kuskusmin of New Guinea, for example, are patrilineal and patrilocal and follow a division of labor where men clear the gardens and women cultivate gardens and raise pigs for subsistence as well as for feasts and ceremonies. But men cultivate the ritually important high-status taro crops. The gardens and the crops are segregated by gender, as is almost every other aspect of life. This division of labor is reflected in their segregated rituals and the opposition between men and women symbolized in their religious beliefs and practices. Some ritual control is exerted over sisters and daughters, but the primary focus is on controlling the much more dangerous wives, especially wives from distant, often hostile tribes—"The alien wife from another tribe . . . is the polluting woman par excellence."[59] Ideas of female pollution and danger to men during menstruation and childbirth are highly elaborated. Yet the reproductive and productive powers of wives are essential to male social status. These people are another example of Sanday's mythical male dominant and dual-oriented societies. They have creation myths depicting androgynous mythical ancestors and a dual sex ideology that reflects the complementarity of males and females. Interestingly, one of their most important ritual roles can be held only by select women who take on both male and female roles symbolizing the androgynous ancestor and acting out in ritual the dilemma of males who must depend on wives from the same groups they fight. Similar dilemmas and practices were found by Strathern for the Hagen of New Guinea.[60] These societies are characterized by fear, conflict, and strife over scarce resources.

Karen and Jeffrey Paige also argue that *reproductive rituals* common among horticulturalists are part of the politics of tribal societies.[61] They are ways that men demonstrate their loyalty and assess the loyalty of others to the fraternal interest groups. They are also ways that men establish and assess support for their claims over women and children—very important and scarce resources in these societies.

Horticulturalists such as the Bimin-Kuskusmin and the Hagen are organized on the basis of patrilineal, patrilocal *fraternal interest groups.* Closely related males share economic and political interests and depend on group solidarity. But they do not have sufficient resources to produce the kind of surplus necessary to sustain powerful, stable fraternal interest groups. Internal conflict and fission are recurrent problems. Leadership is not stable. Leaders have little power to order obedience; they must persuade people to obey. Rituals in these groups tend to focus on monitoring the difficult-to-enforce contracts and maintaining the solidarity of the fraternal interest groups.

Rituals at menarche demonstrate the father's right to bargain for access to his daughter's reproductive powers. *Virginity* is important because it allows the father to demonstrate his control over his property and thereby guarantee clear paternity to the potential husband. The fraternal interest group is used to back up this claim by punishing seducers and keeping the girls under surveillance. Among the Bimin-Kuskusmin, for example, anyone who has sex with an uninitiated girl (easily recognized by the lack of abdominal scarification) faces death.[62] Some groups demand high fines for such "theft" of sexual access. The father also usually tries to marry the girl off as early as is acceptable to reduce the likelihood of such theft. Rituals at menarche help build political support for the father's claims and allow him to assess his political base—the degree of support he has in the group. If significant clan members do not attend or do not bring appropriate gifts, the father knows his political base is weak. Societies with very strong fraternal interest groups do not rely much on menarchal rituals because they can use the power of the group to control access to their women and to avenge any violations. Where fraternal interest groups are weaker, *ritual mobilization* of support is more important and menarchal rituals are more common.[63]

Horticultural societies are also likely to practice *pregnancy and childbirth rituals.* Where the fraternal interest groups are not strong, claims to paternity cannot be maintained simply by the threat of force and violence and the power derived from the group's wealth. Practices such as *maternal surveillance rituals,* requiring food taboos, seclusion, or other behavior limitations on the pregnant woman, and *couvade,* requiring similar observances from fathers (which may include the father "experiencing" the pains of childbirth and needing a recovery period from his ordeal), are likely.[64] This ritually proclaims the father's rights as father. It is also part of the politics of assessing blame if something goes wrong with the pregnancy or delivery. Marriage is a contract transferring the reproductive powers of the female from one kin group to the other. If something is faulty with those reproductive powers, each group seeks to blame the other as not fulfilling their part of the contract. Both kin groups therefore want to avoid any appearance of guilt beforehand by observing all the required behaviors. Couvade and maternal surveillance rituals keep both the father and mother in line and protect the claims of their respective groups.

Menstrual segregation is also related to the political problem of *fission* among horticulturalists. A woman's fertility is potentially divisive because many offspring provide the father with his own power base, which he might use to break away from the group. Wives are also likely to press for such fissions; they are more interested in the conjugal unit than in the husband's wider fraternal interest group. A man has to be careful with the way he displays the power derived from a wife's reproductive powers. He wants to display it for its prestige value, but he does not want to encourage too much jealousy or fears that he is disloyal. Where the fraternal interest group is very strong, this is not such a problem. The strength and wealth of the group keep the man tied to the group. But where the surplus is low and the fraternal interest groups are weaker, leadership is more unstable and fission is more likely.

Ritual disinterest in the wife's sexuality is a partial solution to this dilemma: "He adheres to elaborate public pollution practices to proclaim the continuing fertility of his wife while simultaneously declaring disinterest by avoiding her, abstaining from sex with her and leaving her unprotected [in the menstrual hut] so that rights to her fertility may be claimed by adulterers.[65] He shows therefore that he is more loyal to the fraternal interest group than to his wife and conjugal unit.

The large-scale *initiation rites* for boys and girls widespread among horticulturists also emphasize the differences between their gender roles as they pass into adulthood. Among the Sherbo and Mende peoples of Africa, lengthy and elaborate initiation rites are performed for boys by the male secret societies and for girls by the female secret societies.[66] Boys undergo painful *scarification* of their backs, while girls are subjected to female circumcision, or *clitoridectomies*—the clitoris and part of the labia are excised. Both these practices carry a risk of infection and even death, but they have the psychological impact of searing the cultural lessons included in the ceremonies into the initiates' memories and of enhancing their feelings of solidarity with their co-initiates. The most important social function of such life-threatening rituals is testing the loyalty of the parents of the social group.[67]

In New Guinea male initiation rites also usually include *ritualized homosexuality.* They believe that maleness must be achieved and that semen helps build men. Therefore, boys receive semen from older males so that they too can become adult men. As with the ancient Greeks, there are appropriate stages for homosexual relations. Young males receive semen from initiated older males, who themselves eventually marry and are then expected to practice only heterosexuality. But young men must age many years before marrying young girls, and homosexuality is practiced during the waiting period. Using arguments similar to Sanday's views on mythical male dominant societies, Gerald Creed suggests that this ritualized homosexuality is part of male attempts to affirm male supremacy and the supremacy of elders in the face of female power in everyday life and the strength and vitality of youth. It is a ritual attempt to solve the dilemmas posed by age and gender stratification in a low-surplus society where people cannot be controlled through the power that comes with wealth.[68]

In general, religion and ritual take on more consequential and complex functions in horticultural societies as compared to foraging societies because of the wider prevalence of both incipient and developed forms of social stratification. Religion and ritual are used to legitimate the positions of "big men" among simple horticulturalists and the powers and privileges of the elite class of men and women among some advanced horticulturalists. The gender roles and gender stratification systems of horticultural socie-

ties are also often symbolized, legitimated, and perpetuated by their religious beliefs and practices. Some horticulturalists have also come under the influence of religions developed by more advanced agrarian and urban peoples such as Islam in parts of Africa. These, like other influences from the external world, may emphasize different and even more subordinate roles for women. However, as we pointed out earlier, where such practices interfere with other aspects of the social structure such as female trading or other female work roles, the religious teachings are likely to be ignored. In other circumstances they may become new and often powerful ideological resources for reenforcing and advancing tendencies toward male dominance which have already emerged among specific horticultural peoples.

Forces for Change

Contact with nonhorticultural peoples is probably the most important force for change in these societies. Horticulturalists are often impressed by the goods that can be obtained through trading with or working for more technologically advanced peoples. This sometimes leads to more individualistic practices and the disruption of the traditional corporate kin group patterns. It is also likely to lead to changes in the positions of men and women.

Among the Mundurucu, for example, the rubber trade has led many people to abandon the village life with its collective kinship, work, and residence patterns. The women are particularly desirous of the trade items obtainable through rubber tapping. They pressure their husbands to adopt the new locale and life-style that rubber tapping requires. Paradoxically, however, the new social and economic system typifying rubber tappers undermines the degree of personal autonomy and independence women exercised under the traditional way of life. Both female and male work groups and collective solidarity are terminated by these individualistic economic practices. Each rubber tapper works alone and through his earnings and individual fishing supports his wife and children. Women thus lose their role as primary economic producers. They become firmly tied to the domestic sphere in relatively isolated, individualistic nuclear family units. The separation of the genders and rigidity of the division of labor characteristics of traditional village life do not continue. Women no longer rely on one another for help in manioc processing, gardening, or child care. Instead, they work alone or turn to their husbands and children for help. The men become the heads of these nuclear family households. The woman's domestic authority is lost and the position of Senior Woman becomes obsolete. The women, however, prefer this pattern. Murphy and Murphy argue that women press for these social changes in response to outside contact and new opportunities more than men do because they see it as narrowing the gap between them and men. The women may not gain, but the men lose. A more detached outsider would probably conclude that both genders have lost.[69]

Colonial domination has also been an important force for change among some horticultural societies. In some cases this has improved opportunities for women; in most cases it has reduced them.[70] Colonial governments and their settler populations have sometimes created markets for women's produce, which allow women to increase their economic independence through trade. In other cases, however, they have undermined female economic activities through the imposition of external standards favoring males as workers, businesspeople, or political leaders. Women may thereby be isolated

from the new public spheres the colonizers create.

The Bari, for example, a forest horticultural people of Colombia, unlike the Mundurucu were originally quite egalitarian in family, social, economic, and ritual life.[71] Colonization has destroyed their egalitarian social structure. Outside encroachment by businesses desiring their lands has led to the imposition of capitalism, private property, inequality, and male dominance. Women have lost their important economic roles. They can no longer be healers, the gender symmetry in ritual life has been eroded, and antagonism now characterizes the relations between the genders. The price the Bari have paid for survival has been the "near total destruction of their culture."[72] It appears that the degree of gender equality characteristic of many low-technology societies cannot survive under the pressures created by technologically more advanced systems.

The demise of matrilineality and matrilocality has also been a result of the encroachment of the modern world on horticulturalists. Matrilineality is suited to noncompetitive, stable environments, but such environments are rare in the modern world. Worldwide population increases and the expansion of technologically more advanced peoples have forced the more peaceful matrilineal peoples to change or be conquered. Matrilineality is a way of life that has lost its ecological niche. It is not less "natural" than patrilineality, but it is not as adaptive under conditions of population pressure and competition. The same holds true for inner-oriented cultures with strong religious and symbolic focus on feminine gods and fertility.

Thus, as with the foragers, the roles and statuses for women and men in horticultural societies may rapidly be disappearing from the face of the earth. Some see the turn to more advanced technologies as progress.

But in terms of the position of women in society, and sometimes for the majority of men as well, it has often meant deterioration instead.

Conclusion

The contrasts are marked between societies adapted to the peaceful, abundant environments of the most egalitarian foragers and those adapted to competitiveness, scarcity, aggression, and inequality under the less abundant, more hostile circumstances that characterize most horticulturalists. Simple horticulturalists in less competitive environments retain more of the gender egalitarianism and personal autonomy of the foragers, but ecological and environmental crises increase the likelihood that peoples will turn to strategies that encourage male dominance along with other forms of human aggression and exploitation.

Horticultural technologies can also be combined with social organizational and cultural innovations in propitious material environments to generate the often sizeable surpluses of the advanced horticultural regimes. Under these conditions, the evolutionary origins of steep stratification systems stand out starkly, and structured inequality and repression become dominant features of the everyday lives of men and women. Within the emerging patterns of more generalized forms of inequality, institutionalized inequality between males and females also becomes an enduring feature of human relationships. In Chapter 5, we will examine agrarian societies where these processes reached their most extreme forms of evolutionary development. In the next chapter, however, we will take up the analysis of pastoral societies, unusual in the respect that although they represent a societal form based upon a distinct mode of subsistence technology, they have evolved in close association with horticultural and/or agrarian ways of life.

Notes

1. For a discussion of the economy and social organization of horticultural societies, see Gerhard Lenski and Jean Lenski, *Human Societies: An Introduction to Macrosociology*, 4th ed. (New York: McGraw-Hill, 1982: 132–165); Marvin Harris, *Culture, People, and Nature: An Introduction to General Anthropology*, 3d ed. (New York: Harper & Row, 1980): 289–320.

2. Lenski and Lenski, 91.

3. Lenski and Lenski, 91–98.

4. Ernestine Friedl, *Women and Men* (New York: Holt, Rinehart & Winston, 1975): 53.

5. Friedl, 56–57.

6. Ester Boserup, *Women's Role in Economic Development* (New York: St. Martin's Press, 1970): p. 18.

7. Michael Burton and Douglas White, "Sexual Division of Labor in Agriculture," *American Anthropologist* 86, no. 3 (September 1984): 568–583; Carol Ember, "The Relative Decline in Women's Contribution to Agriculture with Intensification," *American Anthropologist* 85, no. 2 (June 1983): 295–304.

8. Boserup, 88–99.

9. Sidney Mintz, "Men, Women, and Trade," *Comparative Studies in Society and History*, 13 (1971): 266.

10. Kamene Okonjo, "The Role of Women in the Development of Culture in Nigeria," in Ruby Rohrlich-Leavitt, ed., *Women Cross-Culturally: Change and Challenge* (The Hague: Mouton, 1975): 37; see also Caroline Ifeka-Moller, "Female Militancy and Colonial Revolt: The Women's War of 1929, Eastern Nigeria," in Shirley Ardener, ed., *Perceiving Women* (New York: John Wiley, 1975): 136–140.

11. Yolanda Murphy and Robert Murphy, *Women of the Forest* (New York: Columbia University Press, 1974).

12. Harriet Whitehead, "The Bow and the Burden Strap: A New Look at Institutionalized Homosexuality in Native North America," in Sherry B. Ortner and Harriet Whitehead, eds., *Sexual Meanings: The Cultural Construction of Gender and Sexuality* (Cambridge: Cambridge University Press, 1981): 80–115.

13. Bradd Shore, "Sexuality and Gender in Samoa: Conceptions and Missed Conceptions," in Ortner and Whitehead, 192–215; Robert I. Levy, "The Community Function of Tahitian Male Transvestitism: A Hypothesis," *Anthropological Quarterly* 44, no. 1 (January 1971): 12–21.

14. Marvin Harris, *Culture, People, and Nature*, 2d ed. (New York: Thomas Y. Crowell, 1975): pp. 338–341.

15. Lenski and Lenski, 154.

16. Lenski and Lenski, 155.

17. Harris, 1980, 281.

18. George Murdock, *Social Structure* (New York: Macmillan, 1949): 209–210.

19. M. Kay Martin and Barbara Voorhies, *Female of the Species* (New York: Columbia University Press, 1975): 222.

20. Glenn Petersen, "Ponapean Matriliny: Production, Exchange, and The Tie That Binds," *American Ethnologist* 9 (1982): 129–144.

21. Martin and Voorhies, 1975, 234.

22. Karen Sacks, *Sisters and Wives: The Past and Future Sexual Equality* (Westport, Conn.: Greenwood Press, 1979); and "Engels Revisited: Women, the Organization of Production, and Private Property," in Michelle Zimbal Rosaldo and Louise Lamphere, eds., *Women, Culture, and Society* (Stanford, Calif.: Stanford University Press, 1974): 207–222.

23. Marvin Harris, *Cows, Pigs, Wars and Witches* (New York: Vintage Books, 1974): 35–110; *Culture, People, and Nature,* (2d ed., 1975): 258–280; *Cannibals and Kings* (New York: Random House, 1977a): 31–66; "Why Men Dominate Women," *New York Times Magazine,* November 13, 1977b; 46, 115–123.

24. Harris, 1977a, 60.

25. Harris, 1977a, 66.

26. The following discussion of the Iroquois is based largely on Judith Brown, "Iroquois Women: An Ethnographic Note," in Rayna Reiter, ed. *Toward an Anthropology of Women* (New York: Monthly Review Press, 1975): 235–251.

27. Alice Shlegel, *Male Dominance and Female Autonomy* (New Haven, Conn.: HRAF Press, 1972): 59.

28. Martin K. Whyte, *The Status of Women in Preindustrial Societies* (Princeton, N. J.: Princeton University Press, 1979): 112–114.

29. The following discussion is based on David M. Schneider, "The Truk," in David M. Schneider and Kathleen Gough, eds. *Matrilineal Kinship* (Berkeley: University of California Press, 1962): 202–233.

30. Schneider, 229.

31. The following discussion is based on Napoleon Chagnon: "The Culture-Ecology of Shifting (Pioneering) Cultivation among the Yanamamo Indians," in Daniel Gross, ed., *Peoples and Cultures of Native South America* (New York: Doubleday Natural History Press, 1973): 126–144 and *Yanamamo: The Fierce People* (New York: Holt, Rinehart & Winston, 1968); also, Harris, 1975, 83–110 and Harris, 1977a, 31–54; "Yanamamo Warfare: Retrospect and New Evidence," *Journal of Anthropological Research* 40, no. 1 (Spring 1984): 183–201; Janet Siskind, "Tropical Forest Hunters and the Economy of Sex," in Gross, 226–240.

32. Harris, 1975, 89.

33. Boserup, 1970, 37–52.

34. Orna R. Johnson and Allen Johnson, "Male/Female Relations and the Organization of Work in a Machiguenga Community," *American Ethnologist* (1975): 646. For examples of interdependency between husbands and wives, see Stephen Thompson, "Women, Horticulture, and Society in Tropical America," *American Anthropologist* 79 (1977): 908–910; Irving Goldman, *The Cubeo: Indians of the Northwest Amazon,* Illinois Studies in Anthropology, no. 2 (Urbana: University of Illinois Press, 1963); Dennis Werner *Amazon Journey: An Anthropologist's Year among Brazil's Mekranoti Indians* (New York: Simon & Schuster, 1984).

35. Murphy and Murphy, 110.

36. Murphy and Murphy, 137.

37. Alice Smedley, "Women of Udu: Survival in a Harsh Land." in Carolyn Matthiasson, ed., *Many Sisters: Women in Cross-Cultural Perspective* (New York Free Press, 1974): 218.

38. Friedl, 68–69.

39. Marilyn Strathern, *Women in Between: Female Roles in a Male Work, Mount Hagen, New Guinea* (London: Seminar Press, 1972): 164–175.

40. Murphy and Murphy, 136.

41. Strathern; Dorothy Ayers Count, "Fighting Back Is Not the Way: Suicide and the Women of Kaliai," *American Ethnologist* 7 (1980): 332–351; Ronald M. Bundt, *Excess and Restraint: Social Control Among a New Guinea Mountain People* (Chicago: University of Chicago Press, 1962); Andrew Strathern, "Why Is Shame on the Skin?" *Ethnology* 14 (1975): 347–356.

42. Count, 344.

43. Alice Schlegel, "Sexual Antagonism among the Sexually Egalitarian Hopi," *Ethos* 7, no. 2 (Summer, 1979): 124–141.

44. Marilyn Strathern, 159–184.

45. Harris, 1975, 90.

46. Werner, 1984.

47. Alice Schlegel, "The Adolescent Socialization of the Hopi Girl," *Ethnology,* 12 (October 1973): 450–451.

48. Schlegel, 1979, 138.

49. Smedly, 213–215.

50. Peggy Reeves Sanday, *Female Power and Male Dominance: On the Origins of Sexual Inequality* (Cambridge: Cambridge University Press, 1981): 165.

51. Leslee Nadelson, "Pigs, Women and the Men's House in Amazonia: An Analysis of Six Mundurucu Myths," in Ortner and Whitehead, 270.

52. Murphy and Murphy.

53. Sanday, 181.

54. Jane F. Collier and Michelle Z. Rosaldo, "Politics and Gender in Simple Societies," in Ortner and Whitehead, 278–279.

55. Simple horticulturalists such as those of Lowland South America practice brideservice. Judith R. Shapiro, "Marriage Rules, Marriage Exchange, and the

Definition of Marriage in Lowland South America," in Kenneth M. Kensinger, ed., *Marriage Practices in Lowland South America*, Illinois Studies in Anthropology, no. 14 (Urbana: University of Illinois Press, 1984): 1–32.

56. Collier and Rosaldo, 278–279.

57. Collier and Rosaldo, 288.

58. Collier and Rosaldo, 287–308.

59. Fitz John Porter Poole, "Transforming 'Natural' Woman: Female Sexual Leaders and Gender Ideology among Bimin-Kuskumin," in Ortner and Whitehead, 116–165.

60. Marilyn Strathern.

61. Karen Erikson Paige and Jeffrey M. Paige, *The Politics of Reproductive Ritual* (Berkeley: University of California Press, 1981).

62. Poole.

63. Paige and Paige.

64. Paige and Paige, 178–194.

65. Paige and Paige, 220.

66. K. L. Little, "The Role of the Secret Society in Cultural Specialization," in Simon Ottenberg and Phoebe Ottenberg, eds., *Cultures and Societies of Africa* (New York: Random House, 1960): 201; Carol P. Hoffer, "Bundu: Political Implications of Female Solidarity in a Secret Society," in Dana Raphael, ed., *Being Female: Reproduction, Power, and Change* (The Hague: Mouton, 1975): 155–163.

67. Paige and Paige, 124–166.

68. Gerald Creed, "Sexual Subordination: Institutionalized Homosexuality and Social Control in Melanesia," *Ethnology* 23, no. 2 (July 1984): 127–176.

69. Murphy and Murphy, 179–232.

70. Sanday, 113–160; Mona Etienne and Eleanor Leacock, eds., *Women and Colonialization: Anthropological Perspectives* (New York: Praeger, 1980).

71. Elisa Bunenaventura-Posso and Susan E. Brown, "Forced Transition from Egalitarianism to Male Dominance: The Bari of Colombia," in Etienne and Leacock, 109–133.

72. Bunenaventura-Posso and Brown, 131.

CHAPTER 4

Pastoral Societies

Chapters 2 and 3 described the roles of women and men in hunting and gathering and horticultural societies. *Pastoralists* exhibit important similarities with and differences from each of these types of societies, and these are reflected in similarities and differences in their systems of gender roles and gender stratification.

Economy and Social Organization

Pastoralism is defined by its primary reliance on the herding of livestock such as cattle, camels, sheep, and goats.[1] The pastoral life is organized around the needs of the herds, and livestock are of primary importance to pastoralists. Like foragers and simple horticulturists, pastoralists are to some degree *nomadic*. They must move to secure sufficient pasturage and water for their animals. Although pastoralism is usually combined with some cultivation of vegetable foods, these people do not have the high levels of productivity necessary to keep their animals fodder-fed in stalls or in small fields. Their low productivity means they have little surplus. However, they do have a form of important exchangeable concentrated wealth in their livestock, which is extremely vulnerable to theft and raiding.

Production is primarily for use values, especially within the pastoral communities themselves. Exchange within pastoral societies is almost entirely conducted through kinship ties. The selling and bartering of animals among kinsmen is rare, because the animals change hands frequently but not through market relationships. Pastoralists resist selling their animals to outsiders even when such a market exists. Only old, barren, or otherwise useless animals are offered for sale. Maintaining and increasing the size of one's herd is a chief concern of pastoralists. Selling an animal would usually defeat this goal and is therefore done only as a last resort.

The work involved in caring for herds of large animals such as cattle or camels is physically demanding. (The herding of sheep and goats is less strenuous.) In addition to the strength required to handle the larger animals, the herder often has to labor for hours hauling water for them. The livestock also must be continually protected from both human and animal predators. Theft and raiding for livestock are endemic to pastoral peoples.

Despite the importance of herding in their lives and cultures, few pastoralists rely solely on herding for their subsistence. Most do some gardening or foraging as well. Those who combine cultivation with herding are referred to as *facultative pastoralists,* while those who rely almost entirely on herding are *obligative pastoralists.* Martin and Voorhies note that greater reliance on crops limits the nomadism of pastoralists and allows for larger communities and the development of more complex sociopolitical institutions.[2] Obligative pastoralists are generally found in rugged, barren areas that cannot be cultivated. They are highly mobile, live in small camps often with fewer than fifty people, and have uncentralized, tribal-level political structures.

Facultative pastoralists range in population density from small camps for those with less dependence on crops, to villages as large as one thousand inhabitants among those with a higher (up to 50 percent) dependence on crops. The larger communities of pastoralists have more centralized and powerful political institutions such as chiefdoms and even small states. Some very powerful pastoralists can rely almost entirely on their herds and obtain agricultural products through their control of agricultural communities or through raiding or trade with agricultural peoples.

Like foragers and horticulturists, pastoralists rely on a high degree of reciprocity and collective work organization in their economic production. However, pastoralists are stricter than foragers in requiring that each person do his or her share of the work. Robert Paine suggests that while hunters and gatherers' values focus on distributing and consuming food and being generous and sociable, the pastoral economy values focus on owning livestock and expanding the size of the herd: "With 'food' all around them in the herd it is only the size of the herd, not the size of the meal, that really demonstrates merit among pastoralists."[3] Pastoralists are involved in production and are future ori-

ented rather than concerned with gathering for immediate consumption. They have therefore a more severe *work ethic* concerning doing one's share of the collective work. They work longer and harder than most foragers. Also, they place a great importance on inheritance, which is uncharacteristic of foragers.

Gender Division of Labor

Variations

The gender division of labor within pastoral societies is tipped toward male dominance of the economically productive tasks. Probably because of the strength required to handle and care for large animals, males are the exclusive herders of these animals. Females may, however, herd smaller animals and serve as dairy maids for large and small species. Women and children contribute substantially to the care of such domestic animals—gathering food and carrying water for them and processing their by-products such as milk, wool, hides, and dung.[4] Martin and Voorhies' study of forty-four pastoral societies found that the female contribution to the diet of herders is small. Men do almost all of the herding and women dairy in only about one-third of the societies. Men also do most of the cultivation in half of their sample. However, where cultivation is based on horticultural techniques, women are either the exclusive cultivators or men and women share equally in cultivation.[5]

Martin and Voorhies also found significant correlations between a group's dependence on crops, the gender division of labor, and the degree of nomadism. Societies that do no cultivation tend to be highly nomadic and men and women share in the care of the herd. Where there is a low dependence on crops (less than 25 percent of the diet), the society tends to be nomadic or seminomadic and men are the primary herders and cultivators. Where there is a moderate dependence on crops (30 to 40 percent of the diet), the group is seminomadic or semisedentary and men are the primary herders while men and women share in the cultivation tasks. Groups with a high dependence on crops (50 percent of the diet) are sedentary. In some cases men are the sole herders, in other groups men and women participate in herding activities. There is also a strong tendency for men and women to share the cultivation work.

Martin and Voorhies suggest that among herders with a high dependence on crops, the variations found in the gender division of labor may be a result of the influence of the *parent community* out of which the pastoral society developed. Therefore, it might be a carryover of institutions and traditions developed in a different socioeconomic context. Those with a horticultural background are perhaps more likely to share tasks and those with an agricultural background more likely to continue to assign primary productive tasks to men.[6]

Other dimensions of these variations in the gender division of labor can be partially explained by the factor of who goes with the herd and who stays behind. In societies that are completely nomadic, both males and females move with the herd and stay with it throughout the year. There is no period in which women are separated from the herd. Therefore, they can be regularly assigned tasks associated with the herd, such as dairying. This is true also in fully sedentary communities where the herd is usually not moved far from the settled village. However, among groups that practice *gender-segregated nomadism*, where for long periods only the men go with the herd, male dominance of the economic activities results. Women in these societies are usually excluded even from dairying. Similarly, in fully sedentary communities where the women are always

in close proximity to the fields, women's participation in cultivation has a status equal to men's Among gender-segregated, seminomadic peoples, men usually do the cultivation: they plant the crops while on the move with the herds, leave the crops unattended when they move on, and return to the cultivated area with the herd at harvest time.[7]

There is usually a division of labor among herders. The Maasai, for example, believe a man will fall ill and perhaps die if he performs female chores.[8] But this division of labor does not create a sharp dichotomy between domestic and public spheres. Women's tasks are more likely to take place in camp than men's tasks, but they do not isolate women in the household. Much of women's work is done in cooperation with, or at least in the close company of, other women. Both men and women participate in collective work patterns with other members of the same gender. Camps are typically divided into *women's spaces* and *men's spaces*, but almost all activities are carried out in the open, avoiding the development of private domestic spheres for women versus public spheres for men. Women's work may be household work, but it is public household work. Boulding argues that women participate more fully in the total life of these societies than they do in settled agricultural communities.[9] Martin and Voorhies argue, however, that the male dominance of economic production gives rise to male dominance in the wider culture and social structure of pastoral societies. But Lois Beck found a flexible division of labor, economic interdependence between the genders, and low degree of gender segregation among the Qashqái of Iran.[10] Furthermore, because of the small size of the independent households of these pastoralists, males and females were partners in economically independent units, and neither males nor females formed strong separate solidarity groups.

Economic Control

Ownership and control over the disposition of livestock lies predominantly in male hands. However, females are sometimes at least the nominal owners of some livestock through inheritance, dowries, or purchase. But even the owners of livestock cannot usually dispose freely of their animals. They are bound by an intricate web of kinship-based exchanges, which requires them periodically to give large numbers of animals to close kinsmen, as brideprices to the bride's family, as dowries to the groom, and as compensation for violation of certain rules, especially in the case of homicide. Furthermore, certain animals in a herd may be held jointly with others or held in the interests of others and are subject to many limitations on use and disposal.

In brief, males who control large herds do not necessarily derive significant economic power from these herds, since they cannot always use them in their own interests. A large herd, however, brings prestige and influence to the man or family who owns it. But ownership of large herds is often a cyclical or temporary phenomenon. Bridewealth and sometimes bloodwealth (fines for homicide) payments regularly deplete one family's herd while greatly increasing the size of another family's herd. Families are unlikely to maintain a large herd consistently. In addition, kinship obligations often require the owner of livestock to share with less fortunate kin. These exchanges militate against the development of *class inequality* among herders and the concentration of power in the hands of individuals or families. Herding societies are *ranked:* Some individuals or families at any one time have more wealth, influence, and prestige than other individuals or families. But they are not usually *stratified:* No one family or group of families can maintain unequal shares of wealth and power from one generation to the next.

Females usually have little or no control over the disposition of livestock, especially large livestock. However, they do sometimes have economic control over small animals and sometimes can earn income through the sale of handcraft items or domestic produce to outsiders. But more important, among herders who assign women the task of dairying, women generally also have control over the disposition of the dairy products. Their control, however, is often limited by customs requiring sharing with certain kin and neighbors. Where males are not allowed to dairy, an economic interdependence is created between the genders which gives women an advantage they do not have where they are the economic dependents of men.

The Sheikhanzai. Bahran Tavakolian's study of Sheikhanzai nomads in western Afghanistan provides insight into the degree of equality women can achieve in pastoral society when they have significant economic power.[11] The Sheikhanzai are obligative pastoralists, herding sheep and goats with no crop production. Shepherding is done by males, but females are in charge of the dairying and disposition of the milk products. Milk products are used for use value in the household and for providing hospitality. They are also used in market exchanges with villagers. The Sheikhanzai have limited relations with settled peoples except for buying grain and using cash from milk sales to raise funds for bridewealth. Women control these economic transactions. Women are also important in that it is the number of women in the household, not the number of men, that determines the size of the flock that a household can maintain. Women also produce the tents and own them as well as most of the other household goods.

Women are in short supply because of high mortality rates (death in childbirth is common). The birth of a daughter is a happy event. Parents might let a son work for another household, but a daughter's labor is too valuable to lend. This helps account for the very high brideprices required to marry—a wife is very valuable.

The Sheikhanzai are Muslim and their kinship structure is patrilineal and patriarchal. This gives rise to an ideology of male dominance and to males publicly displaying their authority. But this only obscures the fact that women are listened to by their husbands: Women are very active in both household and camp decision making, directly influencing migration schedules and camp locations. Although they are Muslim, women are not veiled or segregated, but they avoid contact with non-Sheikhanzai, partly because outsiders usually insult them for being nomads, saying they smell like animals, for example.

Cousin marriage is preferred. Therefore, although the society is patrilocal, the wife is not separated from her own kin. Camps are cross-cut by many kinship ties, and a wife almost always has kinsmen and kinswomen to come to her aid should she be abused. Women control some livestock, but sisters usually give up their Islamic inheritance rights in exchange for the right to call on their brothers for economic support if needed. Because of the importance of milk products, women's use rights over milk are as important as livestock ownership in this economy. The society is not gender egalitarian in all respects, but women have a relatively high status.

The Shahsevan and the Durrani. Nancy Tapper's research on the Shahsevan of Iran and the Durrani of Afghanistan produce a picture of much more restrictive roles and much lower statuses for these Moslem pastoralists.[12] Women in these two societies help with the milking and processing of milk products, but they do not control any economic products and do not participate in economic exchanges outside the domestic sphere. They therefore exercise much less economic or political power.

But Shahsevan women have a basis for female solidarity, or what Tapper calls a *"women's subsociety,"* which furnishes a network for information exchange, dispute settlement between women, female leadership, and social support in disputes with men. Such a subsociety can emerge among pastoralists if three conditions are met. First, women's activities must be separate from men's to a degree. Among the Shahsevan, gender segregation is marked in the division of labor. Veiling and the social avoidance of men by women are also practiced, although not to the extent as among agrarian Muslims. Second, there must be regular opportunities for women to meet, and third, there must be a purpose for these meetings. Shahsevan women have such purposive meetings in their feast cycle, which allows women to travel in groups to meet with other women from other camps.

Durrani society does not meet these three conditions and the women do not have a women's subsociety. There is much less gender segregation and participation in large gatherings with other women is neither structured nor regular. Durrani women have more freedom of movement and interaction with men in their society but little basis for female solidarity to create a power base to offset the power and authority of men. Unlike Shahsevan women, Durrani women accept the dominant male view of women.

Gender Roles, Gender Stratification, and Warfare

Pastoralism creates forces that tend toward both gender egalitarianism and male dominance. The lack of firm differentiation between the domestic and public spheres is a force toward gender egalitarianism. Where women have some economic control, women's status may be raised. Male economic control and female economic dependence, however, are forces toward male dominance and gender stratification. Other factors of primary importance in supporting male dominance are the defense needs and warfare practices of herders and the patricentric kinship systems that internal warfare and corporate ownership of livestock generate.

In terms of Sanday's categories, pastoralists most often fall under the rubric *real male dominance*, because in most cases the environment is sufficiently dangerous for the society to depend on the strength and aggressiveness of their men for survival. Sanday argues that under such conditions of stress, "for the sake of social and cultural survival, women accept real male dominance. Their lives and those of their children may rest on their willingness to do so. . . . Women willingly accept domination in exchange for protection and food."[13]

Livestock are extremely valuable property among pastoralists. Each camel or head of cattle represents a tremendous investment of material resources and human labor. Yet livestock are easily stolen. If one calculates the relative costs of stealing livestock versus raising livestock, it is usually clear that it is more efficient to steal than to raise your own. In addition, in areas of high population pressure there is competition over scarce pasturage and water holes, both between different camps of pastoralists and between pastoralists and agricultural peoples. Thus pastoralism is often associated with internal warfare. Chapter 3 discussed Harris's theory of the effects of internal warfare between geographically proximate, culturally similar peoples involving shifting alliances and treachery. These factors lead to the development and maintenance of fierce, aggressive, warlike males and a high degree of gender inequality. The situation among many pastoralists supports Harris's model.

Analyses of the warfare complex within and among pastoral peoples indicates that war can become an integral part of the economic and political structure and serve as a type of functional adaptation to the ecology of herding. Louise Sweet, for example, has studied the practice of camel raiding among North Arabian Bedouins.[14] Camel raiding is a primary activity of Bedouins to the extent that

the main occupations of the majority of the men in a Bedouin chiefdom or clan section have to do with keeping and guarding the camels and particularly with prosecuting raiding expeditions. The security of the family, lineage, clan section and chiefdom rests in the possession of adequate numbers and kinds of camels.[15]

Within local groups camels are exchanged through the mechanisms of bridewealth, bloodwealth, fines, gifts, hospitality, and tribute. But between distant groups, raiding is the chief mechanism of distribution. Sweet found that camel raids served to distribute both camels and human populations more evenly, and therefore in a more ecologically adaptive manner, over the desert areas and oases available to Bedouin pastoralists.

Reciprocal camel raiding, as a continuous practice, operating at both long and short distances between tribal breeding areas, maintains a circulation of camels and of camel husbandry over the maximum physical range for camels and the societies which specialize in their breeding and depend upon them. The continued exchange by mutual raids serves thus to recoup local losses owed to failures of pasturage and water, or disease.[16]

The raiding triggers institutional mechanisms that integrate the disparate camps into loosely structured chiefdoms occupying large zones. The threat of raids motivates different camps to enter into truces to limit their number of potential enemies, and the potential spoils of raiding motivate different camps to form alliances for joint raids. Furthermore, a camp suffering from raids often attempts to appeal to the chief to force the guilty group to pay compensation or return the stolen camels. Raiding thus maintains a process of truce making and breaking, alliance making and breaking, and provides a continual basis of integration for the very loosely confederated camps of herders. Confederation is important to maintain, for it is potentially useful in organizing defense against encroachments by non-Bedouins.

Raiding is also practiced against non-Bedouin peoples living in or near the Bedouin zones. Bedouins often obtain goods they do not produce themselves from such non-Bedouins through trade, tribute, and raiding. In this case raiding serves to maintain Bedouin control of the district while simultaneously allowing for the continuation of symbiotic relations between these different peoples.

Sweet states that in addition to these economic and political functions, camel raiding also serves to support the whole culture and social structure of Bedouin life. Male dominance is one aspect of the culture and social structure of raiding. Raiding encourages the development of fierce, aggressive personalities and skills in Bedouin men. These personalities and skills can be used to dominate Bedouin women as well as other men. Furthermore, if Harris's model of warfare and female subordination is accurate, female submissiveness to males constitutes an important reward or motivation for the males to risk the dangers inherent in raiding and defense against raiding.

The Maasai of sub-Saharan Africa have also practiced high degrees of raiding and internal warfare. Men are highly valued and idealized for their bravery as warriors and lion hunters. Women are disparaged for lacking bravery and the self-control and cooperativeness necessary in war parties.[17] During their years as warriors, young men have legitimate sexual access to adolescent girls and are considered very attractive to older, nonwarrior men's wives, who seek the warriors as lovers. There is a strong link between the warrior traditions and conceptions of masculine identity and sexuality among African pastoralists.[18]

Boulding found that the taming of horses by pastoralists in open areas that are conducive to riding great distances at great speeds tended to produce a *warrior aristocracy* and social and gender inequality. However, in areas less amenable to warfare on horseback, the nomads remained more egalitarian and peaceful. The more warlike and richer Mongols of the Asian steppes had more pronounced class inequality and were more strictly patriarchal than the somewhat less warlike Bedouin pastoralists. However, given the nature of internal warfare among pastoralists women as well as men were often trained as aggressive defensive fighters.[19] Although raiding and some more important battles were conducted away from the camps, much of the fighting involved the tent camp itself:

The distinction was not always clear between the "army" and the total tribe. One of the first things Genghis [Khan] did was organize the wagons as part of the tribal battle formation, with women and children trained to shoot and defend the wagons and babies . . . women were also trained to fight from horseback . . . probably only women of the warrior aristocracy received such training.[20]

Furthermore, the women of these pastoral warrior aristocracies were more influential and more openly involved in political affairs than were the women of agricultural warrior aristocracies, who were not typically trained to fight or directly involved in warfare. Boulding has found several examples of *warrior queens* in the history of warring pastoralists. Among state level herders such as the Asian Mongols, the khatun (wife of the khan or chief ruler) had a court and her own diplomatic corps of princesses and shared the duties of state with her husband. Some of them even led armies into battle. However, contact with settled urban populations often undermined the position of women. Assimilation to urban life changed the texture of pastoral life, and one of the consequences was the increase of male dominance and a loss of personal autonomy and public power on the part of upper-class pastoral women.[21]

Although Boulding's examples of warrior queens appear to contradict Harris's theory, it may be that these women's elevated position in the class structure partially neutralized the effect of their gender in learning the skills of mounted warriors. Similarly in our society a wealthy upper-class woman is often in a position to give orders to a working-class man. This does not undermine the gender stratification system in our society, because it is recognized that class position takes precedence over gender status in this context.

Further support of Harris's warfare theory in relation to pastoralists is found in data on the relative gender egalitarianism of the Fulani of Niger in Africa. The Moslem Fulani are pastoralists who must compete for scarce resources. But they have avoided direct involvement in the warfare complex that often accompanies pastoralism in a competitive environment. They accomplish this through a division of labor with closely related Fulani sedentary agriculturalists. The sedentary Fulani act as the fierce, warlike attack force for the more peaceful, accommodating Fulani pastoralists. As the pastoral Fulani migrate into new areas, they are accompanied by their sedentary kinsmen. Opposition to the pastoralists is dealt with by their sedentary kinsmen who readily involve themselves in warfare.[22] Because the pastoral Fulani do not have to fight their own battles

for expansion, they do not have a culture and social structure emphasizing aggressiveness, male dominance, and hierarchy, which usually accompanies local warfare.

The problem of the warfare complex manifests itself in yet another manner in pastoral society and again has important consequences related to gender stratification. Pastoralists are overwhelmingly patrilineal and patrilocal. The ecological conditions of pastoralism and the defense problems engendered by population pressure are functionally related to the pastoral preference for patrilineality and patrilocality and to pastoralists' widespread emphasis on male honor, shame, and female chastity.

These connections are especially characteristic of Mediterranean pastoralists of Europe and North Africa.[23] Population pressure and competition over scarce resources are acute in these societies. Intracommunity conflicts over land, water, and animal theft are common. Such disputes are overlain with an ideology of male honor and shame. Maintaining one's own or one's family's property is a matter of honor. Shame comes to males who cannot defend or increase their property. Furthermore, strong central governments had not, even in the recent past, penetrated these areas sufficiently to maintain law and order and to remove the settlement of disputes from the local areas. The codes of honor and shame are means of social control adapted to a competitive environment in the absence of state level controls.

Since pastoralism requires nomadism, the determination of grazing and water rights is likely to be a problem. Permanent ownership, property lines, and fences are not adapted to a migratory life. Access or temporary property rights are established through the credible threat of force. Maintaining an impressive fighting force is then of key importance to local groups of herders. They achieve this partially through the practice of patrilineality and patrilocality with at least some kin ownership of resources. The kinship and residence system concentrates the power of closely related male kinsmen who are reared together with a strong sense of common identity and common purpose. This maximizes the strength of the collective work group necessary for herding, protection, and aggrandizement.

Bette Denich found that a highly patricentric kinship and residence pattern based on an extended household of brothers and male cousins characterizes Montenegrin pastoralists.

The formal structures . . . are based exclusively upon relations among male kinsmen. The only enduring social units are formed through the male descent line, and women are exchanged among these units to procreate future generations of males, leaving no enduring marks of their own existence in terms of the formal structure. . . . The exchange of women leads to the formation of male groups, not groups acknowledging the equal participation of both sexes.[24]

The Montenegrins do not even count daughters as children.

The Montenegrin male kinsmen own sheep and goats and rights in pastureland collectively and share in the work of herding and guarding them. As Schneider notes, population pressure and the consequent competition for scarce resources creates chronic defense problems. This

requires that herdsmen band together with allies to ward off actual attacks and discourage potential threats to their means of subsistence. The organizational solution to this problem has followed the pattern developed around the world by populations in analogous circumstances: patrilineally related groupings bonded through the dynamics of fusion against common external enemies . . . the public face of

each group vis-a-vis the external world represents its competitive posture toward potential rivals. . . . Since all public arenas have the potentiality for combat, they are designated as male. The household's external environment is exclusively a male domain.[25]

This system is supported and encouraged by the concepts of honor and shame which help to maintain the solidarity of nuclear and extended family groups. Any perceived insult against one member of the group is taken as an affront to the entire group and must be avenged. Feuding among males is endemic.[26] Males are socialized to be quick-tempered, aggressive, courageous warriors. Denich argues as Harris that this aggressiveness is necessary for survival in this context of high population pressure and scarce resources. Furthermore, each domestic unit acts as a fortified household, that is, taking care of its own defense needs and settling disputes through the personal use of violence. As Randall Collins has pointed out, such domestic arrangements focus and consolidate male dominance.[27]

The presence of women actually becomes problematic for these societies. Women are necessary for their labor and procreative abilities, but their loyalty is suspect because they are not members of the patrilineage and because their interests often lie with the nuclear family rather than the extended family. Women are a potentially disruptive and divisive force. Every attempt is made to subordinate women to the authority of the male kinsmen. Females must exhibit deference to the males of the household at all points of contact. Physical punishments are employed to enforce male authority. Denich notes this deference is shown in public by the wife customarily walking several paces behind the husband, carrying his burdens, and walking while he rides. Within the household men are served food first and women eat the leftovers later with the children. *Degradation ceremonies* including such rituals as washing the feet of the men are common. The wife's name also reflects male dominance. Among the Montenegrins, after her marriage the wife is referred to only by the possessive of her husband's first name. Thus a wife might become simply "John's."

The ideology of male honor and shame deflects many of the conflicts among men over land, water, and animals onto women, through its corollary emphasis on females as *sexual property.* Women are treated as another form of male property:

In a sense, they are contested resources much like pastures and water, so much so that kidnappings, abductions, elopements, and the capture of concubines appear to have been frequent occurrences at least in the past.[28]

Virginity and chastity are required of women on the pain of death. A woman who violates these sexual codes dishonors herself and her male kinsmen. But to seduce another group's women brings honor to the seducer. Women are expected to share in the defensive burden of protecting their sexuality by always acting in a chaste manner. They should appear in public as seldom as possible, and when they do, they must dress conservatively, deemphasize sexual attractiveness, and keep their eyes lowered so as not to invite any male advances. Women are socialized to regard themselves and are regarded by men as shameful temptations who are potential traitors to the household.

The demonstration of female virginity can be so important to family honor that virginity tests such as bloody sheets or undergarments are sometimes required for public display after the consummation of a marriage. *Infibulation,* the cutting and fusing together of the sides of the vulva, sometimes in conjunction with clitoridectomy, is practiced by Somalian and Egyptian Nubian pastoralists

as a means of ensuring and proving virginity beyond a doubt.[29]

Purdah, or the veiling and physical seclusion of women, is practiced by some pastoralists, but not to the extent found among Muslim agrarian peoples. It has often been adopted as a direct result of outside contact or domination, but this does not mean it had to be forced on the pastoralists. Carol Pastner points out that in the case of Baluchistan nomads of Pakistan, purdah was consistent with their traditional values of male honor and shame. With increased social mobility, the destruction of their feudalistic and warrior-based social structure, and the introduction of a more stable centralized political order, Baluchistanis adopted veiling and seclusion from their new sedentary neighbors on the oasis. Purdah should be viewed as "the ritual aspect of the ideology of honor and shame" and as such is "a symbolic statement about social order in its ideal form."[30] It is a symbolic means of making claim to high social status (implied by the expenses of maintaining purdah) and of the separation of insiders from outsiders in the more heterogeneous and socially fluid village world. Such ritual had been unnecessary in the strictly nomadic community of kinsmen.

But even in the purely pastoral community, controlling the sexuality of their women is a primary concern of males. An unmarried girl's loss of her virginity or adultery on the part of a wife brings tremendous shame to her family. The family's honor must be avenged and this requires the joint efforts of all close male kinsmen to kill the seducer or at least to obtain some compensation for the insult. The concern in maintaining the modesty of women and avenging violations serves to solidify the male kinsmen in the face of divisive pressure.[31] In addition, this intense concern with controlling female sexuality derives from the need to present a fierce public face to ward off potential attacks on livestock and pastures: "Evidence of lack of control over women would indicate weakness and possibly reveal the men's vulnerability to other external challenges."[32]

Patrilineality, Organizational Flexibility, and Male Dominance

Although patrilineality is functional for the maintenance of a unified male core for collective work and fighting, it is also associated with a high degree of internal competition and divisiveness. The divisiveness is kept under control to a degree by the solidarity generated by common interests and the ideological supports of honor and shame. However, the divisiveness itself can be adaptive when the household and its herds get too large for the available resources to support. Both the processes of *fusion* and *fission* among pastoralists can generate male dominance and female subordination.

Like the nomadic foragers, nomadic herders require an organizational flexibility based on kinship ties, which allows them to fuse into larger groupings to take advantage of temporarily lush pasturelands, and more important, for defense against external enemies. They also must break up into smaller units, sometimes down to the nuclear family unit, to spread over and utilize the largest area possible. The feuding and raiding among camps and villages partly serves the function of dispersing the population over wide areas as defeated groups move on to avoid further losses. However, the fissioning and dispersal processes are regularly required within the patrilineages or extended family households themselves.

When too many brothers, cousins, sons, and grandsons are within the same domestic group, there is an intense pressure to divide. The amount of pasturage and water necessary to maintain a very large household and its herds are difficult to find without breaking into smaller units and migrating in different directions. There is therefore a critical point at which a household that is large enough to defend itself and obtain sufficient grazing lands and water becomes too large for the ecologically allowable population density. Fission is regularly necessary, but the group cannot afford to allow the pressures for division to separate it too soon into units too small for the collective work and defense needs of herding. The problem is thus to maintain household solidarity while simultaneously providing a basis for the eventual destruction of that household. Again, degradation and subordination of women are used to symbolize these processes and to deflect the competitiveness of the men onto women as the enemy. Thus conflicts between brothers are often said to be caused by disputes among wives—"The system can deal with dissension from women more easily than it can with disputes among its male members."[33] As a household becomes too large for environmental conditions, the pressures from wives in the interests of their children become the acknowledged reasons for brothers to divide up their patrimony and set up separate households with their sons. This prevents too much hostility among brothers from accompanying the fissioning and allows the brothers to remain close enough to come to one another's defense whenever necessary. Females are used as scapegoats to diminish the impact of the actual rivalries between the male kinsmen.[34] Among the Shahsevan of Iran, for example, overt camp conflict is minimal, but real conflicts of interest over inheritance and leadership are brought into the open as conflicts between the wives of the involved men.[35] Women's quarrels are the ostensible cause of fission. Women fall into this role as a result of their being in-marrying outsiders to the patrilineages, connected to the lineage primarily through their own children whose interests they place above those of the wider patrilineage.

Relations between the Genders

Religion and Ritual

The cultural and structural subordination of women is supported by the religions of most herders. *Islam* is widely accepted among herders of Asia and Africa, while *Christianity* predominates among European and New World pastoralists. Both of these religions support male dominance; Islam specifically requires female subordination and seclusion. However, the impact of these religions' teachings supporting patriarchy appears to depend on the existence of wider socioeconomic forces toward gender stratification or gender egalitarianism. That is, where conditions support a high degree of male dominance and patriarchy, the religious practices of these structures are more strictly adhered to, such as among the Mediterranean herders. Where conditions do not so strongly support male supremacy, people are more likely to practice these religions indifferently, for example, the Fulani and the Tuareg Moslems.[36] The Tuareg are often noted for the high status of their women despite centuries of adherence to Islam. They have many institutions supporting male dominance, but they are still not as patriarchal or male supremacist as we might expect on the basis of their religion alone.

The Tuareg woman enjoys privileges unknown to her sex in most Moslem societies. She is not kept in seclusion nor is she diffident about expressing her opinions publicly, though positions of formal leadership are in the hands of the men. . . . She places little value upon pre-marital chastity, stoutly defends the institution of monogamy after marriage, maintains the right to continue to see her male friends, and secures a divorce by demanding it—and she is allowed to keep the children.[37]

The Moslem Durrani of Afghanistan adhere strongly to the principle of male superiority, but do not practice veiling or the seclusion of women. Control over women is important for a family's honor, but it must be publicly visible control to demonstrate familial strength and prestige. Restricting women to women's quarters is a sign of weakness.[38]

Elaborate veiling and seclusion are not usually necessary among most Islamic pastoralists, because their communities are more homogeneous and kin-based than those of urban dwellers. Women therefore require less protection.[39] Close kinsmen are more likely to cooperate in the mutual control of the group's women. Seclusion is also not very practical in tent-based communities where women must help with the herd. These communities can rely on the "social walls" erected by the male fraternal interest group. Nomads, however, often resist living in settled communities, even when drought threatens their existence, because they do not have sufficient material resources to build the mud walls necessary in the heterogeneous village to shield their women from contact with outsiders.[40]

Not all pastoralists have come under the control of the great universal religions such as Islam or Christianity. The Maasai retain their own religious myths and practices, which exemplify Sanday's pattern of a dual orientation and a prehistoric time when females held power. Originally, there were female warriors and young male warriors. The women were braver than the men, but there was no fertility; women had no vaginas. The males used their arrows, which women did not have, to create vaginas in them. Women lost their bravery and men gained control. Since then, women have been devoted to caring for children, while men care for the herd and defend the group. Another myth also emphasizes women's concern for children over livestock. Women had been in charge of all the animals but when they stayed home with their children and let the animals go out alone, the animals became wild and men had to take over to support the group.[41]

Nuer *creation myths* emphasize women's role as creators of life and in the creation of society. In the beginning women were the cattle herders while men were forest-dwelling buffalo hunters. Women could give birth, but only to females, without men. Men eventually came out of the forest and marriage and bride-wealth institutions were established. There is both an *inner orientation* and *outer orientation* in this myth. Women are associated symbolically with fertility, and the fertility of both human beings and cattle are crucial to the survival of pastoral society. Although males are dominant in many respects among the Nuer, the gender division of labor is complementary, and strong tendencies toward gender equality are apparent in everyday life and in the peoples' attitudes.[42]

Paige and Paige argue that male circumcision rites are common among pastoralists because of the problem of fission and the strong tendencies encouraging men to break off from the group to found their own group.[43] The rites are a means of testing the loyalty of men with sufficient sons to consider separation—"Every man is a potential lineage head and, therefore, also a potential traitor to his lineage."[44] The Maasai place a great deal of emphasis on both male and female circumcision, perhaps because children of both sexes are so valuable in achieving high position in their ranking system.

Male circumcision is done when a boy is in late adolescence and ready to become a warrior. In addition to testing his parent's commitment to the wider group, being performed at this late age rather than in infancy or early childhood, it is also a test of the boy's bravery and self-control and serves as a strong psychological reminder of his soli-

darity with his age mates who undergo the rite with him. He and his family and his entire age set suffer severe humiliation if he so much as flinches during the cutting of the foreskin. This is evidence that he can stand up to the demands of warfare and lion hunting and be depended on in times of extreme danger. Females, however, do not cause great shame if they express pain during circumcision. Their self-control and bravery are not necessary to group survival.[45]

Female menarcheal ceremonies are not common, however. The strength of the male group allows men to control women and make marriage contracts without having to resort to such *social mobilization rituals*.[46] Similarly, birth rituals and couvade are rarely found among pastoralists. Nor are menstrual huts and elaborate pollution practices needed for men to express ritual disinterest in their wives' fertility. The power of the kin group allows, even encourages, men to display openly their wives' fertility and wealth in sons. Power is stable enough among pastoralists that such ritual solutions to the divisiveness of jealousy are unnecessary.[47]

Marriage

As we have already noted, pastoralists are predominantly patrilineal, and marriage often entails the exchange of women between male-dominated patrilineages. Marriages are often arranged by families to cement political and economic alliances. They usually involve the exchange of large numbers of livestock as brideprices (goods received by the bride's family from the groom's family) and as dowries (goods given to the bride or the groom by the bride's family), which further stabilize the marriage arrangements and solidify the interfamily alliances.[48]

Bridewealth is common in pastoral societies because they have large, stable resources and strong fraternal interest groups. Contracts involving large transfers can be made and enforced and the wealth retrieved if the bargain is violated. Moreover, because bridewealth benefits the daughter's family, there is a strong tendency toward early marriage for girls.[49]

Among the Nuer of Africa men view their herds in terms of the number of wives they can bring.

Cattle stand for a wife and are therefore the most important thing in a Nuer's life, because a wife means to him his own home and that he becomes a link in the lineage by fathering a son. Nuer do not grudge the loss of a herd to obtain a wife. They lose cattle, but the wife will bear them daughters at whose marriage the cattle will return, and sons who will herd them.[50]

Some pastoralists such as the Durrani view the exchange of women in purely market terms, using economic concepts such as "sale" and "price," and fathers often seek to marry their daughters to social superiors and to obtain the highest brideprice possible. The father is dishonored if he must marry her to a man of lower standing or for a low brideprice. But the Shahsevan refuse to view marriage in such crass economic terms. Brideprices are seen as somewhat shameful, and much of a brideprice is actually given to the bride and groom and not kept by the father. The Shahsevan do not like the idea of treating women like livestock.[51]

But bridewealth serves an important function in the relatively nonstratified pastoral societies. It regularly disperses the wealth and keeps it from being concentrated in the hands of a few families generation after generation. It is a mechanism for economic leveling among peoples who do not produce sufficient surpluses to support full-blown class inequalities.[52]

Martin and Voorhies found that polygyny characterized the majority of their sample of pastoral societies, and they found a high correlation between the incidence of polygyny and the type of cultivation practiced by pastoralists. The nuclear family predominated among those using agricultural techniques, whereas polygyny characterized those practicing horticultural cultivation.[53] This is in accord with the hypothesis that polygyny is more likely to be practiced where additional wives lend increased productivity to the domestic unit, as is usually true in horticultural but not in agricultural societies.

Polygyny with a wealthy older male married to many younger wives is common among some pastoralists. But among the Maasai, young wives of polygymous older men may discreetly take lovers from the unmarried warrior class. The women exhibit strong solidarity in maintaining the secrecy of one another's affairs. Even mothers-in-law will not inform their sons of their daughters'-in-law adultery. The only exception to this tolerance of adultery is for women who have sex during pregnancy. This is believed to harm the infant, and women will severely punish other women whom they believe have violated this taboo. The children that result from these unions belong to the husband and further increase his wealth and prestige. This is especially true for old men with many wives. Similarly, a young man may take his first wife while still serving as a warrior. If she bears a child by another man while he is away at war, that is simply proof of her valuable fertility and helps him build his power base in children and cattle sooner.[54]

Divorce is common among many pastoralists, and men generally have more freedom to obtain divorces than women do. This is particularly true among Moslems, who allow men to divorce their wives by merely announcing the divorce in the presence of reliable witnesses. Wives, however, have to undertake litigation to obtain a divorce and the grounds are quite limited. The litigation process, furthermore, usually requires extensive support from some influential male, maintaining the dependence of the woman on men even if allowing her a chance for freedom from her husband. Among the Durrani and the Shahsevan, divorce is strongly disapproved and extremely rare.[55]

Sexuality

Mediterranean and Asian pastoralists often place great emphasis on female virginity and chastity for the reasons discussed earlier. They also practice a strong sexual double standard. However, some pastoralists, in particular those of the Sudan and sub-Saharan Africa, allow premarital and sometimes extramarital sexuality for women as well as for men.

The Nuer, for example, like the Maasai are sexually permissive and allow girls as much premarital freedom as they do boys. Sexual play is an important part of childhood, and after initiation at the age of twelve or thirteen girls begin taking lovers and having both serious and casual affairs. Boys are initiated at about fourteen to sixteen years of age. They are then expected to take on the rights and duties of manhood in work, play, and war. But during this stage, courtship, dances, and affairs are of primary importance. Being attractive to girls in personal appearance and the demonstration of strength and bravery is crucial.

Girls have a great deal of personal autonomy in the Nuer courtship system. The girl may reject or accept a boy's advances. She may want to withhold sexual access to demand marriage. However, boys often promise marriage with no intention of actually marrying the girl they are attempting to seduce. It is also possible for the girl to propose marriage to the boy.

After marriage, a sexual double standard is applied. Nuer women should not participate in extramarital sex. A man is supposed to settle down, but if he desires an affair, his wife should not object. Furthermore, a husband can claim compensation for adultery but a wife cannot. Adultery is, however,

frequent. It is illegal among the Nuer, but it is not considered immoral. Moreover, the Nuer do not attach much importance to physiological paternity. It does not shame a man to raise children he did not beget.

Female Subordination

Women are subordinate to men in most pastoral societies. Wives are expected to obey their husbands and show respect within the home and in public, for example, eating only after the men have eaten or walking behind men. Close emotional ties are not likely to develop within these marriages. Women maintain close ties with their children and sometimes with kinsmen and kinswomen and cowives, but not with their husbands.

Husbands usually have the right to mete out physical punishments to their wives whenever they deem it appropriate. Wife beating is common among pastoralists. But the man who exceeds the culturally acceptable standards of wife beating is likely to be the object of ridicule as one who prefers to fight women rather than men.

Given the subordinate nature of her position in marriage, the pastoral woman typically uses three main tactics in defending her own interests against the power of men: "playing men off against each other, seeking alliances and support from other women, and minimizing contact with her husband."[56] The opposition built into marriage among the Marri Baluch Arabs, for example, leads men and women to view each other as enemies. Love is considered antithetical to marriage.

Marri men see themselves as opposed by women, as fighting a continuous battle against female recalcitrance and laziness. Women . . . see themselves in a conspiracy of opposition against men.[57]

Among the Marri Baluch, it is not uncommon for wives to hate their husbands and in extreme cases to poison them. The men, in turn, regard their wives as polluted, as filth. Sexual intercourse is believed to be polluting. A menstruating woman pollutes anything she contacts, and a new mother is polluting for forty days after childbirth. Men express strong disgust with women in general and with their wives in particular.

The Durrani, however, place a great deal of emphasis on romantic love. Yet this produces an ambivalent view of women. Women can be intelligent and desirable companions and can associate quite freely with men. But men fear them and view them as "quarrelsome, sexually voracious and unclean as compared with men."[58] The emphasis on love and companionship exists alongside very negative stereotypes of the female character. Women are seen as so inferior and ungodly, so easily possessed by evil spirits, that they may not enter the mosques or participate in other public religious practices. "Such ideas are used to justify the literal powers of life and death a household head has over the women of his household as well as to debar women from all control of produce and capital goods."[59] Durrani women bring in extremely high brideprices but they may inherit nothing from their natal families and own little in their own right. By contrast, the Shahsevan idealize and honor women, exhibit little sexual antagonism, allow some respected females to participate in public affairs, and allow women to go on religious pilgrimages, but have very low brideprices and firmly segregate and seclude women.[60]

The power of the husband over the wife is typically limited by the continued guardianship of her kinsmen. In general, females cannot defend their own interests or rights but must depend on some male or males. The woman's father and brothers are expected to protect her interests against her husband and to intervene on her behalf whenever the husband exceeds his proper

authority. Among some groups the father has the right to take his daughter away from her husband if he feels she is being abused.

Relying upon male kinsmen for protection, of course, exacts its costs in terms of female subordination. Among the Egyptian Awlad 'Ali, for example,

it is basically through blind obedience to her father or closest kinsmen that the woman secures the protection and backing of her kin—family, which is the major guarantee of her marital rights. And it is mainly through forfeiting her rights of inheritance that she is able to maintain such protection.[61]

Bedouin females in Libya also ignore Islamic law and refuse inheritance rights as daughters to maintain the corporate property of the patrilineage intact. But women can and do use this sacrifice as a basis to make claims against their kinsmen. They are not meek or submissive in pressing their rights.[62]

Where there is a high degree of economic interdependence between the sexes and where women can obtain a divorce or separation easily, there is greater equality between husband and wife. If losing his wife means losing his household, his cook, his dairymaid, and sometimes his children, as it does among the Nuer, the husband is more careful not to motivate her to leave. The divorced or separated woman may lose the protection of her kinsmen (especially where they have to return the brideprice to the husband) and find herself in an even more vulnerable and desperate situation than she was with an abusive husband.

Not all pastoral women passively accept abuses by their husbands, however. Evans-Pritchard notes that Nuer women often physically attack their husbands during disputes:

Should she in a quarrel with her husband disfigure him—knock a tooth out, for example—her father must pay compensation. I have myself on two occasions seen a father pay a heifer to his son-in-law to atone for insults hurled at the husband's head by his wife when irritated by accusations of adultery.[63]

Even though pastoral husbands may have the culturally legitimated authority to dominate their wives and homes, they do not necessarily exercise total power over the women or women's activities.

Child Rearing

Pastoralists' emphasis on the use of force and violence is reflected in their child-rearing practices. Like foragers, they encourage a high degree of independence and individualism in their children. But unlike foragers, pastoralists also encourage aggressiveness. Evans-Pritchard notes that among the Nuer, for example,

from their earliest years children are encouraged by their elders to settle all disputes by fighting and they grow up to regard skill in fighting the most neccessary accomplishment and courage the highest virtue.[64]

Children are expected to begin working at an early age in the sex-segregated division of labor. Boys learn herding and fighting skills from their male kinsmen and neighbors, and girls help with the household tasks and learn from female kin.[65] Among pastoralists who emphasize female chastity, young girls are also taught to be extremely modest and to feel great shame about their bodies. Boys often have to undergo a period as warriors before being allowed to marry, again reflecting the important role of warfare and feuding among herders.

Forces for Change

The pastoral way of life is threatened by the increasing penetration of strong national central governments into the pastoralists' previously remote lands. These governments typically attempt to remove the set-tlement of disputes from local control. They try to suppress internal warfare, feuding, and raiding. This disrupts the culture, social structure, and ecology of many pastoral peoples, making their way of life unviable. This type of change may be of some benefit to women, as a lessening of the warfare complex may allow some lessening of the male dominance complex that so often accompanies it. But other forces may maintain male dominance and aggressiveness against women even when the warfare complex has been suppressed.

Contact with nonpastoralists has long had a disruptive effect on pastoralism. However, it has not usually brought about an improved status for women. Since more often than not it has introduced sedentary life-styles and social structures to these peoples, the subordination of women practiced by sedentary peoples has often been part of the assimilation process.[66] The adoption of the practice of purdah by Baluchistanis separated men and women, allowing men to become more "modern" through outside contact but encouraging women to become more "traditional" in their isolation.[67]

Settled agriculture or wage labor does not liberate women. Yet these are often the paths forced on pastoralists by strong central governments seeking to apply national economic development schemes.[68] For example, the World Bank and the Afghan government tried to entice and coerce the Sheikhanzai into a modernization project that would have transformed them into settled meat producers for urban slaughterhouses.[69] Their plan would have destroyed the traditional community and kinship-based reciprocity, political, and economic structure. The plan assumed male dominance and male economic control and would have undermined all the bases for female power. The Sheikhanzai refused to participate. Women were particularly outspoken in camp against the plan. The reforms introduced by the communist government after the 1978 takeover were no more enlightened in their appreciation of communal, nomadic life or of the interests of nomadic women.They also sought to introduce individual male property ownership. Other researchers have also complained that development plans ignore the often negative impact their schemes would have on women.[70]

Pastoralists, like the Sheikhanzai, themselves may moderate the amount of social change they accept or reject. Emmanuel Marx has found that Arab pastoralists in Israel have maintained ties with external markets for centuries without cultural disruption. Today many men move their wives and children with them into nuclear family houses. But unless they establish a truly secure niche in the urban economic system, they carefully maintain their ties, and especially their reciprocal relationships, with the tribal community. They do not want to lose their access to tribal lands. Savings are still invested in the traditional forms—in jewelry and polygynous marriages. The only new investment type is trucks and tractors. But this fits with pastoral nomadism: These goods are portable and help protect against unexpected political and economic disruptions.[71]

Bedouin women in Israel welcome some of the changes brought by contact and colonization. They have taken advantage of their rights under the government-enforced Islamic laws and the civil law, which among other things forbids polygyny. Bedouin men still sometimes circumvent the law by refusing to register their marriages. But social security benefits provided to families of registered marriages is an important inducement to registration.[72]

Women can also use the urban setting to escape from the extended household ruled over by the mother-in-law. They gain more influence over their husbands and children in the nuclear family sedentary home, which separates the husband from his fraternal interest group as well as from his mother. Wives also use the urban setting to demand a standard of living from their husbands that matches town rather than desert standards. However, the urban way of life creates a higher degree of gender segregation, with men leaving the domestic sphere to work as wage laborers in the public sphere. This is perhaps offset by the greater independence and free time available to the women, which they use for visiting and maintaining ties with other town-dwelling tribal women. Some also earn money by selling their handicrafts in the marketplace. This money can be used for reciprocal gift giving and feasting to maintain solidarity among women.[73]

Pastoralists can sometimes escape pressures for change altogether if they live in areas too barren for exploitation even by modern scientific agriculture. Yet the existence of collectively owned grazing lands is usually an enigma to government bureaucracies, accustomed to dealing with legal property titles. Modern governments strive to keep close track of their citizens and their resources because they want to know whom to tax and what property belongs to which taxpayer. Such outside controls and influences can disrupt the flexibility of pastoral life. Changes in the basic structure and practice of pastoral life will undoubtedly mean changes in these peoples' gender roles and sexual stratification systems. The changes may not, however, benefit women or lessen gender inequality.

Conclusion

From an evolutionary point of view, there is some usefulness in conceiving of pastoralism as a "stage" between the horticultural and agrarian (see Chapter 5) ways of life.

This conception, however, must be sharply qualified. Although it is hazardous to generalize too sweepingly about the evolutionary origins of the pastoral way of life, the characteristics of historically known and archeologically accessible societies of this type indicate that they have developed in close conjunction with horticultural and/or agrarian communities and societies.[74]

Pastoral societies display a wide range of variation in gender relations and, as Martin and Voorhies have pointed out, some closely approximate horticultural patterns in this respect while others incline toward the agrarian.[75] Certain features reminiscent of foraging bands also appear among pastoralists. Almost all pastoral societies are, however, subsumed by patriarchal values, and their range of variation is effectively confined to Sanday's "mythical male dominant" to "real male dominant" continuum. Distinctive environmental conditions work for the elevation of women's position in some of these societies, while reinforcing patriarchy in others. Historical relations with specific horticultural and agrarian communities and societies and complex cultural interactions with agrarian civilizational religions also affect and complicate the range of adaptive strategies available to pastoral peoples, perhaps especially in the area of gender relations. Pastoral societies, then, are perhaps most interesting from the standpoint of the evolutionary and comparative study of gender relations and gender stratification as kinds of historical laboratories: societies in which the confluence of a number of social, cultural, political, and economic factors emanating from horticultural and agrarian sources impinge on low-surplus producing units of social organization, strategically dependent on nomadism and the male-dominated preindustrial extraction of meat and dairy products from herd animals as the primary basis of subsistence.

Notes

1. For a discussion of the economy and social organization of pastoral societies, see Gerhard Lenski and Jean Lenski, *Human Societies: An Introduction to Macrosociology*, 4th ed. (New York: McGraw-Hill, 1982): 221–225.

2. M. Kay Martin and Barbara Voorhies, *Female of the Species* (New York: Columbia University Press, 1975): 337–338.

3. Robert Paine, "Animals as Capital: Comparisons Among Northern Nomadic Herders and Hunters." *Anthropological Quarterly* 44 (July 1971): 169.

4. Michael L. Burton and Douglas R. White, "Sexual Division of Labor in Agriculture," *American Anthropologist* 86, no. 3 (September 1984): 576–577.

5. Martin and Voorhies, 339.

6. Martin and Voorhies, 340.

7. Martin and Voorhies, 343.

8. Melissa Llewelyn-Davies, "Women, Warriors, and Patriarchs," in Sherry B. Ortner and Harriet Whitehead, eds., *Sexual Meanings: The Cultural Construction of Gender and Sexuality* (Cambridge: Cambridge University Press, 1981): 337; Melissa Llewelyn-Davies, "Two Contexts of Solidarity among Pastoral Maasai Women," in Patricia Caplan and Janet M. Bujra, eds., *Women United, Women Divided: Comparative Studies of Ten Contemporary Cultures* (Bloomington: Indiana University Press, 1979): 206–237.

9. Elise Boulding, *The Underside of History* (Boulder, Colo.: Westview Press, 1976): 288–289.

10. Lois Beck, "Women among Qashqái Nomadic Pastoralists in Iran," in Lois Beck and Nikki Keddie, eds., *Women in the Muslim World* (Cambridge, Mass.: Harvard University Press, 1978): 365–367.

11. Bahran Tavakolian; "Women and Socioeconomic Change among Sheikhanzai Nomads of Western Afghanistan," *Middle East Journal* 36, no. 3 (Summer 1984): 433–453.

12. Nancy Tapper, "The Women's Subsociety among the Shahsevan Nomads of Iran," in Beck and Keddie, 1978, 374–398; Nancy Tapper, "Matrons and Mistresses: Women and Boundaries in Two Middle Eastern Tribal Societies," *Archives of European Sociology* (1980): 59–78.

13. Peggy Reeves Sanday, *Female Power and Male Dominance: On the Origins of Sexual Inequality* (Cambridge: Cambridge University Press, 1981): 181.

14. Louise Sweet, "Camel Raiding of North Arabian Bedouins: A Mechanism of Ecological Adaptation," in Louise Sweet, ed., *Peoples and Cultures of the Middle East: Vol. I:* (Garden City, N.Y.: Natural History Press, 1970): 265–289.

15. Sweet, 272.

16. Sweet, 287.

17. Llewelyn-Davies, 1979.

18. Ali A. Mazrui, "The Warrior Tradition and the Masculinity of War," *Journal of Asian and African Studies* 12, nos. 1–4, (1977): 69–81.

19. Beck, 1978, 355.

20. Boulding, 308.

21. Boulding, 303–312.

22. George Murdock, *Africa* (New York: McGraw-Hill, 1959): 413–421.

23. Jane Schneider, "Of Vigilance and Virgins: Honor, Shame and Access to Resources in Mediterranean Societies," *Ethnology* 10 (January 1971): 1–24; Jean G. Peristiany, ed., *Honour and Shame: The Values of Mediterranean Society* (Chicago: University of Chicago Press, 1966); Julian Pitt-Rivers, "Honour and Social Status," in Peristiany, 19–77; Julian Pitt-Rivers, *The Fate of Shechem: The Politics of Sex* (Cambridge: Cambridge University Press, 1977); J. K. Campbell, "Honour and the Devil," in Peristiany, 139–170; Abou A. M. Zeid, "Honour and Shame among Bedouins of Egypt," in Peristiany, 243–259.

24. Bette Denich, "Sex and Power in the Balkans," in Michelle Rosaldo and Louise Lamphere, eds., *Women, Culture and Society* (Stanford, Calif.: Stanford University Press, 1974): 246.

25. Denich, 248.

26. Joseph Ginat, "Blood Revenge in Bedouin Society," in Emmanuel Marx and Avshalom Shmueli, eds., *The Changing Bedouin* (New Brunswick, N.J.: Transaction Books, 1984): 59–82.

27. Randall Collins, "A Conflict Theory of Sexual Stratification," in Hans Peter Dreitzel, ed., *Family, Marriage, and the Struggle of the Sexes* (New York: Macmillan, 1972); Randall Collins, *Conflict Sociology* (New York: Academic Press, 1975).

28. Schneider, 18.

29. John G. Kennedy, "Circumcision and Excision in Egyptian Nubia," 5 *Man* (1970): 175–191; I. M. Lewis, *People of the Horn of Africa* (London: International African Institute, 1955): 135; Karen Ericksen Paige and Jeffery M. Paige, *The Politics of Reproductive Ritual* (Berkeley: University of California Press, 1981): 89; Tobe Levin, "Unspeakable Atrocities: The Psycho-sexual Etiology of Female Genital Mutilation," *Journal of Mind and Behavior,* 1, no. 2 (Autumn 1980): 197–210; Awa Thiam, "Women's Fight for the Abolition of Sexual Mutilation," *International Social Science Journal* 35, no. 4 (1983): 747–756; Winifred Weekes-Vagliani, "A Practice Known as Going to Granny's," *Women in Development: At the Right Time for the Right Reasons* (Paris: Development Centre of the Organisation of the Economic Co-operation and Development, 1980).

30. Carol McC. Pastner, "A Social Structural and Historical Analysis of Honor, Shame and Purdah," *Anthropological Quarterly* 45, no. 3 (July 1972): 248–261.

31. Schneider, 21–22.

32. Denich, 255.

33. Denich, 256.

34. Denich, 259–260.

35. Tapper, 1978, 390.

36. See, for example, Emrys L. Peters, "Women in Four Middle East Communities," in Beck and Keddie, 1978, 310–350 and Beck, 1978 for discussions of variations in the practice of Islam and gender roles in different socioeconomic situations.

37. Robert F. Murphy, "Social Distance and the Veil," in Sweet, 1970, 297–298.

38. Tapper, 1980, 68–69; Nancy Tapper, "Acculturation in Afghan Turkistan: Pastun and Uzbek Women," *Asian Affairs* 14 (February 1983): 39.

39. Dawn Chatty, "Changing Sex Roles in Bedouin Society in Syria and Lebanon," in Beck and Keddie, 1978, 403.

40. Stephen Pastner, "Ideological Aspects of Nomad-Sedentary Contact: A Case from Southern Baluchistan," *Anthropological Quarterly* 44, no. 3 (July 1971): 178–183.

41. Llewelyn-Davies, 1979, 215, 230; Llewelyn-Davies, 1981, 342, 350.

42. John W. Burton, "Nilotic Women: a Diachronic Perspective," *Journal of Modern African Studies* 20, no. 3 (September, 1982): 467–491.

43. Paige and Paige, 124–166.

44. Paige and Paige, 128.

45. Llewelyn-Davies, 1981, 339, 351.

46. Paige and Paige, 95.

47. Paige and Paige, 177–228.

48. John W. Burton, "Gifts Again: Complimentary Presentation among the Pastoral Nilotes of the Southern Sudan," *Ethnology* 21, no. 1 (January 1982): 55–61.

49. Jack Goody, "Bridewealth and Dowry in Africa and Eurasia," in J. Goody and S. J. Tambiah, *Bridewealth and Dowry* (Cambridge: Cambridge University Press, 1973): 10.

50. E. E. Evans-Pritchard, *Kinship and Marriage Among the Nuer* (London: Oxford University Press, 1951): 90.

51. Nancy Tapper, "Direct Exchange and Brideprice: Alternative Forms in a Complex Marriage System," 16 *Man* (1981): 395.

52. Goody, 1973, 13.

53. Martin and Voorhies, 347.

54. Paige and Paige, 93; Llewelyn-Davies, 1979.

55. Tapper, 1980, 65.

56. Robert Pehrson, *The Social Organization of the Marri Baluch* (New York: Wenner Gren Foundation, 1966): 59.

57. Pehrson, 60.

58. Tapper, 1980, 73.

59. Tapper, 1982, 164.

60. Tapper, 1980, 72–73.

61. Safia K. Mohsen, "Aspects of the Legal Status of Women among Awlad 'Ali," in *Sweet*, 233.

62. Peters, 1978, 327.

63. Evans-Pritchard, 1951, 104.

64. E. E. Evans-Pritchard, *The Nuer* (New York: Oxford University Press, 1940): 151.

65. See Peters, 1978, 314–319 for a description of the labor inputs of Bedouin children and adolescents.

66. Beck, 1978, 367–369; Chatty, 1978, 399–415.

67. Carol McC. Pastner, 1972, 255.

68. See the special issues on pastoralists edited by John G. Galaty in *Journal of Asian and African Studies* 16, nos. 1–2 (1981) and Philip C. Salzman, ed., *When Nomads Settle: Processes of Sedentarization as Adaptation and Response* (New York: Praeger, 1980).

69. Tavakolian, 1984.

70. Vigdis Broch-Due, Elsie Garfield, and Patti Langton, "Women and Pastoral Development: Some Research Priorities for the Social Sciences," in John G. Galaty, Dan Aronson, and Philip C. Salzman, eds., *The Future of Pastoral Peoples* (Ottawa: International Development Research Centre, 1981): 251–257; Michael M. Horowitz, "Research Priorities in Pastoral Studies: An Agenda for the 1980s," in Galaty, Aronson, and Salzman, 1981, 61–85.

71. Emmanuel Marx, "Economic Change among Pastoral Nomads in the Middle East," in Marx and Shmueli, 1984, 1–15.

72. Gillian Lewando-Hundt, "The Exercise of Power by Bedouin Women in the Negev," in Marx and Shmueli, 1984, 97–98.

73. Lewando-Hundt, in Marx and Shmueli, 1984, 90–91.

74. Martin and Voorhies, 1975, 364–366.

75. Martin and Voorhies, 1975, 364–366.

CHAPTER 5

Agrarian Societies
Antiquity and the Middle Ages

As the populations of horticultural and pastoral peoples increase beyond the productive capacities of their technologies and environments, people are motivated to search for more productive means of subsistence. In particular, as land becomes more scarce people can no longer maintain the nomadic life of shifting horticulture or herding. Staying in one place means they must learn to keep the land fertile for continuous use. To deal with this pressure, people developed the technology and social structure of settled agriculture. Agriculture greatly increases productivity and thereby makes possible very different patterns of social organization among sedentary agriculturalists. Out of this process arose such great agrarian civilizations as ancient Egypt, Greece, Rome, and China. The agricultural revolution is usually thought of as progress and often hailed as the "dawn of civilization." However, this progress brings with it a loss of status and power for women relative to men and for the majority of the population relative to a tiny ruling elite.

Economy and Social Organization

Technology

Agriculture involves first and foremost the use of the plow and draft animals and often entails fertilizing and irrigating the soil. These practices increase the productivity of land and allow for denser populations and more complex social organization. But agriculture is much more strenuous and demanding than horticultural or pastoral production. The agricultural laborer works a longer day and longer seasons than workers in other types of economies. Guiding a plow requires muscular strength and stamina, as does digging and maintaining irrigation ditches. Breaking draft animals to take the harness and plow is a demanding and time-consuming task. Oxen and other draft animals are large and can be difficult to handle. Draft animals cannot be allowed to wander freely because of the danger of their ruining crops if left untended, so there is less land for them to roam in. Therefore, they have to be fed and watered. Their manure must also be collected, carried to the fields, and spread as fertilizer.

The work is so much more demanding than horticultural labor that horticulturalists often resist the introduction of agricultural techniques, despite the latter's higher productivity. An agriculture-based economy probably first arose in Mesopotamia and Egypt before 3000 B.C. Agriculture then spread throughout Europe, North Africa, and Asia. Much later it was introduced into the New World and sub-Saharan Africa by European colonists.

Agriculture did not spread to many parts of Africa until forced on the local populations by Europeans, because African peoples' horticultural techniques provided them an adequate living with much less effort expended. Population pressure on the arable land never became great enough to force the people to increase productivity or face mass famine. Such population pressure and scarcity of resources, especially land, appear to have accompanied the development of agriculture and its increased productivity in other parts of the world. However, the benefits of this increased productivity do not remain in the hands of the producers. Increased production also often leads to the rise of a social stratification system in which an elite few live luxuriously off the labor of many.

Class Structure

The level of productivity achieved through plow agriculture allows the production of *surpluses* on a scale unimaginable in hunting and gathering, horticultural, or pastoral societies. For the first time, large segments of the population can be freed from primary subsistence production.* This allows for the rise of urban communities, complex governmental institutions, empires, writing, and a high culture for the elite.[1]

Agriculture transforms the great majority of the world's population into *peasants*. Unlike horticultural farmers in nonstratified societies, peasants must give up much of their produce to the ruling class in the form of taxes, rent, tithes, unpaid labor, and gifts. This often amounts to as much as one-half and sometimes more of the peasants' harvest. Except in times of labor shortages caused by wars, famine, or plague, there is a surplus of peasant labor and the elite can afford literally to work peasants to death and replace them. The level of class oppression found in agrarian societies is rarely matched in the horticultural or pastoral societies and never found among foragers.

Slavery is also widely practiced in agrarian societies. Slaves are, of course, even more firmly controlled by their masters than are peasants. Slaves are an especially important benefit of military conquest.

The peasants' high birthrates mean that many of the children are forced off the land. These landless peasants are often driven by necessity into the cities and towns and become part of the *urban artisan classes*, who are sometimes even more despised than the peasantry. They produce necessary goods and services, but many live degraded, poverty-stricken lives. The artisans, however, do not constitute more than a small percentage of the population of agrarian societies.

---

*A very few horticultural societies were sufficiently productive to allow for large urban populations, craft specialization, and leisure classes, but these never reached the scale of the great agrarian civilizations.

Agrarian societies often have *degraded* or *unclean classes* below the artisan class, such as the Untouchables of India and the Burakumin of Japan. These people perform the most despised tasks in the societies such as tanning leather and working with animal carcasses.

Overpopulation among the masses also produces a substantial *expendable class* of criminals, beggars, and chronically underemployed itinerants. Although despised and often living on the verge of starvation, these people provide an important reserve labor force that can be drawn on in times of labor shortage among the peasantry or artisans.

Above the common classes, agrarian societies have important urban *merchant classes* who handle the local and regional commercial activities and trade. This is low-prestige work, but it sometimes produces significant wealth.

The *retainer class* of lower governmental officials, professional soldiers, household servants, and personal retainers who serve the rulers and the governing classes constitute a higher-prestige class. These people mediate between the tiny governing elite and the masses. They are often the ones who perform the tasks directly involved with expropriating the surpluses from the merchants, peasants, and artisans in the form of taxes, rent, and forced labor. Along with the merchants, they deflect the hostility of those being exploited away from the elite onto themselves. The retainer class is not, of course, as wealthy as the governing classes, but its members use their positions to amass wealth and live comfortably.

The highest classes in agrarian society are the *governing classes* of top governmental bureaucrats or nobles and the *ruler*—the king or emperor. These people are sometimes fabulously wealthy. They benefit the most from the surpluses produced by the merchant, peasant, and artisan classes.

Agrarian societies contain one more important class—the *priestly class*. The top leaders of organized religion are drawn from the governing class. These people are often very wealthy and powerful. The lesser clergy may be drawn from the lower classes and have little wealth or power. The priestly class serves the governing class and ruler by lending legitimacy to their power and privilege and by helping to control the masses. However, they sometimes challenge the power of the rulers and governing class on the basis of their status as the representatives of god or the gods.

As the preceding description of the class structure indicates, agrarian societies are characterized by marked social inequality. Exploitation is built into the economy and social organization of great agrarian civilizations.

Community Size

The increased productivity of agriculture makes possible much larger and denser populations than had previously been possible. The cities of agrarian societies have as many as one million inhabitants and societies such as mid-nineteenth-century China had 400 million people.[2] These societies also control vast territories containing ethnically, linguistically, and racially diverse peoples.

Agrarian societies are much more complex than societies based on simpler technologies. Although the rural peasantry constitutes the great majority of the population and provides the productive backbone, the societies exhibit a high degree of occupational specialization, both regional and local. Trade between different areas is an important benefit of expansion and imperial domination. Transportation and communication systems are needed to maintain the complex political and economic systems.

Leadership and Government

Agrarian societies are held together by powerful central governments or by local warlords. Control of governmental machinery can be used effectively for personal aggrandizement. For this reason there are continual struggles over power and the privileges that accompany it. There is also continual struggle between the ruler and the governing classes. Most of the time an unstable balance is maintained, giving the ruler certain powers and the governing classes other powers. In some societies, however, one or the other group dominates. In Ottoman Turkey, for example, the ruler was so powerful that even the members of the governing class were his personal slaves, while in medieval Europe the kings had little power compared with the nobility.

Political power and military might are in the hands of the few. Advances in agricultural productivity are accompanied by advances in military technology. The new military technology is used to increase the power of the state and the governing classes at the expense of the masses. The political system is tightly integrated with the economic system. Land is the basis for both economic and political power in agrarian societies. The chief rulers, bureaucrats, and nobles are also the chief landlords.

Warfare

Warfare is chronic in most agrarian states. The societies themselves are formed primarily through conquest. The productivity and technology of agrarian economies make warfare almost inevitable, and the surpluses produced make conquest profitable. The forcible subjugation of foreign peoples as peasants or slaves increases the exploitable labor supply and expands the wealth available to the conquering elite. Historically, inventions such as the wheel and the sail and the domestication of the horse allowed for the rapid transportation of soldiers, weapons, and supplies over long distances and thereby facilitated external war against foreign enemies. Technological improvements in weaponry also increase the efficiency and destructiveness of warfare.

Warfare is often the chief preoccupation of the ruling classes in agrarian states. Control over the means of violence and warfare such as weapons, transportation, and training is the primary distinguishing characteristic of the elite as compared with the masses. The elite classes gain power and status through warfare and skill in fighting. Warfare pervades their life-style, self-concepts, and culture.

Moreover, as mentioned above, warfare is internal as well as external. The gains from political office are so great that they encourage continual struggles among members of the elite and continual jockeying for power among the different elite classes.

Religion

The religions of the agrarian states reflect the wider social and economic situation. The great universal religions—Christianity, Islam, Hinduism, Buddhism, and Judaism—spread and became institutionalized largely within agrarian societies. Unlike the religions of foragers and horticulturalists, these religions do not emphasize local cults and local gods or original female or couple creators. Rather, the religions are outer oriented; the god or gods tend to be masculine and reign over all people regardless of residence or group membership. This mirrors the empire building of these states and the rule of their male monarchs.

Religions also support and legitimate the power of the ruling classes. An extreme example of this is found in ancient Egypt where it was believed that the pharaoh was god and ruled because he was divine. But most agrarian states were not such complete theocracies. Instead, the rulers were seen as ruling because of "divine right" given by God, but not because the rulers themselves were gods. Religion was used to enforce the power of the rulers, and it served as a relatively effective noncoercive means of encouraging the peasants both to produce a surplus and to give much of it up to the secular and sacred rulers.

The priestly class is itself often comprised of members of the governing classes. Many of them are the younger sons of the nobility who cannot inherit the family estate because of the rule of primogeniture (the eldest son inherits the entire estate). They often live a luxurious life at the expense of the peasantry. Furthermore, religious institutions often own large amounts of land and many peasants and slaves, just as the governing classes do.

While reflecting and legitimating the stratification of agrarian states as a whole, the religions also legitimate the gender stratification system, patriarchy, and male dominance. The teachings of Christianity, Islam, Hinduism, Buddhism, and Judaism all prescribe female subordination to greater of lesser degrees and emphasize a predominantly masculine image of God.

Family, Kinship, and Child Rearing

As the state takes over the integrating functions of agrarian societies, family and kinship ties decline in importance. Political and economic functions are performed by non-kinship-based institutions. (An important exception to this was China, which retained an elaborate clan network as the basis of its economic, political, and class structures.) As land ownership and use rights come to be more and more invested in the individual instead of the corporate kinship group, the unilineal kinship groups or clans, which are so important in horticultural and pastoral society, give way to bilateral kinship systems. Large extended families and patrilocal residence patterns decline as *neolocal residence* and smaller domestic units become important.* Polygyny also declines among the bulk of the population as the economic productivity of wives declines under the male-dominated agricultural production. Polygyny continues to be practiced, however, among some of the elite. In this case polygyny is a form of conspicuous consumption or political alliance making, rather than a means of increasing productivity through increasing the family labor force.

Kinship ties remain important in politics and in the inheritance of position and wealth. This, of course, affects only the upper classes, but among the common classes family ties remain important in economic matters as well. Businesses are usually family businesses and agricultural land is usually worked by families.

Marriages are made as economic alliances among all but the poorest people and for political alliances as well among the upper classes. It can be important to join two plots of farm land together through marriage or to cement a truce by marrying one's sons and daughters appropriately. Love and attraction are not important considerations in making marriages. Close emotional bonds are not crucial for families or couples.

Child-rearing practices reflect the wider political and social stratification system. Discipline and obedience are emphasized; love and affection are not. Among the common classes children are put to work at an early age. Socialization is highly gender segre-

---

Neolocal residence: the married couple lives separately from either the husbands or the wife's kin.

gated. Girls are taught domestic skills in all classes. Among the elite they are also expected to learn the feminine social graces for pleasing men. Girls are also taught modesty and submissiveness to men and sometimes the skills required to manipulate men. Commoner boys are taught nondomestic economic skills. Elite boys learn the arts of warfare and politics and sometimes art, literature, and high culture in general.

Gender Roles and Gender Stratification

Agrarian societies are characterized by marked gender stratification as well as class stratification. The subordination of women reaches its highest degree in agrarian civilization. One of the important factors in reducing the status of women in agricultural as compared with horticultural societies is the gender division of labor. As we pointed out earlier, agricultural labor requires muscular strength, long hours, and often takes the worker far from home and places him in dangerous work situations. Much of it is not compatible with pregnancy or child care. Women thus lose their roles as primary economic producers under agriculture.

Peasant women do not remain idle, however. They work long hard hours within the home processing the products of men's labor: baking, preserving food, weaving, and sewing. Women undertake a great deal of agricultural labor, but the tasks are of a secondary nature. They usually do not clear the land, plow, or dig the irrigation ditches. They also become intensive breeders of the labor supply. Agricultural women have more children more closely spaced than horticultural women. Peasants react to their poverty by trying to produce large numbers of sons. The birthrate in agrarian societies is higher than in any other type of society, and the spacing between children is much shorter. Rae Blumberg notes that peasants have little control over the amount of land or capital at their disposal, but they can attempt to expand their labor supply through having children.[3] In terms of the short-run interests of individual peasants or peasant families, large families may increase their chances for survival. A large number of children, especially sons, may allow them to increase productivity through increased labor input. It may also help ensure that the aging peasant man and woman will have someone to care for them when they can no longer produce for themselves. However, in the long run the high birthrate can undermine the position of the peasantry as a whole by keeping the overall labor supply high. Any individual peasant is often expendable and easily replaced by other hungry, eager workers.

Women also constitute an important reserve labor supply that can be used in periods of peak labor demand such as the planting and harvest seasons. Blumberg suggests that the chronic labor surpluses of agrarian societies are more important in explaining women's lowered status than is the strenuous nature of the work.[4] Women can perform the agricultural labor, but they are not likely to be as efficient as male laborers. Since these societies usually have an abundance of laborers, males are given first preference as workers. Women are in that sense another group of expendables who can be kept out of primary production or paid a lesser wage than men. They can furthermore be kept busy at auxiliary tasks and child care and still be available when male labor is insufficient. In highly labor-intensive areas such as China, women remained a part of the regular labor supply. No one was kept in reserve because extra labor could almost always be used to increase productivity without expanding the amount of land under cultivation.

This gender division of labor gives rise to a separation of the genders and a strong public/domestic split. As women lose their productive roles in agriculture, they become more economically dependent on their husbands and more isolated into smaller domiciles. Large collective female work groups and the bases for female solidarity decline. Martin and Voorhies note:

Female labor, encapsulated as it is, becomes focused upon repetitive, monotonous tasks inside the domicile. Their isolation from "outside" activities eliminates access to avenues of political power and the control of property, both real and portable. In sum, the overall status of women in agricultural or peasant society is one of institutionalized dependency, subordination, and political immaturity.[5]

The dependency may not, however, be as extreme as these writers suggest. The genders are really interdependent. Men need the labor of their wives and women need the labor and protection of their husbands. But it is an unequal interdependence because of the male control over primary economic production and the female relegation to secondary tasks.

The low status of women in agrarian societies is probably also related to the militaristic nature of these societies. Warfare is endemic, increasing the male emphasis on aggressiveness and bravery. The concentration of military might in the hands of powerful warlords is likely to lead to females becoming just another form of property to be conquered and ruled. Such control over women is a matter of male honor among many agrarian men. This pattern of warfare and female subordination is likely to occur when warfare is conducted close to home. However, when warfare takes the men away for long periods of time, women are often left in control of the family holdings. Enterprising women are sometimes able to turn this opportunity into power, privilege, and personal autonomy for themselves.

Sexuality

The isolation of women in the domestic sphere and the view of women as a form of property for men are accompanied by strict controls on female, but not male, sexuality. Agrarian societies tend to place extreme importance on premarital virginity and chastity for married women. Women are not supposed to exhibit the slightest suggestion of sexual activity or interest. Violations of these sexual taboos for females are often severely punished. To help ensure the sexual purity of the family's females, they are subjected to spatial separation and isolation in the home. The less contact with nonkin males, the better. This is difficult to enforce among poorer families who cannot afford separate living quarters, courtyards, high walls, and elaborate veils to protect their women from view. But upper-class women are so isolated. The practice of purdah among Moslems is an example of such seclusion. Females of the wealthier classes are expected to live their entire lives without being seen by a nonkinsman. Separate female quarters are maintained in the home. If male guests are present, females retire to their quarters or serve them from behind screens. Errands outside the home are performed by males or lower-class servant women. If the woman has to leave the home, she goes accompanied by servants and covered from head to toe in a veil with only small slits for her eyes. When railroads were introduced into India, special windowless cars were made available for women practicing purdah.

Although some upper-class women in agrarian societies become influential behind-the-scenes manipulators and many enjoy the luxurious life-style afforded by great wealth, they are still likely to be isolated and subordinated to the men of their class. Upper-class females are also likely to be used to advantage in male political and economic alliances. Their class status gives them some privileges and some power over lower-class males and females, but it does not necessarily lessen the gap between them and their men.

Ideology and Gender Role Stereotypes

Agrarian societies also develop elaborate religious, moral, and legal justifications for their gender stratification systems. Thus the religions of agriculturalists emphasize male dominance and female subordination and often female inferiority and uncleanness as well. They legitimate the patriarchal family structure and rationalize women's isolation in the domestic sphere. Martin and Voorhies note that ideologies of agriculturalists come to include gender role stereotypes that emphasize the male's physical, intellectual, and emotional fitness for public roles. Females are often viewed as inherently suited for domestic tasks and as incapable for assuming public political and economic roles. Furthermore, stereotypes of females commonly present women as needing male direction, supervision, and protection.

Sanday also found that in agrarian societies, particularly as the agricultural technology becomes better developed, there is a tendency toward male-oriented religious symbolism.[6] A masculine orientation emphasizing a male creator and males as the source of power in the universe often develops. But much depends on the nature of previously prevailing creation beliefs and sex role symbolism. A people coming from a culture emphasizing a feminine creator and female power or an original creator couple with males and females both holding power may retain that orientation or parts of it and respond to the stresses associated with adopting an agrarian way of life with less male dominance than a people whose cultural background has long focused on masculine gods.

We next turn to specific historical ex-amples of agrarian societies, beginning with the maritime society of ancient Crete and the full-fledged agricultural society of ancient Greece.* This is followed by examinations of ancient Rome and medieval Europe.

Ancient Greece

A review of the changing positions of women and men in Greek society from the Minoan civilization on the island of Crete to the Hellenistic period in Athens and Sparta illustrates some of the evolutionary changes in gender stratification that accompany the rise of agrarian society.

Minoan Civilization

Minoan civilization arose and flourished on Crete from about 3000 B.C. until it was destroyed by earthquakes in 1500 B.C.[7] Crete never developed a true agricultural economy, nor did it ever exhibit a truly patriarchal, strongly male-dominant gender stratification system. The primary source of wealth on Crete was seafaring trade. The fertile land supplied the people with food, and population pressure was never so great as to force them into more intensive agricultural practices or into exploitative compulsory systems of production and exchange. Instead, they retained the horticultural pattern of small-scale, independent female gardening, although they used such technological advances as irrigation.

The lack of defense needs also helped keep the independent farmers from being

---

*The evidence for reconstructing men's and women's lives in these ancient societies is inadequate and often unreliable. Myth, drama, oratory, vase painting, and funeral inscriptions provide some clues, but the resulting descriptions are based heavily on scholars' conjectures.

transformed into a heavily taxed peasantry. Minoan civilization was not militaristic or warlike. They increased their wealth through trade, not through internal or external conquest. No large powerful warlords or landlords arose. Their island location protected them from outside attack, so they did not require centralized military leadership or taxes or forced labor for making weaponry and fortifications. Political power remained decentralized among the merchants with a great deal of struggling among rival houses. But there was no need for males to develop fierce aggressive personalities at the expense of women's autonomy and social position.

In the absence of pressure to increase agricultural productivity and in the absence of war, the development of a wealthy stratified society and high civilization on Crete did not bring an end to female economic participation nor the decline of the matrilineal clan structure. Women continued to be the primary food producers and participated with men in the trading and commercial activities that were the backbone of the Cretan economy. Women also hunted and practiced various arts and crafts. They were not the economic dependents of men, nor were they isolated in the domestic sphere away from the public worlds of the economy, polity, or society. The high status of women may be reflected in the religion of Minoan Crete. Goddesses were of great importance, but no powerful king or dominant male god has been found.

Bronze Age Society

Because it could maintain a peaceful society without population pressure or war, Crete seems to have followed a very different pattern than that found during the Bronze Age on the mainland of Greece.[8] Mainland Greeks were extremely vulnerable to attack. It was a society ruled over by military kings who were seafaring warriors. The local peoples were reduced to peasant status. The peasant surpluses and the booty from conquest were used for weaponry, fortified palaces, and strong walls. Women did not have as high a status as among the Cretans. However, the women of the dominant warrior classes were not totally stripped of power, nor were they secluded, because the distant wars kept the warrior males away for long periods of time. This left the chief woman in the household in charge of its management. Although a patriarchal family structure was becoming the established norm, women were still not considered inferior or incompetent. Thus male absence diluted somewhat the male dominance that accompanies a militaristic society.

The religious myths, although they emphasized Zeus as the most powerful of the gods, point to a distant past where Zeus had to overcome threats from females, and many powerful goddesses as well as gods were said to rule. The sources of power in the universe were not seen as being entirely in the hands of males,[9] and females as well as males served in priestly roles.

But the fierce aggressiveness and competition among males did render females as prizes to be won by the bravest warriors. The women of a conquered people were taken as slaves and concubines of the victorious group. Domination over women accorded prestige to men, and an extra measure of prestige accrued to the man who held as slave a wife or daughter of a high-status male opponent. The female slaves were, of course, sexually available to their masters, although virginity and chastity were required of these same males' daughters and wives. But violation of the sexual code by females was not as severely punished during this period as it came to be later. Bronze Age women were expected to be modest, but they were not as firmly secluded in the household as women in Classical times.

Recently uncovered evidence indicates

that women were important as both skilled and unskilled laborers and in general occupied a more equal socioeconomic position in this society than in other Near Eastern societies of the time or in later Greek cultures.[10] But a division had emerged between the domestic sphere for females and the public sphere for males. Free women and slave women worked primarily at the household chores, while free men busied themselves with matters of war and politics. The lower classes and slave men and women carried out the menial work of the society.

The kinship system of Greece during the Bronze Age reflects its transition to an agrarian way of life from simpler, nomadic foraging and horticultural practices. Matrilineal and matrilocal traditions gave way to patrilineality and patrilocality as the constant threat of war produced a need for strong male leadership.

The Dark Ages

The Bronze Age ended in the twelfth century B.C. Writing disappeared and Greece entered its Dark Age followed by the Archaic Period.[11] These were periods of great internal strife among local warlords. Gender roles continued to emphasize the male as warrior and the female as the producer of warriors. Marriage alliances between powerful warrior families were an important part of the political structure. Women as well as other gifts were used to solidify agreements between powerful families.

Greece was underpopulated during the early part of this period but suffered a dramatic rise in population after 800 B.C., creating a problem of population pressure.[12] As Harris's theory would predict, not only was warfare a problem, but infanticide, especially female infanticide, was also practiced. (The usual practice was to abandon unwanted infants. Not all of these died, however. Infants could be picked up by others

to be used as prostitutes or servants.)[13] The status of women was low, although variations did occur among the different city states and among women of different classes.

In Athens free women were firmly tied to the domestic sphere. Although poor women and slave women were often forced to work in the public sphere, the only respectable public roles for women were centered around religious festivals and funerals, which often afforded women an opportunity to get together and maintain some nondomestic ties.[14] Women had very prominent roles in Greek religious practices. Both the gods and women were considered "uncivilized," closer to nature, and more unpredictable than the more comprehensible (to men) male world.[15] Both were also necessary for men, even though relations with them were often dangerous.

A strong sexual double standard already existed in Athens by the Dark Ages. The warrior class came to view women as sexual property and male status in terms of control over property in the form of land, livestock, and women. Male honor depended on controlling the sexuality of women.

The position of women in Sparta was quite different from that in Athens. Although they never exercised the same political rights as men and although men did not consider them as equals, free women had more personal autonomy in Sparta. The Spartans were a highly militaristic society, but they were more involved in long-distance war than Athens. Males were absent for long periods of time. The men also lived most of their adult lives in the military barracks and visited their wives only briefly at night.

Adultery was not condemned for women. But it was probably not the wife who had the initiative in extramarital sex. A husband could allow another man to use his wife to bear children for the husband himself or for the other man and obedience was expected of the wives involved.[16] The emphasis was on the production of healthy Spartan children in the service of the state.

Spartan women were not tied to the household or housework. The huge slave class performed the menial labor. Citizen women, like citizen men, were expected to spend their time carrying out civic responsibilities and maintaining physical fitness in the service of the state. Spartan women were treated equally with men in matters of health and nutrition. Athenian women by contrast did not exercise or receive the same food allotment as men.

The different role of Spartan women is also reflected in their dress. They wore short, loose-fitting dresses that left their legs bare and afforded easy movement. Athenian women wore heavy, voluminous gowns that inhibited their freedom of movement.

A greater equality of Spartan women and men is also seen in the customary age at marriage. They did not practice child marriage for females. Athenians, however, married their girls at the age of twelve to sixteen to help ensure their virginity. Child marriage also encourages dependency in the wife, as it is very difficult for a child bride to be the physical or intellectual match of an adult husband. The Spartans did not institutionalize this type of male advantage in their marriage practices, and male dominance and control over wives was not as significant to Spartans as it was to Athenians. Athenian women were controlled largely by the family. In Sparta there were concerted efforts by the state to depreciate the family. The primary allegiance was to the state. The authority of the family was replaced by overlapping male groups—age-graded army classes, homosexual pairs, elite military groups, and the public mess.[17] Women were free from the kind of domination by the paterfamilias that Athenian women experienced, being neither as bound to nor protected by the family as Ath-

enian women were, but they were not free in the modern feminist usage of the word.

Male absence due to warfare also seems to be important in explaining the relative freedom and autonomy of Spartan women. Gortyn, one of Sparta's closely related neighbors, had less male absence and accorded women much less freedom. Gortyn women were not, however, as restricted as Athenian women.

Homosexuality was common among males during this period, encouraged by the long military campaigns and the separation of the genders. There is also evidence of homoerotic ties between older women and girls in Sparta. The island of Lesbos is best known in this regard through the often homoerotic poetry of Sappho.

As Greek society continued to evolve during the Dark Ages and Archaic Period, the class structure became more rigid. The upper class or aristocracy increased in power and wealth. In Sparta the change from the rigorous simplicity of earlier years to more luxurious living and the susequent decline in military power were blamed on women. In Athens women were also penalized for the excesses of the aristocracy. Solon codified the laws of Athens in the sixth century B.C. To curb the activities of the aristocracy, he institutionalized a great many legal restraints on the already restricted Athenian woman. He made a legal distinction between good, pure women and bad, sexually available women, for example, giving a male guardian the right to sell into slavery or prostitution an unmarried girl who lost her virginity, even if it was due to rape. Solon established state-owned brothels to make Athens attractive to foreign businessmen. He limited the amount of jewels, clothes, and food and drink that free women could have and limited their public freedom of movement to restrain the practice of displaying male wealth through the flaunting of expensively adorned wives and daughters. Solon considered women a source of strife among men and attempted to solve this problem by isolating women from the male public sphere. Citizen women were to serve the family and the state by producing children to perpetuate the lines of descent and the ancestor cults based on them. Citizen men were to serve the state through their political and military roles. M. I. Finley argues that as Greek society became more politically centralized in the eighth and seventh centuries B.C. citizenship in the polis took on greater importance. The legitimacy of citizens became the concern of the state. The determination of who was a wife and a producer of citizens and who was a mere concubine passed from the males of the family to the male head of the state.[18]

The Classical Period

Solon's restructuring of the Athenian law code ushered in the Athenian democracy and what has come to be known as the Classical Period beginning in the fifth century B.C.[19] Athens was the leading political, economic, and cultural power in Greece despite crippling wars with the Persians and Spartans. The position of women reached its lowest point in this period known for its democracy.

Guttentag and Secord suggest that Athens had many more men than women and this helps account for the differences between Athenian and Spartan gender stratification systems.[20] They argue that because the Athenians exposed primarily female infants while Spartans exposed both weak male and female infants in their attempt to rear the strongest warriors, there was a shortage of citizen women in Athens but a more equal numerical balance in Sparta.

Where females are in short supply, Guttentag and Secord maintain, they become the objects of male competition, and high-status men acquire more than their "fair share" of the women. In Greece this probably meant having a wife and concubines or *hetaerae*. When there is an imbalance, women tend to be more firmly secluded and protected as valuable property from outside males and have little opportunity to compete in the public world with men. Because of their value, they are married off very young. This description characterizes what we know of Athenian women, but not Spartan women.

In Classical Athens the restriction of the public activities of women evolved into full-fledged seclusion of some women. Respectable women were to remain in the home almost all the time except for certain festivals and funerals. The home itself was divided into the public rooms for males and women's quarters or *gynaeceum*.[21] The gynaeceum was the most isolated part of the house and no males except close kinsmen could legitimately enter it. Here the well-to-do citizen woman and her children and slaves carried out the domestic routine. The work of the citizen woman was sometimes the same as that of the slaves she directed. She prepared food, made wool, and wove cloth. The work was important to the Athenian economy, and women took pride in and were praised for their cloth-making skills.

Respectable women were under the perpetual guardianship of men. As daughters they were under the authority of their fathers. Authority passed to the husband at marriage and to the son if a woman were widowed and not remarried. Women were often married several times during their lives because of the large age difference between the girl and her first husband. Marriages were arranged by fathers and it was important that the girl be a virgin. If it were discovered on the wedding night that she was not a virgin, the husband had to renounce her and her family was publicly humiliated.

Similarly, the husband was required by law to divorce a wife caught in adultery. Men were greatly concerned with the possibility of adulterous wives, and adultery did seem to occur despite the severe penalties. The wife became a social outcast and lost her rights as a citizen. The husband had the right to kill the seducer or to demand compensation for the damage done to his "property." The penalties for rape were less severe for the male, who had to pay a fine for compensation. The women, however, was still "ruined property" and had to be divorced and possibly sold as a slave or prostitute.

Women had few independent economic or political rights. Classical law vested almost all authority in the hands of the male head of the household, who was expected to act in the interest of the women, slaves, and minors who composed his household. The law did, however, attempt to provide some economic security for the wife by protecting her dowry. To marry, the daughter had to be given a dowry commensurate with her family's wealth and social standing. The dowry was passed to the husband who could use it as he saw fit but could not sell it. It had to be maintained intact and be returned to the women's guardian for her support if she were divorced. Divorce was easy to obtain, and the futures of women would have been even more insecure if their dowries had not been so protected. In the case of women with substantial dowries, the law served to inhibit men from divorcing their wives in order not to lose control over such important wealth or property.

Classical Marriage. The marriage relationship was not one of close emotional companionship in Classical Athens. Wives were less educated and more isolated than their husbands. The age gap might be large. Most of them could not be expected to provide

the stimulating companionship of the husband's male friends or the noncitizen female companions of men called hetaerae. Close relationships between men were encouraged and homosexuality accepted. Marriage was intended to produce heirs for the patrilineage. But because population pressure and the costs of endowing a daughter and supporting a son were great, small families were desired. Few families reared more than one daughter, and two sons were usually sufficient. The relationship between husbands and wives could be so distant that a citizen man who married an orphaned girl without brothers was required by law to sleep with her at least three times a month. (This was an attempt to ensure the continuation of her father's lineage.)

Despite this gulf between men and women, Greek literature suggests that some couples did develop close loving relationships. This was not a necessary part of a good marriage, however. The good wife was one who provided the husband with legitimate male heirs, ran her household well, and increased her husband's property. It was especially important in this highly competitive society that she bring no shame on her husband. Her name should not even be mentioned in public. The orators, for example, took care not to refer to respectable Athenian women by name.

Classical Child-Rearing Practices. Child-rearing practices in Greece reflected the wider social structure. Girls and boys were socialized into almost opposite personality traits. Girls were reared to be silent and submissive and to abstain from men's pleasures such as sex, politics, and learning. They were taught domestic skills and were married off at an early age: "While her male contemporary was living in his parents' house and developing mental and physical skills, the adolescent girl was already married and had young children."[22] But most upper-class girls received some education and they were certainly literate.[23]

Philip Slater develops the controversial argument that the Athenian subordination and seclusion of women in the domestic sphere led to the development of psychologically destructive child-rearing practices, especially in the raising of sons.[24] Fathers kept their distance from the household and involved themselves very little in child rearing. Mothers acquired by default a great deal of power over the children. Slater maintains that women's resentment of their low status was focused on their sons. They simultaneously hated their sons as members of the powerful privileged gender and idealized them and desired to experience the public world vicariously through the achievements of their sons. The son was reared in a male-dominated culture, yet his first years of life were spent in a female-dominated environment. According to Slater, this produced men who feared women and were anxious about their manhood. Such men developed narcissistic personalities and exhibited great concern with how others viewed them and an intense preoccupation with honor, glory, and competitiveness. Slater argues that this was one reason why "life in fifth-century Athens seems to have been an unremitting struggle for personal aggrandizement—for fame and honor, or for such goals as could lead to these (wealth, power, and so forth)."[25]

Male Fear of Women. Slater suggests that the male fear of women at least partially explains the high incidence of homosexuality among Greek males. Adult males, especially in the period from age sixteen until marriage at the age of about 30, often preferred anal intercourse with young boys to sexual relationships with either adult males or females. The boys sought these emotional and sexual attachments with adult men to free themselves from attachments with their mothers. As they grew older, however, taking the passive feminine role in homosexual relationships became unacceptable. It was viewed as degrading, as too feminine for men.

This same fear of women is also supposedly seen in some of the beauty practices of Greek women. Slater notes that it was customary for women to remove their pubic hair, and he related this to a male disgust for or fear of the female genitals. Removal of the hair makes the mature woman seem like a less-threatening, immature girl. The practice of marrying adolescent girls may be of similar psychodynamic origin. But Martin Kilmer has pointed out that it was primarily hetaerae who removed pubic hair and even they did not remove it all. They merely shaped it to enhance their sexual attractiveness to their clients.[26]

Slater offers as partial proof of his theory the powerful and often dangerous women of Greek myth and literature. He sees these as mirrors of the male fear of women, and less extreme, less Freudian scholars also find a strong fear of women among the Athenians.[27] They probably had reason to fear women as outsiders to the patriarchal family structure and male political community. Women are the weak points in the structure. John Gould argues that in Greek mythology women play important roles that are fraught with fear, tension, and ambivalence. Men are brought into the world and reared by these outsiders to the male community, and it is incumbent on men to control, tame, and civilize these wild creatures who are also their mothers, wives, and daughters. Women embodied the irrational, and this must not be allowed to spread to men.

One problem with Slater's theory is that socially acceptable homosexuality was more widespread than the family structure of fifth-century Athens, which he argues is the cause. Homosexuality was practiced both before and after the Classical Period and it was widespread in non-Athenian areas with different gender stratification systems and family practices, such as in Sparta. It was also known among members of the lower classes who could not afford to seclude their women.

Perhaps homosexuality is simply related to the gender segregation of men in military units and their absence for long-distance wars. The late age at marriage for men in Athens provided a hiatus between sexual maturity and sexual outlet through marriage. Prostitutes and hetaerae cost money, while a relationship with an older man would afford the boys gifts (but not payment—male prostitution was illegal for citizens) and yet not be outrageously expensive for the older partner. It also gave the younger partner access to education; the older man was to train the younger and received respect for this role.[28] The relationship also provided an important social and political alliance. The subordinate role in the homosexual sexual relationships ended with adulthood, but the social and political benefits could continue as the relationship changed from lover to friend. All in all, the homosexual tie was probably a better bargain for the youth than were slave girls or prostitutes. Deep-seated psychological conflicts are not necessary to explain why large numbers of upper-class youths followed this socially acceptable path.

Nonstereotypical Female Roles. Although the practice of secluding women existed, seclusion was not characteristic of all Greek women. Only the well-to-do could afford it. Some women may have chose the secluded life rather than face the insults and dangers of Athenian streets. But poor women had to work, and the available sources show them in a variety of occupations inside and outside the home. Foreign women could also move freely through the city, exempt from the laws imposed on citizen women. Some women of very high status had great freedom because of their social position. Perhaps more important, however, was the large class of women known as hetaerae who stood outside the legitimate Greek family and citizenship systems.

These women are often lumped together as high-class prostitutes. Many were prostitutes, but not all sold their sexual services. Boulding notes that it is more accurate to distinguish three classes of hetaerae. Some were scholars, such as Plato's pupils Lasthenia and Axiothea. These women were true contributors to the intellectual and political life and the advancement of knowledge in Greece. A second group was made up of poets. The modern emphasis on Sappho makes it appear that she was unique in Greek history, but she was one of many female poets. The third group consisted of the sexual companions of men, some of whom were very skilled entertainers, cooks, and nurses.

Sexism and Greek Science. Despite the participation of the hetaerae in Greek intellectual development, the Greeks developed "scientific" explanations supporting female subordination and inferiority.[29] Although Plato has been considered somewhat of a feminist by some scholars because of certain passages in the *Republic,* his work is quite misogynistic. In developing his image of the ideal society, he argued for greater public responsibilities for women. He wanted to open public life to women to a degree and allow a talented elite few to become Guardians along with the elite of men. But this plan was part of his general disparagement of the private sphere and family life and his desire to eliminate the private family. It was also central to his genetic engineering scheme to reproduce superior children. The elite female guardians would among other tasks ensure the survival of talent into the next generation.

Plato felt that women should be educated, although women were intellectually inferior to men. He would allow women to compete equally with men but expected all but a few to fail. A woman's main function in society was still childbearing. Moreover, in his later work *Laws* he reversed many of his quasi-feminist positions and asserted the importance of the patriarchal family and male dominance. Plato also idealized nonsexual love and companionship between men rather than love between men and women. He condemned physical love between men, possibly because it required men to act like women.[30]

Plato's pupil Aristotle also idealized the public roles of aristocratic males and derograted the world of family life. He can be credited with introducing "scientific" proof of female inferiority into Western thought. According to Aristotle, nature created females the physical, mental, and moral inferiors of men. Such inferiority was built into the female physiology and biology: Male dominance was nature's plan. Aristotle argued this was the case even in reproduction: The male semen played the active role in creating new life, whereas the female was merely the field for sowing the male seed. (This belief and analogy reflect the agrarian base of Greek society and culture.) Aristotle concluded that nature intended the female to be passive. He was horrified by the freedom accorded Spartan women.

The Hellenistic Period

This period of Greek history was brought to an end by the consolidation of the Greek city states into the Macedonian empire of Alexander the Great, whose father, Philip, conquered Athens and its allies in 338 B.C. This imperial era is known as the Hellenistic period of Greece.[31] The Greek city states lost their independence. The local control of weaponry by citizen males shifted to the standing armies of the central governments of Alexander. The removal of arms from the control of the local patriarch should decrease the power of these men and afford a degree of independence for women. This appears to have been true in Hellenistic Greece. Women were not so firmly suppressed and isolated as they had been in Classical Athens. Education, including physical education, was extended to more of the daughters of the well-to-do. Female poets reemerged. Women were able to raise their positions within marriage and the family setting. The marriage relationship became emotionally closer, love matches increased in importance, and private family life was idealized.

During the Hellenistic period, women gained in economic and legal freedom, except in Athens, which firmly held to the principle of male guardianship. But many of the previously male rights that now extended to women were not as valuable as formerly since decision making and power now lay with the monarch rather than with the citizens. Women did, however, become less isolated, even in Athens; and other cities, where women gained legal and economic rights, a few women came into control of substantial fortunes and used their wealth for pursuing political office and political rights. But these women were exceptions. Women in general continued to be excluded from full citizenship and political participation.

One impetus toward greater freedom and public involvement of women came from the example of the Macedonian queens and princesses. Because of the long absences of their male rulers in the wars creating the empire, royal wives and mothers were often ruthless in their quest for power for themselves and their sons. Alexander's mother, Olympia, presided over the court in his absence; her intrigues included the murders of competing family members. She eventually failed in her power-hungry quests and was stoned to death by other royal relatives. The Macedonian princesses could not legitimately rule in their own right, but they were active forces in the political arena. Their public roles provided the example for nonroyal women of the empire and brought some wealthy women out of seclusion. However, even the wealthy women could not come close to attaining equality with men.

Ancient Rome

The history of ancient Rome spans a dozen centuries. The *Archaic Period* began in 753 B.C. with Rome's monarchical and feudal stage as an agricultural society. It ended with the overthrow of the kings and the establishment of the Republic in 509 B.C. Rome was involved in almost constant internal and external warfare. Its success in external wars, in particular the Punic Wars with Carthage in the third century B.C., resulted in the establishment of a great empire. With imperial domination abroad lubricating the trade routes to Rome, business and commerce, an urban way of life, and extensive slavery increased in importance. The period of the *late Republic* was one of great internal strife and jockeying for power among members of the upper class. It ended with the defeat of Antony and Cleopatra by Octavian in 27 B.C. Octavian then declared himself emperor, took the name of Augustus, and set about trying to curb the excesses and decadence of the Roman upper classes through his strong centralized rule. The *em-*

pire continued for five more centuries until internal disruptions and external threats finally led to its dissolution and Europe entered its *Dark Ages*.

The positions of women and men in Rome and the nature of the gender stratification system underwent important changes as the Roman economy and society evolved.[32] As is typical of an agrarian society, a greater or lesser degree of female subordination characterized all the periods of ancient Rome, although the Roman woman was never as subjugated and secluded as was the Athenian woman of antiquity.

Rome Before the Punic Wars

In the early or Archaic Period, Rome was a strongly patriarchal, feudal, agrarian society. The head of the household, or *paterfamilias*, was the legitimate authority in the patrilineal, patrilocal extended family. He could control the lives and fortunes of his wife, children, servants, and slaves including having them put to death or sold. A newborn infant was accepted into the family only if the father allowed it. Otherwise, it was exposed and either died or was picked up by slave traders. Female infanticide was probably more common than male infanticide.

The extended family household and the wider patrilineal clan structure were key institutions in Rome's early history. The household was largely self-sufficient, producing and processing its own food, clothing, and shelter. Thus Rome was an agricultural society with production primarily for use value. In conjunction with the wider clan structure, the household solved its own political, economic, religious, educational, defense, and social security problems. It was stratified and not egalitarian because power was concentrated in the heads of the extended families. However, the upper class was not a leisure class: Its men and women were heavily involved in productive labor. Males concerned themselves primarily with running and defending the agricultural estates, while the women devoted themselves to the domestic sphere of housework, child care, and spinning and weaving. Poor men and women did the heavy and menial work for the estate holders.

During this early stage, women were under the authority of their fathers first and then of their husbands. Marriages were arranged by the fathers in the interests of the families involved. Romance and personal attraction were not very important. Girls typically married at about twelve to fifteen years of age.[33] A dowry was required for a fully legitimate marriage, and it became the unquestioned property of the husband. But the law said a husband could not sell his wife to steal the dowry. Her family could look out for her interests to a degree. Since Romans did not usually marry close relatives as the Greeks did, the continued surveillance by her family was often crucial to the wife's well-being if she had an abusive husband.[34]

Virtually everyone married. The society at this time had no place for unattached adults. Marriages and families were stable and divorce was rare. Monogamy was the rule for men as well as women, but adultery was dealt with much less harshly for men than for women. Virginity was highly valued for unmarried girls. Husbands and fathers had the right to kill unchaste wives and daughters to maintain family honor.

The earliest form of marriage, which transferred guardianship to the woman's husband, was gradually replaced by the practice of fathers retaining guardianship throughout the daughter's life. This was called marriage without *manus:* without turning over authority to the husband. This gave the father the right to continue to direct the daughter's life after she left his household. If the woman's own relatives were greedy and corrupt, instead of protecting her, they could dissolve her marriage against her will and regain control of her dowry. A daughter's marriage could also be part of the game of alliance making and alliance breaking. She could be forced into a marriage that benefited her family or forced out of one that had ceased to be of benefit. (In this patrilineal system, the children belonged to the father and remained with him in the case of divorce.) Some women actively participated in this political alliance system by choosing their husbands and lovers with an eye to the fortunes of their own families. But a woman's fate often depended heavily on the nature of the men who held authority over her. Sons could gain legal independence, daughters could not.

Although marriage without *manus* affirms the legitimacy of the power of the paterfamilias, it probably gave the wife more actual freedom than marriage with *manus*. Through it she could have some physical separation from those who had authority over her.

Although the ideal woman remained at home working her wool and wore a veil that covered all but her face when she did go out, the Roman woman did not have to practice such seclusion. The upper-class woman directed the household and the slaves and in the early stage participated in the work herself. She could leave for shopping, the theater or game, dinner parties, visiting, walking, and in extreme circumstances to protest at political gatherings. Females had access to education almost as freely as males. They were, however, forbidden to drink wine. Romans believed that alcohol consumption in women inevitably led to adultery, and husbands could order the death penalty for either activity.

Rome After the Punic Wars

In Rome too, one of the important factors in granting women greater personal autonomy was the involvement of men in distant wars that took them away from the city and their homes for long periods of time. In addition, the high male death rate in war freed many women from their male guardians. War thus left women in charge of the management of the family estates and in control of their personal lives. Since in some families all adult males were killed in war, many females came to inherit great wealth. Although they were never granted full legal rights to control their wealth, they could usually manipulate the guardianship law by choosing a guardian willing to forego his legitimate right to intervene. Thus by the late Republican Period some women were wielding significant economic power. This upset Roman leaders if for no other reason than that women did not have to pay the military taxes required of male property owners. The Romans firmly believed that women should have no part in that ultimate male domain, the military.[35]

Role of the Roman Upper Class. Success in war led to the concentration of political power in the hands of Rome's important military leaders. The tremendous wealth and numbers of slaves that flowed into Rome after the Punic Wars allowed for a more powerful central government to develop, run by representatives of a now exceedingly wealthy aristocratic class. This small upper class came to dominate the economic, political, and social structure of Rome. The large slave class and poor free men and women did the bulk of the menial labor. A gentleman now disdained any labor except the law profession; even commerce should be left to their inferiors.[36]

Since women were barred from military and political participation, the new wealth freed upper-class women from almost all productive roles in society. Even child rearing was turned over to slaves and tutors. Child-rearing practices changed from an emphasis on stern discipline to indulgence. Although the choice of a husband continued to be the right of the father, mothers often exercised a good deal of influence and control over their daughters' lives, including the choice of spouse. Women were not as limited as a strict reading of the law might suggest.[37]

Decline of Traditional Values. As the upper classes became wealthier, they were more and more given to extravagant displays of homes, carriages, clothing, and jewels. Women are often accused of having caused the decay of Roman society by their luxurious life-style. However, this luxury was often a means for men to flaunt their wealth and status and was not entirely initiated by women, who were sometimes merely objects for conspicuous consumption. Some women were driven to excessive display and leisure pursuits by the boredom forced on them by their unproductive lives. Some managed to obtain behind-the-scenes manipulative political power through their sons or husbands, but this required great skill, a strong personality, and pliable men.

The luxurious life-style for men included the services of the courtesan: elegant, talented female entertainers modeled on the Greek hetaerae. Rome had long had brothels and they were socially accepted, but the wealth of the empire encouraged what the conservatives saw as moral decay: expensive banquets and drinking parties with dancing girls and "fancy boys" for the sexual pleasure of the male guests. But even worse in the eyes of the conservatives was the development of long-term attachments to courtesans, which separated men from their wives and families and often from much of their wealth as well.

This world of sexual license was open at first only to men, but by the first century B.C. many women were addicted to these pleasures as well. Some of these "amateur courtesans" became as skilled at makeup and entertaining as the professionals. Not only were men turning away from their traditional obligations, losing their heads in romantic love, but they were also "violating other people's marriages" in adulterous relationships with married women of citizen rank.[38]

Political leaders spoke openly and vehemently against women. In Roman literature women served as scapegoats for almost all human failings and problems. Livy, for example, repeatedly blames tragic events in Roman history from military defeats to tyrannical regimes on the machinations of women. His ideal women were chaste and proper and loyal in their service to the state and their families.[39]

One seeming exception to this view of women is seen in the love poetry extolling the charms of the poet's mistress.[40] Judith Hallet argues that the love poetry shows how exciting these professional or amateur courtesans were in contrast to the drab, unappealing ideal of the homebound wife. She sees a kind of protofeminism in the gender role reversal implied in the lovers' declarations that they are devoted to or enslaved by their often cruel and demanding lovers. But Lyne's more thorough analysis of these poets portrays their work in a less-feminist light. These poets condemned the traditional virtues of marriage, military service, political office, and the pursuit of wealth. They present their search for love and sexual pleasure as the most important goal of life. But their poetic imagery of themselves as slaves of their lovers was more hedonistic than feminist in spirit. Tribullus, for example, writes about his devotion to and domination by his married lover Delia, but in the same book tells of a similar love for and abuse by a young male. Horace speaks of his love for thousands of girls and thousands of boys. Devotion and enslavement are temporary for most of these poets.

The lives of men described in Latin love poetry fit well with Guttentag and Secord's thesis that in periods when females are not in short supply, women have greater freedom and sexual license is more widespread. During this period men were very reluctant to marry, and political leaders tried to force or at least encourage them to do so. Wives and marriage lost in social value, and many upper-class men rejected the commitment that marriage entailed.

Marriage and family among the upper classes lost the stability that had characterized earlier Roman society. Divorce became common and acceptable grounds became more and more trivial. Divorce was easier for the husband to obtain than for the wife, but wives could initiate divorce through their guardians. Concubinage became more common, especially for men who desired partners of lower social status. This practice was not as openly permitted to high-status women. The sexual double standard remained strong, at least in the eyes of the law.

Laws against adultery continued to exact severe penalties, especially for women, but they failed to control the practice. The Emperor Augustus sent the love poet Ovid into exile for extolling adulterous love, but the latter's popularity continued. Some Roman matrons went so far as to register as prostitutes to protect their lovers from prosecution under the adultery statutes. This loophole in the law was later closed.

Marriage and birthrates steadily dropped. Contraception and abortion were practiced although they were unreliable and dangerous.[41] The low birthrate was a grave concern to the rulers, who feared negative consequences from a decline in the numbers of the citizen population and available military personnel. Laws were passed requiring all adult males and females to marry, but laws were rarely enforced on males. Some people evaded the law by marrying in name only or repeatedly making and breaking betrothals. Divorce laws were also tightened, but the overall decline in family life remained a problem among the upper classes.

One law to encourage larger families was of particular importance in increasing the personal autonomy of some women. Citizen women who bore at least three children and noncitizen women who had four or five children were granted full legal independence from the guardianship law.

One of the reasons family life lost ground was that the family lost many of its functions. The central government and the developing market economy took over more and more of the power, authority, and functions that the family had previously controlled. The household and its head were no longer the center of political, economic, religious, educational, and social life. People could live their lives effectively as individuals independent of wider family or kinship structures. This greatly undermined the control the family could exert over its members.

The government repeatedly passed legislation to curb female behavior. The Oppian law, for example, was passed in 215 B.C. during the second Punic War to prevent women from using their wealth for gold, clothing, ornaments, and chariots; but it remained on the books long after the war was over. Women had to demonstrate for its repeal and were finally successful, but other laws were passed that attempted the same ends, limiting inheritance by women and limiting the display of wealth by women. Pomeroy notes, however, that the state eventually turned its attention to controlling the display of men's wealth rather than women's especially as upper-class women became more independent of their male relatives:

> Wealthy upper-class women were considered less as appendages of men, and their displays of wealth brought them status in the eyes of women. But whatever women did independent of men was futile and, though potentially irritating to men, ultimately of minor importance to the state.
> When men participated in status seeking by means of the clothing of their women, then regulation was required.[42]

Women's lack of political power also resulted in poor women being discriminated against in the distribution of welfare benefits. Beginning in the late Republic, the government and some wealthy individuals instituted several relief programs. Extensive unemployment and poverty threatened Rome's stability, and these programs were intended to quiet unrest and to maintain support for the rulers. Since woman could not vote or openly take an active role in politics, they did not receive the free grain. Also, men were not given enough to help a wife or family. Some additional programs were set up to care for children, but since their goal was to produce future soldiers, they also discriminated against girls.

Women's Role in Roman Religion. In Roman religions women held high status and could participate actively. The Vestal Virgins were the most prestigious, privileged, and influential of Roman priestesses. The safety of Roman society was believed to depend on their correct practice of ritual and the protection of their virginity during their terms as priestesses. Occupancy of these positions had important benefits and costs. From childhood through her thirty-year term, the Vestal Virgin's life was severely controlled. Her chastity had to be above suspicion. Furthermore, when calamities did strike Rome, the Vestal Virgins were likely to be blamed and accused of violating the requirements of their office. This could result in the death penalty for the priestesses.

Pre-Christian Rome had many other cults and religious groups in addition to the Vestal Virgins. Some of them were exclusively female, others were all male. Many allowed both males and females to participate equally. Husbands and wives also participated in the family ancestor cults of their households, although these declined in importance in the later period. Rome had important goddesses such as Isis, as well as gods like the militant Mithras, popular among soldiers.

The Rise of Christianity in Rome

Christianity arose and spread within the Roman Empire. Since Christianity developed within the more capitalistic market economy of urban Rome instead of the more agrarian or pastoral societies of the ancient Hebrews, Muslims, Hindus, Buddhists, and Confucians, it is less patriarchal than these other great universal religions. It was probably even less misogynistic in its early years when it appealed to the less powerful, non-aristocratic segments of Roman society.

Pagels's study of the texts of the gnostic gospels suppressed as heresy by the early church fathers finds a blending of feminine as well as masculine symbolism of God—an image of God, the Mother, as well as God, the Father.[43] Orthodox Christianity seems to have become more masculine oriented as it developed. The earliest Christians broke with traditional gender role divisions. Expecting the end of the world soon, they minimized gender differentiation and advocated celibacy. They were detached from traditional family roles. This new belief system was attractive first to the working classes, merchants, and people in the provinces—people marginal to Roman society.[44] Women of these groups were especially attracted to the new religion. The opposition to them from non-Christians was fierce. A great many women as well as men were persecuted and suffered horrible deaths. But despite the active roles of women in the early church by the year 200, Pagels found that the majority of Christian churches accepted the doctrine that females should not have authority or leadership roles within the church.

With the conversion of the Emperor Constantine in A.D. 313, Christianity became the state religion of Rome and was incorporated into the male-dominated Roman power structure. (But even when it spread to the upper class, converts were found among women first.) The church more and more adopted hierarchial, male-dominated Roman administrative practices and soon developed a powerful centralized leadership of males. Furthermore, as the Roman Empire declined, its more centralized political, military, and economic institutions were replaced by the decentralized agrarian feudalism of the Middle Ages. Christianity therefore continued to develop and evolve within a traditional, agrarian, antifemale context and incorporated aspects of female subordination and male dominance characteristic of such societies.

As the Christian movement grew and the end of the world seemed more remote, the concept of celibacy was also questioned. In place of celibacy for everyone, the idea of a *calling* arose. This meant that some people were called to raise families, while others were called to celibacy and would serve the wider society outside the family. The latter group would not allow sexual interests to interfere with their single-minded service to God. Many celibates chose to live lives of solitude in the desert. However, the large numbers of people who chose to withdraw from the world eventually resulted in the founding of monastic communities for communal living. These communities required celibacy, but they were not usually gender segregated. By the fourth century, the unmarried ascetic life had become an acceptable alternative to marriage for many aristocratic women. The monastic movement was itself a reaction against the new centralized church government. Boulding notes that women were an important part of the monastic movement because "women would have even more reason to protest that hierarchy than would men, since it was crowding them out more than it was crowding men."[45] As women came to be second-class citizens within the church, one of the few outlets for strong women was the monasteries. As canonesses and as members, they could work and participate in religious and political activities.

The church itself continued to become more and more hostile to females. They lost their public roles and were more firmly assigned to domestic roles under the authority of their husbands. Only older widows and consecrated virgins seemed safe for active church service. The church fathers came to equate women with sex, temptation, and sin. But women could find little positive imagery even as wives or mothers in the early church. The disgust with sex was so pronounced that marriage was disparaged also. Church fathers such as Jerome argued forcefully for virginity and against marriage and sex. The only positive point in marriage's favor was that it kept the church supplied with virgins to serve God as nuns with purity and humility.

The church survived the fall of Rome and continued to be a powerful influential force throughout the Dark Ages of Europe. Although Christianity had begun as a religion offering women spiritual equality with men, by this time it had become male dominated and suspicious of women.

Medieval Europe

The Early Middle Ages

Little record remains of life in the early Middle Ages in Europe.[46] The Roman Empire was overrun by nomadic tribes of herders and horticulturalists. Various Germanic tribes conquered different areas of the old empire and introduced their own customs, which mingled with the old Roman customs. As we could expect on the basis of our previous discussion of horticulturalists and herders, these tribal peoples had significantly different gender roles and gender stratification systems than the Greeks and Romans. Women were the subordinate gender among these war-like nomads, but they had greater freedom in some respects, for example, being less isolated in the domestic household. Consequently, women were less isolated in the early Middle Ages than they became in later periods.

Under the Germanic tribal customs that were incorporated into Roman areas, women were under the guardianship of men, first the father and then the husband. Women were also discriminated against in the inheritance of land and movable property. This originated under war conditions in which conquered land was given to distinguished warriors who were then expected to hold and defend it and provide military service to the lord. Females were excluded from warrior roles and therefore were not considered safe defenders of land nor valuable for military support. This tradition persisted, however, long after military support and defense ceased to be important concerns.

Adultery was often punishable by death for both males and females. Virginity was highly valued in females, and virgin girls were valuable property for exchange for high bride prices. For this reason, the fines for killing a virgin were double that for killing a man. High fines were also levied for rape and for looking at the body of a virgin girl. To discourage attempts to avoid the high bride prices by abducting girls, the fine for abduction was nine times that of the normal bride price. But the practice of abduction continued, especially when the man felt more powerful than the girl's family. The only real barrier was the threat of revenge, and although brothers might compete among each other, defending one's sisters was a matter of honor that could unify the brothers against the abductor.[47]

The high bride prices and marriage by abduction resulted from the severe shortage of women in the early Middle Ages. Emily Coleman found that agricultural productivity was fairly low during this period and land was scarce. Population pressure was a problem and female infanticide was probably practiced.[48] The shortage of women helped control population growth and kept the many men who could not acquire a wife from seeking land of their own. But this situation also increased the tendencies toward violence and internal warfare. The shortage made women valuable as sexual property, but it did not afford them high status or power. Husbands had the right to beat their wives. Wives were expected to please their husbands, but husbands were under no ob-ligation to please their wives. In fact, the shortage of women was also partly the result of women so often being the victims of the violence rampant in early medieval Europe. Thus the high degree of internal warfare probably served to keep the female's status low.

Guttentag and Secord view the situation in a more positive light.[49] They note this was a period of high sex ratios, and in line with their theory, women were highly valued "in their place." What they call role complementarity prevailed, with the wife in charge of the private sphere and the man in charge of the public sphere. According to Guttentag and Secord, marriage and family life tended to be stable; women had little fear of being abandoned on their own resources and therefore did not express much discontent with their social place.

This was perhaps true in the lower classes, but among the upper classes powerful men did abandon their wives whenever they were tired of them or whenever political or economic considerations made it desirable. Few barriers existed to divorce except for the wife's ability to resist her husband through the power of her own familial or extrafamilial alliances.[50] The aristocracy and the church struggled over the control of marriage from the tenth until the thirteenth century. The church eventually succeeded in imposing monogamy and forbidding divorce. Aristocratic males resisted primarily because making and breaking marriage was an accepted and important part of their political and economic maneuverings. Once divorce was impossible, marriage choices became of crucial importance to the family and sons' marriages were given the same close supervision as had previously been given to daughters'.[51]

The early medieval period was characterized by a domestic/public dichotomy in women's economic and political roles. David Herlihy describes women as working very hard in the domestic economy—baking, brewing, and caring for the barnyard animals and gardens.[52] Men were usually kept busy with the heavy cultivation and fighting. The upper-class lady, however, was not isolated. The important affairs of the estate took place in the *donjon*, the center of the castle. In this open space, which afforded no privacy, the lady as well as the lord participated fully. Noblewomen often accompanied and advised their husbands on their travels administering their realms;[53] and when war and emigration took the men from the home, women assumed management of the family property. Herlihy's study of the records found women as landowners and managers throughout the early Middle Ages. Similarly, wives of married clergy often assumed control of their husbands' estates, freeing their husbands to practice their professions. In fact, the prominent economic roles played by many women were reflected in the widespread use of matronymic names from the mid-tenth century through the eleventh and twelfth centuries.

Royal women were also often important players in the court politics of the time. They did not have a legitimate right to rule, but some were able to gain substantial power through their husbands and sons.[54] Their positions in the domestic sphere could be converted to power in the political sphere. While the king was away, the queen was guardian of the treasury and could use it, as well as property given to her by her husband, to build her own power base of alliances with her family, other important aristocratic families, and church leaders. If she could maintain her sexual attractiveness or usefulness to her husband, she could keep her position as queen and persuade him to name her son, rather than sons by other wives or concubines, as successor. Since she

was often much younger than the king, if she outlived him she might rule the kingdom as regent for her son for many years. Much depended on her ability and resources for maintaining alliances and keeping her son and husband under control. When such a queen failed, her fate could be a brutal death.

Royal sons and daughters, as well as wives, were sources of competition for the king's power. He kept his sons under control by waiting to name a successor while they vied for his favor. He could use the princesses as part of the system of marriage diplomacy, marrying them to princes or kings in distant kingdoms. Young girls only ten or fourteen years old were sent to foreign lands with foreign tongues, yet many served admirably as diplomats for their fathers.[55] This kind of banishment also kept them from marrying into the local powerful aristocratic families who could use the marriage tie to compete more effectively for the throne itself. For this reason, Charlemagne did not allow his daughters to marry, though they could take lovers at will. Others placed princesses as abbesses in the nunneries, a practice that could cause power struggles in the nunneries also.[56]

Women of all classes served as an important reserve labor force that could be called on whenever men desired. The roles they assumed during these periods of male labor shortage could be sources of power and autonomy while they occupied them. But when the males decided to reassume the roles, most females could not prohibit them from doing so. Use of women as a reserve labor force may look like significant social change, but it usually did not result in permanent improvement in this position.

The concept of the reserve labor force can even apply to women's roles in the development of high culture. In the early Middle Ages when the men were concerned with internal strife and the external wars of the Crusades, upper-class women received more education than men. Women were primarily responsible for the development of culture. According to Emily Putnam,

in places where men have leisure for culture, it is believed to belong more or less exclusively to the male type. . . . The learned or the thoughtful woman is rather ridiculous, and certainly a bore. Probably she neglects her children. On the other hand, when men are as a class engaged in the subjugation of the natural world or in struggles with each other, the arts of peace naturally fall into the hands of non-combatants, and are then believed to belong more or less exclusively to the female type. . . . culture is felt . . . to be unbecoming in man.[57]

In the early Middle Ages women also had important roles in the church. Monasteries were highly autonomous and were often influential and powerful institutions. They introduced Christianity to the tribal peoples and maintained what little educational instruction there was during this period. Women as well as men were drawn to the monastic movement, although because there were fewer women's orders, it was more difficult for a woman to become a nun than for a man to become a monk. The convents were populated by the daughters of the nobility who either did not desire to marry or could not for lack of a husband or parental permission. Lower-class women could not take vows, but they could often enter the convent as lay sisters and servants to the aristocratic nuns.

Control of the convent gave the lady abbess in particular a powerful position in medieval feudal society. Convents were often large landowners with many peasants attached to them. The lady abbess was sometimes as powerful as a baron or other important lord. Some of the abbesses even headed double monasteries that had a male order as well as a female one. During this early period, nuns were not secluded in the cloister. Great freedom of movement and action were allowed to the religious woman.[58]

But the positions and powers that some upper-class women gained in both sacred and secular worlds during the early Middle Ages could not be sustained. Male dominance was reasserted in all spheres when external warfare diminished and men remained at home, as the central political institutions strengthened and gained control over the society, and as the sex ratios changed, leading to a relative excess of women.

The Later Middle Ages

Kinship and family ties had been important integrating and organizing principles during the tumultuous centuries of the early period. Women could sometimes share in the wealth and power of their families, especially when there were no strong male members to challenge them. But during the later Middle Ages after the year 1200, kinship began to give way to governmental control of the society. Where power resided in the domestic sphere, some women had some opportunity to share it. When it was removed to the public sphere, they lost those opportunities and women's status in European society appears to have declined in many respects. However, Herlihy notes that women's position improved in at least one respect in the late Middle Ages: "The curtailment of violence in medieval life aided them. . . . The emergence of effective governments assured them greater personal security and protection against rape, abduction and enslavement."[59]

This also meant that the shortage of women characteristic of the early period was transformed into a surplus of women. Increased agricultural productivity allowed more female children to be fed.[60] The practice of female infanticide dwindled. The loss of men in war and the celibacy now imposed on the priesthood meant that more women than men were available for marriage. Women no longer held a high value in the marriage market. High bride prices gave way to dowries payable by the bride's family to the groom. Dowryless females could not marry. Marriage decreased in value and sexual libertarianism grew.

In the later Middle Ages the control of the great estates, the state, and the church came increasingly to reside in the hands of men exclusively. In their power struggles with the kings, nobles disinherited their daughters and younger sons to maintain the size, wealth, and importance of the family.

In this period written laws came to replace unwritten tradition as the important ordering principle of society. Women were not treated equally with men under the new laws. Men received rights; women received restrictions.

As the state governmental machinery and bureaucracy expanded, the positions were opened only to males. Education was necessary to fill such jobs. Education was removed from the convents and monasteries (where women had had some access to learning) and placed in the cathedral schools and universities, which barred women. Women were excluded from culture as well as politics now that men had the time and interest to pursue both.[61]

Women who could not marry often had to rely on their own earnings to support themselves. This drew them out of the domestic sphere into increased competition with men for the scarce resources of the public sphere, producing hostility, misogyny, and antifeminism in the latter. This was countered by the vocal protests of some women. The widowed noblewoman Christine de Pizan wrote about women's problems, sometimes from personal experience. She argued that the economic insecurity of

women, even married women, meant women needed better educations and more economic and political rights. Despite the need, they did not obtain these rights.

The church also moved toward a more male-dominated, highly centralized structure. During the later medieval period, every attempt was made to reduce the influence, power, and participation of women in church affairs. The great abbesses and convents were stripped of their power and brought under the direction of the male church hierarchy. The important turning point for women and the church came with the Gregorian reform of the late eleventh century:

This reform demolished the double monasteries of the earlier era and quite effectively walled women's houses off from the church. The great medieval church women . . . all belong to the earlier period. As the influence of church women waned, church writings on women showed a greater tendency to regard women as the "other," the basis for a growing misogyny.[62]

As an outlet for the frustrations deriving from their lower status, loss of public roles, and the difficulties of finding a husband and performing a domestic role, women turned to the new heretical movements. In the twelfth and thirteenth centuries, single women enthusiastically embraced the Beguine movement, a lay religious movement not under the direction of the male-dominated church. Beguines lived and worked in all-female communal households and workshops. These communes contained women from all classes, but all the members lived simply and worked diligently. Their autonomy frightened the church fathers. Independent women did not fit with the church's teaching.

The Gregorian reforms also imposed strict celibacy on the clergy. Bullough argues that much of the misogynistic, antisex stance on the part of the church was the result of the psychological reactions of the clergy to their difficulties with celibacy. Women reminded them of sex and sex was sin; therefore, women represented sin. Eve, the evil temptress of man, came to dominate the church's view of women. Fear of women was widespread among laymen as well as clerics. Menstrual blood was viewed as particularly dangerous, and women were linked with magic and the black arts.[63]

Paradoxically, the emphasis on Eve was paralleled by a new emphasis on Mary, the virtuous virgin mother of God. The Virgin Mary had long been a popular cult figure among the common people in many areas, but the elevation of the Virgin Mary by the church leaders went hand in hand with an increasing fear of women by the church fathers and a negative view of earthly women in the church's teachings. Furthermore, the witch hunts condoned by the church that swept Europe in the fourteenth through the eighteenth centuries were aimed primarily at women and were especially concerned with female sexuality, in particular, with female sexual relations with the devil.[64]

All of the church's new teachings were not harmful to women, however. In the early Middle Ages the church had increasingly taken control of marriage, divorce, sex, and child rearing from the secular authorities. Divorce, which had been easy for males to obtain in the early period, was forbidden to males as well as females. This aided women as it gave them some protection against repudiation by their husbands at a time when they were becoming ever more economically dependent on men.

The church was highly antisex, but it took a long time to impress this view on the people. Bawdy plays, tales, and humor were an accepted part of medieval life. Women, even nuns, were not isolated from this aspect of the culture. Boulding argues that

this shared sense of humor between women and men had egalitarian aspects to it. When

men started to creep away to tell funny stories about sex, it was a sign of something more than emerging puritanism. It was a signal that an important dimension of man-woman relationships had atrophied.[65]

This double standard of enjoyment of sexual humor emerged as the concepts of romantic love and the idealization of women developed. Women could only maintain their position on the pedestal and reap its advantages at the expense of segregating themselves from the real world of politics, economics, and sex.

Upper-class women supported the developing concept of romantic love as a means of adding interest to their restricted lives. If she could not enjoy the public world of men, the lady could luxuriate in being on the pedestal. But even romantic love was a double-edged sword of gender stereotypes: "The growth of romantic and devotional literature extolling women only strengthened the belief in the moral and social dangers of feminine wantonness."[66]

Guttentag and Secord note the paradox of the theme of courtly love flourishing in this low sex ratio, high misogynistic context.[67] They point out, however, that while the sex imbalance was fairly equal in the population as a whole, among certain groups it was not. This was a period of *hypergamy,* men marrying women from the social class above them.[68] There was an acute shortage of noblewomen for the growing numbers of upwardly mobile knights wanting to marry them. These men idealized the ladies of the class they hoped to enter. Marriage was delayed for these knights until they had sufficient resources to be acceptable for marriage to a lady of high birth. This left years for the bachelor life of adventure and for the development of courtly culture.

The marriage relationship itself was not affected by this new emphasis on love. Love was to occur only outside of marriage. In the courtly poetry, the knight admired and loved his lady, usually the wife of his lord, chastely and from a distance. (In reality, adultery and rape were not unknown in court life.) She inspired him for battle. He wrote poetry and music extolling her beauty and charms. But he could not marry her because she was married to another. Marriages among the upper classes continued to be made for political and economic reasons, not for love or companionship.

Despite the restriction of their public roles, women continued to serve as a reserve labor force whenever this met the needs of the man in authority. Because the number of foreign wars decreased and because the clergy could no longer marry and have wives as managers of their estates, there were fewer opportunities for upper-class women to manage family holdings. When necessary, however, ideological and religious prohibitions against public roles for women were relaxed in favor of preserving male and family interests. For example, Susan Mosher Stuard found that among the noble merchant class of Ragusa, an Adriatic city state, women were important participants in business.[69] The laws of Ragusa severely restricted women's public roles, but merchants who went on distant trade expeditions preferred to leave their businesses in the hands of their wives while they were away, rather than bring nonaristocratic or foreign families into the businesses. This important source of economic power and control was extended to noblewomen, not because of a commitment to women's individual freedom or rights, but to preserve the interests of the family business and the wider aristocratic merchant class.

The women of Ragusa were the exception rather than the rule. As JoAnn McNamara and Suzanne Wemple describe it, "In the upper reaches of later medieval society, apart from bearing children and acting as sex objects, companions in social functions, and sources of religious or poetic inspiration, women lost their usefulness."[70]

Peasant women and merchant women led very different lives from those of the nobility. Peasant women worked hard, both in the fields during peak labor seasons and in the homes. Despite the restrictions on their activities outside the household, they were an important source of labor to their families and their feudal lords.[71] The husband had the legal right of control over all their goods and property, and the wife was legally allowed to dispose of only small sums of money. The wife was expected to be subservient to her husband in all matters. For example, she served him at meal times and stood behind his chair awaiting further orders while he ate. She typically ate after the men of the household had had their fill. Gender stratification even superseded economic stratification. The peasant wife did not give orders to her husband's male hired hands. Couples who broke the practices of male dominance and female subordination could be subject to public ridicule by the community.

Women of the merchant class remained active in their family businesses even in the later Middle Ages when noblewomen's economic activities were curtailed. Wives of merchants often had control over the household and family business because their husbands were often away on business for long periods of time.[72] Town women in general worked in many fields and were members of many of the guilds regulating the crafts and trades. Women's guild membership did not make them the equals of the male craftsmen and tradesmen, however. Instead, the guilds operated to control the women and often to forbid their competition with men.[73] During periods of high unemployment, women workers were likely to face even more active discrimination in employment.

Common women were also potential targets for sexual exploitation by powerful upper-class men. A few women could benefit economically and in terms of prestige as a mistress to a king or noble.[74] Organized prostitution also flourished during this period.

Medieval Child-Rearing Practices

Child rearing in the Middle Ages appears to have been quite different from today's Western practices.[75] Infants and small children were not lavished with love or attention; tenderness and maternal love were not emphasized. The death rate was so high, even among the upper classes, that parents could not emotionally afford to become too attached to children. Among the lower classes was the added distraction of the parents' heavy work loads. Neither mother nor father had much time or energy to devote to child care. Discipline was strict. Obedience was an important virtue and was beaten into the child if necessary. The child learned early to show deference and respect to the father in particular.

Children who survived were treated as miniature adults. Phillippe Aries argues that childhood as a separate stage of development was not recognized in Western Europe until agrarian feudalism declined and capitalism developed. Children were, for example, not isolated from adult sexuality. The lack of privacy in medieval homes gave them sufficient opportunity to observe sexual practices. Early marriage also meant that they became sexually active soon after puberty.

Children were also put to work at early ages, and the tasks they were given reflected the adult gender division of labor. Girls learned domestic skills and reserved behavior. Boys learned their fathers' occupations or were apprenticed out to others to learn their trades. Even among the upper classes,

it was common to send young boys for training into the homes of other nobles, often the boy's maternal uncle to solidify the relationship with his mother's higher-status family. The boy served as a page or servant to an older knight where he learned the skills and etiquette of knighthood. In particular, he served the knight in preparation for battle and was taught the skills of warfare and combat.

Upper-class girls might be sent as children to the families of their future husbands. Some were well cared for, but others were abused, even raped, and then returned home unmarriageable if the other family decided to break the marriage agreement. Girls were also offered in trial marriages to men of high social standing in the hopes that if she proved to be really attractive, the man would marry her to the economic and political benefit of her family. More often than not, he did not choose to marry the girl and returned her to her family in disgrace when he tired of her. The church condemned this practice but placed most of the opprobrium on the poor girl. Other girls were kept secluded either at home or in convents, which were sometimes located inside the castle grounds of a great family.[76]

Non-Western Agrarian Societies

These case studies of Greece, Rome, and medieval Europe, which provide a brief description of the agrarian experience as it affected the West, are not necessarily representative of all agrarian societies. For one thing, there was a great intermingling of tribal traditions with agrarianism in the West. Another distinction lies in the fact that none of these societies ever developed the truly despotic, highly centralized stable agrarian regimes that characterized many areas of the East. The positions of women

and men in these societies differed significantly from those in the West. We briefly
consider these differences in the discussions
of China and Japan in Chapters 7 and 9.

Forces for Change

In the Western world agrarian practices lost
their position as the dominant form of economic production. Capitalist trade and commerce came to be the chief sources of wealth
and power. Industrialization soon followed
the rise of capitalism and made manufacturing the primary economic basis of European
society. Gender roles and gender stratification underwent important changes as Western societies evolved from agrarianism to
industrialization.

Some parts of the world remain agrarian
based. However, they have tended to come
under the influence of the more powerful
industrialized countries. Large peasant populations still exist today, but their gender
roles and gender stratification systems are
not duplicates of what was found in past
agrarian societies. We examine contemporary peasants and the underdeveloped nations, or Third World, in Chapter 8.

Conclusion

Agrarian civilizations represent the high
point of the preindustrial societal capacity to
generate economic surplus. At the root of
this capacity were technological innovations
which transcended the productive potentials
of horticultural techniques.

The large surpluses created by many of
these civilizations would, however, have
been unachievable if it had not been for the
equally revolutionary innovations in social
organization and ideology. The main effect
of the latter innovations was the widening

of the range and complexity of available social, economic, and political means of subordinating and controlling human populations—not only to achieve new productive
goals, but also to enhance the power, prestige, and privilege of ruling elites and the
ascendent classes who served them and
prospered under their protection.

Agrarian societies gave rise to larger and
denser human populations; truly urban
forms of social life; arts, crafts, and occupational specialities undreamed of under
horticultural conditions; and a vast extension of the activities, achievements, and influence of intellectual specialists. They also
produced two of humankind's most mo-
mentous historical experiments in political
control: feudalism and centralized bureaucratic states.

Of all the perfected forms of human subordination that emerged from agrarianism,
none was more significant than the restructuring of "women's place" in society, along
with the intensive and simultaneous idealization and degradation of female imagery in
culture. A separate domestic sphere for
women, a sphere in which they were either
excluded from extra-domestic production or
radically circumscribed and controlled by
men when participating in such production,
was one of the most important legacies of
agrarianism. To be fated to perform household labor, bear and nurture children, and
serve fathers, husbands, and brothers was
agrarian civilizations' gift to women. The
fate was economic and political in origin,
conditioned by forces making for more generalized inequality among classes in society.
But through the creative activities of ideological specialists it was also an idealized
fate, elaborated in religion, ritual, philosophy, and proto-sciences: woman as the "natural" inferior of man, one whose person-
hood and human worth were to be defined

by her obedience and subordination to another.

The world is no longer dominated by the great agrarian civilizations, but their impact is still with us. Modern industrialized societies, both capitalist and socialist, are rooted firmly in the soil of these civilizations. The evolution from one socioeconomic system to another does not destroy all of the old patterns. Modern gender roles and gender stratification systems still partially reflect their agrarian origins, as we see in the following chapters. Moreover, in both the capitalist and the socialist Third World, agrarian institutions live on in ways that have been transformed but not obliterated by the advent of the modern world.

Notes

1. The following discussion of agrarian societies is indebted to Gerhard Lenski and Jean Lenski, *Human Societies*, 3d ed. (New York: McGraw-Hill, 1978): 177–230; and Gerhard Lenski, *Power and Privilege* (New York: McGraw-Hill, 1966): 190–296.

2. Lenski and Lenski, 192.

3. Rae Lesser Blumberg, *Stratification: Socioeconomic and Sexual Inequality* (Dubuque, Iowa: William C. Brown, 1978): 45.

4. Blumberg, 51.

5. M. Kay Martin and Barbara Voorhies, *Female of the Species* (New York: Columbia University Press, 1975): 295.

6. Peggy Reeves Sanday, *Female Power and Male Dominance: On the Origins of Sexual Inequality* (Cambridge: Cambridge University Press, 1981).

7. The following discussion is based on the work of Mary Kinnear, *Daughters of Time: Women in the Western Tradition* (Ann Arbor: University of Michigan Press, 1982): 13–18; Ruby Rohrlich-Leavitt, "Women in Transition: Crete and Sumer," in Renate Bridenthal and Claudia Koonz, eds., *Becoming Visible: Women in European History* (Boston: Houghton Mifflin, 1977): 36–59; and Verena Zinserling, *Women in Greece and Rome* (New York: Abner Schram, 1972): 10–13.

8. The following discussion is based on Jon-Christian Billigimeier and Judy A. Turner, "The Socio-Economic Roles of Women in Mycenean Greece: A Brief Survey from Evidence of Linear B. Tablets," in Helene

P. Foley, ed., *Reflections of Women in Antiquity* (New York: Gordon and Breach, 1981): W. K. Lacey, *The Family in Classical Greece* (Ithaca, N.Y.: Cornell University Press, 1968); Sarah Pomeroy, *Goddesses, Whores, and Slaves: Women in Classical Antiquity* (New York: Schocken Books, 1975): 16–31; and Zinserling, 14–21.

9. Mary R. Lefkowitz, *Heroines and Hysterics* (New York: St. Martin's Press, 1981): 1–11, 41–47.

10. Billigimeier and Turner.

11. The following discussion is based on Paul Cartledge, "Spartan Wives: Liberation or License?" *Classical Quarterly* 31, no. 2 (1981): 84–105; K. J. Dover, *Greek Homosexuality* (Cambridge, Mass.: Harvard University Press, 1978); Moses I. Finley, "Marriage, Sale and Gift in the Homeric World," in M. I. Finley, ed., *Economy and Society in Ancient Greece* (New York: Viking Press, 1982; orig. 1953): 234–245, and "Sparta and Spartan Society" in Finley, 24–40; Lacey; Lefkowitz, 1981; Mary R. Lefkowitz and Maureen B. Fant, *Women's Lives in Greece and Rome: A Sourcebook in Translation* (London: Duckworth, 1982); David Schaps, *Economic Rights of Women in Ancient Greece* (Edinburgh: Edinburgh University Press, 1979); and Anthony Snodgrass, *Archaic Greece: The Age of Experiment* (London: J. M. Deal, 1980).

12. Snodgrass, 20.

13. Donald Engels, "The Use of Historical Demography in Ancient History," *Classical Quarterly* 34, no. 2 (1984): 386–393; Donald Engels, "The Problem of Female Infanticide in the Greco-Roman World," *Classical Philology* 75 (1980): 112–120; Mark Golden, "Demography and the Exposure of Girls in Athens," *Phoenix* 35 (1981): 316–331; William Harris, "The Theoretical Possibility of Extensive Infanticide," *Classical Quarterly* 32 (1982): 114–116; and Sarah Pomeroy, "Infanticide in Hellenistic Greece," in Averil Cameron and Amelie Kuhrt, eds., *Images of Women in Antiquity* (Detroit: Wayne State University, 1983): 207–219.

14. Amy Swerdlow, "The Greek Citizen Woman in Attic Vase Painting: New Views and New Questions," *Women's Studies* 5 (1978): 275.

15. John Gould, "Law, Custom and Myth: Aspects of the Social Position of Women in Classical Athens," *Journal of Hellenistic Studies* 100 (1980): 38–59.

16. Cartledge, 102–103.

17. Finley, "Sparta and Spartan Society," 28.

18. Finley, "Marriage, Sale and Gift in the Homeric World," 243.

19. The following discussion is based on Marilyn Arthur, " 'Liberated' Women: The Classical Era," in Bridenthal and Koonz, 62–89; Marilyn Arthur, "Classics: Review Article," *Signs* 2, no. 2 (Winter 1976): 382–397; Marilyn Arthur, "Women and the Family in Ancient Greece," *Yale Review* 71, no. 4 (Summer 1982): 532–547;

Vern Bullough, *The Subordinate Sex: A History of Attitudes Toward Women* (Baltimore: Penguin Books, 1974); Cartledge; Dover, 1978; K. J. Dover, "Classical Greek Attitudes to Sexual Behavior," in John Peradotto and J. P. Sullivan, eds., *Women in the Ancient World: The Arethusa Papers* (Albany: State University of New York, 1984): 143–158; Helene P. Foley, "The Conception of Women in Athenian Drama," in Foley, 1981, 127–168; Gould; Sarah C. Humphries, *The Family, Women and Death: Comparative Studies* (London: Routledge & Kegan Paul, 1983); Lefkowitz, *Heroines and Hysterics*; Mary R. Lefkowitz, "Princess Ida, the Amazons and a Women's College Curriculum," *Times Literary Supplement*, November 27, 1983: 1399–1401; Mary R. Lefkowitz, "Wives and Husbands," Greece and Rome 30, no. 1 (April 1983): 31–47; Lefkowitz and Fant; Pomeroy, 1975; Donald Richter, "The Position of Women in Classical Athens," *Classical Journal* 67 (1971): 1–8; Schaps; Wesley E. Thompson, "The Marriage of First Cousins," *Phoenix* 21 (1967): 273–282; Dyfri Williams, "Women on Athenian Vases: Problems of Interpretation," in Cameron and Kuhrt, 92–106; and Zinserling.

20. Marcia Guttentag and Paul F. Secord, *Too Many Women? The Sex Ratio Question* (Beverly Hills, Calif.: Sage, 1983): 37–52.

21. Susan Walker, "Women and Housing in Classical Greece: The Archaeological Evidence," in Cameron and Kuhrt, 84–91.

22. Pomeroy, 1975, 74.

23. Susan Cole, "Could Greek Women Read and Write?" *Women's Studies* 8 (1981): 124–155.

24. Philip Slater, *The Glory of Hera: Greek Mythology and the Greek Family* (Boston: Beacon Press, 1968); Philip Slater, "The Greek Family in History and Myth," *Arethusa* 7 (1974): 9–44.

25. Slater, 1968, 4.

26. Martin Kilmer, "Genital Phobia and Depilation," *Journal of Hellenistic Studies* 102 (1982): 104.

27. Gould, 55–57; Charles Segal, "The Menace of Dionysus: Sex Roles and Reversals in Euripides' *Bacchae*," *Arethusa* 11 (1978): 185–202; Helen King, "Bound to Bleed, Artemis and Greek Women," in Cameron and Kuhrt, 109–127; Peter Walcot, "Greek Attitudes towards Women: The Mythological Evidence," *Greece and Rome* 31 (1984): 37–47; and see Helene P. Foley, "Sex and State in Ancient Greece," *Diacritics* 5 (1975): 31–36, for a critique of Slater's use of the mythological evidence.

28. Elise Boulding, *The Underside of History* (Boulder, Colo.: Westview Press, 1976): 263.

29. The following discussion of sexism in the works of Plato and Aristotle is based on Bullough, 58–69; Elizabeth V. Spelman, "Woman as Body: Ancient and Contemporary Views," *Feminist Studies* (1982): 109–132; Susan Moller Okin, "Philosopher Queens and Private Wives: Plato on Women and the Family," in Jean Bethke Elshtain, ed., *The Family in Political Thought* (Amherst: University of Massachusetts Press, 1982): 31–50; Jean Bethke Elshtain, "The Public Private Split," in Elshtain, 51–65; Jean Bethke Elshtain, *Public Man, Private Woman: Women in Social and Political Thought* (Princeton, N.J.: Princeton University Press, 1981); Mary R. Lefkowitz, "Influential Women," in Cameron and Kuhrt, 49–64; Sarah Pomeroy, "Plato and the Female Physician (*Republic* 454d2)," *American Journal of Philology* 99 (1978): 496–500.

30. Spelman, 116.

31. The following discussion of the Hellenistic period is based on the works of Arthur, 1976, 73–78, and Arthur, 1977, 73–78; Boulding, 265–266; Elaine Fantham, "Sex, Status, and Survival in Hellenistic Athens: A Study of Women in New Comedy," *Phoenix* 29, no. 1 (1975): 44–74; Lefkowitz, "Influential Women"; Lefkowitz and Fant; Grace Harriet Macurdy, *Hellenistic Queens: A Study of Women's Powers in Macedonia, Seleucid Syria, and Ptolemaic Egypt* (Baltimore: Johns Hopkins University Press, 1932); Julia O'Faolain and C. Laura Martines, eds., *Not in God's Image: Women in History from the Greeks to the Victorians* (New York: Harper & Row, 1973): 29–32; Sarah Pomeroy, "Technikai Mousikai: The Education of Women in the Fourth Century and in the Hellenistic Period," *American Journal of Ancient History* 2 (1977): 51–69; Riet Van Bremen, "Women and Wealth," in Cameron and Kuhrt, 223–242.

32. The following discussion of Rome relies on Arthur, 1976, 399–403; Arthur, 1977, 78–89; J. P. V. D. Balsdon, *Roman Women: Their History and Habits* (Westport, Conn.: Greenwich Press, 1962); Boulding, 339–379; Bullough, 77–120; Teresa Carp, "Two Matrons of the Late Republic," in Foley, 343–354; Gillian Clark, "Roman Women," *Greece and Rome* 28, no. 2 (October 1981): 193–212; Mary R. Lefkowitz, "Influential Women"; Lefkowitz and Fant; R. O. A. M. Lyne, *The Latin Love Poets: From Catullus to Horace* (Oxford: Clarendon Press, 1980); Anthony J. Marshall, "Tacitus and the Governor's Lady: A Note on Annals iii, 33–4," *Greece and Rome* 22 (1975): 11–18; Antony J. Marshall, "Roman Women and the Provinces," *Ancient Society* 6 (1975): 109–127; Jane E. Phillips, "Roman Mothers and the Lives of Their Adult Daughters," *Helios* 6, no. 1 (1978): 69–80; O'Faolain and Martines; Pomeroy, 1975, 149–226, Sarah Pomeroy, "The Relationship of the Married Woman to Her Blood Relatives in Rome," *Ancient History* 7 (1976); 215–227; Stuart Queen and Robert Habenstein, *The Family in Various Cultures*, 4th ed., (New York: J. B. Lippincott, 1974): 174–219; Amy Richlin, "Approaches to the Sources on Adultery at Rome," in Foley, 379–404; Susan Treggiari, "Jobs for Women," *American Journal of Ancient History* 1 (1976): 76–104; and Zinserling, 48–73.

33. M. K. Hopkins, "The Age of Roman Girls at Marriage," *Population Studies* 18, no. 3 (March 1965): 309–327.

34. Pomeroy, "The Relationship of the Married Woman to Her Blood Relatives in Rome," 215.

35. Marshall, "Roman Women and the Provinces," 112–113.

36. F. R. Cowell, *Everyday Life in Ancient Rome* (London: B. T. Batsford, 1961): 112–113, 128.

37. Phillips.

38. Lyne, 14.

39. Charlayne Allan, "Women in the Books of Livy," paper presented to the NEH seminar, "Women in Antiquity," Wellesley College, August 1984.

40. Lyne; Judith P. Hallett, "The Role of Women in Roman Elegy: Counter-Cultural Feminism," in John Peradotto and J. P. Sullivan, 241–262.

41. K. M. Hopkins, "Contraception in the Roman Empire," *Comparative Studies in Society and History* 8 (1965): 124–151.

42. Pomeroy, 1975, 182.

43. Elaine Pagels, *The Gnostic Gospels* (New York: Random House, 1979); Elaine Pagels, "What Became of God the Mother? Conflicting Images of God in Early Christianity," *Signs* 2, no. 2 (1976): 293–315.

44. Averil Cameron, " 'Neither Male nor Female,' " *Greece and Rome* 27 (1980): 63–67.

45. Boulding, 369.

46. The following discussion of men and women in medieval Europe draws on the works of Derek Baker, ed., *Medieval Women* (Oxford: Oxford University Press, Basil Blackwood, 1978); Susan Groag Bell, ed., *Women: From the Greeks to the French Revolution*, 2d ed. (Stanford, Calif.: Stanford University Press, 1980; Boulding; Brenda Boulton, "Mulieres Sanctae," in Susan Mosher Stuard, ed., *Women in Medieval Society* (Philadelphia: University of Pennsylvania Press, 1976): 141–158; Diane Bornstein, *The Lady in the Tower: Medieval Courtesy Literature for Women* (Hamden, Conn.: Archon Books, 1983); Bullough; Emily Coleman, "Infanticide in the Early Middle Ages," in Stuard, 47–70; Georges Duby, *The Knight, The Lady and the Priest: The Making of Modern Marriage in Medieval France*," trans. Brenda Brag (New York Pantheon, 1983); Bernard Hamilton, "Women in the Crusader States: The Queens of Jerusaleum (1100–1190)," in Baker, 143–174; Sybylle Harksen, *Women in the Middle Ages* (New York: Abner Schram, 1975); David Herlihy, "Life Expectancies for Women in Medieval Society," in Rosemarie Morewedge, ed., *The Role of Women in the Middle Ages* (Albany: State University of New York Press, 1975): 1–22; David Herlihy, "Land, Family, and Women in Continental Europe, 701–1200," in Stuard, 13–14; David Herlihy, "The Natural History of Medieval Women," *Natural History* (March 1978); 56–67; JoAnn McNamara and Suzanne Wemple, "The Power of Women through the Family in Medieval Europe: 500–1100," in Mary Hartman and Lois Banner, ed., *Clio's Consciousness Raised* (New York: Harper & Row, 1974); Angela M. Lucas, *Women in the Middle Ages: Religion, Marriage and Letters* (New York: St. Martin's Press, 1983); JoAnn McNamara and Suzanne Wemple, "Sanctity and Power: The Dual Pursuit of Medieval Women" in Renate Bridenthal and Claudia Koonz, eds., *Becoming Visible: Women in European History* (Boston: Houghton Mifflin, 1977); Michael Mitterauer and Reinhard Sieder, *The European Family: Patriarchy to Partnership from the Middle Ages to the Present*, trans. Karla Oosterveen and Manfred Horzinger (Chicago: University of Chicago Press, 1982, orig. 1977); Janet Nelson, "Queens as Jezebels: The Careers of Brunhilde and Balthild in Merovingian History," in Baker, 31–77; Joan Nicholson, *"Feminae Gloriosae:* Women in the Age of Bede," in Baker, 15–29; O'Faolain and Martines; Eileen Power, *Medieval Woman*, ed. by Michael M. Postan (London: Cambridge University Press, 1975); Emily Putnam, *The Lady* (Chicago: University of Chicago Press, 1970, orig. 1910); Queen and Habenstein; Shulamith Shahar, *The Fourth Estate: A History of Women in the Middle Ages*, trans. Chava Galai (New York: Methuen, 1983); Pauline Stafford, "Sons and Mothers: Family Politics in the Early Middle Ages," in Baker, 79–100; Susan Mosher Stuard, "Introduction," in Stuard, 1–12; Susan Mosher Stuard, "Women in Charter and Statute Law: Medieval Ragusa-Dubrovnik," in Stuard, 199–208; Suzanne Fonay Wemple, *Women in Frankish Society: Marriage and the Cloister, 500 to 900* (Philadephia: University of Pennsylvania Press, 1981).

47. Wemple, 1981, 32–36.

48. Coleman, 47–70; Wemple, 1981, 59

49. Guttentag and Secord, 53–77.

50. Duby, 1983; Wemple, 1981, 40–60.

51. Wemple, 1981, 75–96.

52. Herlihy, 1975, 10; see also Lucas, 131–134; Bornstein, 94–96.

53. Nicholson, 19.

54. Nelson; Stafford; and Hamilton.

55. Boulding, 429–439.

56. Stafford.

57. Putnam, 131.

58. Putnam, 84.

59. Herlihy, 1975, 15.

60. Coleman, 50–51.

61. Patricia Labalme, "Introduction," in Patricia Labalme, ed., *Beyond Their Sex: Learned Women of the European Past* (New York: New York University Press, 1980: 3; Joan M. Ferrante, "The Education of Women in the Middle Ages in Theory, Fact, and Fantasy, in Labalme, 17–18; Lucas, 136–179.

62. Stuard, "Introduction," 8.

63. Shahar, 73; Duby, 46, 144; Lucas.

64. Bullough, 173; Nancy Van Vuuren, *The Subversion of Women as Practiced by Churches, Witch-Hunters, and Other Sexists* (Philadelphia: Westminster, 1973); Rosemary Reuther, "Misogynism and Virginal Feminism in the Fathers of the Church," in Rosemary Reuther, ed., *Religion and Sexism: Images of Women in the Jewish and Christian Traditions* (New York: Simon & Schuster, 1974): 150–183; Duby, 177.

65. Boulding, 499.

66. Bullough, 171; see also Shahar, 79–80; Duby 1983, 215–225; Georges Duby, *Medieval Marriage: Two Models from Twelfth-Century France* (Baltimore: Johns Hopkins University Press, 1978): 12–15.

67. Guttentag and Secord, 53–78.

68. Duby, 1983, 144; Herbert Moller, "The Social Causation of the Courtly Love Complex," *Comparative Studies in Society and History* 1, no. 2 (January 1959): 137–163.

69. Stuard, "Women in Charter and Statute Law," 114.

70. McNamara and Wemple, 1977, 114.

71. Harksen, 10; Edward Shorter, *The Making of the Modern Family* (New York: Basic Books, 1977).

72. Harksen, 23; Bornstein, 96–98.

73. Harksen, 11; Bornstein, 99–113.

74. Bullough, 169.

75. Phillippe Aries, *Centuries of Childhood* (New York: Vintage Books, 1960); Shahar, 98–99; Duby, 145, 223–224.

76. Duby, 1983, 255–260; Wemple, 1981, 92–95; Lucas, 85, 89.

CHAPTER 6

Capitalist Industrial Society
The United States

Capitalist commercial and productive enterprises developed gradually within the medieval agricultural economy. Small-scale merchants, traders, artisans, and craftspeople became more numerous as medieval society became centralized under the rule of powerful kings. These monarchs' central governments stimulated capitalist development through the provision of standardized laws, money, highways, and the physical protection of the merchant and his or her wares. Cities and towns grew dramatically. Agriculture declined in relative importance in the economy and so did the power of the landed aristocracy, which depended on agriculture. The capitalist class was in ascendancy.

The capitalists eventually became powerful enough to limit or overthrow the power of the kings themselves. Parliamentary democracies replaced the rule of absolute monarchs in England, Western Europe, and the United States. These parliamentary governments were run by and for the newly powerful male capitalists. While these changes were taking place in the political and class structures, the process of industrialization was transforming the economy, which developed from small-scale cottage industry and shops to large-scale factory production. And as these evolutionary and revolutionary changes in society from feudal agrarianism to modern industrial capitalism were taking place, they had important effects on the gender roles and gender stratification systems of these societies.

Economy and Class Structure

The capitalist economy is dominated by commodity production and exchange value. Simple use values continue to be produced within the home as women cook, clean, and care for children without direct monetary compensation. The trend, however, is for the production of use values to be replaced by the production of exchange values. Market relationships come to characterize the society. Productivity is vastly increased under capitalism and industrialization. This allows for the production and consumption of surpluses impossible under previous modes of production. People become dependent on the money economy for their subsistence as well as their luxuries.

The economy is based on individual ownership of private property, but most people own little or no important private property. A very few, the capitalists, own or control the important income-producing property such as factories and industrial corporations.

To run their profit-generating enterprises, they depend on the existence of a *free labor force*. "Free" in this sense does not imply a true personal freedom for the individual. Instead it refers to the individual workers not being bound to a particular employer or occupation as serfs, indentured servants, or slaves. The individual is thus free to sell his or her labor at whatever prices he or she can command from an employer. The employer is also free from the traditional obligations of the lord-peasant, master-slave relationship. He or she can dismiss the employees whenever their labor is no longer needed or desired.

This is adaptive for fluctuating labor requirements as businesses go through "boom" and "bust" periods of expansion and recession. It is also adaptive for the changing needs for different types of workers. Technological change is rapid under industrialization. It renders some occupations obsolete and increases the demand for others. Workers, therefore, have to adjust to the highly variable needs of a capitalist economy through their "freedom" to be unemployed, to move from areas of low employment to areas of high employment, and to undertake training to obtain skills that are still in demand.

Class Inequality

There is, therefore, marked class stratification and inequality under capitalism. Some people become wealthy and powerful capitalists while others are left with nothing but their labor to sell in the market economy. Some workers can make a better bargain for their labor than others: that is, they receive better salaries, job security, or better working conditions. For example, those with desirable skills can obtain a better contract than unskilled workers. The working class does not, therefore, constitute a class-conscious, unified group. It is divided and weakened by any number of cleavages such as distinctions between skilled and unskilled or white collar and blue collar workers. Two very important bases for dividing the working class against itself are race and gender. Workers of different races are pitted against one another so that racism keeps them fighting with each other instead of uniting against the power of the upper classes. Men are similarly pitted against women, with sexism focusing their discontent on demands or competition by female workers instead of on the powerlessness of workers in general.

Gender Division of Labor

Work inside and outside the home is characterized by a high degree of gender segregation. As capitalism develops, some jobs come to be defined as "feminine" and others as "masculine." Sometimes the definitions undergo change. For example, teaching began as a male occupation and later came to be dominated by females and redefined as feminine. Similarly, before World War II, the job of librarian had been feminine. After World War II many men used the GI Bill to obtain college degrees in library science and gradually took over the administrative and higher-level librarian posts.

As capitalism and industrialization develop, work is separated from the home. The domestic/public dichotomy is more fully realized under industrial capitalism than it is in any of the societal types we previously considered. Within the domestic sphere the gender division of labor manifests itself in assigning primary responsibility for the housework and child care to women. This is functionally related to the needs of capitalist business and industry. As Heleieth Saffioti points out, family responsibilities *marginalize* women in the labor force and turn them into a vast *reserve labor force*.[1] By being assigned the household and child-care tasks, women are limited in their ability to compete with men for jobs in the public market economy. Yet they can still be drawn upon as workers whenever the male labor supply is inadequate to meet production needs. A capitalist industrial economy rarely needs all of its potential labor supply. Labor shortages sometimes occur, however, especially in times of mass mobilization for war or during periods of tremendous economic growth. Extra workers are kept available within the family as housewives. When job opportunities draw them out of the home, the women assume the dual role of worker and housewife, thus allowing employers to take advantage of both their paid and unpaid labor. Their role in the family justifies returning them to the home when their labor is no longer needed. And it justifies discriminating against women in favor of male employees and thus provides a basis for dividing the working class against itself. Gender segregation of jobs, in turn, creates and amplifies specific demand patterns for "women's work" in the paid labor force.

The domestic role also allows employers to draw upon the unpaid labor of women to make the male employees more efficient workers. As women take care of the male workers' food, clothing, household maintenance, and child-care needs, they free the men to concentrate on their public jobs. Women's unpaid labor is also used to produce and socialize future generations of the labor supply. Mothers consciously prepare their children, especially their sons, to become obedient, diligent, responsible workers. They aid them in obtaining the necessary education and skills to be more productive and valuable employees.

Women and the family situation they maintain also create a buffer against the intense competitiveness and alienation of the work process. This helps to maintain the emotional and psychological fitness of the workers. Eli Zaretsky states that one of the effects of participation in capitalist work structures is an increase in *individualism* and emphasis on *personal life*.[2] That is, people come to value personal self-development and intimate interpersonal relationships to compensate for the depersonalization and alienation they experience in their work. He argues, moreover, that individualism was first extended only to men. Women's role was to make the personal self-development of the male possible. Men thus were freed to pursue a personal identity and personal life, while women were bound to the needs of the family and expected to sacrifice their personal needs and self-development whenever they clashed with family priorities.

John Kenneth Galbraith points out another function of the domestic role of women for capitalism.[3] The housewife has been a main support for *consumerism* and this underlies the continued profitability and growth of capitalist business. Idealizing women's roles as wives and mothers is what Galbraith calls a "convenient social virtue"— convenient for business and industry. It assigns to women the often onerous tasks associated with consumption. Purchasing, maintaining, sorting, and storing consumer goods are often time-consuming and boring jobs. If each person had to assume responsibility for his or her own consumption, it could limit the desire to consume. However, if some of the burdens of consumption can be shifted to someone else, there are few limitations on one's consumption wants. Women are convinced to assume these burdens by defining the tasks as "virtuous." Thus a "good wife" may take care of purchasing her husband's ties and taking his suits to the cleaner, and the "good mother" shops for the appropriate educational toys for her children. The housewife's assumption of the role of consumer for the family is, of course, profitable for business, which depends on constantly increasing sales.

Although women's role in the family justifies limiting their participation in the public sphere, it should be realized that this family organization and these gender roles for women are the result, not a cause, of the industrial capitalist mode of production and gender division of labor. As Eleanor Burke Leacock states it:

It is not the family that keeps women in an inferior position in the labor force and in society, but the need for women's marginalized role as workers and as the unpaid producers and reproducers of the labor force that is responsible for family organization and its social-psychological concomitants.[4]

It should be kept in mind that the domestic specialization of women was also deeply rooted in the historical legacy of agrarianism.

The marginalization of women from the paid labor force and the domestic/public dichotomy also have an important effect on men and serve the interests of business in yet another way. If women and children are turned into the economic dependents of men, then the responsibility for their maintenance devolves solely upon men. Instead of joint familial responsibility for subsistence needs, the husband becomes the sole breadwinner for the family. This is, of course, a great burden for the husband/father, and this responsibility binds him firmly to his job. He usually cannot afford to quit his job without already having found another. He cannot decide to tell the boss off and suffer the deprivations of unemployment because he will not be the only one to suffer. He must always think of the needs of his family as well. Therefore, placing the burden of economic support on the husband is a means of enforcing labor discipline. The married man with children is easier to exploit as an employee than the single man who has only himself to provide for.

Gender Stratification

Male dominance is thus encouraged by the gender division of labor and the family structure it promotes. Male workers are exploited and alienated in their role as workers. Their exploitation is softened by their being rewarded with the subservience of their wives. Wives are expected to tend to the physical, emotional, and sexual needs of their husbands. They are to relieve the males of household and child-care responsibilities and provide them with an emotional haven from the wider world. In return, wives are to receive economic support from their husbands.

However, as capitalism and industrialization have evolved, important changes have taken place in the relation of the family to the market economy. The needs of the economy have drawn increasing numbers of women out of the private household into the labor force. Even though these women usually retain the dual role, paid employment still has important liberating effects. It improves women's bargaining positions in relation to men by giving them a degree of economic independence. It furthermore develops the skills of the public world in women. Their new skills and economic independence often combine to give women the confidence and motivation to demand an end to sexism and gender stratification in both the domestic and public spheres. Thus feminist movements tend to arise. Women begin to demand that individualism, self-development, and the pursuit of a personal identity be extended to them as well as to men. These may be elusive goals for both men and women under capitalism. The nature of work and social organization may very well make it impossible for either gender to find a truly satisfying personal life without a reorganization of society. However, many women no longer accept the gender stratification system which puts them at a disadvantage relative to men.

The Interaction of Class Stratification and Gender Stratification

Just as gender stratification creates an important cleavage within the working class, so does class stratification create important divisions among women. Women from different socioeconomic classes are likely to view each other with hostility and misunderstanding. The interests of working-class women, for example, do not always coincide with those of middle-class or upper-class women, and sometimes they may actually clash. Black women and white women may find it difficult to unite in feminist causes. Full-time housewives may distrust career women and fear feminists.

Class stratification also sometimes obscures the pervasive effects of gender stratification. The well-to-do upper-class or middle-class woman may be able to direct and exploit the labor of working-class men and women while, at the same time, remaining subordinate to men of her own class standing. Furthermore, the fact that some upper-class women can obtain higher educations, pursue prestigious careers, run for political office, or own important property may also make it appear that such positions are as open to women as they are to men. However, it is the class positions of these women that make their achievements possible and give them the resources necessary to overcome to a degree the barriers of gender stratification. Such women do not constitute proof that gender stratification does not exist, but they can be used to keep people from recognizing the continuance of gender inequality. We will explore some of the complexities and contradictions of gender and class stratification in modern American society later in this chapter. First, however, we look at some of the important historical antecedents and earlier developments of gender-relations in the United States.

The Preindustrial Family Economy

In the seventeenth and early eighteenth centuries, agriculture and small-scale capitalist enterprises dominated the economy. Women, men, and children engaged in both forms of economic activity as family units. Among the farmers and working classes, the family was the unit of production and consumption. Family life, women, and children were not cut off from the public world of work. Women pursued a wide variety of occupations both in the home and outside it.

Louise Tilly and Joan Scott characterize this mode of production as the *family economy*.[5] Families worked together in the household, on the land, and in the cottage industries and shops. There was a division of labor by gender and age, but no one was idle. If the family did not require the labor of all its sons and daughters, they were placed in other peoples' homes as domestic servants, laborers, or apprentices and their wages were contributed to the family budget.

Gender Roles

The family work unit was ruled over by the father. Women were viewed as naturally subordinate to men. They were believed to be physically, intellectually, and morally weaker than men. They were not, as they came to be later, idealized as pure mothers who upheld the higher principles of civilization. Instead there existed what John Demos refers to as an undercurrent of fear and suspicion of women.[6] They were often associated with evil and corruption. Such beliefs were, of course, clearly manifested in the witch hunts which continued into the seventeenth century in the United States.

Despite these negative images and stereotypes of women, women were not segregated from men. Their labor was too important for female isolation to be practical. A man had to have a wife as an economic partner if he were to run his household and farm or business. Men controlled the important basis of wealth and power—the land—but they needed a wife to work it and profit from it. Therefore, the lives of men and women were not separate. They worked together and shared the same experiences. As active participants in the family economy, women had a say in the family decision making also.

This situation of full-time female involvement in the family economy, although associated with a high degree of female subordination, did not give rise to an ideology of femininity. Women might be weaker, but they were not delicate. A society that expects strenuous labor from its females producing food, clothing, crops, livestock, and trade goods cannot afford to view these women as frail creatures in constant need of male protection and support.

Women were also not viewed as asexual creatures and the society was not antisex. Even the Puritans accepted sex as an important human activity. Their goal was to confine it to marriage and to stamp out fornication and adultery.[7] It was considered a dereliction of duty for either a husband or a wife to refuse sexual access to the partner. Furthermore, in colonial America it was common for brides to go to the altar pregnant. In many communities engagement made it fairly acceptable for the couple to have sexual relations. If the bride became pregnant before the wedding, the man was expected to marry her immediately. He was not allowed to break his promise of marriage. The families of the couple and the wider community forced him to live up to his obligations to the woman. The pregnancy was no disgrace to the couple or their families as long as the marriage did take place.

Childhood and Child Rearing

If women were not delicate, innocent creatures in need of protection from the realities of the world, neither were children. The importance of children's labor kept children from being characterized as weak dependents, just as women's labor participation prevented the development of a stereotype of feminine weakness. There was a division of labor by age, and the less demanding, less skilled jobs were given to younger family members, but age segregation was minimal. Children were treated as miniature adults and fully integrated into the adult world.[8] They were not viewed as different from adults. In particular they were not believed to be innocent and malleable. Instead children were commonly viewed as innately evil and in need of harsh discipline. Parents were expected to break the child's will and to enforce moral principles of behavior. Moreover, child rearing was not assigned exclusively or primarily to mothers. Fathers were viewed as the most important influence. Both fathers and mothers bore the burden of correct child rearing, and the community felt it had the right and obligation to intervene if parents did not discipline their children in an appropriate manner. Family privacy was not idealized or honored.

Child labor was necessary to the family economy, but infant and child mortality rates were high. Therefore, fertility rates were high to ensure an adequate family labor supply. Women were burdened with many pregnancies, which threatened their own lives. Parents could not afford to become too attached to their infants. The resulting periods of grief would have been too disruptive. Furthermore, the economic demands on the parents' time left them little opportunity for extensive involvement with child care. Infants and small children were therefore often badly cared for. This in turn contributed to the high mortality rate and created a cycle of parental noninvolvement and infant death. Thus, although women were expected to bear many children to reproduce the labor supply, they were not expected to devote their lives to motherhood as such.[9]

Women were expected to adjust the demands of their domestic and child-care tasks to their economically productive tasks. Within the family economic unit, women could combine nursing and the care of infants and small children with their farmyard tasks, their household work, and with such cottage industry work as spinning and textiles. Women who worked outside the home, such as street vendors, solved the problem by taking their children with them. For those who could not or would not combine infant care with their other work, there were wet nurses who nursed infants for pay. The death rate, however, for infants sent to wet nurses was very high. These poor farm women often cared for the babies under the most unsanitary conditions and were tempted to take in more than they had milk for. Well-to-do women also used wet nurses to avoid the bother of infant care. The practice in general, reflected the lack of strong maternal-infant bonds and of an emphasis on maternal nurturing.

The Family and the Community

The preindustrial nuclear family was not a private isolated enclave, and the domestic/public dichotomy was not firmly established. The family and community were closely intertwined. The community was viewed as comprised of families, not of individuals. Heads of households participated in the public sphere. Females, children, and unmarried adults were not accorded full public rights. In colonial America, for example, the term *town fathers* meant just that. The affairs of the town were decided by the fathers, that is, the householders. According to Demos, the head of the family was also the agent of the state.

The family served many important functions that were later taken over by other institutions. In addition to being the primary unit of production and consumption, the family was the center of education for the young and the provider of such social services as care for the sick and the elderly. People who did not live in such household units were viewed with hostility and suspicion. Unattached adults were often refused permission to live in the early New England towns unless they could find a household in which to live and work.

Industrialization

The preindustrial society and its system of domestic production gave way to the forces of industrialization and capitalist growth. Nancy Cott characterizes the years between 1780 and 1830 in the United States as a period of deep and far-reaching transformation:

. . . the beginning of rapid intensive economic growth . . . ; the start of sustained urbanization; demographic transition toward modern fertility patterns; marked change toward social stratification by wealth and growing inequality in the distribution of wealth; rapid pragmatic adaptation in the law; shifts from unitary to pluralistic networks in personal association; unprecedented expansion in primary education; democratization in the political process; invention of a new language of political and social thought, and—not least—with respect to family life, the appearance of "domesticity."[10]

The Wealthy Merchant Families

Barbara Easton notes that a new "ideal of femininity" or "cult of domesticity" was developing in America as early as the eighteenth century among the wealthy merchant class in the commercial towns such as Boston, Fall River, Newport, and Providence.[11] The family domestic economy was already being replaced by the isolated, private nuclear family supported by the father as the sole breadwinner. As businesses grew, they needed more space. It became impractical to continue running the enterprise out of the home. And as the merchants became wealthier, they could afford to establish more elaborate houses in residential areas separate from the business districts. Thus for the well-to-do, the home and the workplace became separated. These merchants could also afford to support their wives and required little in the way of productive labor from them. With the English upper class as their role models, they came to expect more in the way of social graces and decorative qualities in their women. Being able to maintain a well-dressed, gracious wife and daughters in a nonproductive but beautifully appointed private home became a symbol of success. (They did not, however, adopt the English upper-class disdain for male participation in business and other productive labor.) Easton found that by the end of the eighteenth century, literature was being imported from England and some was being

published in the United States directing women in the graces of the lady. At this point, however, the duties of motherhood were still not included in the ideal of feminine womanhood among the upper classes.

The Middle Classes

The aristocratic ideal borrowed from England did not retain a firm hold in the United States. The republican spirit engendered by the Revolutionary War led to an overt disavowal of a class-based society. Even as the United States moved toward more marked class inequality, ideologically the emerging class system was denied. Thus a somewhat different model of womanhood placing less importance on "society" and more emphasis on domesticity was adopted, particularly in the middle classes.

Industrialization gradually removed economic productivity from the homes of the middle classes. Single women left the household for work outside the home, often as domestics in other peoples' homes or as schoolteachers. The change in the location of work had some positive consequences for single women. They no longer had to live as dependents and virtual servants in their parents' homes. Their work and education outside the household gave them greater independence, variety of experiences, and mobility—some undertook careers as writers, religious leaders, and educators. But it also created insecurity. Work, especially work suitable to their class standing, was sometimes difficult to obtain and was always poorly paid. But the single woman did not have to accept the isolation and decreased variety and mobility that increasingly characterized married women's lives.[12]

The Creation of the "Pedestal."   One result of the transformation of the married woman's role due to the separation of economic production from the home was an increased emphasis on the importance of household management and upkeep and of mothering and nurturing children. From her study of sermons, literature, and personal communications in the period from 1780 to 1835, Cott concludes:

More than ever before in New England history, the care of children appeared to be mother's sole work and the work of mothers alone. The expansion of nonagricultural occupations drew men and grown children away from the household, abbreviating their presence in the family and their roles in child rearing. Mothers and young children were left in the household together just when educational and religious dicta both newly emphasized the malleability of young minds.[13]

Simultaneously, the home came to be viewed as a retreat from the public worlds of men, and the family became more private. According to Easton,

the supervision of family life that Puritan courts had engaged in was no longer possible. The individualist philosophy that was coming to pervade the towns and cities of nineteenth century New England allowed for no such intrusions into the family, now seen as the private domain of the husband and father.[14]

The family became an enclave protected from the rest of the world. In it the man could escape the pressures of the competitive capitalist economy. His wife was to provide the emotional support necessary to revive him for the struggle. But the wife with her purity and innocence could never be a part of that public competitive world without losing her ability to maintain the haven so necessary to her husband. Women's and men's experiences thus became increasingly dissimilar. Men were integrated into the time-oriented industrial work world. Women remained in the preindustrial, task-oriented domestic world.

These changes in the nature of the middle-class, married woman's work led to the development of a new ideology of femininity. Barbara Welter and Barbara Easton both document the rise in the nineteenth century of an extensive literature extolling the virtues of the true woman. Martha Vicinus notes that the ideal of the true woman or perfect lady was most developed among upper-middle-class Victorian women.[15] Among those who could afford to practice it, this new ideal served to isolate women firmly in the domestic sphere.

Welter describes the new cult of womanhood as based on four virtues—piety, purity, domesticity, and submissiveness. Women were seen as the virtuous, moral gender, devotedly religious and pure. Purity required virginity of unmarried women and chastity of married women. All manner of flirtatiousness was to be abhorred in women. Young girls were to be kept innocent of the harsher aspects of life. In particular, they were to be denied all knowledge of sexuality and the facts of reproduction. As a result, the onset of menstruation was often a terrifying shock to girls. Women were seen as innately asexual. They were to submit to their husbands' sexual advances only out of duty or to have a child, never out of desire. Their only concern with sex was to be for procreation for they were also believed to have a strong maternal instinct that laid the biological basis for domesticity. The female's life was to be focused almost entirely on her husband, children, and home. Motherhood had become the primary purpose of womanhood, although much of the actual work of child care could be left to nannies and governesses if the husband could afford them. All of a woman's domestic duties were to be carried out with submissiveness and self-sacrifice.

Medical Views of True Womanhood. Middle-class woman's new role "on the pedestal" as a dependent, delicate creature isolated in the household was reflected in nineteenth-century medical opinion and practice.[16] Doctors viewed women as dominated by their uteruses and ovaries. The reproductive role defined woman's body and being, and this was believed to render women particularly weak and subject to illness. Their frailness, in turn, justified isolating women from the public worlds of social activity, work, and politics. Menstruation and pregnancy were believed to require most of the female's store of energy. Women of the wealthier classes were often advised to retire to their beds for the duration of their menstrual periods. Such advice was not, however, deemed appropriate to working-class women. Maids and other working women were given no special consideration for the supposed weaknesses of women.

On the basis of these beliefs about women, physicians advised that women should not take part in education, work, or other outside activities, because these activities might irreparably damage their reproductive organs. Instead, doctors prescribed a domestic routine of housework and child care as the only activity suitable to the female physiology. Furthermore, adolescent girls and young women should avoid an active social life and the expression of strong emotions, especially anger, because such activities might use up the female's scarce energy supplies and cause her reproductive organs to atrophy.

Many women trying to accept the isolated but often demanding role of full-time housewife as well as to live up to the ideal of feminine weakness, dependency, and non-assertiveness succumbed to the disease of hysteria. Hysteria might involve uncontrollable fits, paralysis, depression, and any variety of aches and pains. Carol Smith-Rosenberg argues that hysteria constituted a legitimate alternative to role conflicts for

nineteenth-century American women.[17] After being socialized into passivity and dependency, women were faced with demanding roles as wives and mothers. A housewife was expected to be a strong, self-reliant, efficient household manager. Many women found themselves inadequate to these demands. Furthermore, economic changes meant that some of these ill-prepared women had to seek outside employment to help their families through economic crises. Being diagnosed as hysterics relieved them of these role discontinuities. They no longer had to take responsibility for home, husband, or children. Instead, they could legitimately demand that the rest of the family cater to their needs. This was therefore an alternative source of power for women, since they could use their illness to dominate their husbands. Smith-Rosenberg describes hysteria as a form of passive aggression and exploitative dependency.

The condemnation of female sexual responsiveness and the idealization of the pure, asexual woman were also embodied in the medical practices of the Victorians. From the 1860s until the early twentieth century, physicians frequently performed clitoridectomies (the surgical removal of the clitoris) to prevent female orgasm during intercourse and female masturbation. Female sexual desire was believed to lead to mental and physical disease. Surgical removal of the ovaries and the uterus were also accepted treatments for a variety of emotional and physical problems in women. G. J. Barker-Benfield argues that such practices were part of the wider pattern of male dominance and reflected unconscious fears of women by men.[18] Sexual intercourse, although avidly sought by men, was viewed as debilitating for them. Females could therefore drain men of their strength and power if their sexuality remained unchecked.

Romantic Love. The ideology of romantic love accompanied the high degree of sexual repression that arose in the context of the private nuclear family with the economically dependent wife. Randall Collins argues that the ideology of romantic love, sexual repression, and the ideal of femininity were ways for females to exercise some control over males from their economically powerless positions.[19] These ideals could serve to mute the exercise of power and aggression toward women by requiring husbands and suitors to treat the supposedly delicate and asexual females with tenderness and respect. The practice of sexual repression and the belief in the women's lack of sexual interest gave women a basis for refusing the sexual demands of their husbands, whereas romantic love and idealized marriage bonds could be used to demand sexual fidelity and love from husbands.

These ideas spread in the United States between 1820 and 1860 as women lost their roles as economic producers in the family household economy but became important for their maternal, housewife, and companionship functions in the isolated nuclear family. As women's and men's spheres pulled farther apart, the romantic love ideology helped bridge the gap between the genders.

The euphoric leaps to romantic love could transcend the gulf between worldly men and retiring girls. The fragile, over-specialized female, furthermore, was helpless without a man to support her and accept her emotional riches in return. Romantic love conveyed the urgency of her search for a spouse. Intense heterosexual attraction also helped to wrench a young woman away from the maternal home where she had been thoroughly protected and dearly loved. Finally, a glorified and overpowering sentiment like romantic love could disguise the inequitable relationship a bride was about to accept.[20]

Cott also maintains that the development by 1820 of a separate "woman's sphere" emphasizing the woman's domestic role, religious piety, and moral virtue served to raise middle-class women's status in some respects.

The doctrine of woman's sphere opened to women (reserved for them) the avenues of domestic influence, religious morality, and child nurture. It articulated a social power based on their special qualities rather than on general human rights. For women who previously held no particular avenue of power of their own—no unique defense of their integrity and dignity—this represented an advance. Earlier secular and religious norms had assumed male dominance in home, family, and religious life as well as in the public world.[21]

The new ideology helped to soften male dominance within the domestic and religious contexts. But this ideology also created barriers for women by emphasizing their distinctiveness from men. It was a separate-but-equal strategy that could not be used to achieve true equality for women. The pedestal for women was accompanied by increases in male dominance in many respects. Women lost the limited legal rights they had enjoyed under the Puritans in the United States. They were excluded from the courts and lost their property rights. They were more firmly defined as the legal dependents of men.

Easton argues that the isolation of women into the domestic sphere was not a necessary aspect of industrialization. Things might have happened differently. If industry had drawn middle-class women as well as lower-class women into the paid labor force, different roles, stereotypes, and ideals of woman's place might have developed. But there was little need to utilize middle-class women's labor outside the home. Waves of foreign immigration in the United States provided the necessary expansion of the labor force as industrialization proceeded. The ideal of femininity affected even the lower classes, who could not really hope to achieve it. Men strove to earn enough to allow their wives to become full-time housewives and mothers, and women who worked looked forward to the time they could leave the labor force for the home. Thus the domestic ideal undermined even working-class women's commitment to the paid work role.

Ethnic Groups

Immigrant men and women often brought the strongly patriarchal agrarian values and family roles of the old country with them to the United States. Italians, for instance, were particularly adamant about the need for male dominance and the distinction between the public sphere of men and the domestic sphere for women.[22]

But immigrant men often failed to earn a "family wage" even with the contributions of working children. Women worked whenever they could. Even the more secluded Italian women worked with their children beside them in the fields and canneries during the harvest season. They could also take in boarders and do piecework or sewing in their homes. Polish and Irish women were more willing to work outside the home.

The domestic burdens of the wife and mother along with her frequent pregnancies, however, kept 80 to 90 percent of the married women out of the labor force outside the home; whenever those who did work outside the home could afford to live on their husbands' pay, they quit. The better-educated and better-off Jewish immigrants were more likely to be able to forego their wives' earnings, and allowing them to stay home to encourage their sons' educations. Gradually, the pressures and standards of the wider society pushed the various ethnic groups into the family patterns of the white, Anglo-

Saxon Protestant natives. Eventually, ethnic families saw the careful nurturance and education of children in the home and school presided over by women as their own ideal.

Slavery

While most immigrant groups and working-class and even lower-middle-class men and women could not live up to the domestic ideals, the ideals were not considered applicable to slave women. They regularly worked in the fields alongside the men. No consideration of female frailty or delicacy interfered with the slave owner's profitable exploitation of his slaves' labor. Nor was the slave woman viewed as an innately moral, asexual creature in need of male protection. Slave women were subject to sexual exploitation by their masters and white overseers. Although black men and women tried hard to establish and maintain strong family ties, the slave family was also exempt from the idealization of the family. Slave owners felt free to separate husbands and wives and parents and children when it suited their purposes. However, many of the abolitionists used the Victorian ideals as bases for condemning slavery because it violated the ideal of femininity and the family.

The Family Wage Economy of the Working Classes

Transformations in family structure and gender roles similar to those of the middle classes occurred among the working classes, although not at the same time or at the same pace. The family economy with its household mode of production gave way to the working-class family wage economy as the productive processes moved from the home to the factory.[23]

Several forces combined to bring an end to cottage industry. First, the logic of capitalist entrepreneurship encouraged business-persons to bring more and more of the elements of production under their direct control. Under cottage industry, the family work unit owned its own tools and controlled the productive process. They decided when and how much to work and controlled the quality of the product. This meant that if agricultural or domestic tasks needed to be done, the family would cease spinning and weaving. This left the amount of cloth they could produce unpredictable. The factory system attempted to make production more reliable and predictable. The factory took the workers out of the household. Tools were owned by the factory owner, who also controlled the work process. He told the workers how long and how fast to work. He could also continually oversee the quality of the product.

A second factor moving production from the home to the factory is associated with the technological advances of industrialization. Industrialization first occurred in the textile industry. Technological advances in the eighteenth century greatly increased the productivity of the textile workers. At first, these inventions were incorporated into the household setting. But subsequent inventions, in particular steam power, required a large investment and a great deal of space. The cottage industry household could provide neither the capital nor the space for steam power and the much larger looms that steam power made possible. To utilize these technological advances, the factory was necessary. So the family textile workers followed their work into the factory.

At first, whole families were hired and fathers could maintain their positions of family authority by directing the family labor within the factory. Even where whole families were not hired, however, the family continued to allocate the labor of the family members in the interest of the family econ-omy. But instead of the son or daughter working in the family household, he or she was placed in factory or domestic work to bring wages into the household economy.

Effects on Married Women. Mothers found it difficult to continue combining economic productivity with domestic production and child care. The removal of the productive process from the household made it almost impossible to carry out the two types of work simultaneously. Employers would not allow women to nurse or to care for small children in the factory. Employment opportunities for married women therefore shrunk. Married women were increasingly tied to the domestic sphere while men, single women, and children were incorporated into the industrial labor force.

When economic need was severe enough, however, mothers did join the wage labor force. Tilly and Scott argue that mothers constituted a reserve labor force for their families:

> The survival of the family unit [even] took priority over an infant life. And when need was great and jobs available for them, married women worked even at the point in the family cycle when they were most needed at home.[24]

The work of married women under the family wage economy was, however, irregular. Employers preferred the more reliable men and single women who would not be absent owing to pregnancy or the need to care for sick children. Married women could usually find only the lowest-paying, low-security jobs. This of course increased their lack of commitment to the work role and made it easier for them to justify returning to the home when the family could afford it.

Women, whether working outside the home or not, retained important economic roles within the family as household managers. Besides the demanding tasks of household upkeep, child care, and food processing, they also had to stretch the family earnings to cover all the household expenses. As the family produced less of its own subsistence needs, greater importance was attached to shopping and bargaining. The wife typically handled the family income. A "good" husband turned all his earnings over to his wife and received back for his personal expenditures what the wife deemed allowable. A "bad" husband, however, kept what he wanted to spend on drinking and gambling and other personal expenses and gave his wife the remainder. Wives did not always passively accept this. Payday in early factory towns was often a day of fierce disputes between spouses. Children were, of course, also expected to turn their pay over to their mothers.

Birthrates had begun to drop among the native middle classes, but remained high among the immigrant and native working classes. Infant and child mortality also remained high in the overcrowded, unsanitary, undernourished working-class industrial households and because child labor was still pervasive. Children added more to the family income than they consumed. To increase the family's chances of survival, a large number of children was desirable. Adult children also continued to support their parents. Children were parents' only hope for support if the parents survived to old age or became too infirm to work. Social services for the poor, the unemployed, and the disabled were either nonexistent, degrading, or even life threatening. The poorhouses were to be avoided it at all possible.

The Development of Childhood and Motherhood in the Working Class

By about 1820 technological improvements rendered child labor less practical and less necessary. Factory machines had become too complex and often too physically demanding for children to operate them efficiently. Social movements to abolish child labor received more favorable attention as the practice lost importance to the factory owners. A series of laws was enacted during the nineteenth century to forbid the employment of children in industry.

Expenses associated with rearing and training an educated labor force were forced on working-class families. Laws forbidding child labor and requiring school attendance deprived poorer families of an important source of income and required them to support the now dependent children. Even among the working classes, emphasis came to be placed on the socialization and education of children. This fit the changing needs of the industrial economy: Child labor was no longer necessary, but an educated work force became more desirable as the need for unskilled labor was replaced by an increased demand for skilled workers. Children were thus freed from the labor force to better prepare themselves to enter the labor force at a later date.

The new tasks associated with the care and socialization of children fell to the lower-class mothers, just as they earlier devolved upon middle-class mothers. With the workplace separate from the home, fathers no longer had the opportunity to participate extensively in child care. Moreover, mothers had already been assigned to the domestic sphere because of the incompatibility of factory work with care of young children and the discrimination against married women by employers. Thus greater emphasis was placed on "mothering," and motherhood became an important part of the working-class married woman's role. The decrease in infant and child mortality brought about by better care, a somewhat higher standard of living, and a reduction of child labor allowed parents to invest more in each child emotionally. Women were thus allowed to invest more in the maternal role at a time when their economic roles were being taken from them.[25]

Single Women. The wage economy increased the independence of single women among the working class just as work made middle-class single women more independent. To obtain jobs they often had to live away from home as domestics or in mill towns. Their employers sometimes supervised them as closely as their families would have. But there was a gradual increase in their freedom of movement and personal autonomy. Those who lived away from home sent most of their wages home just as those living at home turned most of their earnings over to their mothers. This was similar to the labor contributions they had made under the family economy of domestic production. But their contributions were individualized with the coming of wage labor. As Tilly and Scott point out, each family member was no longer bound to a family enterprise. Instead, each person worked separately to contribute an individually earned wage to the family budget. Thus although their wages were usually too low to allow them a truly independent life, their individual wage made daughters and sons feel less dependent on their families. With the small allowances they kept for themselves, single women could indulge in fashionable clothes and entertainment. They could go dancing with young men and lead a social life with what little free time they had.

One result of this increased freedom was a lowering of the age at marriage. Since few working-class families any longer held land or important property, it was no longer necessary for young people to wait to inherit property from their parents before they could begin families of their own. They would live on their own earnings instead. Thus parents lost control over their children's marriages.

This lack of control was also manifested in the increasing probability that the parents of the bride and groom would not know each other. Immigration and internal migration from the country to the town and moves from town to town in search of work destroyed community ties. Sons and daughters who went away to work would meet and fall in love with strangers. This increase in freedom for young men and women also led to an increase in vulnerability for the females.[26] In the traditional community, if a man promised to marry a woman, the community would force him to honor the promise, especially if the woman became pregnant. In the more anonymous urban settings, family and community ties were less important. There was often no one with the power to force a man into a marriage he had previously agreed to. Some men, of course, took advantage of the situation to seduce young women with promises of marriage. Others truly meant to marry their lovers, but the loss of their job or some other setback would make it financially impossible for them to support a wife and family. The man would then often abandon the woman. The lot of these unwed mothers was often one of severe hardship.

Despite their increased vulnerability, most of the working girls did marry, and marriage drastically changed their lives. They could no longer indulge in chocolates and clothes. They had to devote themselves to their households and this meant hard work and self-sacrifice. Their own needs and interests were not supposed to interfere with the needs of their husbands or children.

Women's Higher Education

Women's Colleges and Vigorous Femininity. Among the first groups to challenge openly the prevailing stereotypes, in particular the medical view of women as physically frail and prone to insanity, were educators associated with the first women's colleges. Medical opinion advised more strongly against mental activity for women than against physical activity. Only males had sufficient energy reserves to accommodate intellectual strain. Female energy was expended entirely on the reproductive organs.

Despite dire warnings from the medical profession, educational reformers established women's colleges in the post-Civil War era. Vassar, in 1865, was the first well-equipped female college to open its doors. The college designed its curriculum to emphasize a new image of femininity—"vigorous womanhood"—in direct opposition to the image of the delicate woman.[27] The students were required to participate in a strenuous physical education program. This was given a great deal of attention by both educational and medical professionals. To the surprise of many experts, it worked. Instead of succumbing to disease or insanity, these young women were the picture of health. This resulted in an important shift in medical opinion. Instead of prescribing complete rest, physicians began to order programs of exercise for ailing women. The colleges had won the battle over vigorous womanhood. But Rothman argues that they lost the war for equality.

The colleges accepted most of the other tenets of Victorian gender role stereotypes. They organized the colleges like large households to emphasize domesticity and the proper moral environment for the young women. Dormitories were closely supervised and a regimen of early rising and early retiring was imposed on all students. Faculty were chosen for their feminine graces and moral stature; academic qualifications were of secondary importance. The women's colleges did go on to challenge the belief in the female's intellectual inferiority, however.

Students at Vassar, Wellesley, and Smith undertook rigorous academic work. But this again was associated with the view of women as innately more moral and virtuous than men.

With a decisiveness quite different from coeducational institutions, these colleges rejected the role assigned to the Victorian female. Or, rather, they rejected some of that role. Their graduates would be intellectually equipped to work in the male world as partners with men. Equal, but not identical. Indeed, the alumnae—as cultured and chaste as the most orthodox Victorian could ask—would be socially and morally superior to men.[28]

Thus, aspects of the strategy of the ideal of femininity were still being used to raise women's status.

Coeducation in the Midwest. Higher education for females followed a different pattern in the Midwest. Instead of establishing women's colleges, which these frontier states could not afford, females were allowed to enter the previously all-male state colleges and universities. Administrators at institutions such as the University of Michigan approached coeducation with great caution and apprehension, also fearing that it might lead to physical disease, sterility, or insanity in the women. The programs women followed were not the same as men's. They concentrated on subjects related to domestic science and child rearing. Female students gravitated toward the humanities in such numbers that male students all but abandoned them for the more "masculine" sciences.

Thus women's higher education did not undermine the ideal of femininity, nor did it turn most female students toward feminism. The feminists were more likely to come from the ranks of the volunteer workers and clubwomen than from the "cultured intellectuals" or "bluestockings" of the women's colleges or the "educated domestics" of the coeducational institutions. Higher education did encourage and prepare a large number of women for careers, however. Although opportunities were very limited, many of these women persevered. But the choice to pursue a career usually also entailed the choice to remain single. Women could participate in the public domain or in the domestic, but not in both. In 1920, for example, 75 percent of female professionals were unmarried.[29] The cult of domesticity carried with it too many responsibilities and too much self-sacrifice to be easily combined with the demands of a career. Female education failed to emancipate women.

New Job Opportunities

In the post-Civil War era there was a great deal of rhetoric about the increasing employment opportunities for young women, but these new opportunities were not as wide as optimistic observers led people to believe. The job market opened up some new fields to women, but they were highly gender-segregated, low-paid, low-security, dead-end jobs. Better positions were very consciously and openly reserved for men.[30]

The jobs for women that did expand greatly were those of typist and stenographer, department store clerk, and teacher. Originally, the job of office clerk and stenographer was one of some responsibility that required working closely with the owner, learning the business, and eventually rising to more important positions. However, this work was considered inappropriate for women. With the invention of the typewriter and the growth of the clerical staff, the job became routine and dead-end and secretarial work was turned over to women. Employers drew upon women instead of lower-class men because the work did require education. Lower-class men did not have the requisite skills of punctuation, grammar, and spelling. Middle-class men were no longer interested in what had become low-level work. This left only the pool of female high school graduates. The women took these jobs because they were the best they could get. It was clean, safe, respectable work and paid as well or better than factory or domestic work.

The same held true for department store clerical work. Salesgirls were not paid as well as the office workers, but the educational requirements were lower and lower-class girls could more easily qualify for these jobs. Again, sales work opened up for women because middle-class men would not take the positions offered by the new departmet stores. They offered no chance of promotion. The employers refused to hire lower-class men because they believed lower-class women were more honest with money and stock, easier to control, had better manners for dealing with customers, and could be paid even less than lower-class men.

The third area of female employment was teaching. The pay was so low that educated men preferred other employment. When men did take teaching posts, they resented it and used the position as a stepping-stone to something better. School boards of necessity turned to women who had crowded into the new normal schools to obtain their teaching certificates. Again, however, the positions held no hope for advancement. Women could be elementary and secondary school teachers, but the principals, superintendents, and school board members were all male. The few men who became teachers were paid much higher salaries and were quickly promoted out of the teaching ranks into the better paying and influential administrative positions.

As capitalism developed, job opportunities for women increased in some areas, but men monopolized the better paying, more prestigious occupations. Furthermore, women were squeezed out of what had been female specialties, such as medicine and midwifery, as these became professionalized. As the pay and prestige of medicine increased, males entered the occupation and then organized to block females from the new educational requirements necessary to practice. Thus the new economic world was gender segregated, and the ideology of the pedestal and femininity were used to justify the exclusion of women from the men's world. Men's occupations and activities, even those that had previously been assigned to females, were defined as too rough for the female's delicate nature.

But employment, even in gender segregated jobs at low wages, still had an emancipating effect on women. The single, white-collar working woman of the 1890s gave rise to the "New Woman" or "Gibson Girl" image. She violated accepted norms of femininity by working until marriage and by wearing a much simpler style of clothing more suited to a work environment. Yards of petticoats and delicate gowns were replaced by more tailored blouses and by skirts that sometimes rose above the ankles. The tightly cinched eighteen-inch waist also gave way to looser corsets to allow more freedom of movement and fewer fainting spells and damaged internal organs. While the traditional fashions for well-to-do women emphasized woman's lack of important productive roles and her status as an object of display for her husband's wealth, the new style emphasized the new woman's greater independence and her new work roles. Such styles also spread to college women and sportswomen as bicycling, tennis, and golf became popular among middle- and upper-class women.

The Home Economics Movement

As the family consumer economy emerged among the middle class, a new ideology legitimating women's new consumer roles gained currency. Susan Strasser maintains that the home economics movement in the late nineteenth century served to link the large-scale capitalist economy that produced vast quantities of consumer goods to the housewife and the private household.[31] Instead of being told to provide a shelter against the forces of the competitive capitalist economy, women were now told to apply the principles of capitalist business to the scientific management of their households. This meant planning and organizing housework, but more important for the wider economy, it meant developing the skills of the good consumer. This role as director of family consumption integrated women into the economy through the private household. It did not destroy the domestic/public dichotomy; it merely changed the nature of the dichotomy. Women were still defined primarily by their domestic role, but they were encouraged to participate in the public economy as consumers for the domestic sphere. This role would greatly expand the market for consumer goods and was extremely profitable for business. It did not, however, serve to raise the status of women relative to that of men.

The Family Consumer Economy in the Working Class

The middle classes became integrated into the family consumer economy early, but the working classes could not afford such a life style until the early twentieth century. The working-class family remained a family wage economy with each member contributing wages. But as productivity increased, as more cheap consumer goods became available, and as wages, at least for men, rose, the wage-earning unit was increasingly focused on consumption needs. And as among the middle classes, the burden of the consumer role fell primarily to the wife. This made the housewife role more distinct from the other family members' roles and set these women apart from the wage earners.

As the household management and consumer tasks expanded for married women, their opportunities for wage earning declined further. Families still required the wages of mothers in times of crisis, but it was more difficult for them to find such work. The real increases in men's wages between 1880 and 1914 and the decline in married women's work options and wages combined to keep married women out of the labor force.

The choice for married women, when their husbands were present and working, was not between home and paid jobs with good wages, but between market work at poor wages and activity in the household in the service of preferred and better-paid workers. Many wives quite reasonably chose the home role.[32]

Although changes were in many ways forcing married women out of the labor force, another set of forces was motivating women to seek employment. The consumer economy created the desire for more and more consumer goods. Wives who did not have to worry about their families' subsistence needs could now worry about the families' life-style needs. They worked to help keep up their families' standard of living.[33] This was still not work for personal self-development or even personal consumption needs. Their work was in accord with at least one tenet of the domestic ideal—it involved self-sacrifice, not selfishness. So whether they worked entirely within the domestic sphere or held outside jobs as well, women's work was still family oriented.

The First Feminist Movement

1830–1860

Some women used the tenets of the ideal of femininity to avoid the isolation of the domestic sphere. In the early 1800s, church work was the one permissible outlet for the lady's time and energy outside the household. Women simply expanded the boundaries of their charitable volunteer activities. They formed women's clubs and benevolent societies and attacked social problems such as prostitution, alcohol abuse, and slavery. They justified these activities on the basis of the true woman's sense of morality, piety, and justice. Possession of such sensibilities meant that women owed it to society and civilization to exercise their talents in the public arena as well as the domestic. Participation in club work and social reform allowed women to develop important organizational and leadership skills without violating the prescribed feminine role. These skills were powerfully used in the abolitionist movement and in the growing feminist movement.

By the 1830s some women were openly challenging the "women's sphere" and demanding greater political, economic, and social rights for women. A feminist tract had been published in England in 1792—Mary Wollstonecraft's *Vindication of the Rights of Women*—but it had a limited appeal at that time. In 1838 the first American feminist argument appeared, Sarah Grimke's *Letters on the Equality of the Sexes*, followed by Margaret Fuller's *Woman in the Nineteenth Century*. These had greater popular success. Women who had been actively involved in various social reform activities had begun to chafe at their legal and political restrictions. Their attempts to improve society were often thwarted by their lack of political rights. Male domination of the public arena was no longer acceptable to many of these middle-class activist women. As they accomplished more in the public sphere, they wanted to do more still. This led them to demand greater freedom to participate legitimately in what had been defined as the male domain, especially politics. And the reformist activities of middle-class women eventually led many of them toward feminism.

Carl Degler points out that before 1900 the woman's suffrage movement argued that women should receive the vote because as individuals they couldn't be adequately or legitimately represented by their husband's votes.[34] This extension of individualism to women, especially in the public domain of politics, was too radical for the American public or political elite. After 1900 the movement began to emphasize a new ideology. Women deserved the vote, it was argued, not as individuals with rights but because they were different from men, more pure, less corrupt, and therefore would have a positive moral effect on political life.

It is a paradox that the attack on the Victorian conception of woman's place in many ways grew out of the Victorian image of womanhood. By firmly dividing the public from the private, by assigning men the public political roles and yet defining men as innately immoral, Victorian ideology laid the basis for the supposedly moral, domestic, female to demand the opportunity to exercise her moral influence to improve the public arena, which had been so sullied by immoral male control. Furthermore, by emphasizing the virtue of women and the immorality of men, the cult of true womanhood made women the only suitable associates of women. This helped to create a female solidarity, to strengthen ties between women, and to give women a consciousness of kind in opposition to men.

Beginning with the Seneca Falls Convention in 1848, American feminists held state and national conventions throughout the 1850s. Although their numbers were small, they worked diligently to improve women's legal position. They exposed many of the injustices women suffered but they did not achieve significant gains.

Feminism and Women's Suffrage After 1860

The Civil War in America drew many more women into public volunteer work in relief agencies and as nurses; a few became spies and soldiers. William O'Neill maintains that women's war efforts enhanced their self-image and expectations and further convinced women that they deserved the vote. It also gave feminists increased confidence that important changes could be achieved: If slavery could be abolished, so could gender discrimination. After the war, feminist activities increased. Women linked their demand for suffrage to the movement for enfranchising black males. They were rejected even by liberals in this, however. They were told not to interfere with the "Negro's hour." The black man's cause had to be fought and won before attention could be turned to the white or black women's cause. A great many feminists rejected this line of reasoning and lost support from most male liberals.

Another setback in public relations came when some spokeswomen, in particular Victoria Woodhull, linked the feminist cause with "free love" and the sexual revolution. The Victorian era was no period to raise issues of freeing human sexual expression, and the public and the government reacted vehemently. Although most feminists did not support free love, they were tainted by association and their demands for increased legal rights for married women, especially divorce, were suspect. The hostility to any perceived attack on Victorian sexual mores or on the Victorian idealization of the family was so great that feminists dropped most public discussion of changes in the patterns of family life as a matter of expediency.

The repressive social climate led feminists to concentrate on political and legal issues, the vote in particular, to the exclusion of other important women's issues. This meant they ceased to challenge the domestic roles of women and the organization of domestic life in general. The feminist movement became more conservative. Thus they left intact the domestic/public dichotomy, the cult of domesticity, and the ideal of femininity. Their strategy came to concentrate on using these ideals against male dominance: They argued for votes for women on the basis of women's greater virtue and morality.

Many suffragists were participants in more conservative "moral reform" politics as well, such as the Women's Christian Temperance Union (WCTU) and the "social purity" movement in the United States. In addition to its work for the prohibition of alcohol, the WCTU campaigned for stricter moral codes, rational dress for women, kindergartens in the public schools, child labor laws, police matrons for female prisoners, and the peace movement before the United States entered World War I. Women's participation in the WCTU was, furthermore, often a first step toward their involvement in feminism and woman's suffrage. As part of the "social purity" movement suffragists along with other men and women campaigned against prostitution and the sexual double standard that underlay it.

Feminism and the Labor Movement. The feminist movement never forged strong ties with the growing labor movement. Feminism was dominated by middle-class women who had little real appreciation of working-class women's lives. But some middle-class women as well as working-class women

were influential in the founding of the Women's Trade Union League in the United States in 1903, whose aim was to improve working conditions for women. In general, however, even working-class women were not involved in the union movement, primarily because they viewed their work as temporary. Young women planned to work only until they married, and married women expected to work only until a family economic crisis had passed. In addition, their work was often seasonal and unstable. Moreover, their domestic duties as both wives and daughters interfered with their commitment to their work roles and to the union cause. Women workers were, however, often actively involved in strikes. From 1900 to 1910 women were especially active in strikes and were part of some of labor history's most violent confrontations. An important barrier to women's greater participation in the labor movement was also the discriminatory practices of the unions themselves. Women workers often received more help from well-to-do women reformers than they did from the male-dominated, if not exclusively male, unions. Working women were not strong supporters of suffrage. They were more interested in pragmatic issues such as working conditions and job security and could not afford the leisure middle-class women had to devote to the vote and general political issues. They were also too desirous of what middle-class women had to worry about what might be lacking in such economically secure lives.

Other Issues. Organized feminism also never linked itself with the socialist movements among the working classes. The feminist rarely recognized the connections between class stratification and gender stratification even though they had presented analogies between black slavery and women's oppression. The division between working-class and middle-class women was further exacerbated by middle-class prejudice against immigrants. Working-class women not only were in a different economic situation but many of them were also foreign-born. Catholics who were seen as carrying a culture threatening to the Anglo-Saxon Protestant way of life.

Xenophobic fears of immigrants were also expressed by such groups as the WCTU in the late nineteenth and early twentieth centuries in their campaign against the sale of liquor. Drinking alcoholic beverages was a tradition among immigrant groups such as the Irish, the bar was an important social institution for Irishmen. But this represented something foreign and evil to Anglo-Saxons. The campaign for prohibition was therefore in many respects a campaign against immigrant cultural practices and perpetuated a view of working-class men as evil brutes who drank away their families' rent and food money and then went home to abuse their wives and children.

The tendency for most feminists to adhere to the Victorian image of womanhood as asexual also led the early feminists to reject the birth control movement. Since they saw no need to free women to have sexual experiences without the threat of pregnancy, they viewed birth control as a means to gratify male lusts. The dangers of childbirth and the burden of large families on women could be dealt with through abstinence. Women should be free to deny sexual access to their husbands.

The birth control movement was severely repressed by governmental authorities. Abortion, which had been legal until the sixth month of pregnancy under English common law, began to be prohibited by the states—except in life-threatening situations for the mother—after 1860. A high birthrate among the working class meant a large labor supply, and a large labor supply was clearly in the interests of the businessmen and industrialists who controlled the government. It allowed them to keep wages low and to resist worker demands because any one group of workers could be replaced from the large pool of unemployed workers eager for work. The dissemination of birth control information was illegal. Activists such as Emma Goldman who persisted in teaching working-class women about birth control were jailed.

The End of the Feminist Movement. Eventually, after a long and hard struggle that had included massive, sometimes violent, protests and the incarceration of many women, the battle for woman's suffrage was won with the passage of the Nineteenth Amendment in 1920. The vote did not, however, have the wide-ranging impact on women's status that the early feminists had predicted. Because so much attention had been focused on the suffrage issue for so many decades, the movement had lost sight of its original, more comprehensive, goals. The vote had become an end in itself. Furthermore, suffrage was gained in the midst of a conservative political climate. Reformist causes were not popular. Further gains by women in the political, economic, and social spheres were doomed to defeat.

Moreover, since the domestic role for women had not been openly challenged, it retained its hold on most women. Domesticity became even more attractive and popular in the postwar era. For example, the climate of opinion on sexuality had changed considerably by the 1920s. Married women were now allowed, even expected, to find sexual gratification in their marital relationships. In addition, Freudian psychoanalytic theory supported a new ideology of domesticity, which declared that healthy adult women found their meaning and satisfaction through the expression of their maternal instincts. Motherhood was again presented as the only "scientifically" valid role for women. Since the vote had not led to emancipation, this new explanation of the maternal role appealed to women who found themselves barred from other avenues of self-expression. The Victorian cult of domesticity was thus replaced by the Freudian cult of domesticity. The United States entered the modern world with votes for women but without female equality or an active feminist movement.

Reaction: 1920–1940

With the First World War over and woman's suffrage won, women's groups continued their commitment to social reform measures.[35] From 1920 until 1925 they were successful with several congressional bills. The women's vote was still an unknown quantity and the political parties feared it. Women's organizations fed these fears by assuring male politicians that women voters had more humane sensitivities than men and would vote as a bloc to support reform issues.

By 1925, however, it had become clear that the woman's bloc did not exist. Women presented no more unified front in politics than men did. Women were just as divided by class interests and other social divisions as the general population. In addition, women suffered the effects of generations of exclusion from politics. Most women were accustomed to leaving politics to men. Many continued to believe that women should not vote. It was not surprising therefore that women did not vote in as great numbers as men did. Furthermore, those who did vote tended to vote exactly as their husbands and fathers. One historian argues that "for fe-

males to vote at all required a substantial break from their conventional role. To ask that they oppose their husbands or fathers in the process entailed a commitment which only the most dedicated could sustain."[36]

Postwar Conservatism

With their fears of a powerful female voting bloc quelled, the political parties ignored the demands of women's groups. The postwar period was a reactionary political period. A fear of radicalism spread throughout the country. Women's reform groups were suspected of communist leanings. Some women's groups themselves turned right-wing, such as the Daughters of the American Revolution, and added to the hysteria over Bolshevism and anarchism. It was a disheartening period for the liberal, reform-minded women who had fought so hard in the woman's movement.

The vestiges of the woman's movement itself split in particular over the issue of an equal rights amendment and protective legislation. The social reformist segment of the woman's suffrage movement reorganized itself as the nonpartisan League of Women Voters to educate voters and support reform measures. They worked hard for protective legislation for women and children. They remained committed to the belief that women were the weaker gender, physically disadvantaged by motherhood, and therefore in need of special protection in the workplace. Therefore, they supported maximum hours and minimum pay legislation for women even though many employers then used such laws as excuses not to hire women.

The more militant segment of the woman's movement rejected these positions. They saw the vote as only a first step toward the legal equality and emancipation of women and argued that women had to continue to fight for complete equality. The militants rejected working through the existing party system and organized a third-party movement as the National Women's Party. They undertook a vigorous campaign in support of an equal rights amendment that would grant full legal equality to women and men and strike down legislation that discriminated on the basis of gender in any way. This position never gained a large following. Most other women's groups actively opposed it. In the conservative, antireform political climate of the time, this serious division of ranks contributed substantially to the collapse of the woman's movement.

Sexual Emancipation

In addition to these factors, the woman's movement had also lost the younger generation. Women no longer had to fight convention to attend college, join women's clubs, or vote. The woman's movement could no longer offer the spirit of adventure it had offered to previous generations. Instead of rebelling against social convention in the political arena, young women in the twenties rebelled in the social arena as flappers. Adventure came through wearing short skirts, rolled hose, makeup, and bobbed hair. It came through smoking, reading sexual novels, and dancing jazz. And it came through rejecting Victorian prudery over female sexual behavior.

The older generation of feminists could not tolerate this version of emancipation. They clung to Victorian standards of modesty and chastity and found themselves and their political movement rejected by these lightheaded young women caught up in private self-fulfillment and uninterested in political issues. Of course, only a minority of well-to-do or middle-class young women could even approximate the flapper image.

But it was an image that caught the imagination of the country, and single working-class women often spent what little extra time and money they had trying to be flappers.

William Chafe analyzes the impact of this sexual revolution and concludes that it did not undermine the gender stratification system:

Shifts in manners and morals did not interfere with the perpetuation of a sexual division of labor where women assumed responsibility for the home and men went out into the world to earn a livelihood. The nuances of a relationship might change, but the structure remained the same. A career, on the other hand, involved a drastic modification of woman's status and challenged the basic institutions of society. If women took jobs on the same basis as men, they would no longer be able to assume sole responsibility for the home.[37]

These social changes represented a degree of sexual emancipation without women's liberation. Moreover, the double standard of sexuality and morality continued to be reflected in the fact that although males were as involved in this revolution of manners and morals as females, public opinion placed the blame for what was perceived as social upheaval solely on women.

Economic Considerations

The sexually emancipated flapper was, furthermore, an image that supported the growing capitalistic emphasis on consumption. Business was booming. Advertisers encouraged people to buy, buy, buy. Advertising purposefully exploited the new sexuality in sales pitches and product imagery. Woman's economic role as consumer was expanding as the economy expanded.

Economic progress for women was highly touted in the twenties, but it was more apparent than real. Women, especially young single women, did enter the labor force in greater numbers. The increase was, however, due to population increase. Women did not increase the percentage of their representation of the labor force. Moreover, women's job opportunities remained gender segregated, dead end, low paid, temporary, and seasonal. In no way did women approach equality with men in the economic sphere. Female college students did increase in both numbers and proportion to males. Females also increased their representation in the professions. But again the increase came in female professions such as teaching, not in the more lucrative prestigious male professions. In fact, many medical and law schools, hospitals, and bar associations responded to women's entry into higher education by either setting very low quotas for females or barring their entry altogether. But despite discrimination, many educated women attempted to pursue careers. These new career women tried to reject the necessity of remaining single that the older generation of career women had accepted. To facilitate combining career and family, some tried to organize day-care centers and establish egalitarian marriages with their husbands.

Among the working class, unions focused almost exclusively on male workers and most of them actively discriminated against females. Women in the garment industry organized themselves as early as 1909, but this example of female labor militancy did not encourage the male-dominated unions to organize women in other trades or industries. Not only did unions refuse to organize women workers, they also refused to admit women when they organized themselves. The American Federation of Labor (AFL) was so disdainful of women workers that it refused even to issue separate gender-segregated charters to female workers analogous to the racially segregated charters it had given to black locals.

It is true that women were, in general, harder to organize than men. Their commitment to the feminine domestic role led them to view their work as a temporary interlude before marriage and childbearing. And women worked in the most marginal, temporary jobs, which were always hardest to organize because of the high turnover. Although these were sometimes advanced as reasons for the unions' recalcitrance on the issue of women's unionization, the primary reason was the feeling among union leaders and the male rank and file that women belonged in the home and that paid employment, especially the more remunerative jobs, should be reserved for men. The refusal of the unions to take up issues related to the needs of female workers was one reason women workers turned their attention to protective legislation and governmental help.

After 1935 the Congress of Industrial Organizations (CIO) undertook more massive organizing efforts aimed specifically at the harder-to-unionize sectors of the labor force. They included women in these drives. Although they sought female members, they did not treat them equally. Labor contracts with separate pay scales and separate seniority lists for females were ratified. The unions helped to protect male members from competition from female workers. Female members paid the same dues but did not receive the same protection from their unions. The union movement continued to incorporate and support the traditional gender stratification system.

The Crisis of Masculinity

Peter Filene argues that the twenties was a difficult period for males. The definition of masculinity in the modern context was unclear. Work was no longer rugged or individualistic. Bureaucratic or assembly line routine was coming to characterize many men's work lives. Filene suggests that the surge in popularity of spectator sports during the twenties reflected the crisis in masculinity. Men were searching for vicarious experiences of masculinity which they no longer experienced in their own lives. This also accounts for the hero worship of Charles Lindbergh after his solo flight across the Atlantic in 1927. Lindbergh embodied the virtues of rugged individualism at a time when few men could aspire to them.

The crisis of masculinity was also manifest in the widespread fear in the twenties that the family was disintegrating because women were supposedly abdicating their domestic role. "The stereotype of a man's home as his castle was competing in the 1920s with the modern image of the family as a partnership."[38] Married women were trying to improve their position relative to their husbands by idealizing the marriage bond and extending sexual fidelity and mutual devotion to men. This undermined the traditional patriarchal authority of the husband/father, who was now expected to be friend and companion to his wife and children. Such intimacy made the image of power more difficult to manage, leaving many men fearing for their manliness.

The Depression

But if modern bureaucratic work and more egalitarian family structures threatened and confused men concerning their gender identities, long-term unemployment in the thirties was even more devastating. The breadwinner role was cut from under a great many men and those with jobs could not be sure they would be able to keep them.[39]

The Depression beginning in 1929 reversed many of the economic and social gains women had fought so hard to obtain in previous decades. It was the death knell to the remnants of the woman's movement, the flapper, the sexual revolution, and experimentation with new forms of domestic organization. Massive unemployment put both women's issues and privatized self-fulfillment in the background.

Feminist arguments in favor of economic equality for women were based on the assumption that both men and women would be integrated into the economy. They had not considered the possibility of one-third of the male labor force being unemployed. Women's position as a reserve labor force was made especially clear during these hard times. In this period of tremendous labor surplus, women were the first fired. The federal, state and local governments passed laws forbidding the employment of married women if their husbands had jobs. Thousands of women were dismissed, including many who were without employed spouses or whose husbands soon became unemployed. The fears, anxieties, and hostilities generated by the Depression were focused in part on the woman worker. Traditional gender roles and gender stratification were clearly reflected in the popular argument that no women should be allowed to hold a job as long as there were men who needed jobs. These arguments were even advanced against women in jobs for which few men had the necessary training or skills, such as stenographers and typists. In times of crisis the powerless are often the scapegoats; women workers served this function during the thirties.[40]

Moreover, hostility against female workers came from women as well as men. Wives of unemployed males could be as vicious as the men in their attacks on working women. The acceptance of the gender stratification system and its supporting ideology was widespread among both genders. Attempts to expand women's economic opportunities and rights were halted, as were programs designed to ease the burdens of the woman worker's dual role at home and at work. Many wives did take jobs, however, after their husbands' long-term unemployment made it impossible to practice the male-as-breadwinner, female-as-dependent gender roles. This role reversal was very hard for men. The support role was too firmly ingrained in their identities for them to accept easily an economically dependent position in the family. Many swallowed their pride and made the best of the inevitable. Others, however, committed suicide, and large numbers deserted their families in humiliation and joined the ranks of the wandering tramps and hoboes.

Paradoxically, this period of ideological setback gave rise to labor codes and minimum wages that benefitted female workers in lower level jobs.[41] It was also a period of expansion of women's political participation in high levels of government. Under the advice and guidance of his wife, Eleanor, President Franklin Roosevelt actively incorporated women into his administration and into the administrative ranks of his New Deal programs. A women was appointed to the cabinet, as a foreign minister, and to a federal judgeship, and numerous women served in high-level positions in the Works Projects Administration. These high-level political appointments did not, however, herald significant advances in women's legal rights or overall social, economic, or political position. The female appointees were dependent on Roosevelt for their political power. They did not move to the top on the basis of their own constituencies or because of their support for women's issues. Rather, these women represented the old feminine humanitarian social reform tradition. The

New Deal needed people with these kind of beliefs and interests. The appointments represented an advance for social reformist politics but not for feminism. We see evidence of the New Deal's lack of commitment to women's issues in the fact that its National Labor Relations Board allowed for discrimination against women workers in hiring, promotions, and pay.

The New Sexual Repression

The overall effect of the Depression and the decade of the thirties on gender roles and gender stratification was retrenchment and retrogression. Women's gains had been dependent on male prosperity. When men's economic roles were threatened, women's demands were considered trivial at best and dangerous or unpatriotic at worst. By the end of the thirties, the impact of the twenties could no longer be detected. Women preferred not to work. The majority voiced their preference for the full-time domestic role with husbands in full-time breadwinner roles. Skirts were longer, bobbed hair was replaced by long curls, virginity was expected of all "good girls." There were no more experiments in day-care facilities, communal kitchens, or egalitarian marriage. The woman's movement had been forgotten. The vocabulary associated with it even disappeared from the language.

The discipline of psychology and Freudian psychoanalysis in particular expanded its influence and popularity in the thirties and forties. Freud's followers elaborated on his tentative beginnings to develop a full-fledged psychology of women. These theories placed women in the domestic role and declared that any woman who was not satisfied as a housewife and mother suffered from emotional or mental illness. Psychoanalysis thereby provided a scientific basis for the "feminine mystique." According to its practitioners, women should be sexually passive but not frigid. They were to experience orgasm only through the vagina, not the clitoris, which is the true physiological base of sexual response in females. They were to fulfill themselves primarily through motherhood. Mary Ryan argues that from the thirties through the fifties Freudian psychoanalysis helped bring us back almost full circle in terms of the female stereotype and gender role. "Women were directed right back to where they were a century earlier, in the captivity of the cult of motherhood."[42] The only real change from the nineteenth-century cult of domesticity was the addition of sexual attractiveness: Women were directed to maintain their physical attractiveness to better satisfy their husbands' sexual needs. Thus, some of the sexual repressiveness of the earlier era was avoided, but the recognition of sexual needs was still not extended fully to women. Women were to achieve satisfaction through satisfying their husbands.

The Black Family

During the twenties most black Americans lived in stable families in the rural South. Contrary to Daniel Moynihan's thesis that slavery permanently undermined the black family, created pathological matriarchal family structures, and emasculated black males, the black family was quite strong and followed the accepted pattern of male authority and dominance. Poor black women, like poor white women, were more likely to work than were their better-off counterparts. The rural tenant farming situation required the labor of all family members. This created an interdependence of the genders that kept women from being the economic dependents of men and therefore undercut male dominance to a degree, but not in an emasculating manner.[43]

Middle-class black women were as involved in charitable volunteer work as their white counterparts, and the postsuffrage era was as disorganizing for black clubwomen as it was for white clubwomen. The new ideal of femininity and domesticity was accepted by blacks as well as whites.

The Depression hit black people harder than whites. Like the female labor force, black workers constituted a reserve labor force, and they were among the first to lose their jobs when the crash came in 1929. Furthermore, they were less likely to receive charitable or governmental aid than were unemployed whites. One response to the collapse of the economy was massive migration of black people from the rural South to urban areas in the Northeast, Midwest, and West.

Urbanization and massive unemployment and poverty had a disrupting effect on the black family. One-parent households grew in number, throwing primary responsibility for the support of the family on the poor black women. The situation hardly created a matriarchy, but it did cause a lessening of male influence within many poor urban black households. Women came to depend more on one another, on their mothers and sisters in particular, for support networks. Men were often viewed with suspicion or as potential drains on an already precarious household budget. Welfare policies when they were instituted, denied aid to women and children with a male living in the household and exacerbated this situation. An unemployed father often felt compelled to desert his family so they would be eligible for welfare. Black women, however, faced even greater discrimination in the economic sphere than black men. They faced the barriers of both gender and race discrimination.

This required them to develop strong self-reliant personalities to withstand the powerful forces against them.

New Jobs, Old Attitudes: 1940–1960

World War II

World War II brought the Depression to an end, recreated strong masculine roles for men in the military, and greatly increased employment opportunities for black and white men and women. The reserve labor force was fully called upon. The ideology of woman's place being in the home was temporarily replaced by patriotic appeals to women to enter the labor force and take "man-sized jobs" in support of freedom, democracy, and the American way. Domestic considerations were not to be allowed to prevent women from heeding their country's call—and the call was answered.

Women entered the labor force as never before. Young single women were no longer the only female workers. This group was not large enough to meet the needs of the wartime economy. Business and industry, long accustomed to discriminating against married women, resisted hiring married or older women during the first few months of the crisis. But the attack on Pearl Harbor deepened the crisis and more fully involved the United States in the war, taking more men out of the civilian labor force and increasing the level of economic production and the size of the necessary labor force. In the face of these pressures, business and government turned to this last remaining reserve labor force. Women who were already working left the low-paying "feminine" occupational sector for "masculine" jobs in heavy industry, and women who had never worked before entered the labor force by the thousands. With their entry into male jobs, women's pay almost doubled and the unionization of women proceeded quickly. "Rosie the Riveter" became a national heroine.

Women also entered the armed forces in noncombatant roles in large numbers. The idea of the female soldier met with ridicule at first, but these women served their country so admirably that the women's auxiliaries became acceptable though not prestigious. It still compromised a woman's reputation to serve in the military, especially if she was not an officer. (Nurses composed the bulk of the officer ranks.) Soldiering was too independent a role, too masculine, too far from the domestic context to be entirely acceptable for women even during a national crisis. And the female soldier was not treated equally with male soldiers. Entry requirements were higher, pay was lower, promotions were more difficult to obtain, training programs were more limited, and benefits were fewer. Furthermore, women soldiers' duties were usually limited to the traditional feminine spheres of office and clerical work, nursing, and menial labor.

Public attitudes appeared to change during the war years. Opinion polls found a widespread acceptance of the woman worker, whereas the majority of the population had rejected her during the thirties. But this tremendous change in the experiences of women, which came with their full-time participation in paid labor and the widespread public acceptance of work for middle-class as well as working-class women, was not associated with any real shift in gender role ideology. The cult of domesticity and the idealization of the family continued to be primary American values. Women could work to serve their country but not to serve individual needs and not because they had any right to a job.

These feelings were manifested in the un-willingness of business and government to provide adequate child-care facilities for working mothers. The women's labor was needed, but mothers had to find individual solutions to the problem of care for small children. Most depended on friends and relatives. Some children received grossly inadequate care, chained to mobile homes or locked in cars in factory parking lots. Despite the desperate needs for child-care services, the idea met strong opposition. Day care violated American ideals of family life, even if reality did not match those ideals. If children should be raised in the home, alternative institutions implied an acceptance of real change in woman's role. Thus the federal government undertook only a limited program of day-care centers, which never served more than one-tenth of the children who needed them, and quickly abandoned the program at the war's end.

The Postwar Years: 1945–1959

This continued acceptance of traditional gender roles was also revealed in the emphasis on the male breadwinner role when the war ended. Demobilization brought thousands of soldiers back into civilian life in search of civilian jobs. It also meant the widespread closing of munitions plants and other war-related industries. Rosie the Riveter lost her job. Women who had so quickly moved into "man-sized" jobs found out what it meant to be a member of a reserve labor force again. Although many of these wartime women workers wanted to keep their jobs, they were quickly removed from them. Female unemployment rose dramatically with demobilization. But it did not remain high. The wartime economy was rapidly transformed to a peacetime economy and the production of consumer goods, long delayed by the war, boomed. Women were

brought back into the labor force in large numbers, but this did not indicate the coming of equality for the female worker. The massive firings eliminated women from the masculine jobs, and women's work after the war was almost entirely within the feminine sector. A dual labor market reemerged in which males were recruited into the higher-paying, more secure, and more prestigious jobs. Women were left with the positions males rejected.

Despite these increases in the labor force participation of women, there was a clear decline in the overall economic status of women relative to men in the forties and fifties.[44] Except for the feminine occupational sectors such as clerical, sales, and service work female participation declined relative to men's. The absolute numbers of women in the professional and technical fields increased, but these sectors expanded dramatically and men gained much more than women. Furthermore, women professionals were concentrated in the feminine professions of teaching, nursing, and social work, which are not comparable in pay or prestige to the male-dominated professions. Women also did not increase their incomes relative to men. In all occupational spheres women continued to earn a fraction of what comparably educated and employed men earned. Moreover, women declined in educational achievement relative to men. They moved from overall educational attainments higher than men's in 1940 to slightly less than men's in the early sixties. Higher education was now often pursued by young women to enable them to find better husbands and to make them better wives and mothers. Career goals were often absent or secondary as motivations for college. This is reflected in the higher dropout rate for college women as compared with college men.

Furthermore, the justification and motivation for female labor force participation during these years supported traditional gender roles. Women still could not legitimately work for individualistic reasons. They worked for their families. Inflation was a major problem in the postwar years. Middle- and working-class families could not support themselves under the new standards of consumerism without a second income. World War II had set the precedent for married women's employment without any feminist justification. The postwar period merely changed the rationale from patriotic to domestic needs. This justification for women's work also allowed for high levels of female economic participation without ideological change or feminist consciousness. The theory that women worked only for "pin money" or luxuries was widely accepted. This denied the reality that many women worked to support themselves, to support families, or because their husbands' incomes were too low to provide for basic necessities. The "pin money" theory obscured the breadwinner role forced upon a significant number of American women.

The New Domesticity. The cult of domesticity was carried to extremes again in the fifties as it had been during the Victorian era. The postwar baby boom is reflective of this. Couples had more children more closely spaced than had occurred for over a century. Child rearing theories such as found in Dr. Benjamin Spock's best selling manual directed the mother to devote almost full attention to the care and socialization of her children.[45] This socialization included clearcut gender role divisions. Little girls were to be directed toward femininity and little boys toward masculinity from the earliest age. Parents were advised to present the appropriate masculine and feminine role models to their children in their own behavior.

In addition to motherhood, the new cult of domesticity also directed women to devote themselves to furthering their husbands' careers. They were to provide the important backup services such as entertaining business associates and joining the right clubs to maintain the right image and the right contacts for his business interests. Women were still provided few legitimate outlets for the development of their interests. They were to live vicariously through the achievements first of their husbands and later of their children, especially their sons.

This revised version of the cult of domesticity had the further effect of placing women in competition with each other in the marriage market. Winning and keeping a mate was a pre-eminent concern for women in the forties and fifties. These years saw the spread of a new stage of human development, devoted to perfecting the arts of heterosexual attraction and couple formation— the teenager. The teenage girl, in particular, was expected to devote herself to the pursuit of heterosexual popularity without giving in to the male's sexual advances. Movie stars were the important role models and the female stars clearly portrayed this new ideal of femininity. These stereotypes and gender roles took firm hold on the youth of the fifties and early sixties.

The Masculine Role. Filene argues that the postwar cult of domesticity had a double edge.[46] It affected men and masculinity as well as women and femininity. Men were also saddled with the responsibility for family "togetherness." The authoritarian male family role was outdated, especially among the middle class. Father was to be a part of the family team. This coincided with the increased emphasis on teamwork in the bureaucratic work setting. The successful worker was the one who could get along with others. Dale Carnegie's courses on "how to win friends and influence people" were symptomatic of the age. Definitions of masculinity were vague. The middle-class man could not be sure what was expected of him as a man. Strong male roles had been undercut by the cult of domesticity and the cult of teamwork.

Most men tried to judge themselves in terms of economic success. Masculinity came to be measured by the size of the paycheck. But the combined forces of inflation and consumerism meant that men could never earn "enough." In addition, the more time they devoted to economic goals, the less time they had for togetherness with the family. Either way their wives were unhappy. Men were in a no-win situation.[47]

The New Feminism: 1960–1979

Radicalism and the Feminist Revival

The development of the new feminism was part of a much larger movement of generational politics that emerged during the early and mid-1960s.[48] The new generation was rejecting the values their parents had striven so hard for: values related to achievement, material success, political conservatism, acceptance of authority, and eventually ideals of family life and woman's place.

The new radicalism began with the sit-in movement conducted by black college students against racial segregation in the South. Many white college students went south to join in this movement and discovered that American democracy as described in their high school civics texts did not exist. After returning to their northern and western campuses, they cast a critical eye on other aspects of their society. In addition to civil rights and racism, they found the issue of the Vietnam war and the imperialistic involvements of what they had previously believed to be a humanitarian and generous

United States government. Thousands of middle-class college students, male and female, protested against the society that had given them so much. They were not the underprivileged. They came from the best homes and best schools and had the most promising futures. Yet they were attacking these same homes, schools, and futures and demanding a more just, more egalitarian society that benefited everyone, not just themselves.

Women in the New Left. The issue of gender roles and gender stratification was not a part of the early years of the New Left and the youth movement. Women were very active in the movement. Many were beaten and many were arrested, but few found themselves in leadership roles. Their socialization to be submissive and compliant, to defer to male authority and to work in background roles kept them from competing for the limelight with their self-confident, assertive male counterparts who disdained females in leadership positions. Although these young people rejected so much of what their parents' generation held dear, they were following their examples quite clearly in the area of gender stratification. Men were the leaders who dominated the movement; women made the coffee, typed the pamphlets, and ran the mimeograph machines. Female roles were clearly secondary and subservient.

By 1964, however, movement women were comparing their positions, both in society and in the movement, with the position of blacks in white society. Their critical eye was turned on gender roles and they did not like what they saw. Men, however, refused to acknowledge the legitimacy of their analyses of sexism. Women found little sympathetic support among the New Left men who embraced sexual emancipation for women but rejected liberation for women in other areas.

The sexual revolution was a boon for males, giving them sexual access to women without commitment or responsibility. Women's liberation, however, threatened the radical male's privileged position in the gender hierarchy, and the radicals opposed it as vehemently as their more conservative brothers. When the women of the Student Nonviolent Coordinating Committee (SNCC) argued in 1964 for female equality within this activist civil rights organization, their leader Stokely Carmichael replied that the position of women in SNCC was "prone." Women of the Students for a Democratic Society (SDS) met similar hostilities in 1965 when they attempted to present feminist issues and demands at the national conference. By 1967 women were withdrawing from many of the male-dominated radical organizations to organize separate women's groups. In 1968 they held their first national gatherings. Their experiences in the youth movement had led them to disavow formal structure and leadership. Instead they worked through local small groups without any permanent leaders. They had also come to distrust traditional political activity and eschewed working through the system. Therefore, they turned to political education and service projects aimed at building feminist consciousness and self-help networks.

Feminist Tactics. One of the tactics supported by these radical women were the rap groups with their consciousness-raising sessions. Groups of women would come together to discuss their personal experiences with sexism and discrimination. These sessions were effective in building a feminist consciousness, resocializing women to see themselves and the world differently, and changing attitudes. But as effective as they were at the psychological level, they were ineffective beyond that. They provided no structure for action. Therefore, many came to an end or degenerated into bitch sessions. By 1971 they were obsolete. Media attention to the movement and publications by feminist writers had turned women's liberation into a household word. Women discussed the issues with each other spontaneously without needing any groups to organize them. Feminism had become a powerful force in the United States again.

Another important tactic used by the young feminists was the exclusion of men from their groups. In the early stages sympathetic men were allowed to participate in the feminist groups, but it soon became apparent that men always dominated the discussions. Gender role socialization was sufficiently effective that the women deferred to men even in these settings. Men were accustomed to filling leadership roles and asserting themselves while women were not. To solve this problem, the feminists followed the example of black liberation groups which excluded whites: They excluded men. They found that the women could be more open with each other and participate more fully when men were not present.

Women also refused to be interviewed by any male reporters and most female reporters as well. The policy of excluding reporters grew out of the consistently negative experiences these groups had with the media. Women's liberation was treated with ridicule by radical, liberal, and conservative media. Their attempts to discuss the relevant issues were not reported. Instead supposed incidents such as bra burnings (which never occurred) dominated media coverage. Female reporters were often as unsympathetic and lacking in undertanding of the movement as the males. The women therefore refused interviews. This in turn intrigued the reporters. Social movement participants were supposed to seek media attention, not reject it. This led the journalists to begin investigating the movement and studying its issues more thoroughly. One result was better media coverage. Another was the conversion of many female reporters to feminism. Some of them filed suits against their own employers after filing their stories on the movement.

In the fall of 1969 an incredible media blitz occurred. The movement was given extensive coverage by all the major news magazines and networks. This served to introduce the issues to large numbers of men and women who had not previously taken the movement seriously.

The radical groups also used the guerilla theater techniques of the antiwar movement. They often staged bizarre events to dramatize their points. For example, in 1968 and 1969 demonstrations at the Miss America pageant included throwing (but not burning) bras, girdles, and false eyelashes into trash cans to illustrate their rejection of the feminine role of sex object for males and the cult of beauty. They also crowned a sheep Miss America in their alternative pageant.

Radical women's groups have also been important in organizing the women's health movement, aimed at giving women more control over their bodies and helping them to resist authoritarian and sexist practices by physicians. This has involved efforts to teach women about their bodies, reproduction, and contraception and how to examine and care for themselves without the intervention of the medical profession.[49] They have supported the establishment of local abortion clinics, family-planning services, women's health collectives, and more sensitive practices in the delivery rooms of hospitals.

Through their local groups, friendship networks, consciousness-raising techniques, and service projects, the radical women of the women's liberation movement created strong grass roots support for feminist issues and ideas. Their lack of formal structure and national organization, however, kept them from effecting change in the wider political and economic arenas. For such change, the new feminist movement had to rely on the more traditional organizations founded by upper-middle-class career women.

Middle-Class Liberal Women and Feminism

While the young radicals were organizing into small group such as the Redstockings and Witch, older, more conservative middle-class career women were also turning to feminism. In 1961 President Kennedy appointed the President's Commission on the Status of Women. This brought together politically active women from around the country to gather the facts about women's position in American society. The Commission created an important communications network among receptive women that provided facts documenting the extensive discrimination experienced by American women. This was an important catalyst for developing a woman's movement.

In 1963 Betty Friedan published her best seller *The Feminine Mystique,* which analyzed the quiet desperation of middle-class women living out the cult of domesticity.[50] This touched a responsive chord among many white, well-to-do women. This was followed in 1964 by a further impetus to movement organization. Congress amended Title VII of the 1964 Civil Rights Act to include sex along with race, religion, and national origins in its prohibitions against discrimination in employment. The amendment was presented as a joke by conservative Southern representatives who hoped to ridicule the bill and thereby defeat it. The bill passed, however with "sex" in its text, and feminist congresswomen and other feminists took it seriously. However, the Equal Employment Opportunities Commission (EEOC), which was to enforce the bill, refused to pursue cases related to gender discrimination. Betty Friedan and a number of women employed by the federal government were sufficiently incensed that they founded the National Organization for Women (NOW) in 1966 to serve as a pressure group on the EEOC for consideration of women's rights. These well-educated professionally employed women were the most likely to feel relative deprivation. They could see that their education and work skills didn't pay off as well as their brothers', husbands', or male classmates'.

Like the old woman's suffrage association, NOW concentrated on political and legal issues. It emphasized the importance of career opportunities for women to free them from the stultifying effects of the housewife role.[51] Within the context of advanced industrial society women come to demand that the pursuit of individualism be extended to them as well as to men. Women were finally demanding the right to work for individualistic instead of familistic reasons. According to Chafe, a historian of the feminist movement, "Ultimately . . . the feminists traced the 'women's problem' to the fact that females were denied the same opportunity as men to develop an identity of their own."[52]

In pursuing women's right to individual self-development through a career, NOW focused discontent on the EEOC's and the Justice Department's refusal to pursue gender-discrimination cases. They eventually persuaded President Johnson to amend Executive Order 11246 to prohibit gender discrimination in employment by holders of federal contracts. This involved them in battle with the Office of Federal Contract Compliance (OFCC) to get this order enforced. In 1968 two lawyers broke with NOW and established Human Rights for Women as a tax-exempt corporation to research and defend gender-discrimination cases.

NOW demonstrated the potential power of the new woman's movement by calling for a national strike on August 26, 1970, in commemoration of the Nineteenth Amendment giving women the vote. There were fears that embarrassingly small numbers would participate, but the opposite occurred. The strike was supported by feminist groups of all persuasions all over the country. Thousands of women in cities across the nation came out in support of equal job opportunities for women, abortion on demand, and twenty-four-hour child-care centers. The strike also served to expand NOW's membership. Housewives and middle- and lower-class women outside the professions joined in large numbers. So did an increased number of radical women, resulting in a great deal of overlapping memberships among different feminist groups greatly facilitating cooperation and coordination of activities.

The Equal Rights Amendment. NOW also supported the Equal Rights Amendment. The amendment had been brought before Congress in 1923 by the National Women's Party, which was still actively lobbying for its passage. The unions opposed the ERA and NOW lost its offices and clerical staff, which had been provided by the United Auto Workers (UAW). The UAW and later the AFL-CIO reversed themselves on this issue after Title VII destroyed the basis of the "protective legislation" that had been hindering women's economic participation for many years. The unions no longer had to fear that the ERA would hurt women's special privileges.

The ERA was finally voted out of Congress in 1972 after a long, hard lobbying effort in the Senate. The proposed constitutional amendment reads, "Equality of rights under the law shall not be denied or abridged by the United States or by any State on account of sex." No real opposition existed at first, except for a weak organization of right-wing groups such as the John Birch Society and the National Council of Catholic Women. The ERA was ratified quickly by twenty-eight states. But the tide was halted by 1973 with the organization of a well-financed "Stop ERA" campaign led by Phyllis Schlafly, backed by right-wing organizations and conservative business interests. By 1979 thirty-five of the necessary thirty-eight states had ratified ERA and some of those tried to rescind their passage. The original seven-year deadline for ratification set by Congress would have run out in March 1979, but against strong opposition, Congress voted to extend the deadline. But the remaining states were all conservative southern and western states which successfully resisted pressures such as the boycott of their cities as convention centers. The amendment failed to pass. It was introduced into Congress again but did not receive enough votes to be sent to the states for ratification.

Other Issues. NOW's support for abortion on demand lost it the support of its more conservative members, who founded the Women's Equity Action League (WEAL) in 1968 to pursue issues related to legal and economic rights, especially in the areas of education and employment. WEAL itself, however, gradually radicalized and has supported lawsuits on a variety of women's issues, especially those related to higher education. For example, they used the executive order for federal contract holders to file class action suits against hundreds of American colleges and universities for discrimination in admissions, granting of financial aid, hiring, and promotions. At first the Department of Labor moved very slowly on enforcing this executive order, hoping the support for it would die out. But the issue

found ready support among female students and faculty across the country, who kept the issue alive. The departments of Labor and of Health, Education and Welfare were forced to act. This resulted in a large number of legal cases and in the requirement that institutions of higher education file affirmative action plans indicating how they planned to remedy the effects of past discrimination against females.

NOW also supported federally financed child-care centers, and child-care legislation was passed in 1971. President Nixon vetoed it with a call for support for the traditional family structure and the cult of domesticity. NOW has also researched, documented, and attacked gender role stereotyping in children's books and textbooks and in elementary and secondary education. NOW has attempted to persuade television advertisers and programmers to rid the medium of sexist images and gender role stereotypes. The campaigns have been effective in some cases but have failed in many others. NOW and WEAL have pushed successfully for reform in credit and banking practices that discriminate against women. They have met with limited success in equalizing women's opportunities to participate in sports. They have also supported divorce reform, which in many cases benefits men by removing the gender role assumptions that mothers should automatically receive custody of the children and the father should provide alimony and child support.

By 1970 feminist groups were mushrooming. The National Women's Political Caucus was formed in 1971 to increase the number of women in elective and appointive public office. *Ms.*, a profit-making slick magazine devoted to feminist issues, was founded in 1972, and met with immediate financial success. *Ms.* also created a nonprofit tax-exempt wing, the Women's Action Alliance, to serve as an information clearinghouse on women's issues and organizations. Professional women, academic women, black women, and labor union women have also organized feminist groups and women's support networks.

Feminist church groups were founded, and one of the important issues of the seventies was the demand for the ordination of females in the clergy. The Catholic church hierarchy has firmly refused, but the Episcopal church admitted females into the clergy and has subsequently suffered substantial defections from antifeminists in the church.

Black Women and Feminism

The response of black women to feminism in the sixties was largely negative.[53] They perceived the problems of racism as being a greater burden than the problems of sexism. Much of the analysis of sexism put forth by middle-class white women did not sound negative at all. Being isolated in the home, economically dependent on a man, and unable to work sounded like progress to poor women who could not afford to stay home, who could not rely on a man for support, and who worked in low-paid menial jobs. Diane Lewis argues that at this time the gap between black women and white women was larger than the gap between black women and black men.[54] By the late seventies, however, the earnings gap between well-educated black and white women had nearly closed.[55]

Furthermore, the influential black liberation movement in the sixties enphasized the need to reconstruct the damaged black male psyche and supported values associated with male dominance and patriarchy. Black men have often been particularly hostile to women's liberation.[56] Increased interest in cultural practices from Africa and in the Muslim religion also contributed to the

movement's call for women to step back and support their men. Black women accepted this because they perceived their interests as being closer to black men's than to white women's. However, the successes of the black liberation movement changed this. The white male power structure adopted policies that benefited black males more than black females. Consequently, the gap between black males and black females widened while the gap between black females and white females narrowed. This is true in earnings, education, job opportunities, and political participation.[57]

As the feminist ideology gained more adherents in the white community and as it received more public attention, black women were provided with an additional explanation—additional to racism—for their continued difficulties in the public sphere. By 1972 opinion poll data indicated that black women had become more responsive than white women to women's issues and feminist ideas.[58] By 1973 black women were organizing and joining black feminist organizations such as Black Women Organized for Action and the National Black Feminist Organization. Moreover, this interest in women's liberation cut across class lines. Whereas feminist ideas appealed primarily to middle-class women among whites, both middle-class and working-class black women responded favorably. Lower-class black women were also active in the Welfare Mothers Movement, demanding more humane treatment from welfare agencies, more child-care facilities, and better job opportunities to help them get off welfare.[59]

Feminism and the Social Context of the Sixties and Seventies

The social circumstances in the United States in the mid-1960s facilitated the rise and spread of both the liberal and radical wings of the women's liberation movement. As Chafe notes, feminism had historically found its most fertile soil in periods of generalized social reform.[60] This was an era of concern for social problems and for disadvantaged groups. Then too, real changes that had occurred in the lives of many women made them responsive to feminist ideology. The increased participation of women in the economic sphere had brought them out of the home and freed many from their isolation in the domestic sphere. The domestic/public dichotomy had not been destroyed: Private life in the domestic context remained firmly separated from the public sphere, but many women now participated in both spheres. Paid employment in particular provided them with new experiences similar to those of men. The differences lessened between the lives of men and women. Women obtained the opportunity to develop the skills of the public sphere, such as leadership, public speaking, and organizational expertise. The work situation also put many women in day-to-day contact with other women. With a feminist ideology available, they were encouraged to share their experiences with sexism and discrimination. This facilitated the development of female solidarity as a basis for women making greater demands on the male-dominated institutions. If women had remained as firmly tied to the domestic role as many feminists described them, women would not have responded to the feminist call. The most isolated, most subordinated, most oppressed women are the least likely to join a social movement and press for changes in their position. One effect of extreme oppression is to destroy any feeling of personal efficacy in working for change. The increased freedom of women to work, to pursue an education, to move freely through much of the social world, and to meet and organize with other women provided an important, if not essential, base for the women's liberation movement to develop and grow.

The Backlash and the 1980s

The growth and spread of feminism in the late sixties and seventies does not mean that women have achieved equality. Despite these massive efforts in attitude change, cultural change, and change in the political, legal, and economic structures of our society, women are still in an inferior position relative to men. The situation may well deteriorate rather than improve. Historically, the progress of disadvantaged groups has been most active in periods of economic expansion and has been halted or reversed in periods of economic decline. The periods of recession, high unemployment, and inflation in the seventies and early eighties fed the conservative backlash against the women's movement. Conditions improved in the middle eighties, but in the midst of persistent uncertainty concerning the future of both the domestic and international economies.

Gains in the area of abortion rights have met with serious challenges. The Supreme Court struck down antiabortion laws in 1973. Since then the right to life movement has worked to make state governments pass restrictive legislation and to make Congress and the states refuse Medicaid payments for poor women who received abortions. The right to life movement has a large and powerful following. It has mounted massive campaigns against the reelection of senators and congresspersons who support women's right to abortions. Abortion clinics have been driven out of many communities through legal technicalities and some have been bombed or burned.

The backlash was also clear in the Bakke case against "reverse discrimination." The Supreme Court ruled in 1978 in favor of a white male who was denied admission to a University of California medical school because some slots were held open for minority group members. This threw into question the legality of many of the affirmative action plans undertaken by universities and private industry to upgrade minority group representation, including that of women. But the Supreme Court ruled in 1979 in the Weber case that affirmative action quotas set by private industry to aid minority groups are legal. By the mid-eighties, however, the administration in Washington had publicly expressed reluctance to pursue affirmative action goals.

The backlash can also be seen in the scientific and academic community. The growth of the field of sociobiology is an example. One of its assumptions is the biological basis of our traditional gender roles and of male dominance. This assumption is used to challenge the feasibility of any programs of change in the gender stratification system.

The women's movement also gave rise to its opposite—the Total Woman Movement and Fascinating Womanhood. The movements began in 1971 and spread nationwide by 1975, although support or at least media attention later waned. Founders Mirabel Morgan and Helen Andelin supported a return to idealized femininity complete with feigning ignorance, being submissive to husbands, and achieving one's goals through the manipulation of men.[61] The Total Woman Movement placed emphasis on sexual attractiveness, while Fascinating Womanhood leaned toward biblical supports of patriarchy and female subordination and emphasized woman's moral role in society. Over 400,000 women paid from $15 to $30 to participate in short courses designed to teach them to be more feminine and more submissive to their husbands.

These "idealized femininity" movements and continued antifeminist sentiment and activity among many women may well be the result of women's subordination in society. Women whose social recognition and economic security have been linked to the full-time mother and homemaker roles have generally not had the opportunity to develop the skills to compete in the man's world. Some women overcome these limitations, but others do not. They have structured their lives around expectations of economic support from men. Movements that undermine traditional gender roles can be threatening to these women, who want their husbands to remain morally and legally committed to supporting them and their children. Not only have many women been socialized to accept the traditional feminine roles, but for many women their current economic situation provides strong vested interests in maintaining those gender roles and resisting efforts toward change. The prospects of perhaps having to make one's own way in the world are, of course, rendered doubly threatening to such women in a society where economic opportunity is restricted by gender discrimination and institutional and cultural sexism. Finally—despite the liberalized images one may draw from contemporary surveys of changing social attitudes—women still do not enjoy the cultural and moral "freedom" that society tacitly concedes to men to abandon the responsibility for raising their children on the dissolution of marriage.

Economic insecurities of this type reveal themselves in struggles for "cultural hegemony" at the level of public politics. Where competing material bases of personal identity and self-esteem are at stake, different classes of women (and their mates) cannot be indifferent to the question of *whose* values dominate society. Kristen Luker, for instance, in her sensitive study of prochoice and antiabortion activists, reveals how the political struggle over abortion is simultaneously a struggle over the social meaning of motherhood among women whose life chances are rooted in different class locations.[62] This struggle in turn can lead to very different perspectives, even on the fundamental meaning of sexuality, between the types of activists:

> Pro-life women . . . have both value orientations and social characteristics that make marriage very important. Their alternatives in the public world of work are, on the whole, less attractive. Furthermore, women who stay home full time and keep house are becoming a financial luxury. Only very wealthy families *or families whose values allow them to place the nontangible benefits of a full-time wife over the tangible benefits of a working wife* can afford to keep one of its earners off the labor market. To pro-life people, the nontangible benefit of having children—and therefore the value of procreative sex—is very important. Thus, a social ethnic that promotes more freely available sex undercuts pro-life women two ways: it limits their ability to get into a marriage in the first place, and it undermines the social value placed on their presence once within a marriage.[63]

The perspective drawn by Luker casts further light on the material bases of the ready acceptance of certain feminist "ideals" of human sexuality among upper-middle-class prochoice activists. What is at issue here is not the rightness or wrongness of such ideals but rather the illumination of the fact that the cultural functions of feminist ideology as well as opposing ideologies cannot be neatly disentangled from the differing opportunities and resources available to different groups of women and men in the class system:

> For pro-choice women, the situation is reversed. Because they have access to "male" re-

sources such as education and income, they have far less reason to believe the basic reason for sexuality is to produce children. They plan to have small families anyway, and their husbands come from and have married into a social class in which small families are the norm. For a number of overlapping reasons, therefore, pro-choice women value the ability of sex to promote human intimacy more . . . than they value the ability of sex to produce babies. But they hold this view because they can afford to. When they bargain for marriage, they use the same resources they use in the labor market; upper-class status, an education very similar to a man's, side by side participation in the man's world, and, not least, a salary that substantially increases a family's standard of living.[64]

Luker focuses on the implications of the class position of activists at the opposite poles of the abortion issue. We can see, however, how similar considerations apply to those working-class and lower-middle-class women, whom the pressures of maintaining or improving the family standard of living have driven into the permanent world of work outside the home. Here the imperatives for value allegiance *vis à vis* the public goals of the feminist movement may be more ambiguous. But it is clear that alterations in the life chances of such women (and their families and/or mates), due to the nature of their participation in the paid labor market, create new sources for both the reception and rejection of the feminist "agenda."

Gender then becomes implicated in the wider struggles for survival, defense, and ascendancy among social classes in the society. Political control of the "bounds of legitimacy" for the relations between genders in society's system of public values becomes an important prize in these struggles. The championing of "pro-familism" by conservative groups—who obviously have more extensive political and religious agendas in mind and who take advantage of this situation of class conflict (as do the more liberal groups in their own way)—should not be allowed to obscure a central issue for future efforts to achieve gender equality in the United States: The struggle for gender equality cannot be ultimately insulated from the larger issues of social inequality that emerge directly and indirectly from the class systems of capitalist societies.

Luker's analysis of the prochoice and prolife movements also highlights a broader dilemma for the contemporary feminist movement in the United States; a dilemma that is also posed by the mutually reinforcing, as well as conflicting, tendencies of the interpenetration of gender and class stratification. Much of the public momentum of both the liberal and more radical versions of recent feminism has derived from an ideological focus on the values of opportunity ("choice"), achievement, and personal growth ("self-actualization") for the *individual* in our society, irrespective of gender.

Almost inevitably in a market society, the realization of such values becomes linked to the life chances of the individual as defined by one's competitive position in the marketplace and one's degree of access to society's valued (and relatively scarce) forms of consumption. Contemporary ideas of personal growth in particular tend to emphasize the cultivation of flexibility and tentativeness in human relationships. A person is to reject the kinds of commitments in such relationships that may stand in the way of her or his ability to "grow," to move on to new forms of experience, and to experiment with new life-styles. Shorn of its finer ideological pretensions, such attitudes and behavior at the level of personal relationships outside of work can be seen as an analogue to the kind of flexibility and value relativity ("keep your options open") that makes for competitive success in the higher-income sectors of the markets for both labor and consumption.

Not only on the political right but also from within feminism itself, the beginning years of the 1980s witnessed a backlash against certain trends in feminist ideology that seem to champion the ideals of "masculine" personal achievement, self-actualization, and competitive success as the hallmarks of women's progress. To a degree, such a backlash reflects a continuing contradiction of capitalist societies: The capitalist marketplace is not a home, nor is it a community. Even those most deeply immersed in the workings of the market—and those most richly rewarded by the market—are nonetheless constantly susceptible to the longing for forms of human relationships whose value, stability, and substance transcend the relativities of the marketplace, that do not have a "price," that represent social recognition and acceptance for what one *is*, not for what one has or has done.[65]

Despite the permeation of what Erich Fromm has called the "marketing orientation"[66] into almost all aspects of life in advanced capitalist societies, cultural imagery of such communal and unconditional human relationships still abound and are the object of both nostalgic longing and the genuine need for more stabilized and authentic forms of human existence. Two of the most compelling images of this kind remain those of the heterosexually based nuclear family and the compact of lovers who commit themselves to protect their love (or to honor its moral imperatives) through commitment to marriage ("for better or for worse") or to the moral equivalent of marriage. Betty Friedan, who in 1962 assailed the "feminine mystique," in 1981 attacked what she called the "feminist mystique": the tendency of feminism, as she saw it, to denigrate family life, the unique bonds between husband and wife, and the gender-specific values (as she saw them) of female psychology and behavior.[67] Political theorist and feminist Jean Bethke Elshtain published her *Public Man, Private Women* also in 1981,[68] and followed it with a number of articles in politically left publications, criticizing the feminist movement for its politicizing of the private life of the family, its antimale bias in the formation of political agendas, and its failure to recognize the family as a source of communal values which must be preserved and nourished as a basis for the struggle against the humanly deforming tendencies of capitalism. Friedan and Elshtain, along with other feminist spokespersons, have also decried the alleged feminist *animus* against the family as a politically strategic error of profound proportions, alienating ordinary women and men from the feminist cause who otherwise would be attracted to it. Of particular interest has been the recent work of sociologist, Alice Rossi. Rossi, who in 1964 published in *Daedalus* magazine a seminal essay of the feminist movement, "Equality between the Sexes: An Immodest Proposal,"[69] was by the late 1970s and early 1980s, producing a series of studies emphasizing the biological roots of gender differences and the need to take these differences into account in family and general social policy.[70]

Feminist intellectuals and activists on the left have been quick to subject such "in-house" revisionism to (often scathing) criticism, pointing out the potential conservative and sexist uses of such second thoughts on the part of prominent feminists. But in an article that mounts a forceful critique of the recent conservative tendencies within feminism, Judith Stacey acknowledges that the new ideology has identified real problems in theory and in practice within feminism:

As Friedan and Elshtain make explicit, their work speaks from and to a reservoir of unmet needs for intimacy, nurturance, and security that feminists experience as much as other men and women. It is in response to these needs that the family has become so powerfully resonant as a political idiom. Feminist attempts to meet these needs by developing alternative forms of family and community have come upon difficult times. Beyond coparenting we have not succeeded in providing models or visions of alternatives to conventional family structure that are compelling to many others, if even to ourselves.[71]

Feminist critics, particularly those on the left, correctly perceive that appeals to family and community values in a society structured on class and gender inequality are highly susceptible to political manipulation and mobilization for reactionary economic, social, and political goals. At a more complex level, the legitimate emphasis on the potentials of "feminine" values, psychology, and behavioral orientations for the humanization of male-dominated society may have ambiguous political implications where emphasis on the "feminine" continues to be an ideological resource for both gender and class stratification. At the same time, emphasis on contractural relationshps, equality of opportunity, achievement, personal growth and development, and female parity (as opposed to equality) with males may become ideological resources for the entrenchment of class privilege in a society in which the inequalities of gender are not politically perceived as infused with inequalities of class. The 1980s are a time where a variety of economic, social, and political trends have coalesced to produce a societal focus in the United States that might be characterized as "betting on the strong"—the cultural celebration of the splendid achiever. In this setting the friends and enemies of the struggle for gender equality are not unambiguously identifiable by their publicly professed values. The affiliations of class increasingly overshadow the political efforts of feminism to identify and implement an effective ideology and program for the achievement of "gender justice."

Gender Stratification: A View from the 1980s

Cultural Imagery

Although feminist activists and academicians have endeavored to expose and challenge sexist stereotypes and images in areas such as the mass media, advertising, literature, children's literature, music, and the language, little real change has occurred.[72] Movies still focus on male lives and emphasize macho values of violence and the sexual subordination of women. Television has few positive feminist or female characters. Advertisers still appeal to the woman as a domestic, selling cleaning agents and floor polishes to women by using male authorities and scientists to attest to their product's superiority, although the career woman is more commonly used as advertising appeal to the young professional "upscale" market. There has in fact been some deterioration in the female's image in the mass media and advertising. The increased cultural emphasis on sexuality in the seventies and eighties has led to an emphasis on the female-as-sex-object image and this has sometimes included sadomasochism against women in such areas as clothing ads, store window displays, record album covers, and rock videos.

With the exception of feminist literature and some new nonsexist children's books, traditional gender role imagery prevails. Some publishing companies have introduced textbooks that avoid sexist and racist stereotyping, but most school systems have not adopted them. Music, especially the hard

rock, acid rock, and punk rock so popular among youth, has become even more sexist. It has turned from more romantic gender role imagery to outright misogyny and images of violence against women. Suggestions for ridding the language of sexism, such as the use of "Ms." instead of "Miss" or "Mrs." to avoid emphasizing the woman's relationship to men, have met with limited success. Similarly, attempts to replace such male-specific words as "mankind" and "he" to refer to males and females, and "chairman," "businessman," and the like with non-gender-specific forms has been rejected by most people and treated with levity by many. Gender role stereotypes are still firmly engrained in American culture.

Employment

The world of gender relations in employment outside the home exhibited the following major trends and characteristics by the mid-1980s: (1) the continued rise in female labor force participation, (2) the newsworthy but socially and economically ambiguous gains in the rate of entry of women into male-dominated elite professions, (3) the persistence of the dual labor market, and (4) the increased relevance of women's paid labor to the structuring of class inequality and the feminization of poverty.

Labor Force Participation. At the end of 1984, 53.6 percent of working-age women were in the labor force, an increase from 43.3 percent in 1970. More dramatically, 70.5 percent of women between twenty and twenty-nine years of age, 53 percent of all married women with husbands present, 59 percent of married women with children under eighteen, and 48 percent of married women with very young children (under three years old) were working or actively looking for work.*[73] Although part-time work continues to be more characteristic of women than men, 72 percent of all employed women, 71 percent of married women with husbands present, and 67 percent of married women with children under three years of age worked full time.[74] Probably most indicative of these trends was the fact that in March 1984, 46.8 percent of all mothers (married or unmarried) whose youngest child was *one* year old or under were in the labor force, an increase from 24 percent in 1970.[75] Even for the mothers of infants, working outside the home seems to be on the brink of becoming normative in U.S. society.

Female Entry into Male-Dominated Elite Professions. Throughout the 1970s and 1980s, the mass media (especially advertisers) celebrated the rapid rate of entry of women into male-dominated, high-status, and high-paying fields of work.

Given the small level of historical participation of women in these fields, the increases in the percentage of women in these fields may have been impressive, but male dominance has not really been threatened. For instance, the percentage of engineers who were women increased almost *five* times betwen 1973 and 1984; but in fact this is a female representation that was 1.3 percent of all engineers in 1973 and 6.2 percent in 1984. In 1984 women were 16 percent of physicians (12.2 percent in 1973), 16.1 percent of lawyers (5.8 percent in 1973), and 33.6 percent of executives, managers, and administrators (18.4 percent in 1973).[76]

Gender pay gaps remain, even in the elite professions. *U.S. News and World Report*, reporting on a Columbia University study in 1984, indicated that after ten years in business, the average male holding an M.B.A. earned 20 percent more than the average female with the same degree and experience. "In science and engineering, women's salaries range from 10 to 20 percent below men's. In computer programming, women make 81 percent of what men earn."[77] It is also the case that women still find themselves disproportionately assigned to positions that have limited authority and decision-making power attached to them within the elite professions.[78] Time will show whether the very youngest cohorts entering these professions will break these patterns.

The Persistence of the Dual Labor Market. Even if elite women were to continue to register gains in these professions, most women in the 1980s were far more likely to face the persistent gender inequalities embedded in the gender-based dual economy. In the 1980s there was no abatement of the trend in which female-typed jobs were generated in the economy in disproportionate numbers; this pattern of job supply continued to underlie the increasing participation of women in the labor force.

The loss of hundreds of thousands of jobs in the blue-collar manufacturing sector because of competition from Japan, Western Europe, and the third world countries and the increasing internationalization of production (see Chapter 8) combined with longer-term trends in the economy to confine the bulk of new job creation to the nonmanufacturing sectors where women are especially in demand. Service employment plus the jobs the Census Bureau calls "administrative support, including clerical" (the classic office jobs) composed 47 percent of the jobs held by women in 1984 as opposed to 15 precent for men.[79] If we take the per-

---

*These two categories, those working and those looking for work (the officially unemployed), define the labor force.

centage of female workers in a job category as a measure of gender segregation, the 1984 statistics reveal the following examples of persistent "female ghettos": sales workers in apparel (83 percent); secretaries, stenographers, and typists (98 percent); interviewers (89 percent); and financial records processors (90 percent). However, only 2.7 percent of mechanics and repairers, 2 percent of construction workers, and 9 percent of motor vehicle operators were women. In manufacturing industries women were closer to parity with men, but were overly concentrated in lower-paid jobs in the non-durable goods sectors (55 percent) as opposed to the better-paying durable goods sectors (31 percent). In nonelite jobs requiring higher educational credentials, women were 96 percent of registered nurses, 99 percent of prekindergarten and kindergarten teachers, 85 percent of elementary school teachers, 86 percent of librarians, 64 percent of social workers, and 83 percent of all health technologists and technicians.[80]

Gender gaps in earnings *within* job sectors remain diffused throughout the economy, irrespective of whether sectors are male dominated, female dominated, or in rough parity.* Economists continue to debate to what degree education, years of work experience, regularity of work history, and other supposedly gender-blind (from the standpoint of the employers) factors account for the kinds of job segregation and ine-

qualities based on gender that we have described. The fact remains, however, that the job markets open to the majority of women participating in the labor force are organized to channel women selectively into jobs that are charcterized by lower average pay, less chance for promotion, and lower status and that have lower levels of unionization, less security, and more meager fringe benefits. It is also clear that human capital factors (education, training, experience, and the like), which afford men greater opportunities in competitive job markets, cannot be considered in isolation from the persistence of different patterns of gender socialization and of societal expectations of what constitutes legitimate gender roles and particularly from an appreciation of the overwhelming competitive disadvantages placed on women because of their roles as mothers, wives, and domestic workers in the family and the household.

Class Inequality and Feminization of Poverty. As the 1980s reached their midpoint, evidence was beginning to accumulate indicating that inequality among individuals and families in U.S. society was on the increase. The effects of foreign competition, the rise of the services economy, the decline of labor unions, the effects of credentialism in employment, and the general instability of domestic and international economies all seem to be implicated in this process. Intertwined in complex ways with all these factors were the additional effects of the changes taking place in the relations between genders and the linkages that exist between gender status and economic opportunity both within and outside of marriage and the family.

Although women as individuals continue to be disadvantaged in competition with men in the world of work outside the home,

---

*For instance, in the following broad classifications full-time women workers earned these percentages of full-time median male weekly income in 1984: executive, administrative, and managerial, 65 percent; sales occupations, 54 percent; administrative support, including clerical, 67 percent; machine operators, assemblers, and inspectors, 61 percent; and service occupations, 69 percent.[81]

their wages and salaries as wives and mothers have become increasingly important for the economic health of families. Through the economically difficult years of the 1970s and early 1980s, the only category of families that held its own or made small gains in terms of real income was that of families in which both husband and wife were present and employed. In 1983 the median income for married-couple families with the wife in the labor force was $32,107; for those where the wife was not in the labor force, it was $21,890. The difference was even more striking for blacks: $26,389 for families where the wife was in the labor force; $13,821 for those where the wife was not.[82]

College-educated elites, combining high incomes for both genders (although less on the average for women) with delay in the age of first marriage and no-, one-, or two-child marriages, are becoming increasingly important in generating aspirational trends of life-style and consumption for the rest of society. The earnings potentials of such elite two-paycheck marriages and families had become truly remarkable by the mid-1980s. An indication of such potentials in upper-middle-class matchups of the two genders is the fact that the average yearly income of males between the ages of 30 to 34 years with four years of college had already reached $25,960 by 1982 and that of their female counterparts, $18,063—a potential mean income of $44,051 for couples still in the early stages of their careers.[83]

At the opposite pole, households headed by women with no husband present increased rapidly during the 1970s and 1980s. By 1984 there were almost 10 million of such families, 16 percent of all families.[84] Their median family income was $11,789 in 1983,[85] and 55.4 percent were below the official federal poverty line. Minority female-headed households without husbands present were to be found in poverty almost by definition:

68.5 percent of black families in this category were below the poverty line and 70.6 percent of families of Spanish origin.* Forty-three percent of *all* black families fell into this category and 23 percent of families of Spanish origin. The female-headed household was a major factor in explaining why in 1983 16.9 percent of all white children, 46.3 percent of black children, and 37.8 percent of children of Spanish origin were to be found in poverty.[86]

The mix of an uncertain economy, rising age of first marriage,† the "1.8 child family," divorce, rising female labor force participation, entrenchment of economic privilege based on the holding of educational credentials, the perpetuation of labor market segregation based on gender and race, and the lack of economically viable husbands for minority women yields the seemingly paradoxical result in which gender position reinforces in *opposite* directions the polarization of classes at the extremes of the income scale. In the middle the full-time housewife and mother has become an economic casualty, while still remaining an object of cultural veneration among a significant sector of the population.

Education

By 1977 women had achieved parity with men in median years of completed schooling. By the advent of the 1980s female undergraduates exceeded males at the college and university level. As in the labor force, however, women's educational attainments

---

*The figure for whites was 46.9 percent.
†This factor has to be taken into account to explain, among other things, why rates of teenage pregnancy continue to fall in the United States, while the rates of children born to unwed teenage mothers continue to rise.

present a mixed picture of gains in gender equality and the perpetuation of gender segregation, with conflicting implications for the future career advances of the female elite and for those women struggling for mobility in the lower levels of the labor markets. In business and management the proportion of bachelor's degrees awarded to women increased from 8.1 percent to 39 percent from 1970–71 to 1981–82.[87] The proportion of master's degrees earned by women in the same area increased from 3.9 percent to 27.8 percent and of doctor's degrees from 2.9 percent to 17.7 percent during the same period. Bachelor's degrees for women in the computer and information sciences advanced from 13.6 percent to 34.8 percent, master's degrees from 10.3 percent to 26.5 percent, and doctor's degrees from 2.3 percent to 8.4 percent. In the field of engineering the advances were spectacular in the rate of increase from a very low starting point, but extremely modest in terms of end results: Bachelor's degrees awarded to women moved from the 0.8 percent level in 1971–72 to 12.3 percent in 1981–82, master's degrees from 1.1 percent to 9 percent, and doctorates from 0.6 percent to 5.3 percent.

However, bachelor's degrees awarded in allied health services *increased* from 85.3 percent in 1971–72 to 86.2 percent in 1981–82 and health sciences bachelor's degrees from 76.2 percent to 83.9 percent. Library and archival sciences bachelor's degrees declined slightly from 92 percent to 86 percent. Bachelor's degrees awarded to women in education advanced from 74.5 percent to 75.9 percent.

In the more academically and professionally oriented fields, psychology degrees moved to a majority female position at the master's level (from 37.2 percent to 58.8 percent) and increased from 24 percent to 45.4 percent at the doctoral level. In the life sciences the movement was from 33.6 percent

to 41.7 percent at the master's level and 16.3 percent to 29.1 percent at the doctoral level. In mathematics the change was from 29.2 percent to 33.2 percent of awarded master's degrees and from 7.8 percent to 13.8 percent of doctor's degrees. In 1981–82 15.4 percent of dental degrees were received by women (up from 1.1 percent in 1971–72), 25 percent of medical degrees (9.1 percent in 1971–72), 36.2 percent of veterinary degrees (7.8 percent in 1971–72), and 33.4 percent of law degrees (7.1 percent in 1971–72).

Clearly, women's advances in higher education will continue to widen the female competitive pool for a number of elite professions and occupations. But the "ghettoization" of women into more extensive female-typed occupations that require postsecondary school training, but that represent an extension of the conventional gender roles of women into the world of paid work—health care, teaching, and secretarial-clerical work (97.4 percent of "business and office" degrees, generally from two-year colleges, were granted to women in 1981–82) continued as a structural feature of both the system of higher education and the labor force.

The self-selection of women for training in the technical fields, which will likely be of great importance for elite mobility in the economy of the future, may also be losing its initial momentum. Among entering freshmen of 1982–83, 57 percent of intended business and commerce majors were women.[88] Later than men to embrace the competitive attractions of nontechnical business careers, women may be the major victims of a repeat of the familiar shifts in the pattern of preferred credentials required by economic change, labor market saturation, and the outcomes of the largely noneconomic bargains that historically have been struck between business and educational institutions to balance the interests of both. Whether female students as a group are able to be as flexible in adapting to these shifts depends not only on the choices available to them at the college and university level but also on the kinds of interests, course selection, and parental, teacher, and peer support that are cultivated at earlier stages of the educational process. In this regard, it remains the fact that boys move in an educational environment in which the "right" choices for early career preparation and socialization are congruent with the culturally preferred and encouraged pattern of discovering and affirming a male gender identity. Despite some changes in the educational environment, this is much less likely to be the case for girls who are in the process of establishing their gender identity. Even the popularly perceived changes in the educational environment may not be what they seem, since recent research indicates that male students still receive systematic preference from teachers in the classroom in the distribution of the kind of recognition and encouragement that affirms competitive potential and achievement.[89] At the same time, the idea that the schools themselves might serve as an instrument of instilling in both females *and* males a taste for noncompetitive forms of achievement was probably even farther from any possibility of realization in the mid-1980s than at the beginning of the contemporary feminist movement in the 1960s.

Politics

In the aftermath of the 1984 presidential election, women found themselves barely holding their own in terms of nationally elected offices. Geraldine Ferraro had made the historic breakthrough as the first female vice presidential candidate of a major party, but the defeat of the Mondale-Ferraro ticket had ushered in an apparent backlash in the Democratic party against the maintenance

of women as a special constituency within the higher party circles. Only 22 of the 435 members of the House of Representatives were women and only 2 of the 100 senators were women. At the cabinet level, President Reagan had appointed two women and had accomplished another historic first, the appointment of the first female Supreme Court justice, Sandra Day O'Connor. At the state level, there were 2 women governors and 1,096 state legislators (15 percent of the nationwide total, up from 8 percent in 1975). Ninety mayors of cities of 30,000 population or more were female. Both those who wanted to emphasize the slowness of change and the increments in the numbers of women holding political office could find evidence to support their views. But women in office, in whatever numbers, did not indicate victory for "women's" issues. The Equal Rights Amendment had been at last defeated, abortion rights were a continued battlefront, and affirmative action programs were objects of distaste for the second Reagan administration. Women's political groups were in the process of rethinking strategies, not only to reach out to new constituencies, but also to prevent erosion in the ranks of those who were already counted in the camp.

Domestic Organization and Relations between the Sexes

Despite the fact that more than half of American women now hold jobs, they still retain primary responsibility for the home and child care. Husbands help out with cleaning, shopping, and taking care of children, but they do not take major responsibility for these domestic tasks. The egalitarian, shared role pattern characterizes only a small number of modern marriages.[90] The egalitarian marriage receives more attention than it did at any time in the past, but most couples find it very difficult to put it into practice. The weight of tradition and, perhaps even more important, the imperatives of the economy, undermine the attempts of even the most committed.

First, the wife is likely to be better trained at domestic tasks than the husband because of gender role differences in childhood and adolescent socialization into the gender division of labor. This makes it "easier" for the wife to do the work. It is frustrating and time consuming for the husband and wife to undergo the retraining necessary to developing cooking and cleaning skills in the husband and home repair skills in the wife. So they tend to fall back into the old patterns. Second, the rest of society continues to place the responsibility for domestic tasks on the wife. She is the one who is made to feel guilty if the house is dirty or the children's faces need washing. People still will not blame the husband for poor housekeeping. Third, employers are less tolerant of family demands that interfere with a male employee's work than with female's. It is more acceptable for a woman to be absent because of a sick child than it is for a man. Yet this type of absenteeism is later used to justify not hiring or promoting the woman to a responsible position. Fourth, and probably most important, the wife's job is likely to pay less and be less prestigious than the husband's. Therefore, if someone's work is to be disrupted, it seems more rational that it be the wife's, which further inhibits the wife's ability to compete successfully in the labor market. The following report from the *Wall Street Journal* indicates the pressures that separate the ideal from reality even among the most privileged sectors of the population:

Nicholas Gabriel, 31, comptroller of the Ford Foundation, took off three weeks when his son was born, although the foundation offers up to eight weeks *paid* leave. But even those three weeks were spread over three months because the birth coincided with the end of Ford's fiscal year. "You're not expected to take the time," he says. The foundation's reaction was "Do what you want to do, but you know what you've got to do."[91]

The example also illustrates that even in the less likely case that the wife were in the position of facing this dilemma, the implications for the maintenance of *inequality* among marriage partners would still be the same—*someone* would have to choose the "lesser" role. It takes an excessive amount of vigilance on the part of a couple not to fall into these traps.[92] Yet if they do resort to the old patterns, the wife is inhibited in her pursuit of a career through her dual role at home and at work. This is exactly where most working mothers still find themselves. Of course, a large percentage, if not the majority, of couples do not even attempt the shared-role pattern. They continue to assume that the wife has primary responsibility for the domestic chores.

Working wives are, however, more independent than full-time housewives, and they exercise more power in the marital relationship. There does appear to be a greater acceptance of egalitarian relationships and less emphasis on the more overt manifestations of male dominance and patriarchy. But the situation does not approach equality.

Although lack of equality across gender lines is a problem faced by married women of all classes, elite women typically possess more flexibility and resources to deal with the problem. They and their husbands can more easily afford to hire out the performance of domestic services and even many of the major burdens of child rearing, while couples earning lower incomes cannot. A woman's elite status also usually brings with it the power to control more effectively her work schedule to adapt it to the demands of motherhood—*if* she is willing to pay the price of having her chances for mobility *within* her elite occupation slightly (or perhaps decisively) hampered. As the psychologists who authored a recent study of patterns of family life and work among women point out: "A physician can earn a good income on a part-time basis, can arrange her professional life so she can get out to her child's school concert during the day, but a nurse can't. Professors don't ask a boss for permission to bring a child to work, if that's necessary; secretaries do."[93]

Despite their cultural impact due to the attention given them by the mass media and even scholarly researchers, true two-career marriages continue to be—and will continue to be—statisticaly rare.[94] More common, but by no means the norm, is the marriage in which one partner pursues a "career"— most often the male—and the second partner fulfills the duties of a "job"—most often the female. More common than either of these two types of marriage is the situation where each partner works at a job and not a career. In none of these three types of marriage is gender equality the standard of practice, nor perhaps even the standard expectation or ideal. Since 1976 the Institute of Social Research of the University of Michigan has questioned graduating high school seniors on their expectations and plans for adult life. A summary of one of the most recent of these surveys presents the following observations.

"The seniors seem to be saying that, for most people most of the time, there are distinct advantages in the traditional family-role arrangements. . . . And when it comes to their own future marriages, the overwhelming majority prefer to maintain *some* traditional role distinctions." Both the young men and the young women want a family arrangement in which the husband consistently works full-time outside

the home; they rule out any other alternative. When small children are part of the family, the young people say they want a wife who is not spending large portions of her time working in outside employment. "To a very large degree . . . these restrictions seem to be internalized and thus self-imposed by the time a young person reaches the end of high school."[95]

How much these attitudes are attributed to the holding of certain values or to realism is debatable—ultimately, values themselves cannot be separated from the constraining influences of realistic expectations.

Alternative Life-Styles. In the early seventies some people tried to alter the traditional domestic organization and relations between the genders by experimenting with communal forms of household organization in both urban and rural settings. Despite their rejection of established practices, gender roles quickly reemerged in most of the communities. Rejections of monogamy usually gave rise to serious problems with jealousy. Responsibility for the burdens of pregnancy and child care almost always fell to the female while the male felt free to move on whenever he wished. The communal alternative is less popular today than it was several years ago. But it is a utopian alternative deeply rooted in the American tradition and may well be expected to revive as a focus for experimentation in new forms of gender relations.

Other forms of experimentation are widespread. A large number of couples, for example, are choosing to live together either temporarily or permanently without legal marriage. This life-style is no guarantee against having a relationship based on traditional gender roles, but some hope it will help them to maintain a sense of individuality and personal autonomy, which they feel legal marriage undermines. Research on such relationships, however, indicate they are primarily a stage toward marriage and as yet have shown no major departures from the gender division of labor characteristic of most marriages.[96]

Remaining single has also become a more acceptable and more widely practiced alternative than it was in the forties and fifties. Many people find themselves living as singles because of the high divorce rate. The increased availability of employment makes this a more viable alternative for many women.

With improved contraceptive technology and greater sexual freedom, singleness does not mean celibacy. Similarly, more couples are remaining childless voluntarily. Both of these alternatives free women from many of the burdens of the domestic roles. But they of course entail certain costs as well. The choice between a career and a family is still more likely to have to be faced by women than by men.

A few couples are attempting to give a higher priority to the woman's career by maintaining separate residences when their career development takes them to different geographical locations. Others have deemphasized careers for both husband and wife by seeking to share one job or alternating working and staying home at different points in the life cycle. However, these experimental forms of domestic organization are confined primarily to the well-educated upper middle class. Couples with fewer educational and economic resources cannot usually afford this type of innovation and may be faced with inflexible employment situations that force them into the traditional molds.

The actual extent of changes in domestic organization may be more apparent than real. Media attention goes to the unusual, not the mundane. But even if only a relative few are living according to different patterns, recognition of such alternatives does help to undermine the taken-for-granted nature of traditional arrangements.

Changes in domestic organization are also evidenced in the high divorce rate. With increased economic independence, many women no longer have to accept and try to maintain unhappy marriages. Similarly, it is easier for a husband to pursue a divorce if the wife can work to support herself. Two incomes give greater personal autonomy to both parties and contribute to the increased emphasis on individualism found in advanced industrial society. Thus if the marriage relationship is not perceived as a satisfying one, the individuals involved feel freer to end it. The divorce alternative should not, however, be overromanticized, especially for women. For large numbers of women and their children it is still a form of "liberation" that comes with great economic cost, exacerbating whatever psychic costs may also be involved.

Sexuality. Women have gained more freedom in the realm of sexual behavior. The sexual double standard has not been destroyed, but emphasis on virginity and chastity has been significantly reduced. Contraception and abortion have freed women to participate in sexual relations with less fear of unwanted pregnancy. The increased economic independence of women has given rise to women's demands for sexual attractiveness and pleasing personalities in men. Women are on more equal bargaining terms with men in the sexual marketplace. Thus we see a greater emphasis on male cosmetics, hair styles, clothing, weight control, and muscle development. We also see an increased emphasis on male sexual performance, since the male is considered responsible for sexually satisfying the female. This is reflected in the immensely popular literature on the techniques of lovemaking.[97]

But new myths and performance standards have also emerged for women, for example, the multiorgasmic response. These new standards may be as personally debilitating as the old sexual myths and standards when individuals fail to measure up.[98] One woman discussed oral sex with Lillian Rubin, "Even though I hate it, if he needs it, then I feel I ought to do it. After all, I'm his wife."[99] Other wives reported fears that their husbands would lose respect for them if they gave in to demands for new forms of sex. The public attention given to sexual liberation for women can also serve to obscure the lack of progress toward equality in other areas of life.

Support for the woman's control over her own sexuality is also evidenced in the recent movement against sexual harassment on the job. Women are often threatened with loss of job, pay, or promotion if they do not submit to the sexual demands of male superiors or coworkers. Feminist groups have been working to expose this type of exploitation and are giving support to women in legal suits against individuals and companies that practice this type of discrimination and sexual exploitation.

Child Rearing. There has been a move away from sexist and gender role stereotypical modes of child rearing. Dr. Spock revised his best-selling parents' manual in 1976 to rid it of sexist assumptions and to advocate more androgynous socialization for both boys and girls. However, the unisex direction of child rearing is usually merely a deemphasis of traditional feminine traits and a greater acceptance of traditional masculine traits for girls as well as boys. Thus girls now wear t-shirts and pants, but boys do not wear skirts or dresses. Girls are encouraged to be aggressive and to involve themselves in sports, but boys are not encouraged to develop tender, emotional traits or to involve themselves very often with dolls or playing house. This is an implicit acceptance of the gender hierarchy. Masculine traits are still viewed as superior to feminine traits: The loss of the traditional feminine interests and personality characteristics may be a loss for both genders instead of a gain. It also appears that young girls are more accepting of feminist ideas than boys are. Young boys and teenagers are still apt to support male dominance and to subscribe to macho values, again because female traits are still devalued in our culture.

Another important change in child rearing has been an increased recognition of the father's role in child development. This may still be more characteristic of better-educated, middle- and upper-class couples.

There has also been an increased acceptance of and utilization of day-care centers and nursery schools. In fact, parents are often encouraged to place their children in the group-care situation for the good of the child, that is, to allow the child to develop social skills earlier. The expansion of such facilities, although they are still expensive, has freed many women from some of the more limiting aspects of the maternal role, allowing them to participate in paid employment and other outside interests and activities. The availability of day-care facilities is still, however, woefully inadequate, their quality often indifferent or poor, and their cost beyond the reach of large numbers of working mothers (or those who want to work).[100] Despite the developments described previously, the 1980s are also a time of renewed emphasis by political spokespersons, portions of the mass media, and not a few scholars on the "specialness" of the mother-child relationship and the necessity for the health of the child of at least one full-time parent, usually the mother.

Violence. Violence against women is one aspect of male dominance that does not seem to be on the wane.[101] The problem of battered wives has received a great deal of public attention in recent years. It is difficult to determine if it is on the rise because wives have not been encouraged to report it until recently. Rape does appear to be on the increase, however, although it is also an underreported crime. This type of violence against women may represent a reaction against the increased freedom and autonomy of women by some men who feel threatened by changes in the traditional sexual hierarchy. The increased incidence of rape indicates a high level of hostility against women by at least a small percentage of the male population. This in turn operates to decrease women's sense of autonomy. Fear of rape and physical assault can prevent women from taking a job with late hours or in an unsafe location. It can prevent them from going out alone at night. It can force them to live in more expensive neighborhoods than they can afford or would prefer. Women's groups have responded to the problem by lobbying for better rape laws, demanding more humane treatment of rape victims by police and medical authorities, and establishing rape crisis centers to give the victim emotional and psychological support and to help her prosecute the assailant. But arrest and conviction rates remain very low.

Conclusion: Future Prospects

The debate over the future of gender relations in the United States centers on (1) the prospects for the growth and transformation of the economy, especially in regard to the patterns of demand and supply for female labor; (2) the significance of shifts in the demographic balance of generations and the genders; (3) the relative permanence of the changes in gender-related attitudes, values, and patterns of relationships that emerged in the last two decades; and (4) the future development of gender politics.

Economic Prospects

Despite the period of economic recovery that was still underway at the beginning of 1985, the prospects for the growth and transformation of the U.S. economy and the world economy as a whole were clouded by many uncertainties. The failure of the major capitalist economies to find new forces of worldwide dynamism equivalent to the spent forces of the post-World War II boom period would mean, at the very least, the perpetuation of a domestic and international economic environment in which all economic decisions and planning would be rendered problematic by the continued threat of instability. In regard to women's work outside the home, present trends would seem to confirm the continued expansion of many sectors of female-typed jobs in the service economy while threatening the curtailment of others in the administrative assistance/clerical areas because of office automation and related technological advances. Even with the latter development, however, current prospects are for the brunt of job creation to continue to be in areas where female ghettoization is most prominent. The U.S. Bureau of Labor Statistics has projected that the ten areas which will have the largest job growth between 1982 and 1995 will be (in order): building custodians, cashiers, secretaries, office clerks, sales clerks, registered nurses, waiters and waitresses, kindergarten and elementary teachers, truck drivers, and nursing aides and hospital orderlies.[102]

In the more favored and protected sectors of the elite occupations and professions, women continue to acquire the credentials that should improve their competitive position vis-à-vis to men. But it is reasonable to expect in the future, as in the past, shifts in the patterns of demand for different types of credential holders. This takes place not only because of technological and organizational change in the economy but also because "credentials revolutions" (drastic changes in the demand for different types of credentials) are one of the major means that the modern middle and upper-middle classes restructure competitive advantages among themselves over time. These revolutions are the means by which educational institutions struggle to maintain their own interests in their ongoing trade-offs with the demands of the business world.[103] Such shifts are also subject to periodic changes in political entrepreneurship linked to technological and military competition with the Soviet Union and, more recently, to the competitive challenges of Japan, Western Europe, and newly industrializing countries of the Third World. Males, by virtue of both the trajectories of their childhood and adolescent socialization and their location within networks of communication and influence that are more sensitive to the advent and implications of such shifts, still maintain considerable advantage over females in responding to them. Men bail out of declining credentials markets before women, and women find men already beginning to flood new markets when they make the collective decision to enter these markets themselves.

In respect to the supply of female labor, economists and other social scientists have emphasized three major factors: (1) the response of women, particularly married women, to the continual expansion of female-typed jobs, which although often low-paying and low-status nevertheless often provide the flexibility to adapt paid labor to the demands of family life; (2) the economic necessity of wives' "supplementary" income to maintain or increase the family's standard of living, particularly in the face of inflation, economic stagnation, and the increasing costs of raising and educating children; and (3) the opportunity costs* of women remaining in the home in the face of expanding opportunities to earn income outside the home.[104] There is little to indicate that these factors will change in a direction that will reduce real incentives for married women to work outside the home as the United States moves toward the twenty-first century. Perhaps of equal or even greater importance will be the fact that two-earner families are in the process of decisively changing what is in fact an acceptable standard of living in U.S. society. "Once established, a widespread pattern of two-earner young families may tend to persist, because one-earner couples will feel relatively deprived."[105]

Changes in the Demographic Balance of the Genders

Demographer Richard Easterlin has argued that the life changes of individuals and the families they establish are crucially linked to the relative size of the cohort (generation) into which they are born.[106] Members of large birth cohorts meet stiff competition among themselves for jobs and income, leading, according to Easterlin, to

---

*"Opportunity costs" refer to the income foregone by wives/mothers by *not* taking advantage of available employment opportunities in the paid labor market.

greater levels of frustration in the realization of their economic aspirations, delay of marriage, delay in having children, smaller numbers of children, more wives and mothers having to work outside the home, and a variety of related social and psychological problems. But members of small birth cohorts grow up to face less competition among themselves, relatively benign conditions for the realization of their economic aspirations, and a generally more benign social climate. Thus they are able to marry earlier, have children earlier, have more children, and relieve wives of the burden of working outside the home. The fifties are viewed as an example of the fate of the relatively small cohort and the late 1960s and 1970s (the maturing of the baby-boom generation) as an example of the destiny of the relatively large cohort.

To the degree that demographic factors described by Easterlin are actually important determinants of family formation, marital fertility, and the labor force participation of married women, the relatively small birth cohorts who come of age in the 1980s and 1990s should marry earlier, produce children earlier (and more of them), and provide an economic atmosphere that will allow wives to remain in the home.

Marcia Guttentag and Paul Secord have also argued that the *ratio* of males and females of appropriate marriageable ages is an important determinant of the relative gender roles and cyclical changes in the emphasis on familism that exist in a society.[107] In this view, when women of marriageable age are scarce relative to men (as in the 1950s), women's marital chances are enhanced, and marriage and family life and the maintenance of conventional gender roles rise in value in society. Conversely, when marriageable women are in oversupply relative to their potential male partners, women's marital opportunities are restricted, and marriage and family life and the maintenance of conventional gender roles decline in societal value (as in the later 1960s and 1970s).

A related theory is that of Hugh Carter and Paul C. Glick and other demographers who call attention to the fact that because women tend to marry men a few years older than they are, cyclical "marriage squeezes" appear in society.[108] From this perspective, women born during the early baby-boom period came of marriageable age during the 1960s and 1970s and found that their likely male partners were fewer in number, because they had been born two or three years earlier during a period of rising birthrates. The consequence was that more women delayed marriage with consequent effects on family formation, fertility, and women's work experience.

Guttentag and Secord's theory as well as the implications of the marriage-squeeze perspective would also tend to support Easterlin's prediction of the renewed emphasis on conventional familism in the late 1980s and 1990s, although for different reasons: The demographic balance would be seen as shifting toward enhancing marital opportunities for females born during a period of falling birthrates.

The Relative Permanence of Changed Attitudes and Relationships

How important are the predictions that may be derived from the demographic theories just described depends to a considerable degree largely on how permanent we are to regard the more recent changes in attitudes and behavior surrounding gender relations in U.S. society.[109]

If, in effect, women and men—and especially women—have remade the culture in terms of gender expectations, demographic factors may pressure toward a restoration of familism in the late 1980s and 1990s, but these pressures may be essentially neutralized by new cultural norms in respect to gender. This would especially be the case if economic forces continue to place a premium on the participation of women, particularly married women, in the paid labor force.

Strong arguments can be made on empirical grounds that the value revolution towards greater gender equality actually came after and was largely provoked by the strong upswing of wives' and mothers' entry into the world of paid work. But once this value revolution has taken place, can the genie be put back in the bottle? Anthropologist Marvin Harris, for instance, argues forcefully that the cultural dominance of familism (or what he calls the "procreation ethic") and related gender role expectations has been decisively broken in American culture.[110] Probably the majority of demographers and other social scientists share this view. In regard to women's market labor in particular, it is evident that despite the continuation of discrimination and structural barriers to achievement, many women, perhaps most women, derive extraeconomic satisfactions from the opportunity to work outside the home. It would also appear just as evident that the economics of child rearing in the contemporary United States has made one child or two children—or even childlessness—the realistic expectation for most married couples for the foreseeable future. This makes it more and more difficult for most women to see motherhood as a plausible "career."

But neither value stability nor value change exist in a political vacuum. The future of the relations between the genders in the United States also depends as much on how women and men collectively and consciously attempt to reorder their lives together as it does on the more impersonal forces of the marketplace and demographic change.

The Future of Gender Politics

The mid-1980s, as we have already indicated, is a time of backlash against feminist issues. Not only are the organized movements of the New Right attempting to reinstate the homemaking role as the essential role for women but also many women who have most clearly benefited from the feminist movement now look upon that movement with indifference. Young, well-educated, career-oriented women increasingly emerge from an environment in which gender equality is ideologically taken for granted. Such women attribute their opportunities and relative successes to themselves alone.

A recent survey of women found this to be a common response. "I don't see what the fuss is all about." One woman holding Rhodes scholarship at Harvard in 1977, the first year in its seventy-four years that the scholarship was open to women said, "I guess I don't see myself as a feminist. I've never had to come to terms as a minority because I haven't been discriminated against."[111]

The new spate of books designed to teach women how to compete effectively in the higher reaches of the corporate world portray it as an individual matter, not a cause for social movement pressure. Gender discrimination is viewed as a thing of the past. You can "get yours" if you dress for success, understand corporate politics, and play the game right. The woman must become a company woman, just as men are company men, and sever any potentially embarrassing ties to feminism. It might hurt her new corporate image.[112]

The widespread denial of feminism among the younger generation may be as dangerous to future progress in dismantling gender stratification as the openly antifem-inist attacks of the New Right. The belief that the problem has been solved lulls many young women into complacency. Such atti-tudes are not just the result of the partial victories of feminism toward the achieve-ment of equality of opportunity between the genders, they are also a reflection of the fact that liberal feminism in particular has not been able to establish a vision of gender equality that is based on something other than equal access to the marketplace. With-out major changes in the dominant institu-tions of the society—which currently pro-mote competitive material success as the prime key to entry to the "good life"—even the most vigorous pursuit of equality of op-portunity for the genders, while laudable and necessary, will end in reenforcing the system of *class* stratification. To believe, without such changes, that the mere entry of women into positions of importance in these dominant institutions will in itself serve to humanize the society or to make greater room for the celebration and practice of genuine feminine values is politically na-ive.[113] It is also ultimately subversive of the effort to give *nonelite* women a greater share of society's rewards and greater opportunity to attain equality, not only with men, but with other women.

Notes

1. Heleieth Saffioti, *Women in Class Society*, trans. Michael Vale (New York: Monthly Review Press, 1978).

2. Eli Zaretsky, *Capitalism, the Family, and Personal Life* (New York: Harper & Row), 1976.

3. John Kenneth Galbraith, *Economics and the Public Purpose* (New York: Houghton Mifflin, 1973): 31–40; Carl Degler, *At Odds: Women and the Family in America from the Revolution to the Present* (New York: Oxford University Press, 1980) traces the difficulties encountered in the attempt by early feminists to extend individualism to women.

4. Eleanor Burke Leacock, "Introduction," in Saffi-oti, xiii.

5. Louise A. Tilly and Joan W. Scott, *Women, Work, and Family* (New York: Holt, Rinehart & Winston, 1978). See also Julie A. Matthaei, *An Economic History of Women in America: Women's Work the Sexual Division of Labor and the Development of Capitalism* (New York: Schocken Books, 1982); Mary P. Ryan, *Womanhood in America: From Colonial Times to the Present*, 3d ed. (New York: Franklin P. Watts, 1983).

6. John Demos, "The American Family in Past Time," in Arlene Skolnick and Jerome Skolnick, ed., *Family in Transition*, 2d ed. (Boston: Little, Brown, 1977): 59–77.

7. Ryan, 1983.

8. Phillippe Aries, *Centuries of Childhood* (New York: Vintage Books, 1962).

9. Edward Shorter, *The Making of the Modern Family* (New York: Basic Books, 1977).

10. Nancy F. Cott, *The Bonds of Womanhood* (New Haven: Yale University Press, 1977): 3.

11. Barbara Easton, "Industrialization and Feminin-ity: A Case Study of Nineteenth-Century New Eng-land," *Social Problems* 23 (April 1976), 389–401.

12. Cott, 55–57.

13. Cott, 46.

14. Easton, 394.

15. Barbara Welter, "The Cult of True Womanhood: 1820–1860," in Michael Gordon, ed., *The American Family in Social-Historical Perspective* 2d ed. (New York: St. Mar-tin's Press, 1978): 313–333; Easton, 1976; Martha Vici-nus, "Introduction: The Perfect Victorian Lady," in Mar-tha Vicinus, ed., *Suffer and Be Still* (Bloomington: Indiana University Press, 1973):vii–xv.

16. Ann Wood, "The Fashionable Diseases: Wom-en's Complaints and Their Treatment in Nineteenth-Century America," in Mary Hartman and Lois Banner, eds., *Clio's Consciousness Raised* (New York: Harper & Row, 1974): 1–22; Carol Smith-Rosenberg, "Puberty to Menopause: The Cycle of Femininity in Nineteenth Cen-tury America," in Hartman and Banner, 23–37; Regina Morantz, "The Lady and Her Physician," in Hartman and Banner, 38–53; Linda Gordon, "Voluntary Moth-erhood: The Beginnings of Feminist Birth Control Ideas in the United States," in Hartman and Banner, 54–71; Elaine Showalter and English Showalter, "Victorian Women and Menstruation," in Vicinus, 38–44.

17. Carol Smith-Rosenberg, "The Hysterical Woman: Sex Roles and Sex Role Conflict in Nineteenth- Century America," *Social Research* 39 (Winter 1972): 652– 678.

18. G. J. Barker-Benfield, *The Horrors of the Half-Known Life* (New York: Harper & Row, 1976).

19. Randall Collins, *Conflict Sociology* (New York: Ac-ademic Press, 1975): 238, 242–249.

20. Mary P. Ryan, *Womanhood in America: From Colonial Times to the Present* (New York: Franklin P. Watts, 1975): 154.

21. Cott, 200.

22. See Degler, 132–143; Ryan, 1983, 154–158, 167–216; and Charlotte G. O'Kelly, "Public Schools, Compulsory Schooling, Child Labor and the Construction of Idealized Motherhood and Childhood in the Immigrant Family in the United States," *Kyushu Annual Review of Sociology* 13 (1983): 38–74.

23. Tilly and Scott.

24. Tilly and Scott, 133.

25. Shorter, 1977.

26. Tilly and Scott 96.

27. Sheila M. Rothman, *Woman's Proper Place* (New York: Basic Books, 1978): 26–42. See also Degler, 307–314.

28. Peter Filene, *Him/Her/Self* (New York: Harcourt Brace Jovanovich, 1975): 26.

29. Ryan, 1975, 236.

30. Rothman, 42–60; Matthaei, 1982, 218–223.

31. Susan M. Strasser, "The Business of Housekeeping: The Ideology of the Household at the Turn of the Twentieth Century," *Insurgent Sociologist* 8 (Fall 1978): 147–163; Susan M. Strasser, *Never Done: A History of American Housework* (New York: Pantheon, 1982); Matthaei, 157–186.

32. Tilly and Scott, 198–199.

33. Tilly and Scott, 202–203.

34. Degler, 348–359.

35. This section draws on the following works: William H. Chafe, *The American Woman: Her Changing Social Economic, and Political Role, 1920–1970* (New York: Oxford University Press, 1972); Peter Filene, *Him/Her/Self* (New York: Harcourt Brace Jovanovich, 1975); Mary Ryan, *Womanhood in America from Colonial Times to the Present* (New York: New Viewpoints, 1983); William O'Neill, *Everyone Was Brave: A History of Feminism in America* (Chicago: Quadrangle Books, 1971); Jo Freeman, *The Politics of Women's Liberation: A Case Study of an Emerging Social Movement and Its Relation to the Policy Process* (New York: David McKay, 1975); Alice Kessler-Harris, *Out to Work* (New York: Oxford University Press, 1982); Alice Kessler-Harris, *Women Have Always Worked: A Historical Overview* (New York: McGraw-Hill, 1981).

36. Chafe, 1972, 33.

37. Chafe, 1972, 96.

38. Filene, 163.

39. Joseph Pleck, *The Myth of Masculinity* (Cambridge: MIT Press, 1981).

40. Kessler-Harris, 1982, 250–260.

41. Kessler-Harris, 1982, 260–270.

42. Ryan, 1975, 285.

43. Daniel Moynihan, *The Negro Family: The Case for National Action* (Washington, D.C.: U.S. Government Printing Office, U.S. Dept. of Labor, 1965); Ryan, 1983, 291–295; Degler, 1980, 127–132.

44. Dean Knudsen, "The Declining Status of Women: Popular Myths and the Failure of Functionalist Thought," *Social Forces* 48 (1969): 183–193.

45. Benjamin Spock, *The Common Sense Book of Baby and Child Care* (New York: Duell, Sloan & Pearce, 1945); see also Ferdinand Lundberg and Marynia Farnham, *Modern Woman: The Lost Sex* (New York: Harper, 1947); Lynn White, Jr., *Educating Our Daughters: The Challenge to the Colleges* (New York: 1950); Ashley Montagu, quoted in Chafe, 1972, 206–207.

46. Filene, 179–180.

47. Barbara Ehrenreich argues that already in the 1950s, ideologies of "male liberation" (such as the *Playboy* philosophy) were emerging, which would eventually aid men in their efforts to escape the "trap" of marriage and the family and to legitimate the kind of behavior that fueled the rapid rise of female-headed households and the feminization of poverty. Barbara Ehrenreich, *The Hearts of Men: American Dreams and the Flight from Commitment* (Garden City, N.Y.: Anchor Books, 1984): 64–66.

48. The following discussion of the rise of feminism in the sixties and seventies relies on Freeman, 1975.

49. See, for example, Boston Women's Health Book Collective, *Our Bodies, Our Selves* 2d ed. (New York: Simon & Schuster, 1976); The Diagram Group, *Woman's Body: An Owner's Manual* (New York: Bantam Books, 1977).

50. Betty Friedan, *The Feminine Mystique* (New York: Dell, 1963).

51. Eli Zaretsky, *Capitalism, The Family and Personal Life* (New York: Harper & Row, 1976).

52. Chafe, 229.

53. For discussion of this phenomenon see Diane K. Lewis, "A Response to Inequality: Black Women, Racism, and Sexism," *Signs* 3 (Winter 1977): 339–361; Charlayne Hunter, "Many Blacks Wary of Women's Liberation Movement in U.S.," *New York Times*, November 17, 1970: 47. For examples of the early opposition to feminism, see Toni Cade, ed., *The Black Woman* (New York: New American Library, 1970); Jean Cooper, "Women's Liberation and the Black Woman," *Journal of Home Economics* 63 (October 1971): 521–523; Nathan Hare and Julia Hare, "Black Women 1970," *Transaction* 8 (November–December, 1970): 68, 90; Mae C. King, "The Politics of Sexual Stereotypes," *Black Scholar* 4 (March–April 1973): 12; Linda J. M. LaRue, "Black Liberation and Women's Lib." *Transaction* 8 (November–December 1970): 59–64; Inez Smith Reid, *"Together" Black Women*

(New York: Third Press, 1972). For a recent discussion of black women and feminism, see Paula Giddings, *When and Where I Enter: The Impact of Black Women on Race and Sex in America* (New York: William Morrow, 1984), and *The Black Scholar* vol XVI, No. 2 (March/April 1985). [Special issue devoted to "Black Women and Feminism."]

54. Lewis, 345–346.

55. Donald J. Treiman and Heidi I. Hartman, eds., *Women, Work and Wages: Equal Pay for Jobs of Equal Value* (Washington, D.C.: National Academy Press, 1981).

56. William A. Blakey, "Everybody Makes the Revolution: Some Thoughts on Racism and Sexism," *Civil Rights Digest* 6 (Spring 1974): 19.

57. Lewis, 349–358; Treiman and Hartman, 1982, 14.

58. Louis Harris and Associates, *The 1972 Virginia Slims American Women's Opinion Poll: A Survey of the Attitudes of Women on Their Roles in Politics and the Economy:* 2, 4.

59. Susan H. Hertz, "The Politics of the Welfare Mothers Movement: A Case Study," *Signs* 2 (Spring 1977): 600–611.

60. Chafe, 232.

61. For a statement of these women's conceptions of woman's place and their recommendations to women see their best selling books: Mirabel Morgan, *The Total Woman* (New York: Pocket Books, 1973); Helen Andelin, *Fascinating Womanhood* (New York: Bantam Books, 1975).

62. Kristen Luker, *Abortion and the Politics of Motherhood* (Berkeley: University of California Press, 1984).

63. Luker, 209. Emphasis in the original.

64. Luker, 209–210.

65. The classic work on the historical contradictions of capitalism in this respect remains Karl Polanyi's *The Great Transformation: The Political and Economic Origins of Our Times* (Boston: Beacon Press, 1957); see also Ross Poole, "Markets and Motherhood: The Advent of the New Right," in Alisa Burnes, ed. *The Family in the Modern World: Australian Perspectives* (Sydney: George Allen & Unwin, 1983) and Christopher Lasch, *Haven in a Heartless World: The Family Besieged* (New York: Basic Books, 1977).

66. Erich Fromm, *Man for Himself: An Inquiry into the Psychology of Ethics* (New York: Holt, Rinehart & Winston, 1947): 67–82.

67. Betty Friedan, *The Second Stage* (New York: Summit Books, 1981).

68. Jean Bethke Elshtain, *Public Man, Private Woman: Women in Social and Political Thought* (Princeton, N.J.: Princeton University Press, 1981).

69. Alice S. Rossi, "Equality Between the Sexes: An Immodest Proposal," in Robert J. Lifton, ed., *The Women in America* (Boston: Beacon Press, 1964): 98–143.

70. For example, Alice Rossi, "A Biosocial Perspective on Parenting," *Daedalus* 106 (Spring 1977): 1–32 and Alice Rossi, "Gender and Parenthood," *American Sociological Review* 49, no. 1 (February 1984): 1–19. For examples of the resurgence of interest in the question of the distinctive capacities of women for nurturance and emotional receptivity, see Carol Gilligan, *In a Different Voice: Psychological Theory and Women's Development* (Cambridge: Harvard University Press, 1982); Sara Ruddick, "Maternal Thinking," *Feminist Studies* 6 (Summer 1980): 342–367; and Mary-Joan Gerson, Judith L. Alpert, and Mary Sue Richardson, "Mothering: The View from Psychological Research," *Signs* 9, no. 3 (Spring 1984): 434–453.

71. Judith Stacey, "The New Conservative Feminism," *Feminist Studies* 9, no. 3 (Fall 1983): 575.

72. See for example Gaye Tuchman, Arlene Kaplan Daniels, and James Benet, eds., *Hearth and Home: Images of Women in the Mass Media* (New York: Oxford University Press, 1978); Mary Anne Ferguson, ed., *Images of Women in Literature* (Boston: Houghton Mifflin, 1973); Molly Haskell, *From Reverence to Rape: The Treatment of Women in the Movies* (Baltimore: Penguin Books, 1974); Joan Mellon, *Women and Their Sexuality in the New Film* (New York: Dell, 1973); Lenore Weitzman, "Sex-Role Socialization in Picture Books for Preschool Children," *American Journal of Sociology* 77 (May 1972): 1125–1150; Robin Lakoff, *Language and Woman's Place* (New York: Harper & Row, 1975); Erving Goffman, *Gender Advertisements* (New York: Harper Colophon, 1979).

73. U.S. Department of Labor, Bureau of Labor Statistics, *Employment and Earnings* (Washington, D.C.: U.S. Government Printing Office, January 1985): 155–156.

74. U.S. Department of Labor, Bureau of Labor Statistics, *News* (Washington, D.C.: U.S. Government Printing Office, July 26, 1984): 2.

75. Howard Hayshe, "Working Mothers Reach Record Number in 1984," *Monthly Labor Review.* Vol. 107, no. 12 (December 1984): 31–34.

76. U.S. Department of Labor, Bureau of Labor Statistics, *Employment and Earnings* (January, 1985): 176. "She's Come a Long Way—Or Has She?" *U.S. News and World Report*, August 6, 1984: 47.

77. Ibid., 46.

78. Elliott Currie and Jerome H. Skolnick, *America's Problems: Social Issues and Public Policy* (Boston: Little, Brown, 1984): 219. Chapters 6 and 7 of this book provide excellent overviews of the dimensions of female employment in U.S. society and their impact on the family.

79. U.S. Department of Labor, Bureau of Labor Statistics, *Employment and Earnings,* (January, 1985): 37.

80. Ibid., 176–179.

81. Ibid., 79.

82. U.S. Department of Commerce, Bureau of the Census, *Money Income and Poverty Status of Families and Persons in the United States: 1983* (Washington, D.C.: U.S. Government Printing Office, August 1984): 5, 7.

83. U.S. Department of Commerce, Bureau of the Census, *Money Income and Poverty Status of Families and Persons in the United States: 1982* (Washington, D.C.: U.S. Government Printing Office, February 1984): 164, 165.

84. U.S. Department of Commerce, Bureau of the Census, *Households, Families, Marital Status, and Living Arrangements: March 1984* (Washington, D.C.: U.S. Government Printing Office, August 1984): 3.

85. U.S. Department of Commerce, Bureau of the Census. *Money Income and Poverty Status of Families and Persons in the United States: 1983*, 5.

86. Ibid., 20–21.

87. All statistics on higher education in this section are taken from U.S. Department of Education, National Center for Educational Statistics, *The Condition of Education, 1984* (Washington, D.C.: U.S. Government Printing Office, 1984): 92, 100.

88. Edward B. Fiske, "College Freshman Better in Basics," *New York Times*, March 20, 1984.

89. Myra and David Sadker, "Sexism in the Schoolroom of the 80s," *Psychology Today* (March 1985): 54–57.

90. Jessie Bernard, *The Future of Marriage* (New York: Bantam Books, 1972), 142–143.

91. David Wessel, "Working Fathers Feel New Pressure Arising from Child-Rearing Duties," *Wall Street Journal*, September 7, 1984: 22.

92. For a description of one couple's difficulties and solution to overcoming the traditional gender division of labor, see Susan Edmiston, "How to Write Your Own Marriage Contract," in Francine Klagburn, ed., *The First Ms. Reader* (New York: Warner Paperbacks, 1973): 91–107; see also Grace Baruch, Rosalind Barnett, and Caryl Rivers, *Lifeprints: New Patterns of Love and Work for Today's Women* (New York: McGraw-Hill, 1983).

93. Baruch, 1983, 248.

94. Harold Berenson, "Women's Occupational and Family Achievement in the U.S. Class System: A Critique of the Dual-Career Family Analysis," *British Journal of Sociology* 35, no. 1 (March 1984): 19–41.

95. *ISR Newsletter* 10, nos. 1–2 (Spring/Summer 1982). The comments within quotation marks are those of A. Regula Herzog and Jerold G. Bachman, authors of the study *Sex Role Attitudes among High School Seniors: Views about Work and Family Roles* (Ann Arbor: University of Michigan, Institute for Social Research, 1982).

96. See Eleanor D. Macklin, "Nonmarital Heterosexual Cohabitation: An Overview," in E. D. Macklin and R. Rubin, eds., *Contemporary Families and Alternative Life Styles: A Handbook of Research and Theory* (Beverly Hills, Calif.: Sage, 1983).

97. For an assessment of how much gender role change has actually taken place in the area of sexuality, see Eleanor D. Macklin, "Effect of Changing Sex Roles on the Intimate Relationships of Men and Women," *Marriage and Family Review* 6, nos. 3,4 (Fall/Winter 1983): 97–113.

98. Alix Kates Shulman, "Sex and Power: Sexual Bases of Radical Feminism," *Signs* 5, no. 4 (Fall 1980): 590–604; Ethel Sepctor Person, "Sexuality as a Mainstay of Identity: Psychoanalytic Perspectives," *Signs* 5, no. 4 (Fall 1980): 605–630; Rosalind Pollack Petchesky, "Reproductive Freedom: Beyond a Woman's Right to Choose," *Signs* 5, no. 4 (Fall 1980): 661–685.

99. Lillian Rubin, *Worlds of Pain: Life in the Working Class Family* (New York: Basic Books, 1976): 139.

100. Marian Blum, *The Day-Care Dilemma: Women and Children First* (Lexington, Mass.: Lexington Books, 1983); Sheila B. Kamerman, *Parenting in an Unresponsive Society* (New York: Free Press, 1980); Sheila B. Kamerman, "Child Care Services: An Issue for Gender Equity and Women's Solidarity," *Child Welfare*. Vol. LXIV, no. 3 (May–June, 1985), 259–272.

101. Wini Breines and Linda Gordon, "The New Scholarship on Family Violence," *Signs* 8, no. 3 (Spring 1983): 490–531; Allan Griswold Johnson, "On the Prevalence of Rape in the United States," *Signs* 6, no. 1 (Fall 1980); see also Susan Brownmiller, *Against Our Will: Men, Women, and Rape* (New York: Simon & Schuster, 1976).

102. "Women in the Workforce," *Economic Notes*. Vol. 53, no. 4 (April 1985), 6–9.

103. For a theoretical and empirical perspective on this issue, see Randall Collins, *The Credential Society* (New York: Academic Press, 1979).

104. For a useful review, see Linda J. Waite, *U.S. Women at Work* (Washington, D.C.: Population Reference Bureau, 1981), 36, no. 2 of the *Population Bulletin*. See also Valerie Kincade Oppenheimer, *The Female Labor Force in the United States: Demographic and Economic Factors Governing Its Growth and Changing Composition* (Berkeley: University of California Population Monograph Series, no. 5, 1970); Victor R. Fuchs, *How We Live: An Economic Perspective on Americans from Birth to Death* (Cambridge, Mass.: Harvard University Press, 1983); and Marvin Harris, *America Now: The Anthropology of a Changing Culture* (New York: Simon & Schuster, 1981).

105. Andrew J. Cherlin, *Marriage, Divorce, Remarriage* (Cambridge, Mass.: Harvard University Press, 1981): 64.

106. Richard Easterlin, *Birth and Fortune: The Impact*

of Numbers on Personal Welfare (New York: Basic Books, 1980).

107. Marcia Guttentag and Paul F. Secord, *Too Many Women? The Sex Ratio Question* (Beverly Hills, Calif.: Sage, 1983).

108. Hugh Carter and Paul C. Glick, *Marriage and Divorce: A Social and Economic Study*, rev. ed. (Cambridge, Mass.: Harvard University Press, 1976).

109. Cherlin, 1981, chap. 2 summarizes succinctly the main issues involved in the debate over the relative importance of demographic and attitudinal factors.

110. Harris, 1981, chaps. 5 and 6; see also Cherlin, 1981, 60–64.

111. Baruch, Barnett, and Rivers, 1983, 23; see also Susan Bolotin, "Voices from the Post-Feminist Generation," *New York Times Magazine*, October 17, 1982: 28–31, 103ff.

112. Suzanne Gordon, "The New Corporate Feminism," *The Nation*, February 5, 1983: 143–147.

113. Gordon, 147.

CHAPTER 7

Capitalist Industrial Society

Sweden and Japan

Capitalist advanced industrial societies are not alike in their gender roles and gender stratification systems. Depending upon their unique historical backgrounds and the different social, economic, and political forces that come to bear upon them, they can vary greatly. We have already considered the United States in some detail. The cases of Sweden, a nation committed to developing the welfare state and supporting gender equality to the greatest extent possible, and Japan, a country reluctant to institute extensive welfare state policies or to encourage gender equality, illustrate the diversity within this type of society.

Sweden: A Committed Welfare State

Historical Background

Sweden and the other Scandinavian countries have a significantly different past from other European countries.[1] Sweden's remote location, rugged environment, poor soil, and low population densities isolated the country from many of the political and social developments and conflicts that characterized the rest of Europe. For example, Sweden

escaped Roman domination and did not come under the influence of Christianity until the twelfth century. Protestantism replaced Catholicism early. The Lutheran church became the established national religion in 1593. Sweden never became as committed to the ideal of the Roman *paterfamilias* or to the rigid gender roles, marriage practices, and religious devaluation of women that came to be a part of Catholic theology and culture. Moreover, feudalism never really gained hold here; Sweden retained its tribal structures longer. Sweden came to rely on small independent farmers running local popular governments. Peasant surpluses were too small to support much of an aristocracy or the institution of knighthood. Consequently, the roles of the lady versus the warrior were never as fully developed or idealized in Sweden as in the rest of Europe.

Economics, Class, and the Division of Labor. Swedish men were often involved in seafaring trade and, during the Viking period from the eighth through the tenth centuries, in long-distance warfare and colonization. This, of course, took many men away from home for long periods of time, often leaving women in charge during their absence. This was especially true in northern Sweden. Women were economically productive and independent. Men were away much of the time hunting, fishing, lumbering, and at distant markets leaving women in charge of the farms and livestock. In the summer unmarried young women took the flocks to the mountain pastures for several weeks. Class distinctions were minimal in such a poor land. Marriages therefore involved few economic or political advantages; families tended to leave it to the young people to choose mates. Little control was exercised over young women and premarital chastity was not highly valued. Engagements could be very long and continue even after the birth of one or more children.[2]

The practice of primogeniture, that is, the eldest son inherits all the family's property, was widespread, and it was very important for the eldest son to have a son to ensure the continuation of the family over the generations. It was therefore often preferable to wait till the intended wife was pregnant or until she had actually born a son before finalizing the marriage. But even when family property was not at stake, engagements were often very long as people waited until they could afford to marry. With the long distances and cold winters, the practice of. "night courting" allowed young men to visit the young women and share their beds rather than undertaking a dangerous trip home. If the woman got pregnant, it was not a matter of shame for her or her family; it simply meant that it was time to marry.[3]

In the south there was greater wealth and more class inequality. It was consequently more important that marriages be arranged between families of appropriate statuses. Since marriages were of greater social significance, closer control was exercised over daughters' sexual behavior to protect her value in the marriage market. But even in the south the men were often out to sea for long periods, which provided wives a high degree of personal and economic independence.

In both the north and the south there was a rather strict gender division of labor. Males were unwilling to take on female chores such as milking. Men and women were, however, economically interdependent; a household required the work of women as much as it required the work of men. But as is typical of agrarian societies, the man was considered the absolute head of the household despite the woman's obvious contribution to that unit.

Swedish history provides several examples of strong female leaders despite the society's patriarchal structure. The Vikings had some warrior women as well as warrior men. Blenda is credited with having led an army that repelled a Danish invasion of Sweden, and in honoring her feat women were given better inheritance rights.[4] Much later in the fourteenth century, Queen Margrethe succeeded in uniting all the Scandinavian countries under her rule until her death in 1412.

Sweden remained a land of poor farmers, fishermen, hunters, and woodsmen well into the nineteenth century. It was "the poorhouse of Europe" with little industrialization until the late nineteenth century. The land could not support all the people, and between 1860 and 1910 there was massive emigration primarily to North America. This emigration, however, coincided with Sweden's late-developing industrialization and created important labor shortages. Single women were drawn into the labor force by the existence of jobs and the difficulties in finding a marriage partner. Poverty had sent many men to America and many of those who remained were too poor to take a wife. The marriage rate was very low, the age of marriage very high, and the number of single adults high. This early reliance on women's labor may help account for Sweden's acceptance of the principle of gender equality much earlier than other industrialized nations. But women were not treated well at this early stage. The traditional beliefs that the male is the primary breadwinner and the devaluation of women's labor under agriculture, where women were traditionally paid half of what a man earned as a day laborer, meant that women entered an industrial labor market that also paid them much less than men and provided little training or opportunity for advancement. Despite the labor shortages, the industrial labor market was as highly gender segregated as agrarian labor.

Although Sweden was one of the poorest countries in Europe, it used its late industrialization to its advantage and avoided some of the social problems that plagued early industrializing nations such as England. Urban slums and massive urban poverty were averted early by Sweden's acceptance of rational social planning. This early recognition of the problems of the underprivileged also helped set the stage for greater official recognition of women as an underprivileged social group.

Early Feminism. Feminism preceded industrialization in Sweden. The first wave included mainly upper-class women in the 1830s. Conventional marriage came under attack in the novel *That Will Do*, initiating social debates about marriage and women earlier in Sweden than in other parts of the world. There was some expansion of rights for women. In 1842 Sweden established a national elementary school system that admitted girls as well as boys. In 1845 women were given equal inheritance rights, and in 1846 women were given the legal right to practice professions, to operate businesses in

their own names, and to take paid employment. But these rights were not the result of organized pressure from women or women's groups. Parliament led the way in these reforms, trying to keep up with the social changes accompanying the economic transformations the country was undergoing. Many young women were leaving the poverty-stricken countryside for employment in the city. Without the legal right to be paid, they could only accept room and board as live-in domestics. After 1846 many middle-class women ran small shops, while lower-class women operated as street vendors.[5]

A second wave of feminism arose in the 1850s and derived partly from the example set by American feminists. But both the American and the Swedish movements arose out of the dislocations of industrialization and urbanization. Frederika Bremer led the movement demanding legal equality for women and better educational opportunities. She founded the first women's emancipation organization in Europe in 1845, and her novel *Hertha*, published in 1856, was avowedly feminist in content. Support for women's rights was strong in Swedish literary circles, but it remained a movement among urban intellectuals and middle- and upper-class women with little real impact on policy makers.[6]

The upper- and middle-class orientations of early feminists were also clear in the goals of other women's organizations. In 1871 the Society for Married Women's Rights was founded to seek legislative protection for women's property from husbands who received automatic guardianship over the wife on marriage. In 1884 the Frederika Bremer Association was founded to seek equal rights for women. Poor women, however, were less interested in equal rights than they were with immediate economic survival. Author and lecturer Ellen Key departed from the mainstream by actively advocating "free love" in the late nineteenth century.[7] Other women established women's aid societies to help poor urban women with food, shelter, work, and protection from prostitution. This was also a period of interest in revivalist religious movements and the temperance movement for Swedish women. As in the United States, participation in such social movements often gave women the necessary experience and self-confidence to branch out from Bible study groups and protests against alcohol to more overtly feminist causes as the demand for the vote. But in Sweden the suffrage issue never became paramount; property rights and jobs were more important.[8]

In fact, in Sweden women were not alone in demanding the vote. Universal manhood suffrage was still an issue and women's suffrage was linked with the demand for extending the vote to the nonpropertied classes in general. Nonproperty-owning men were successful before women, however. All men received the vote in 1909; women had to wait till 1919 when the example of other countries finally led Sweden to accede to the demand for women's suffrage.[9] But the struggle for the vote reflects the organizational path that feminist issues have continued to follow in Sweden. It was carried out within the major political parties and not in opposition to them. The Social Democrats and the Liberal Party were both founded at the turn of the century and both supported suffrage for women as well as men. Women's issues have continued to be accepted within the important institutions of Swedish society such as the political parties, the labor unions, and the employers' associations. This differs from the United States where women have had to organize separately as women in opposition to parties and unions. One consequence has been that women's issues in Sweden have cut across gender lines and have not engendered the same hostile op-

position that they have in other countries. They have been part of wider programs of social reform with broadly based social support.

Social Policy, Gender Roles, and the Rise of the Welfare State

Another benefit of arriving at industrialization as a latecomer was that Sweden could solve some of the issues of class conflict without the same degree of violence and opposition that England and the United States experienced. It could also view socialistic programs for change with a more objective, less hostile eye. The Social Democratic Party, founded in 1889, was able to avoid the Marxist emphasis on class conflict and revolution yet follow a clearly Marxist policy of redistribution of wealth.[10] Since the Social Democrats came to power in the 1930s battling the massive problems of the Great Depression, they have built an economy in which almost all production is in the hands of private capitalists but a society in which the surplus of this amazingly productive economy has been redistributed to meet the needs of the weaker members of society with dignity. Sweden has one of the highest standards of living in the world, ranking ahead of the United States on per capita income, health care, infant mortality, life expectancy, and many other measures of health and well-being. Yet Sweden's social and economic organization is the antithesis of what neoconservatives, New Rightists, and much conventional wisdom in the United States says is necessary for economic productivity and strength. The welfare state has not sapped the energy and vitality of Sweden, nor have equal rights for women destroyed the fabric of the family or society.

Full Employment. One of the key elements in Swedish social policies for gender equality is their idea of full employment—that every adult has the right to a job. The Social Democrats began their struggle for full employment in 1913, long before Keynesian economics. Unemployment was a crucial issue in Sweden in the 1920s. They had moved from a labor shortage to a labor surplus, with more than one-quarter of the labor force unemployed for the entire decade. Despite a high level of industrial strife and labor unrest, business and industry opposed programs to combat unemployment for fear that such programs would drive wages up and profits down. In the 1930s the Social Democrats finally had enough power to control the government and put their policies of public-sector spending to produce jobs into effect. In the 1950s they revised their model to include, in addition to job creation, shifting and retraining workers, eventually including unemployed housewives, from labor surplus occupations and areas to labor shortage areas. Sweden pulled out of the Depression before the rest of the West. The Social Democrats remained in power uninterruptedly from 1932 until 1976 and returned to power in 1982. During this time the Swedish government has been the world leader in almost every type of social legislation. The commitment to full employment has carried with it the gradual acceptance into social policy of the view of women as national resources.[11]

The Population Crisis.   At the same time that the Social Democrats came to power, Sweden also recognized the beginning of a population crisis. Gunnar and Alva Myrdal published their influential book *Crisis and Population* in 1934. In it they outlined the extent and implication of the decline in the birthrate that Sweden experienced during its long bout with widespread poverty and unemployment. They argued that to avoid imminent population decline, the government

had to take responsibility for making it easier for people to have and support children. Children should be viewed as a valuable contribution to society, and society should shoulder much of the burden associated with having and rearing children. Like other countries Sweden had previously attempted to halt population decline by making it illegal in 1910 to disseminate birth control information.[12] The National Association for Sex Education finally won repeal of this law in 1938. Since then Sweden has been committed to the principle that every child should be wanted.[13]

Contraception and Sex Education.
Sweden's pronatalist policies have not included support for a marital and procreative imperative to force people to marry and to limit sex to procreative sex.[14] Swedish policies, unlike the pronatalist policies of Hitler's Germany, do not attempt to lock the women in the domestic sphere with no choice but to reproduce. The Swedes have simultaneously developed policies to make contraception available to all sexually active individuals who do not desire conception. This has included a program of sex education in the schools begun in the 1940s and made compulsory for everyone fourteen years of age and older since 1956. The sex education includes detailed information on contraception and avoids taking a moral stand against premarital sexuality. The principle is that sexuality is the right of the individual, but it should be approached in a rational and responsible way, which includes protection against unwanted pregnancies. In recent years school nurses have been empowered to write prescriptions for contraceptives for schoolgirls. There has been some opposition to such programs by conservative medical doctors who pressed the government to have sex education courses advocate sexual abstinence to avoid pregnancy and veneral dis-

ease, but the government has not accepted this position as a realistic one.

The Swedish official response to the population problem and the issues of contraception and sex education reflects its basic outlook that government should take the lead and work with the people rather than against them, on such problems. Adams and Winston point out that three different models have been proposed to explain why governments accede to feminist demands. One is getting women into key political office so they can use their official power to support policies of gender equality. The second is organizing mass support for candidates, male or female who support these issues. The third is creating a general climate of opinion favorable to feminism so that the politicians will support such reforms. But Adams and Winston point out that as logical or necessary as these three paths may seem, none of them characterize the Swedish situation. The government has not waited for widespread public support or feminist-backed male or female politicians to take the lead. The government has pursued policies it considered necessary for the good of the nation and in doing so has become increasingly involved in social policy supportive of gender equality and women's issues.[15]

Family Policy.   Simply ordering people not to use contraception in order to increase the birthrate did not fit the model of working with the people for a better society. The freedom of the individual and individual rights were more important than the need for population growth. Instead of forcing people to have children, the government adopted a family policy to allow people more easily to choose to have children.

Most of these programs were implemented in Sweden before they had even begun to be suggested or debated as realistic possibilities in the United States. For example, in 1937 Sweden began providing free prenatal and postnatal medical care. The services have continued to expand to the point that virtually all health-care problems are covered today; a special concern is ensuring that children get the best preventive care with regular checkups. Guaranteed maternity leave for up to six months without pay was instituted in 1945. In 1954 a bill requiring maternity leave with pay for three months was passed. Today Sweden has the most generous *parental leave policy* in the world. Either parent is entitled to nine months leave at 90 percent of regular pay and an additional three months at a flat-rate payment. Either parent can take all of it or it can be divided between the two parents. In addition, both the mother and father get an additional sixty days per year off with pay for each sick child. The government actively encourages fathers to take advantage of the parental leave and is considering allocating each parent nontransferable parental leave to force fathers to share in early child care.[16]

In 1938 the government set up loans to newlyweds to purchase household goods; such loans were extended to unmarried parents in 1953. Subsidies for neighborhood laundries were added in 1939. In 1943 the government subsidized the Social Home Help program to provide household help for the elderly, the ill, and other families experiencing a crisis.[17] During the 1930s it also experimented with forms of housing that would allow many of the household chores to be taken care of centrally. In 1948 a *family allowance* for each child regardless of family income replaced the system of allowing a tax deduction for each child. Poor families did not benefit from tax deductions as much as well-to-do families did. Extra money is given to single parents and to parents with extra financial problems.[18]

Public assistance is also provided to any-one who needs it at a much higher level than in the United States. The Swedes do not feel they have to starve people into accepting a job by providing unrealisticaly low assist-ance rates or policies designed to humiliate the recipients. The rationale is that anyone who stays home to care for children is pro-viding a public service and should not be punished. The government is especially re-sistant to pushing single parents to work outside the home while their children are young, because such parents have a partic-ularly difficult time combining work and child rearing. The official view is that it is more likely to be detrimental to the children when a single parent works than when both parents in a two-parent family work outside the home.[19]

Public financing of *day care* began in the 1940s. There have never been enough spaces for all the preschool children of working mothers, and the government continues to increase its support for child-care facilities. The government has also gradually ex-panded its support for education. Today ed-ucation is free at all levels including the uni-versity. This includes a stipend for living expenses regardless of parental income.[20]

The policies of the Social Democrats and the general economic upturn during the 1940s and 1950s resulted in an increase in the marriage rate, a decrease in age at mar-riage, and a slight increase in the birthrate. Sweden's history of low birthrates, however, combined with more time devoted to edu-cation meant that labor shortages reemerged with prosperity. Demand for women's labor was high because of both the labor shortage and the great expansion of public service jobs that men did not want. Women's par-ticipation levels in the labor force continued to rise, but married women were still likely to opt for full-time housewifery, especially when their children were young.

Two Roles vs. Shared Roles. The need for women's labor gave rise to a debate about "women's two roles" and how to best ease some of the burdens of those roles. Alva Myrdal and Viola Klein published another very influential book in 1956, *Women's Two Roles*, in which they described women's par-ticipation in the labor force as basically se-quential. Women work before they have chil-dren, then they devote themselves to full-time motherhood and housework, and when the children are older they return to the labor force. Although the ideal was for husbands to share in the child care and housework, in reality wives did almost all of it. Myrdal and Klein recognized that women went back to work for real economic motives. The stand-ard of living rose rapidly in the 1940s and 1950s, and even well-off husbands could not always afford what a family felt it needed. The problem described by Myrdal and Klein dominated public discussion of gender roles during the 1950s—how could government and industry work to make it easier for women to combine their responsibilities as mothers, housewives, and workers.

The nature of the debate changed consid-erably after Eva Moberg published a chal-lenge to the "two roles" position in an essay entitled "The Conditional Emancipation of Women." She argued that two roles for women and only one role for men was in and of itself unequal and should not be sup-ported in public policy. Instead, policy should focus on both men and women shar-ing both the domestic and the work roles. After considerable public debate, this view was widely accepted and by 1968 it had be-come government policy.[21] One result has been the development and expansion of pa-rental leave and the government's attempts to encourage men to accept half of the pa-rental responsibilities.

Combining their long-standing commit-ment to full employment with their more recent commitment to gender equality as shared roles, the Social Democrats are now actively pursuing policies to pull married women, who constitute "hidden unemployment" and whose full-time provision of household services deters the sharing of these roles by men, into the labor force. Sweden has long had exceptionally high female labor force participation rates, always higher than in the United States. In 1979 about 65 percent of Swedish women worked (compared with about 79 percent for men) with females constituting about 45 percent of the labor force.[22]

In 1971 tax laws were changed to eliminate joint tax accounts for married couples. Everyone now is taxed as an individual regardless of marital status. This was intended to encourage married women to work and to discourage husbands from trying to earn more in order to retain the full-time household services of their wives. Under Sweden's sharply progressive tax structure, if a man earning a good salary takes an extra job to earn more income, the extra income will be taxed at his highest marginal rate and most of it may be paid out in taxes. But if his previously unemployed wife goes to work, she will pay taxes at her probably much lower individual tax rate. Her income will not be added to his and taxed at the higher marginal rate. If both work they will pay lower taxes than if only one worked and earned the same amount that they earn jointly.[23]

Gender Segregation in the Labor Force. Another program is designed to encourage unemployed housewives into the labor market and at the same time to attempt to break down some of the gender segregation that continues to characterize the Swedish labor force. It is called the *Kristianstad model* and involves job information programs, job placement, and job training to place women in male-dominated blue collar work and subsidies to both companies and individuals willing to participate in this program. In regions and industries suffering labor shortages, the government will undertake to find unemployed women willing to consider previously all-male work assignments, usually unskilled or semiskilled factory jobs. The policy has worked quite well in some factories and some areas where employers have been desperate to find workers. It gets little support, however, from employers who have adequate supplies of male laborers. The government also offers extra incentives and subsidies in many other occupational areas to encourage members of the underrepresented gender to enter a largely one-gender work category. For example, males are given preference in many female-dominated social service jobs.[24]

Gender Discrimination Legislation. Many of the improvements that have occurred in women's job situation are not the result of direct governmental legislation. Rather the Social Democrats have preferred to encourage the major trade unions and employers' organizations to negotiate the issues with the workers. Since almost all Swedish workers are organized into highly centralized unions, this is not as elitist a policy as it would be in United States where most workers, especially female workers, are not unionized. One policy that has helped narrow the wage gap between men and women in Sweden is the "solidarity wage" adopted by the major labor federation. Each time it negotiates a new contract, instead of accepting a percentage wage increase for all workers regardless of current wages, it negotiates for a larger percentage increase for those with the lowest wages. The aim is to gradually raise the wages of those on bottom without directly penalizing the higher-paid workers.

The wage gap for industrial workers has narrowed. In 1960 women earned 68.8 percent of what males earned; by 1977 the figure was up to 87 percent.[25]

The Social Democrats continued to block attempts to pass legislation specifically barring discrimination on the basis of gender. They felt it would undermine attempts to make up for past discrimination through reverse discrimination programs. But while the Social Democrats were out of power, the coalition government headed by the Center Party tried to pass a nondiscrimination law. It failed narrowly and was followed by a substitute bill offered by the Social Democrats that outlawed discrimination on the basis of gender in employment only and with the specific exception of "positive discrimination" to help improve the representation of the underrepresented gender. To further weaken the nondiscrimination clauses, they removed specific implementation procedures of enforcement machinery. The Social Democrats lost the battle for nonimplementation. With enforcement machinery restored, the Act on Equality between Men and Women at Work became law in 1980.[26]

How Much Equality Has Been Achieved?

With more than fifty years of official commitment to gender equality, how much social support has there been? The impressive amount of material support for child care and child rearing relieves Swedish parents of much of the crippling financial burden that American parents face. Swedish taxes are, of course, very high to pay for the welfare state, but until the recent economic recession and increases in inflation there had been little public resentment of the high taxation.[27] Most people realize that with lower taxes they would have to pay for more goods and services out of their income that now come from the government. Lower taxes probably mean a net loss rather than a net gain for all but the wealthiest Swedes.

Low Birthrates vs. The Cult of Motherhood. Despite family support systems the birthrate remains low (1.62 in 1979).[28] This is below replacement levels, and natural increase has all but ceased in Sweden's population. Only the limited amount of immigration keeps the population from actually declining. The birthrate has also declined to below replacement levels in the United States, and similar factors are probably at work. The high cost of living associated with high levels of consumption and inflation make children expensive even in Sweden and especially in the United States. Furthermore, women's participation in the labor force and higher levels of education have long been associated with lower birthrates.[29]

An additional factor in Sweden to account for low birthrates may be the lack of a cultural tradition glorifying and idealizing motherhood. Sweden never developed the "cult of motherhood" so characteristic of the late-nineteenth-century middle classes in the United States. Instead of focusing on the need for the moral mother to mold her children correctly, Swedes tend to view children as innately good and set on a path for healthy development unless something deters them. Hence mothers (or fathers or society) may get the blame if a child turns out badly, but the child will get the credit for turning out well. Swedes also emphasize early independence and separation from the parents. The hovering, overprotective mother is not encouraged in Swedish culture. This makes it difficult for mothers to overidentify with their maternal role. It simply is not as all-consuming as the mother role can become in other cultures. Sweden is not a child-centered society. They make it convenient to have and rear chldren, with playgrounds in shopping areas, ramps for strollers, and traffic-free paths between residential areas and schools. But they do not idealize or mystify child rearing.[30] Ann-Mari Sellerberg describes how even in cramped apartments, working-class Swedish mothers are concerned to establish "boundaries" that segregate adult from child space. Here is a typical response from a shop assistant, mother of two:

They aren't allowed in the big [living] room. And they don't go there either. I have many ornaments on low tables and shelves in there. And when they are playing with hockey sticks and things like that . . . We have a color television set and a vase might easily crack. The furniture is robust but you do want to have some place which is tidy, don't you?[31]

Marriage, Cohabitation, and Sexuality. Intimate relationships in Sweden are left entirely up to the couple with little control exerted by wider social groups. Neither kinship groups nor government have the right to intervene in an adult's private relationships unless someone is being seriously abused. Sweden abandoned its more patriarchal traditional marriage laws with the Marriage Code of 1921, which declared the equality and legal independence of the husband and the wife, equated housework and earned income as contributions to the unit, and declared both partners joint owners of any property they held. This law still assumed that the man would be the breadwinner and the woman the housekeeper, but it was very liberal for its time.

In the 1970s the marriage law underwent more reforms to embody the new concept of shared roles.[32] The state now makes little distinction between legal marriage and voluntary cohabitation. Both qualify for the same government benefits and most legal protections. The only exception is that the state protects the individuals' right not to accept an implied contract of marriage. Therefore, legal spouses have specific inheritance rights and joint property ownership unless they agree contractually to forego those rights, but cohabiting couples do not have joint inheritance or property unless they contract specifically to do so.

Legitimacy. Children of unmarried parents are not treated any differently than children of married parents by government or society. Illegitimacy was removed from the law books in Sweden as early as 1917.[33] The government does insist on determining the paternity of children born out of wedlock, but in 90 percent of the cases the father accepts paternity voluntarily. Fathers are charged with half of the support for the child till its adulthood, and the government is in charge of collecting it for the mother. If it is insufficient or if the father does not pay, the government provides the money to the mother and then attempts to deal with the recalcitrant father if he can afford to pay.

Little or no pressure to marry is placed on a couple with a child. Forced marriages are condemned as bad for everyone involved. The illegitimacy rate and the premarital conception rate are both very high in Sweden, but neither is considered a real social problem. In 1975 35 percent of Swedish births were out of wedlock, the highest rate in Europe. An unwanted pregnancy is considered undesirable, but out-of-wedlock and premarital conceptions are not necessarily unwanted or even unplanned.

Abortion. Since 1973 abortion has been readily available to Swedish women.[34] But abortion has been somewhat controversial as a moral issue and Sweden was reluctant to liberalize its laws to encompass abortion on demand as the right of any pregnant woman. Since 1938 Sweden has allowed abortion for serious problems such as rape, incest, severe fetal defects, or threat to the mother's health. But even this limited liberalization indicated Sweden was in the forefront of change. Only Iceland and the Soviet Union preceded them with such laws.

Illegal abortions were, however, widespread in the 1930s and continued to be a major social and health concern. After years of debate the law was liberalized in 1973 partly to end the illegal abortion trade. Currently, the government is under some pressure to return to a more restrictive law. There is particular concern over the high rates of teenage abortions. Why teenagers allow themselves to get burdened with an unwanted pregnancy in a society with compulsory sex education and easy access to effective contraception remains a puzzle to the Swedish government and people. The state Health Education Committee is trying to bring discussion of the problem into the open among young people as a means towards a solution. For example, a play entitled *Knocked Up or Cracked Up*, using language often shocking to parents and teachers, has been presented at schools and youth organizations, followed by group discussions of sexual inequality, freedom, and responsibility.[35]

Premarital Sexuality. Unwanted pregnancies and abortions are disapproved, but premarital sexuality is considered normal. Premarital virginity was never as highly valued in Sweden as in other countries and today premarital sexuality is universal.[36] Little of the sexual double standard remains in Sweden. Relations between the genders, especially among young people, are said to be more relaxed and more focused on friend-

ship rather than sexuality because it is simply taken for granted that if a couple grow to like each other, they will have sexual intercourse. Sex is seen as a natural part of a close loving relationship between men and women. As one young woman visiting the United States as an exchange student expressed it, "There is much more pressure to have sex in America. Boys seem to think they have to press for it whenever they are out with a girl. In Sweden we can wait till a relationship develops without the boy's masculinity depending on 'scoring.' " She added that she was eager to return to the more easygoing male-female relations in Sweden.

Extramarital Sexuality. Despite the widespread acceptance of premarital sex, extramarital sex is merely tolerated and not approved.[37] Sexual fidelity in relationships is still highly valued. While most Swedes will not condemn adultery in others, they see it as a form of losing control which may be excused but not endorsed. Adultery may also be less common in Sweden than in the United States because of less opportunity in a less mobile society and because egalitarian relationships make it less likely for a wife to suffer in silence with a philandering husband because of her dependence on him.[38]

Sexual Freedom. In keeping with the principle that the sexual lives of adults are private, Sweden outlaws sex only when it involves the exploitation of children or infringes on the rights of others. Prostitution is legal as an agreement between two people, but public solicitation is not. Newspapers have mutually agreed not to publish advertisements for thinly veiled sexual services or ads with provocative sex illustrations.[39] Since there is practically no poverty in Sweden, prostitution is not the major problem that it is in the United States. The benefits of the welfare state keep women from being driven into prostitution through economic deprivation.[40] There has been, however, recent concern over growing numbers of teenage girls turning to prostitution, probably as a result of illegal drug use.

Sex with children under the age of fourteen is illegal. Incest is illegal only if it involves children under eighteen years of age. Marriage between close relatives may be approved after examination for potential genetic problems. Homosexuality is also considered a private matter. It has been legal since 1944, but legal toleration does not indicate widespread approval, and there is an activist movement today opposing prejudice against homosexuals.[41]

Pornography has been legal and widespread since the 1960s, but it cannot be displayed in public where it could offend others.[42] Child pornography was specifically banned in 1980.[43] Women's organizations have actively opposed pornography in recent years. The government is not pleased with the popularity of pornography, but is reluctant to ban it and create a criminal supply network. Unlike the United States, the debate over restricting pornography in Sweden has focused on assessing its effects on men and women and the sexual inequality that it represents, rather than on the principle of freedom of the press. But as pornography is such a profitable industry, it would be difficult to suppress it.[44] Many argue that the bulk of the customers are foreigners, not Swedes; but it is certainly not an exclusively foreign market.

Protest over the use of scantily clad or nude women in advertisements has been more effective. The problem gained official recognition in the early seventies and such ads are relatively rare today.[45]

Sweden has long been concerned with venereal disease as a public health problem, and through requiring and encouraging swift medical treatment has kept its rate lower than in the United States despite the acceptance of sexual activity among its population.[46] Combating the spread of AIDS (acquired immune deficiency syndrome) currently threatening the homosexual population is a public health problem today.

Violence Against Women. In the past decade increased attention has been given by the women's organizations and the government to the problem of violence against women including rape. Both rape and other forms of violence are increasing though the levels are much lower than in the United States. A new rape law was drafted in 1976 but was rejected after women protested that it placed too much attention on the behavior of the victim rather than concentrating on the behavior of the rapist.[47]

Cohabitation. One reason that the marriage rate is so low in Sweden today is that the incidence of couples living together without marriage is quite high. Combining all couples living together (legal and nonlegal), the rate of actual couple formation has not been declining over the past decade, although the legal marriage rate has declined.[48] Many people choose cohabitation as a form of trial marriage. If the relationship works, they may eventually decide to have a child; most couples get legally married shortly before or after conception or the birth of the child. If they do not plan a child, there are often no pressing reasons to legalize the relationship. If insoluble problems arise, they can separate with no formalities required.

Jan Trost suggests that one of the most important reasons for the dramatic rise in cohabitation since the mid-sixties is the greater social acceptability of the custom. Cohabitation has been more widespread and acceptable in Sweden than in other parts of the West for two centuries.[49] But recently, the last remaining imputations of immorality have been laid aside. Some unmarried couples even place newspaper announcements similar to engagement or wedding announcements to publicly advertise their new status as cohabitants, using the label "conscience marriage," an old Swedish term for such relationships. Another important reason for the increase in cohabitation is that legal marriage has become unfashionable in some circles. Trost does not view cohabitation as resulting in the eventual demise of marriage as a Swedish institution; he sees it as continuing the old Swedish custom of premarital cohabitation.[50]

Divorce. Divorce rates are very high in Sweden.[51] The social and legal emphasis is on the compatibility of the couple. The marital and procreative imperative is not strong in Sweden. Marriage is not considered a necessary part of a healthy adult life (low marriage rates and a late age at marriage have a long tradition in Sweden).[52] It is also not a requirement for the economic support of women, men, or children. Sex is acceptable and legitimate without marriage. That leaves the main functions of marriage as long-term companionship and intimacy. If the relationship fails to provide these, many Swedes see little reason to continue the marriage.

If the couple has no minor children, divorce is as simple and immediate as marriage is. The government sees no reason to intervene. However, the state always recognizes its duty to protect its weaker members, so a housebound wife or husband may be protected by an alimony award. This is not likely to be large or permanent, and it depends on the extenuating circumstances of the individual case. Children are also weaker members of society, and the government takes a hand in deciding who gets custody and who should pay child support. Mothers are, however, still much more likely to obtain custody. Seventy-two percent of the awards in Stockholm in 1977 gave custody to the mother, compared with only 6 percent to the father, 10 percent joint custody awards, and 9 percent in an arrangement where one child lives with one parent and another child with the other parent.[53] Alimony is rare, but child support is considered a legitimate parental obligation of mothers as well as fathers.

Role Sharing. Swedish women undoubtedly have a stronger structural and cultural basis for establishing equality in their marriage or cohabitation with men. The welfare state and full employment policies make them less dependent on their mates, and the culture upholds the value of gender egalitarianism. But the reality of individual relationships can still be quite unequal with the woman feeling greater dependence on and need for the man and greater insecurity should the relationship fail. For example, one thirty-two-year-old divorced mother of two told Hilda Scott, "Nothing has really changed for us. My friends are preoccupied with their bodies, how they look to their men. The older women in this neighborhood are worried about what will happen to them if their husbands leave them or die suddenly.[54]

The difficulties of moving from a shared-role policy to a shared-role reality are clear in the parental leave program. The government wants men to take part of this generous leave to stay home full time with their infant children. But the program has met with limited success outside of a small circle of well-educated professional and civil service workers. Only 12 percent of the fathers actually take parental leave. As one male factory worker described it, " 'A man's not made for looking after a bundle like that. And I would definitely feel inadequate. We haven't got the mother instincts, the mother's feeling or the patience. After a fortnight a man would say, "I can't stick it. It's not my line." ' "[55] Several of the workers ventured that they agreed with parental leave for fathers in principle, but not in practice. " 'I'd like to but couldn't. Of course I could learn to look after a baby. But I wouldn't be able to stand being at home for three months. I need people around me.' "[56] But another fully intended to take the leave for the baby he was anxiously awaiting.

However, some working-class males feel at ease with helping with housework " 'He cleans all the windows outside and I clean them inside. He does the weekly cleaning: I do the washing. He buys the food and I go along perhaps once a month, when I feel like it. He cooks the dinner every other week and he looks after the car too, but we clean the garage together.' "[57] But another female factory worker replied that " 'if I asked him to do the cleaning, he'd throw the vacuum cleaner at me!' "[58] One solution working couples use to share the burdens of child care and housework and avoid outside child care is shift work. This allows one of them to be at home whenever the other one is at work, but at considerable sacrifice to their own relationship. "When Lars comes home from work, Isa and the children are asleep. He finds it difficult to fall asleep immediately. . . . The children wake Lars up in the morning. People on evening shift schedules seldom get enough sleep. When he wakes up, Isa has already gone to work. When Isa comes back, Lars has left. Isa goes to bed before Lars comes home. This married couple see each other on Saturdays and Sundays."[59]

It is not always the reluctance of the individual man to embrace the shared-role model that keeps fathers from exercising their legal right to parental leave. Swedish employers often oppose male employees' taking the leave. Representatives of companies participating in the *Kristianstad model* to integrate their work force with women were, however, clear in their resistance to parental leave for men. Their attitude is that men's jobs are too important, too difficult to fill while they are away. " 'I'd be disappointed if one of the male employees came and asked for leave to look after the new baby.' " or " 'As men usually have jobs which are more important to the company, we prefer the wives to stay home.' "[60] By 1980 it appeared, however, that most men were taking the ten-day leave allowed at the time of the birth of the baby and that one-third had taken leave to care for sick children. Three-quarters of the men approved of the leave and felt men should take it.[61]

Swedish women themselves often resist or hinder the implementation of shared roles even when they desire it. They may complain about the quality of the husband's cooking or cleaning or assume he is incapable of caring for small children. But those who do share the burdens with their husbands are the most positive about working outside the home.[62]

Women may also resist an equal sharing of the full breadwinning role. Some continue to view their work as "helping out" and feel freer to quit work if they are dissatisfied.[63]

Child Rearing. Early child care, despite structural and cultural support for shared roles, remains primarily the responsibility of women. Even if the mother works and places the child in a day-care center, as most mothers do, the caretakers are still likely to be female, in keeping with women's traditional roles. These jobs are not attractive enough in pay, prestige, or promotion opportunities to attract men. The government and social service agencies encourage men to apply and practice positive discrimination in favor of men, but other social forces work against this. One male preschool teacher described his situation: " 'But I was brought up to be a man, and I have this career idea in my mind. It's there. My mother and father, they say you have to get a real job. And I don't want to be like that because I really enjoy this work, but my surroundings are telling me of course you should be—well, you shouldn't stay there. Work with children? It couldn't be? It's a woman's job!' "[64]

Thus children continue to grow up in a society with a gender division of labor that incorporates greater male access to rewards such as high prestige and high-paying jobs and female work in less prestigious jobs and as child rearers. "Much of what the child is taught about equality from preschool on is clearly contradicted by the child's own observations."[65] Rosen argues that although Swedish children grow into adults who show more gender role transcendence than do Americans, they still abstract from society ideas of gender appropriate activities and interests and are still motivated to practice these activities rather than opposite gender activities as part of the process of acquiring a sense of gender identity.[66] Thus a vicious cycle continues influencing females into certain skills and interests and boys into others.

Education. In Sweden girls as well as boys were allowed into the new public elementary school system in 1842, but it was not until 1920 that girls could join the boys in the public high schools. Since 1969 the National School Board has set gender equality as a goal.[67] Despite years of effort to remove gender segregation and inequality from the schools, girls still go into female-dominated specialties and boys into male-dominated ones. To counteract these trends, schools now require that both boys and girls take home economics, child care, coed gymnastics, and industrial arts courses. Schools are required to emphasize gender equality and textbooks are regularly scrutinized for gender stereotypes. Research, however, still finds that teachers pay more attention to boys and give boys more encouragement to persevere and succeed in scientific and technical fields. Females enter postsecondary training in as great a number as males do, but they are likely to choose shorter courses of study and to prepare for jobs in the female sector of the labor force.[68] One vocational guidance counselor describes her job as nagging the girls into considering nontraditional educational programs. " 'Ninety-nine percent want to be telephone operators, nurses, dressmakers, or secretaries. Or go into child-care.' "[69] Another notes that there has been some change: " '*Every* girl now thinks in terms of a job. This is progress. They want children, but they don't pin their hopes on marriage. They don't intend to be housewives for some future husband. But there has been no change in their vocational choices.' "[70]

The Dual Labor Market. Women's labor force participation in Sweden has been consistently ahead of their participation in the United States. Economic expansion in the late forties, fifties, and sixties pulled married women into the labor force earlier and faster than similar factors operated in the United States. The proportions of mothers in the labor market have increased steadily, sometimes dramatically, over the past few decades. The Swedish government recognized early the importance of women's labor in their zero population growth society. The goal of full employment has been interpreted as including even mothers of young children. This was vigorously pursued in public policy even when the unemployment rate began to rise in the sluggish economy of the 1970s. Some politicians began to discuss upgrading the position of household work as an alternative to employment outside the home, but the general commitment has been to avoid that type of "hidden unemployment." Unlike the United States, Sweden has not accepted higher and higher unemployment rates as natural; in the past Sweden has been able to keep its rate at about 2 percent for women and men even during recession. Recently, however, constraints on worldwide economic growth have caused even the Swedes to accept higher rates than this. Their most persistent unemployment problem is among youths of both genders, but the unemployment rate is somewhat higher for the females.[71]

The most striking inequality between male and female workers in Sweden is the extent and persistence of gender segregation in the labor market. Over 50 percent of the working women are in the public sector, double the rate for men. They are still primarily in clerical, secretarial, nursing, teaching, and retail sales—the typical "pink collar" jobs of the United States.[72] Occupational segregation persists as in the United States, but the pay gap has been narrowed more effectively in Sweden.[73] Females from better-educated families are now more likely to pursue male-dominated professions and occupations, but other women are not.[74]

Gender inequality in the labor market is probably most marked in the ranks of Swedish management. Women have made few inroads here. Women hold only about 1 percent of the private-sector managerial positions, and even in public administration where women are better represented, the higher the position, the fewer the women.[75] Birgitta Wistrand notes that government and industry are sensitive to the problem and are trying to encourage women to prepare for

such positions and employers to adopt non-discriminatory hiring and promotion policies. But one problem is a growing lack of enthusiasm among many young males and females for the stresses of managerial-level work.[76]

One of the main reasons Swedish women continue to earn less than men is that almost half of the women work part time (less than thirty-five hours per week).[77] Swedish women use part-time work to solve the dilemmas posed by their continued acceptance of most of the household responsibilities. They want to work and they need to work, but if they must do most of the housework and child care as well, they opt for shorter hours despite the fact that, just as in the United States, part-time work places severe constraints on career development. Part-time work for women cannot be seen as entirely negative, however, since it represents an option not available in societies with a strong full-time work imperative such as the Soviet Union, and part-time work does not result in the lower hourly wages or loss of important benefits such as health insurance, pension plans, and parenthood leave, which occurs in the United States and Japan. The Swedish government would like to make it easier for women to work full time and thereby be more competitive with male workers for higher-ranking positions, but current economic problems make that difficult to achieve for the present.

Political Participation. In some ways women have gained greater equality in the political sphere than in the economic sphere, but their share of political power is far from equal. Swedish women hold a far higher proportion of political offices in Sweden than in the United States. Compared with only 3 percent representation in the Congress and Senate of the United States, Swedish women hold 26 percent of the seats in Parliament and this has been increasing rapidly, from fifty seats in 1972 to eighty-nine in 1979. They also hold one-quarter of the cabinet-level ministries and have strong representation in all of the major political parties. Women also hold about 25 percent of the local offices and 45 percent of the seats on the Stockholm city council.[78] The most powerful positions and the well-paid, full-time positions are still held by men, however.

Political participation is high in Sweden. Ninety percent of both men and women vote. But Wistrand maintains that politics remains the bastion of the "unliberated men" because women and men practicing shared roles have less free time to devote to political activities.[79] But where women hold office, it does seem to make a difference. In localities where female officeholders are particularly numerous, expansion of child-care facilities has proceeded much more rapidly than in other areas.[80]

All of the major parties, both on the left and the right, are supportive of gender equality, and most have special women's sections to pursue women's issues and make recommendations. The parties had to be pressured in the 1970s to increase the number of female candidates for office. They did not struggle vigorously against the mass media's and women's organizations' demands for more females in public office. But with women constituting 51 percent of the electorate, women are still underrepresented at all levels of government in numbers as well as in the power of the positions they hold.

With 90 percent of the workers unionized and much of labor policy being decided within the union negotiations, union leadership constitutes an important locus of political power in Sweden. Here women are much more underrepresented. They are union members in large numbers, but they hold only a relatively few, lower-ranking union offices.

Women also participate in large numbers in Sweden's popular movements, but with the exception of the women's movement, they are generally underrepresented in the leadership positions of these movements. Women hold relatively few positions on the important public boards and committees; and on the boards of the private companies there are almost no women. Combined with their lack of leadership in the unions, this leaves the major economic decision making almost entirely in the hands of men. Women's organizations such as the Frederika Bremer Association are pressuring for women's integration into these positions and maintain lists of qualified candidates, but they have not met with success.[81]

As Sweden reached the midpoint of the 1980s, conditions of slow growth and uncertainty in the worldwide capitalist economy placed great strains on the ambitions of its Social Democratic government to continue to pursue the goals of greater equality for its people. Higher rates of unemployment, signs of a tax revolt, the spread of an underground economy, erosion of harmonious labor-management relations, and a general sense of insecurity in the face of the future have made their appearance in Sweden as elsewhere in Scandinavia and Western Europe. Women are especially vulnerable to the consequences of such developments, and Sweden may once again be placed in the vanguard of nations in attempting to answer the question: Can progress in women's position be maintained when rapid economic growth proves elusive while the pursuit of affluence remains a dominant social and individual goal?

Sweden through its policies of the committed welfare state has created what is perhaps the most gender-equal society in the modern industrialized world. It is still far from equal, but in comparison with Japan, a reluctant welfare state, Sweden is indeed on the opposite side of the earth.

Japan: A Reluctant Welfare State*

If Sweden shows the greatest commitment to the principle of gender equality in the modern industrialized world, then Japan is probably the country with the least commitment. Male dominance is still the norm culturally and structurally in Japan.

Historical Background

Early and Feudal Japan. Unlike Sweden or the United States, Japan has a long history of feudalism and internal warfare.[82] Little is known about earliest Japan, but the people probably lived by fishing, hunting, and horticulture. Rice-based agriculture was introduced about 300 B.C. giving rise to more stable agricultural villages.[83] Japan gradually emerged as a nation as the stronger clans subjugated weaker ones and integrated more and more territory under their leadership. By the fourth century the Yamata clan had succeeded in establishing a confederation of clans under its authority as an imperial lineage.

Japan has since gone through periods of relative centralizaton and decentralization;

periods of relative peace and chronic feuding and warfare. The Nara period (710–794) was followed by the Heian period (794–1185), which saw a change in the ruling clans and a move of the capital to Kyoto. Both were periods of relative centralization and stability with a powerful aristocratic class and nobility. This disintegrated into the feudalistic periods of the Kamakura shogunate (1192–1333), the Muromachi shogunate (1338–1573) and the Tokugawa shogunate (1603–1867). The Tokugawa shogunate was eventually in firm enough control to establish peace. But warfare had already been endemic for centuries. The Samurai warrior had become the cultural ideal for men, and his loyal, cloistered, cultured, and beautiful lady was the ideal for women. Centuries of warfare and rigid class inequality set their mark on gender roles in Japanese society. Prehistoric patterns of more equal participation by men and women were gradually but finally lost.[84] Japan did not move as Sweden did from a land of decentralized small independent farmers to a modern industrialized society.

Religion. Japan also did not escape the influence of patriarchal universal religions. It did not come under the domination of Christianity, but it has been greatly influenced by the sometimes even more strongly patriarchal traditions of Confucianism, Buddhism, and Taoism introduced from China and Korea. The indigenous religion of Japan is Shintoism, which evolved out of local rituals, legends, and myths. It was essentially a folk religion that helped preagricultural and agricultural peoples solve many of their problems through social ritual. In its early form it emphasized what Sanday has called both feminine and masculine orientations. Women's procreative abilities were an important part of the sacred symbolism.

*This section is based partly on research conducted in 1983 in Japan while Charlotte O'Kelly was a Fulbright Lecturer at Seinan Gakuin University and Kyushu University and Larry Carney was a Visiting Scholar at Kyushu University. The work was also partially funded by a grant from the Providence College Fund for Aid to Faculty Research, 1982–1983. The authors would like to thank all these sources for their support.

Creation myths postulate an original creator couple; in Japan the sun goddess Amaterasu Omikami is the original ancestress of the imperial family and the most important divinity of the Shinto pantheon. Shintoism was at first a local religion with rituals suited to the occupational pursuits of the local village: agricultural rites for farmers, different rites for fishermen and craftsworkers. As the clans fought for dominance, Shintoism took on a more supralocal aspect as the clans worshipped their special divinities who helped them in their quest for power. Clans that won in the struggle for power could then use their versions of Shintoism to legitimate their rule. Shintoism became an organized religion in this manner.

Buddhism was introduced into Japan in the sixth century. Shintoism and Buddhism were both used by the ruling classes to legitimate their positions and to foster behaviors and attitudes beneficial to their rule in the wider population. At different times Buddhism and Shintoism have each been declared the state religion.

Confucianism has never been the state religion, but it has been influential as an ethical system, in the area of education, and as a system of political thought and social philosophy. Its stress on hierarchy and loyalty has fit with patterns of feudal fealty between lord and vassal and with the loyalty owed to imperial regimes. Filial piety was stressed in relations between children and parents, but loyalty to one's leader took precedence in Japan.

Women's position was clearly subordinate and inferior in both Buddhism and Confucianism.[85] Their practices came to supplant the more egalitarian religious practices and symbols of ancient Shintoism. Gender stratification emerged and spread in the agrarian, feudal environment of Japan and was reflected in and supported by these religions imported from the already highly class- and gender-stratified Korean and Chinese societies.

Modernization. After centuries of isolation, Japan was opened to modern influences with the Meiji Restoration in 1868, which overthrew the crumbling Tokugawa shogunate and reinstated imperial rule. The Meiji period (1868–1912) was a period of rapid modernization and social change. Japan undertook to catch up with the West in industrialization. The feudal social structure was dismantled. Shintoism was established as the state religion as part of an attempt to increase nationalist identity, fervor, and patriotism. The emperor was declared a god directly descended from Amaterasu Omikami. But the other religions were allowed to practice and Christianity was reintroduced into Japan.

During this period of change many aspects of traditional society were challenged, including gender roles.[86] Young women as well as young men were sent to the West to study. A feminist social movement emerged and its base was particularly strong among the Westernized, educated, urban, upper-middle-class women who had embraced Christianity. The egalitarian aspects of Christian belief were particularly attractive to these women. Western missionaries, horrified by the degree and forms of female subordination in Japan, often encouraged women to resist traditional practices. Christians set up schools for girls, organized an antiprostitution movement, the Women's Christian Temperance Society, the Salvation Army, and the Young Women's Christian Association, bringing Japanese women into new public social reform roles and providing them with education and the experience of leadership and organization.

The Meiji government did not approve of attempts to undermine its power and soon adopted a policy of allowing only limited "modernization," meaning it would accept changes that increased the government's strength and power but suppress those that might undermine it. Traditional gender roles were reaffirmed in the *Imperial Rescript on Education* issued in 1890. This embodied the values of loyalty to the emperor and state, filial piety, patriarchal dominance in the family, and women's roles as "good wives and wise mothers." Education for girls would be education for their domestic roles. The new Civil Code adopted in 1898 retained traditional family law and ideology, limiting women's rights and giving husbands full guardianship over wives.

But as Japan industrialized, it turned to a predominantly female labor force. To fund its adoption of Western technology, Japan relied on profits provided by its textile industry, and young girls labored, often under life-threatening conditions, in these mills. Labor recruiters went into the countryside to "buy" or contract daughters' labor from financially hard-pressed peasants. Peasant families in desperate situations had long accepted the necessity of occasionally selling their daughters into prostitution to raise money, and the factory seemed to be no worse than the licensed prostitution district of a distant city. The girls were honor bound not to shame their parents by breaking their parents' contracts by running away. But conditions were so inhumane that many did attempt to run away and many committed suicide to escape these conditions. By the 1880s some of these workers were willing to go out on strike, and in the early 1900s labor organizations became interested in their plight and a small socialist movement with some female activists turned their attention to the textile workers.

In 1911 the first feminist organization, *Seitosha*—the Bluestocking Society—was founded following the pattern of Western intellectual women's groups. They were dedicated to higher education for women and to finding an outlet for the literary and intellectual interests of women and openly expressed concern for women's issues and other social problems. *Seitosha* was influential as a pathbreaker but short lived. By 1916 it had disbanded but was soon followed in 1920 by the New Woman's Association, dedicated to pursuing greater legal rights and the vote for women. "New Woman" was a popular phrase describing educated Westernized women. The organization also lasted only two years, but it was influential in repealing the law forbidding women's attendance at political rallies. In 1924 Ichikawa Fusae founded the Women's Suffrage League to lobby for the vote and other women's rights issues. Universal manhood suffrage finally passed in 1925, but women's efforts were not rewarded until after World War II when women's rights were incorporated in the new constitution written under the influence of American occupation forces. A socialist women's group, the Red Waves Society, was also founded in 1924. It argued that women's inferior position was the result of capitalist developments in Japan. Others were more likely to see women's inferiority as deriving from the feudalistic past.

A major force in opposition to greater equality for women was Japan's increasing militarism. The Japanese leaders clearly had expansionist goals. With the defeat of Russia in the Russo-Japanese War in 1904, Japan established itself as an imperial power with colonies in Manchuria and Korea. Nationalism, patriotism, and militarism pervaded the population in the aftermath of the war. Japan had emerged as a world power with an industrialized economy wedded to many feudalistic institutions and values.

The Meiji era ended with the death of the emperor in 1912. It was followed by the Taisho era (1912–1926) and then the Showa (1926–present). Japan became even more militaristic and aggressive in its foreign policy as its interests clashed with other imperialist powers. Women's protest over their situation came to be defined as unpatriotic. National policy enunciated the importance of the patriarchal family, filial piety, samurai values or the "way of the warrior," and female subordination. It condemned Western influences that emphasized individualism and democracy including, of course, women's rights proposals. World War II drew everyone into war-related production. Women, children, and the elderly were left to produce in the fields and the factories. Women's organizations had to be supportive of the government and the war effort or face severe repression.

Japan's defeat in the war was a severe blow to the Japanese faith in the traditional way of life. This jolt in their collective self-perception opened the way for Westernization on a scale unimaginable even during the Meiji era.[87]

Japan Since World War II

Under the direction of General Mac-Arthur, commander of the American occupation forces, Japan drafted a new constitution and proceeded to rid its political structure of many of the vestiges of feudalism including a disavowal of militarism.[88] MacArthur insisted on including equal legal rights for women in the Japanese constitution; he felt that women's influence on the Japanese government would be a brake on any future tendencies toward militarism. Therefore, Japan has the equivalent of the Equal Rights Amendment in its constitution, although the United States still resists including such an amendment in its own constitution.

Protective Legislation. Japanese legal commitment to equal rights and equal pay for equal work provides us with an interesting example of ineffective legislation on gender equality.[89] The laws are there in Japan, but the political leadership does not support them and they are ignored rather than enforced. Japanese feminists, unlike American feminists, tend to focus their attention not so much on getting new legislation passed but on getting the existing laws enforced. In the 1980s they have met with a few successes, but it remains a difficult battle. They face strong opposition from business and industry and have only lukewarm support from women themselves.

Japanese feminists are not even sure themselves how strictly they want the equal rights provisions enforced. The issue of *protective legislation* for women workers remains controversial. Women's exploitation in the early factories was particularly harsh in Japan, with many young women dying of tuberculosis, malnutrition, and accidents and by suicide. The passage of laws guaranteeing minimum working conditions in the Labor Standards Act of 1947 and the Law Concerning Welfare of Working Women in 1972 were seen as major advances for working women. Today, even though working conditions are quite good, women fear that if they relinquish their rights to protection they may lose something without gaining any better economic rights in return.

Ambivalence toward the recent abolition of protectionist laws is heightened to the degree that Japanese women cannot anticipate emancipation in the family sphere. As one married respondent told us, "I think we need those laws. Single women don't need the restrictions, but we married workers need them. . . . A married woman's time is limited, they have to be back home early. If they don't have such laws, we'd have to work until late and do a lot more things, so I think we need them."

Until 1985, the law limited women's working hours, forbidding most overtime work and most night work. This led to incongruous situations. For example, nurses were given an exemption and allowed to work at night, but female doctors were not. One obstetrician told us, "Of course babies are often born at night so I have to punch out of the hospital officially and remain on duty unofficially in order to care for my patients." Everyone knows that female doctors did this but little concern was given to revising such archaic laws. Female taxi drivers began to complain in the early 1980's that the law "protected" them from earning the wages of male taxi drivers. The biggest fares come after the trains and buses cease operations, that is, during the hours when women were forbidden to work. But again, rather than challenge the law itself, female taxi drivers merely wanted an exemption. Given the large number of women employed in bars, restaurants, and night clubs in addition to hospitals, a significant proportion of the female labor force was already exempted.

This law made it difficult for women who want to pursue professional, managerial, or even many kinds of white-collar careers. Men in such positions show their loyalty to the company or office by staying at their desks long hours even if there is little or no work to keep them there. If women had to leave, then that was proof they were not as valuable to the company and therefore did not deserve promotions or pay raises. But those few women who do attempt such careers in combination with marriage and motherhood sometimes found the legal limit on work hours at least a temporary salvation. Forced to leave one's infant from 8 A.M. until 8 P.M. and sometimes even later for a department store position is bad enough. But without the limitation on night work and excessive overtime, one young management trainee said she would never see her baby, which, of course, is the case for most fathers.

Female workers have also been barred from many types of work that are defined as too dangerous for women. The law is said to "protect motherhood." The protection of motherhood also accounts for the requirement that women get six weeks' maternity leave before and after childbirth. Most employers observe this, but at least a few apply the law in an inflexible manner. For example, one department store employee took the six weeks before delivery at the date set by her physician, but as is common, her baby was late. The store would not extend her maternity leave to the actual six-week period after delivery and she had to return to work after only four weeks.

A more controversial aspect of "protection of motherhood" is the monthly menstrual leave, which female employees are supposedly guaranteed by law. Many women workers do not avail themselves of this leave because they do not need it. But others find it too embarrassing to go through the procedure of declaring the onset of their menses to a male supervisor and filling out appropriate forms to be granted the leave. Others feel quite certain that their loyalty and commitment to their companies would be questioned if they took such leave. Menstrual leave is rarely paid leave, so most women cannot afford it. Japanese employers offer little or no sick leave benefits and actually expect male employees to come to work even if they are ill. The only women who regularly take this leave in large numbers are women who belong to strong unions with a large female membership such as some local government unions and the telephone workers union, which often encourages the operators to take the leave so that the benefit will not be lost in future contract negotiations. A negative side effect of this is that union leadership is almost always male and often takes the attitude that if it has protected the "menstrual leave" for the women, the women should be satisfied and make no further demands on the leadership for women's interests.

Discriminatory Employment Practices.
Japanese law may forbid discrimination, but it certainly has not abolished it.[90] The law only encourages employers not to discriminate in hiring, but it includes no sanctions against discriminators. Employers feel quite free to hire males and females on totally separate career tracks. Women, even those with degrees from top-ranking universities, will have a difficult time finding anything but dead-end, routine work at fairly low pay. Very talented and skilled women may end up as "office flowers" expected to serve tea, to be gracious to guests, and in general to add an air of beauty, charm, and gentility to the office setting.[91] As one talented and ambitious woman told us, "For very obedient, docile women, Japan is a very easy place to live. But, on the contrary, for very active women, for those who want to do something, it's a very difficult place to live."

Companies expect women to work only between school and marriage, which should occur between the ages of twenty-three and twenty-eight.[92] For a college graduate, this means she will be expected to work for only two to five years, a junior college graduate for four to seven years, and a high school graduate for six to nine years. Many employers use these calculations as a reason to exclude four-year university graduates from consideration altogether.[93] They almost certainly consider them as sufficient reason to deny women the extensive job training that goes to almost all their male employees. In an economy that values lifetime commitment from its employees, women's discontinuing work for marriage and child rearing deals a fatal blow to female career aspirations and policies of nondiscrimination in the labor force. At all educational and skill levels, women earn much less than males. The pay gap between men and women is wider in Japan than in other industrialized countries.

Women earn only 54 percent of what men earn.[94]

Until a recent court ruling, companies often forced women to retire at the age of thirty or thirty-five. Others allow them to continue working but offer them only minimal pay raises and benefits and never another promotion. Official retirement from full-time careers is still age fifty for most women, but fifty-five for most men, despite the longer life expectancy and better health of women. In 1981 the Supreme Court ruled against Nissan's mandatory five years' lower retirement age for women.[95] But court decisions in Japan do not have the far-reaching implications they have in the United States. Previous court decisions are not as binding on future decisions.

For many young women, this is no problem because it fits with the life course they have charted for themselves. They work for a few years, save money for their wedding and trousseaux, spend the time enjoying themselves, buying clothes, traveling, and being frivolous before settling down to the serious duties of a wife and mother.[96] But for those who do not marry or who genuinely desire a career, the situation is frustrating at best, impossible at worst. The genuine careerists may try to avoid the Japanese situation by seeking work in a foreign-owned company where more liberal policies often prevail. College women are often particularly desperate to improve their English-speaking ability to compete for these scarce jobs.

1985 Anti–Sex-Discrimination Law. After seven years of political debate and considerable public controversy, the Japanese parliament finally passed an anti–sex-discrimination employment law in May 1985. The law provides no legal sanctions against gender discrimination in employment but *en-*

courages, as a matter of public policy, employers not to engage in such discrimination in hiring, job assignment and promotion.

The law also abolishes many, but not all, remaining restrictions on women working overtime and at night. Female taxi drivers and women in managerial, executive, and professional positions will be among those who benefit.

The passing of the law received little positive comment from any sector of the Japanese public, including feminist groups and legislators. It was generally regarded as a compromise without teeth. Guidelines as to how the government would expect employers to implement the law were to be drawn up by the Ministry of Labor, and these guidelines were to go into effect in April 1986.

Although the law lacks legal sanctions, the Japanese government does have considerable informal power and resources to pressure employers to conform, if it so chooses. In mid-1985, expectations were not strong in Japan that the government would in fact lend its power and prestige to exercise such pressures.

Labor Force Participation. Female labor force participation in Japan is higher than one would expect given Japanese perceptions of low female work commitment. Women constituted 35.3 percent of the paid labor force in 1983 and their participation has been rising steadily. Half of Japanese women are employed.[97] They seem to be following the pattern established earlier in the West. First young women are employed in large numbers, then mothers whose children have grown up are drawn into the labor force, then mothers of younger and younger children enter the labor force. Japanese mothers are going to work today for the same reasons American women poured into the labor force in the 1950s and 1960s—for their families standard of living.[98] As the cost of living and the standard of living creep upward in Japan, mothers go to work to provide their children with what were once luxuries, but now are necessities.

Clothing, toys, and vacations are expensive, but the crucial factor in the desire of women to work is the cost of education. Education theoretically is almost free in Japan. Some of the very best schools and universities are public and cost very little to attend. But if your child fails to gain entrance into a good school, and even the public junior and senior high schools require a competitive entrance examination, then you must pay for a place in a good private school to have any hope of his or her getting into a good university. But this is not the only problem. Whether your child is in a public or private school, to ensure success in the all-important standard examinations, you must provide the child with extra study guides and probably the services of private tutors, who for a considerable fee drill children after school in memorization exercises designed to improve their examination performance. The Japanese examination system is based on meritocracy: Those with the highest scores get in, those who fail must look elsewhere. But families with enough money for these extras can increase their child's chances, and one of a mother's primary responsibilities is the educational success of her children. Thus, if the pressure to keep up with the Sato's levels of consumer goods is insufficient to drive the mother out to work, fear of her children's examination failure often is.[99]

"Part-Timers." Women returning to the labor force face bleak prospects, however. Business and industry are eager for their labor in the expanding tertiary sector and in

low-skill factory jobs, but they are not eager to pay them well. These women often earn only two or three dollars per hour with few benefits. They are referred to as "part-timers," but the Japanese definition of part time is quite different from that in the United States. It does not refer to the number of hours worked. Part-timers very often work the same hours and work week as full-timers. "Part-timers" really means a temporary worker without the usual lifetime job security or benefits.[100]

The use of part-timers and the even lower-paid "piece workers" gives the Japanese company the flexibility in labor force size that American employers take for granted. Japanese business can justify the practice ideologically on the grounds that these women are working only for extras; they are not real breadwinners, and therefore it is of little consequence that they can be fired at any time and are paid much less than full-timers doing exactly the same work. As economic pressures increase on Japanese firms to cut labor costs to stay competitive in world markets, the use of part-timers to avoid traditional labor practices is expected to increase.[101]

Taxes and Benefits. Unlike Sweden, Japanese tax laws discourage married women from working full time. If a wife earns more than about $3750 per year, she loses her status as her husband's tax dependent and has to pay higher taxes. Some women are careful to keep their earnings below this very low ceiling to keep from losing much of it to taxes. A wife may also lose her health insurance coverage on her husband's family policy if she earns more than a small amount yearly.

In Japan, as in the United States, most fringe benefits come primarily from full-time employment. Wives are further discouraged by company policies of providing a "de-pendency allowance" to men with nonworking wives that is revoked if the wife takes a job. Women with unemployed husbands do not qualify for such payments. Adding in the high costs of child care, for most wives employment is a net financial loss while their children are young and not very remunerative after the children are older.

As more jobs are available to returning women, the women take them often without complaint, feeling lucky to be able to work and pay for some of their children's needs and appreciating the opportunity to get out of the house and meet people. But if the American precedent holds for Japan, women's experience of discrimination in the workplace increases the likelihood of widespread discontent and fuels movements for social change in women's position in society. Women who are still quite willing to accept a subordinate position in the domestic sphere may still bristle at discrimination in the labor market.

Educational Achievement. Despite their poor showing in the employment sector, Japanese women are highly educated. Females were allowed into the prestigious national universities after World War II, and many of today's career women recall the difficulties of being the first or one of only a few females attending the university. Brave and dedicated women took advantage of these new opportunities immediately, sometimes having to overcome strong familial opposition. But now, almost thirty years later, females still represent less than one-quarter of the student bodies of these institutions. Females go on to college in the same numbers as males. In 1955 only 5 percent of the girls attended college: in 1983 it was 32 percent, down slightly from the high of 34 percent in 1976. Thirty-eight percent of the boys go on to college.

The important difference lies in the type of college and program of study chosen by the girls.[102] Ninety-five percent of the males go to four-year universities, while 62 percent of the females attend junior colleges. A four-year college education can be a liability for females in finding work, but it may make them more attractive as wives for upper-middle-class men desiring educated women to raise their children.[103] Boys, of course, choose majors from the entire gamut of university offerings; girls primarily study Japanese or English literature or education in the university and nursery school teaching and clerical or home economics courses in junior college.[104] Families are also much more likely to insist that a girl continue to live at home and choose her college from the limited selection within commuting distance. Boys are expected to go to the best university that will accept them, wherever it might be located. A young reporter told us of her efforts to persuade her parents to allow her to follow the precedent of her brother and enter a prestigious university for which she had qualified. They refused and told her "that's the way it is in this world—it's like burning money to send a girl to a very expensive university."

Professional and Managerial Careers. Females with a university education often enter elementary school teaching.[105] It is one of the few professions that is truly open to them and in which they can usually combine marriage, motherhood, and a career. But even there they face some discrimination. Mothers often prefer that their children have male teachers and complain that female teachers are too picky, too apt to take maternity leave and force the children to undergo the disruption of a temporary teacher, and too "hysterical." The relative few who enter high school teaching may find it rather pleasant at first, but if they reach the age of thirty without marrying, they can become the object of ridicule by students and other teachers alike.

An even smaller number of women hold university-level positions, and they are concentrated along with the female students in the junior colleges and in literature, child development, and early education departments. Rising in the academic world depends very heavily on having an established scholar act as your mentor. The powerful academic positions are almost always filled by males, and they feel little pressure to recognize and promote the interests and careers of even the most talented female students. Such women often pursue study at prestigious universities abroad to build sufficiently impressive credentials to be competitive with males for university appointments. A woman must usually be much better qualified than her male counterpart to be recognized as competent. A young English professor who had been fortunate enough to secure a position at a prestigious Tokyo university described to us a "sympathetic" greeting she received from a male colleague on her first day of work: "The first day I went to the school, one of the men said, 'You know Miss X, we really wanted a man, but there wasn't any as good as you, so we hired you.' What could I say? 'Oh, thank you, I'm glad I was accepted'!? He didn't mean anything bad. He was just telling the truth. He thought he was being nice!"

Most Japanese firms have no women in managerial-level positions. Women can sometimes forge a career in research, government, or the media, but manufacturing, finance, and trading are almost impossible.[106] In 1974, while female employees claimed 26 percent of the jobs in Japan's large corporations, they held only 0.12 percent of the managerial positions.[107] Those few women who are in management-level positions have faced innumerable obstacles.

They have had to obtain much better credentials than similarly employed males, and they have sometimes started in much lower positions than men and faced much slower promotions. Their success has usually required an almost superhuman dedication to their careers. Many have remained single and even remained in their parents' homes, leaving the domestic chores to their mothers.

Politics.   Women gained the vote in 1946 and have exercised it in large numbers, but female representation in politics has remained very small. The number of female Diet members has ranged from a high of thirty-nine in 1946 when women could first stand for elected office to a low of twenty in 1960 and only twenty-six in 1980.[108] Women hold less than 5 percent of the Diet seats. Ichikawa Fusae, the indefatigable defender of women's rights and interests, held office off and on from 1953 until her death in 1981. She was the highest vote receiver in the nation and was held in great respect by men and women, but one important figure does not represent real integration into the political power structure.

Although women are grossly underrepresented at all levels of the Japanese political structure, women are not politically inactive. Their political participation has been focused, however, on political problems associated with the female role. Many middle-class women are active in the consumer movement, lobbying for policies to ensure pure food, safe products, and fair prices. Women also form the backbone of the peace movement. Organizations such as the League of Women Voters continue to be strong in Japan. A few women participated in the radical movements of the 1970s.[109]

As of now there are no large-scale feminist social movements in Japan, despite a flurry of interest during the United Nations International Women's Year in 1975. But there are small, active, and increasingly vocal groups at work pressing for change and encouraging women to change their attitudes about their rights.[110]

The Domestic Sphere

Rigid gender roles within the family would make it difficult for married women to compete equally with men in the labor force even if all the overt forms of discrimination by employers were suddenly lifted. The patriarchal *stem family* of ancient Japan is no longer the predominant family form. Instead of an extended family including the parents and their eldest son and his wife and children operating as a corporate residential and economic unit, Japanese families today are more likely to be nuclear families (63 percent of the households in 1980). In 1967, 58 percent of the households with persons over sixty years of age contained three generations; in 1982 the figure had fallen to 44 percent.[111] Despite its more modern form, traditional gender divisions have been adapted to the changed circumstances and remain strong.

In the traditional agrarian based *stem family,* the father was the head of the family with authority over his wife and children and over his married sons' wives and children as well. He was responsible for the economic survival of the household and could arrange the occupations and marriages of his dependents. But the patriarchal structure allowed women considerable authority over household matters. As a young bride the wife held the lowest position in the household and was often treated as little more than a servant. But after she produced children, especially a son, for the lineage, her position began to rise. Eventually, she would take over the position of her mother-in-law as head of the domestic sphere, and the mother-in-law would then depend on her. [112]

The modern wife does not have to work as hard as the wife in past times, and many of them never have to live with a domineering mother-in-law. But the modern wife is still responsible for the domestic sphere with little or no help from her husband. The "shared role pattern" finds little support in theory or practice in Japan. [113]

Men's lives, especially those in managerial positions, are structured by their work in a manner that makes it virtually impossible for them to help with either housework or child care. [114] Not only are men expected to stay on the job extremely long hours, from eight or nine in the morning until eight or even eleven at night, five days a week plus Saturday mornings, but in addition they are expected to go out after work with their coworkers to bars, restaurants or cabarets. Social life with coworkers is further proof of one's commitment to the company. It is important to show this type of solidarity. A man who goes home to his family is viewed as untrustworthy; his first loyalty should be to the job. On Saturday afternoons and Sundays he may sometimes be expected to play golf or games of chance with coworkers or bosses. His "free time" is rarely his own.

When he does actually get some time at home, he is likely to be so tired from getting up early, making a long commute to work, staying out late with coworkers, and getting very little sleep night after night that all he wants to do is sleep and watch television with no disturbances from his family. The husband and father is, therefore, a distant, shadowy figure whom the children rarely see. He leaves for work early in the morning. They may see him at breakfast if his commute is not so long that he has to leave before they awaken for school. But they rarely see

him at night. When he returns at night, he may be too drunk to talk with them anyway because of the necessity of drinking in his after-work social life. A good wife will, however, wait up for her husband no matter how late or how drunk he might be and have a meal and a bath ready for him. Her job is to help him refresh himself in the brief time he has before returning to the company. She should not burden him with domestic chores or concerns or with demands that he help build and maintain a close marital relationship. A common criticism of wives is that they "nag" their husbands when they get home. [115] Not rarely, Japanese housewives view the situation with a mixture of resignation and compassion. A forty-seven-year-old wife and mother told us, "Well, I've gotten used to it. Of course, I wish we could enjoy a family holiday; but it is his job, so I can't complain—of course, I do complain, but there is no way to change it. . . . I rather feel sorry for him. He often says, 'I wish I could get three consecutive days off; I'd like to go to the hot springs and spend three days reading.' That is his dream, but until he quits his job, it can't come true." Men in nonmanagerial positions do not have to devote themselves as fully to the company, but their free time is limited compared to Western men. Japanese men, therefore, devote little or no time to housework. The prevailing attitude is still that "men work, women stay home." The commitment to this pattern is weakening somewhat among the younger generation, but the acceptance of a rather strict division of women in the domestic sphere from men in the public sphere is stronger in Japan than in any other modern industrialized society. [116] Most men of all ages still feel that it is preferable for a woman to quit work and devote herself to her family full time. Most women agree that they should quit work when they have children, but feel it is desirable to resume work later when family responsibilities lighten.[117] Even when the wife resumes outside employment, her mother or mother-in-law is more likely to help with the household tasks than her husband. But the husband may help with some things.[118] In 1982, 67 percent of Japanese women agreed that men receive preferential treatment in the family, compared with 48 percent of American women and only 31 percent of Swedish women. In Sweden 63 percent felt women and men are treated equally in the family; 40 percent of the American women agreed, but only 27 percent of the Japanese women said men and women are treated equally in the family.[119]

Arranged marriages are still common in Japan, constituting 27 percent of the marriages in 1980, partly because the emphasis on romantic love and companionship in marriage is less developed in Japan than in the United States and Sweden.[120] The laws supporting the old family system giving parents the right to choose spouses for their children and viewing marriage as a contract between two families were abolished after World War II and replaced by laws treating marriage as a contract between two equal individuals. But it is still very important for the couple to be from similar socioeconomic and familial backgrounds. No one is forced into a marriage by parents attempting to force the right political, economic, or social alliances today, but parents run careful checks on prospective spouses, even for "love matches," to make sure that nothing in their background would cause embarrassment.[121]They are particularly concerned that there be no non-Japanese ancestry, no ancestors from the outcast group, no history of mental illness or genetic disorders, and no history of scandal of any type.

The prevailing belief is that it does not matter whether a couple meets on their own in a "love match" or through an arranged introduction. If the backgrounds are similar with no problems, they will fall in love after the marriage if they are not already in love before the marriage takes place. People repeatedly told us that the relationship will not be any different for couples brought together in arranged marriages than for couples brought together in love matches. This may be true partly because the marriage relationship does not force the couple into high expectations for emotional intimacy or for close day-to-day cooperation. If certain role expectations as a wife and as a husband are fulfilled, then the marriage relationship is a satisfactory one and the couple is "in love."[122] A widowed mother responded to a question about whether emotional closeness between partners was good or bad for the health of a marriage: "After the honeymoon, they are close for a few months, but after that they belong to different societies and don't depend on each other so much anymore. It's not a problem of being good or not, society doesn't give you a choice."

Divorce. The factors described above result in a high degree of marital stability. The divorce rate is very low in Japan and divorce is still disapproved. Seventy-three percent of the men and 70 percent of the women disagree with the attitude that people should feel free to divorce if they are dissatisfied with their spouse.[123] Divorce creates somewhat of a scandal and can hurt the marriage chances of one's children. The prevailing opinion is that divorce is always bad for the children and that couples with children should abandon the idea of divorce.[124] This keeps some couples from divorcing until after their children are safely married off. The divorce rate has been rising since 1963, but primarily among older couples, and among this group it is usually the wife who initiates the divorce.[125] Husbands are said sometimes to be taken by surprise when an otherwise very dutiful wife declares that she wants a divorce now that they are older and their parental responsibilities have been completed.[126] Husbands who saw nothing wrong in their marriages can be faced with wives who suddenly tell them they have loathed them for years. There is some public concern about the increase in divorce among couples in their fifties. But the divorce rate is still very, very low among all age groups.

Divorced women are very likely to suffer financial hardship.[127] (Widows suffer similarly.)[128] There is no provision for alimony in Japanese law and child support is minimal or nonexistent. In half the cases of divorce, women get nothing from their husbands in the way of money or property.[129] Japanese social services and public assistance programs provide some help, but there is no commitment at the level of Sweden's welfare policies. The usual practice is for the couple to make a "clean break," with the parent not receiving custody never or only very rarely ever seeing the child again. Traditionally, members of the family only included those who actually lived and worked together, so if a parent moved away, he or she was no longer a part of that group. Under the traditional family system, children were viewed as the father's property and he almost always retained custody in the case of separation or divorce. In the extended family setting, he would usually have female relatives available to care for the children. In 1950 in 49 percent of the divorces the father still got custody, the mother in only 40 percent. The movement away from traditional patterns is reflected in the fact that in 1981 the mother received custody in 69 percent of the divorces and the father in only 24 percent.[130]

Child Rearing. The marital relationship is not as important as the parental role for an adult. Everyone is expected to marry and to have children.[131] The person who does not marry is to be pitied, and there is always a suspicion that there is something wrong with the individual or his or her family background. Cohabitation is rare. Premarital sexuality is much less common than in other industrialized countries and still disapproved for girls while young men are expected to go to prostitutes.[132] Japan's illegitimacy rate is one of the lowest in the world.[133] It is every man's duty to marry and become a breadwinner. It is every woman's duty to marry and take care of all of her husband's domestic needs and be a good mother to his children.

The husband and wife may not have a close relationship, but a mother must have a strong emotional bond with her children.[134] Children must develop feelings of total devotion to her and dependency on her. Japanese mothers achieve this relationship by devoting themselves fully to their children. They are rarely apart from them the first few years of life. The baby is strapped to the mother's back as she does her domestic chores, as she bicycles through the neighborhood on her errands, and while she shops in the stores or visits her friends. She controls her child by anticipating its needs, feeding, changing, or entertaining the child before the child demands such attention. Such child-rearing practices foster dependence rather than independence. Where American and Swedish mothers encourage early independence and psychological differentiation of the child from the mother, Japanese parents do just the opposite. The mother-child bond even takes precedence in the sleeping patterns of the household. The mother sleeps with the child rather than with the husband. The husband may sleep with an older child who has been displaced by the birth of a sibling or he sleeps on his futon alone or beside the mother-child pair.

Such dependency-inducing practices have come under criticism by some of the more Westernized, well-educated, upper-middle-class wives.[135]

Day Care. Such child-rearing practices require full-time mothering, and child-care substitutes are frowned upon in Japan. It is permissible to leave the child with a grandparent sometimes, but ideally he or she should not leave the mother before the age of three or four. Baby-sitters are almost unheard of; a mother should not make a practice of going out at night, not even with her husband, who has to be out with his colleagues in gatherings that never include wives. With this the ideal for mother-child relations, it is almost impossible for women to work when their children are young. Some young mothers are violating that ideal today through either desire or necessity, but they face severe criticism from family and friends and will most certainly be blamed if the child fails in any way at any time during childhood or adulthood.

There is some provision of subsidized and licensed child care facilities by local governments and by some businesses trying to attract more women workers, but the number of places is woefully inadequate. Mothers who cannot find a place for their children or who must work longer or different hours than the typical 8 A.M. to 6 P.M. schedule often must turn to unlicensed, unsubsidized centers of questionable quality referred to as "baby hotels." These women suffer a lot of anxiety about their children.

Many women who work when their children are young depend on their mothers or mothers-in-law to take on much of their domestic burden of housework and child care.[136] This is particularly true for married women with demanding careers. There are very few such women in Japan compared with other modern societies, and their so-

lutions are very individual ones. They have little or no help from nonfamilial sources in juggling the demands of their domestic and work roles. Very few husbands share in even the child-care burdens, no matter how demanding the wife's job or how much money she earns. She usually accepts it as her sole responsibility to manage these problems. It is a source of pride that her husband is only rarely called into service in the domestic sphere. It is a deeply felt duty even among many "liberated" women that if they want a career as well as marriage, their husbands should not be inconvenienced in any way.

The full-time contact period between mother and child ends even for the full-time mother when the child begins school. With the current emphasis on education, school begins earlier and earlier. A particularly eager mother may investigate good preschools to prepare her child for the "entrance examinations" of the best kindergartens to get the child on the track to a top university from the earliest possible moment. Once the child is in school, the mother is free to move about the community on her own while the child is in school.

She is now sharing her burden with the teachers and may work during these hours if she can find a job and if she does not have a younger child to care for. If she cannot or does not need to work, she will most likely devote this free time to visiting with friends, shopping, and taking lessons in traditional subjects such as flower arranging and tea ceremony, which demonstrate the high cultural level of her family. Earning money through teaching such traditional arts as tea ceremony and flower arranging can add to the prestige of the family in a way other part-time work cannot.[137] Lessons in tennis or English are also proof of ability to consume conspicuously and are therefore also status-enhancing for her and her family in addition to being enjoyable leisure pursuits.[138] An important function of the wife is maintaining and displaying her husband's status achievements through both the conspicuous display of material goods and generosity and display of cultural achievements.

Birth Control and Abortion. The birthrate has been very low since the brief postwar baby boom ended in 1949. Most Japanese families have two children. They do not marry until their late twenties. Marriage indicates that a couple now has enough money and maturity to start a family, so the birth of the first child is usually about one year after the wedding. A second child will usually follow in a few years and the wife then ends her childbearing period.

Japanese women had begun to control their fertility as early as during the Tokugawa shogunate.[139] The population stabilized partially through the use of infanticide, referred to as "thinning out." Infanticide was the husband's and his family's decision, not the mother's.[140] Killing or selling daughters, and more rarely sons, has never been as strongly denounced by Japanese religions as it has in the Christian tradition. But Japanese religion and culture do oppose abortion, and the people express negative attitudes toward it, despite their very high abortion rate.

Economic deprivation and a lack of contraception encouraged people to rely on abortion as the primary fertility control measure in the immediate postwar period.[141] The government had made abortion and infanticide illegal during its militaristic, imperialistic period as part of its unsuccessful pronatalist campaign to keep women producing new soldiers and workers.[142] But with these motivations removed after its defeat in World War II and the surplus population engendered by the repatriation of millions of overseas Japanese after the loss of the colonies, the government legalized abortion in the Eugenic Protection Act of 1948.

Today couples rely primarily on condoms and the rhythm method. IUDs are available but used by only 10 percent of the married women. Fewer than 1 percent use diaphragms because of the traditional reluctance of women to touch their own genitals, and the pill is prescribed only for menstrual problems.[143] The government prefers to promote condoms with abortion as the backup for the method's low reliability. Abortions are therefore quite common. The rate is higher than in Sweden or the United States and most are performed on married women.[144] The law does not permit abortions for unmarried women. Perhaps one-third of all married women have had at least one abortion. Physicians often do little to give women good contraceptive information, partly because of the reluctance of Japanese women to initiate discussions about sex, but primarily because abortions can be a substantial source of income. A doctor may perform as many as twenty abortions per day charging several hundred dollars each, paid primarily by the patients themselves, who in their desire for secrecy avoid insurance claims. The doctor may also see a full list of outpatients as well as carrying on his daily abortion practice. To maintain their high incomes from abortion, the ob-gyn association does not support legalization of oral contraceptives.[145]

Japanese women remain woefully ignorant about reproduction and contraception despite their high levels of education and their otherwise excellent health-care system. One woman interviewed had had seven abortions at the insistence of her doctor who told her she should not bear children for some vague health reason. She finally summoned sufficient courage to resist his advice and had two uncomplicated pregnancies producing two healthy children

There are periodic attempts by the government to repeal the economic necessity provisions of the Eugenic Protection Act, but so far this has failed. Doctors oppose restricting abortion, and many women feel it is crucial to the well-being of their families to have this backup for contraceptive failure. Some feel, however, that human life should receive more respect and abortion should be limited to serious circumstances. Others think the government is not really concerned with the value of human life; rather, it is attempting to return to the prewar militaristic policies of encouraging a high birthrate to increase the number of potential soldiers.[146]

"Education Mamas." But the birthrate is low, primarily due to the expense of raising children in the modern context. Combining the low birthrate with one of the longest life expectancies in the world leaves Japanese women with many years of relative unemployment if they do not work outside the home. The full-time devotion to children can be extended through a careful overseeing of the child's studies through high school. Such intensive mothering is referred to as being an "education mama."[147] This can include keeping distracting friends and phone calls at bay, keeping the child up until after midnight every night and on weekends and school vacations studying, rewarding the child's efforts with tea and snacks at regular intervals, and waking the child early in the morning for more study before school. Child-rearing practices that create high dependency needs in infants and toddlers facilitate this type of control when they are older. Obedience is further encouraged by full-time service and respect from a deferential mother.

Japanese children are allowed relatively little time for play compared with Western children. Fifty percent of the children devote two or more hours to study or tutoring after school. Only 22 percent of American children study that long after school.[148] Schoolwork is of such importance that Japanese children are given almost no responsibilities for household chores. The mother takes care of everything for the child; he or she studies full time just as the father works full time. Japanese mothers do not actually spend a great deal of time with their children. Contact is less than between American mothers and their school-age children. But Japanese mothers must devote a great deal of time to organizing their children's activities and studies and serving their needs. Even mothers who feel uneasy with this role believe that the competitive nature of the Japanese educational system and its links to the economy trap them into acquiescence. One mother told us, "When I think about the circumstances in Japan, I can't help but be an education mama. Even if it is against a mother's will, she must be." Eventually, even the most diligent mother has her children grow up and leave her for college or work and for marriage.

Financial Management. Women's domestic responsibilities also place them in charge of the family budget. The husband typically turns his entire pay over to his wife's management and receives an allowance for personal expenses from her. Eighty percent of Japanese wives manage the household finances alone; only 12 percent of the couples share this responsibility. This is in marked contrast to the United States where 46 percent of the couples share this task and in Sweden where 60 percent share the responsibility.[149] This practice is often used as proof that women hold significant power in Japan. But it appears to be more a burden than a sign of power in most families. The husband's monthly allowance may in fact be a relatively large sum compared with the household expenses the wife must meet. He will want money for cigarettes, lunches, and for that all-important and quite expensive after-work socializing. If he is a "bad" husband, he may also spend money on excessive gambling and other women.

The Japanese wife's control over the family budget does not seem to indicate real power; her husband always has the legitimate right to retrieve control of his pay wages. He has delegated a reponsibility to his wife but he is not really sharing power with her.

In Japan the husband is seen as holding the real power in the family in 66 percent of the marriages, with husband and wife sharing the power in only 13 percent. In the United States husbands hold the real power in only 31 percent of the marriages; it is shared by 57 percent of the couples. In Sweden 76 percent of the couples share the power and only 12 percent report that the husband is the primary decision maker.[150]

The wife is charged with managing the household with what her husband leaves for her. This can be an awesome task in a country with as high a cost of living as Japan has. She will keep very careful records of every yen she spends and she will usually be a very careful shopper.[151] In addition to providing for the daily household needs and the education expenses discussed above, it is also her responsibility to see to it that enough money is saved to purchase a house and pay for it in full before the husband's retirement at age fifty-five and to save money to help see them through the twenty or more years of retirement. Japan is not a committed welfare state like Sweden, and pensions are usually very inadequate to meet the needs of people living so many years in retirement. Money problems are sometimes a source of marital discord. One young wife whom we interviewed was almost driven to divorcing

her husband who ran up large debts to loan sharks to pay his gambling expenses and to maintain his mistress, but the man's boss intervened and offered to help her husband keep his job and retrieve his financial situation if she would stay with him. Another young wife could simply not manage on the money left over after her husband's expenses for entertainment were subtracted from his income. They fought often over money matters and the fights sometimes ended in her receiving a beating. These problems subsided, however, as his income and work situation improved.

These onerous financial management responsibilities drive many women into the labor force. Even at the low wages they receive, they see any small amount as helping out. Women in their forties and fifties also often seek jobs when their husbands retire in order to make ends meet on a small pension. Sometimes the men also seek work after forced retirement from their careers. It is not unusual for a man to go from a middle-class, white-collar position to menial labor as a janitor after his forced retirement. A substantial number of couples open a small shop or run a small farm to support themselves after "retirement." Many couples often find it difficult to be thrown together in a small apartment or house after years of separation.[152] An often-used phrase to describe retired husbands translates as "unwanted lump of trash." Wives do not always welcome the full-time intrusion of their husbands into their domain. Some wives seek employment to get away from their housebound husbands.

Home Nursing. Women's domestic role in Japan continues to include providing home care for bedridden elderly husbands and parents. Husbands are likely to become ill and bedridden while their wives are still healthy, and the wife is expected to care for the husband at home no matter how burdensome the task is unless hospital care is absolutely necessary.[153] Nursing homes and old-age homes are still rare. If the wife becomes bedridden while the husband is still healthy, he will care for her, but this is much less likely to occur. Ninety percent of the caretakers for the elderly are female.[154] When the wife becomes too old to care for herself, she is likely to depend on her daughter-in-law. One woman reported that she felt like her life had begun anew when her mother-in-law finally died; she had cared for her full time the first twelve years of her marriage. Several women stated that they had refused to marry any man who was an eldest son precisely because they did not want to shoulder the burdens of caring for his aging parents. It is still considered primarily the responsibility of the eldest son to live with the parents if the need arises and have his wife care for them until they die.

Violence, Prostitution, and Pornography. Although women occupy a clearly secondary position in Japanese society, in one area they have a clear advantage over American women. They can feel personally secure that they will not be raped or attacked. The crime rate is very low in Japan for all types of crime, and violence against women is also relatively rare. Interestingly, family violence takes a very different form in Japan. Rather than being predominantly wife abuse or child abuse, family violence in Japan is increasingly a problem of children abusing their parents. Because mothers are responsible for their children's examination performance, a frustrated child who does poorly may respond by beating up his mother.

Young women and girls do not face much threat of rape, but they face a high likelihood of physical assault in the form of men who take advantage of the crowded buses and trains to fondle the bodies of girls. There is also a likelihood of encountering "flashers." Such men concentrate almost exclusively on adolescents and teenagers.

The Japanese sex industry and "prostitution tourism" are a current source of international embarrassment and a focus of small-scale feminist protest in Japan. Concubinage has disappeared in Japan, and the elegant, intensively trained *geisha* is an expensive rarity. But prostitution continues to flourish as the law turns a blind eye. The businessman on an expense account can choose from any number of sex-oriented entertainments for his clients or associates, ranging from out-and-out prostitution to coffee shops with "no panties" waitresses and mirrored floors.[155] But "buying a woman," the traditional Japanese term, is expensive in today's inflationary economy. Some businesses sponsor meetings or conventions in countries such as Korea and Thailand and include the services of prostitutes as part of the entertainment. There are tourist agencies that specialize in such arrangements.[156]

Japan has what are in some ways very strict laws on pornography. But these laws coexist with an inundation of the society with pornographic magazines and movies. Crowded street corners and bus stops will often have numerous coin-operated pornographic magazine machines. Passers-by constantly face lurid magazine covers and movie posters depicting graphic sex and especially violent or sadomasochistic sex. Television after 11 P.M. often includes very "blue" movies and television shows. Even the children's comic books and television cartoons sometimes contain sexual scenes, female nudity, and violence against women. Japanese women, except for a few feminists, express little concern about this. They see it as simply a fantasy world that some men and a few women enjoy. Perhaps because the level of crime and violence is so low, any connection with female subordination or the cultural devaluation of women seems remote.

Forces for Change in Sweden and Japan

Sweden has long been committed to promoting social change in gender roles and gender stratification. Whether the government can sustain such a commitment in the face of slowed economic growth may be problematic. Integrating women into the public sphere and men into the domestic sphere depends heavily on the achievement of full-employment policies and a finely woven safety net of social services replacing the unpaid labor of women in the home.

By contrast, the Japanese government has shown little interest in promoting gender equality and no interest in supporting a "shared-role pattern." Yet business and industry are eager for married women's services in the labor force. The pull created by the increase in employment opportunities is matched by the push of inflation, higher levels of consumption, and more free time for women. Women's experiences in the public sphere may well encourage them to challenge their traditional gender roles at home and at work. A stronger feminist movement might be in the offing for Japan. But a downturn in their economy could also make it very difficult for feminism to promote real change. The remarkably effective national consensus—maintained by government, business, educational institutions, and the communications media—that the Japanese must pull together to advance their competitive position in the world market also

serves in ways direct and subtle to mute and diffuse efforts to raise public consciousness concerning women's issues.

Conclusion

Consideration of the historical development and contemporary structure of gender relations in the United States, Sweden, and Japan demonstrates that although advanced capitalism may be a system of socioeconomic relations that exhibits many common features in different societies, it does not force these societies to a common convergence in the patterning of relations between males and females. Relatively unique features of the mix of cultural, social, economic, and political events and developments over time must be considered for each society. Yet our three cases lead us to some tentative conclusions about the possibilities and limits of the progress toward gender equality in such societies.

First, we see that there is nothing intrinsic to the development of market forces and the generalization of capitalist market relations that will in itself secure equality between genders, any more than such forces and relations will guarantee equality (of opportunity or of social position) among social classes, races, ethnic groups, or other important divisions in society. Second, what progress has been made toward gender equality in such societies has depended very heavily on pressures exerted by political movements and various types of intervention by the state. Third, although sustained economic growth and the achievement of relatively comfortable standards of living for the majority of the population in these societies do not in themselves guarantee sustained progress in gender equality, increasingly they seem to have become prerequisites, or minimal conditions, for such progress.

This last consideration leads us to a final and more challenging observation. The varying forms of progress that have been made toward gender equality in these advanced capitalist societies continue to be constrained by the particularities of the institutionalized relationships between the family and the economic system. The political impetus toward equality between the genders has as yet in none of these societies succeeded in transcending the stubborn fact that the organization of work and the demands of work commitment embedded in the competitive economic system push toward minimal domestic and child-rearing involvements by its most successful (or those who would aspire to be successful) members. Even the occasional shift of the breadwinner role in the family across gender lines is the exception that seems to prove the rule; and the economic capacity of affluent two-career families to purchase domestic and child-care services from others is hardly a pattern generalizable to the larger society.

Gender distinctions can perhaps be partially unlinked from total association with one sex or the other, but the gender division of labor implied by the distinct imperatives of the labor market and domestic sphere still remains. Moreover, these are not matters to be determined by the values and choice of individuals, but are subject to the winnowing and selective effects of international and national competitive markets which "bet on the strong." As economist Julie A. Matthaei observes, "I question whether capitalism can survive without 'men' willing to dedicate themselves to its service in exchange for self-advancement, at the price of all else."[157] In Chapter 9, we address the question whether contemporary socialist societies have more adequately confronted this dilemma. First, however, we must survey the rawer edge of capitalism in today's world—the capitalist societies of the "Third World."

Notes

1. Shari Steiner, *The Female Factor* (New York: Putnam's, 1977): 244–253; Ira Reiss, "Sexual Customs and Gender Roles in Sweden and America: An Analysis and Interpretation," in Helena Z. Lopata, ed., *Research in the Interweave of Social Roles: Women and Men. A Research Annual*, Vol. 1 (Greenwich, Conn.: JAI Press, 1980): 191–195; Jan Trost, "Married and Unmarried Cohabitation in Sweden," in Marie Corbin, ed., *The Couple* (Harmondsworth, Eng.: Penguin Books, 1978): 158–159; Rita Liljestrom, Gunilla Furst Mellstrom, and Gillan Liljestrom Svensson, "Sex Roles in Transition: A Report on a Pilot Program in Sweden." (Stockholm: Swedish Institute, 1975): 8–12; Elisabet Sandberg, "Equality Is the Goal: A Swedish Report," (Stockholm: Swedish Institute, 1975): 11–14.

2. Liljestrom, Mellstrom, and Svensson, 1975, 9.

3. Martin Schiff, "Sexual Liberation, the Welfare State and Sexual Malaise in Sweden: An Analysis of Popular Myths Concerning the Swedish Way of Life," *Sociological Analysis and Theory* (October 1975): 360.

4. Steiner, 249.

5. Carolyn Teich Adams and Kathryn Teich Winston, *Mothers at Work: Public Policies in the United States, Sweden, and China* (New York: Longman, 1980): 113–114.

6. Adams and Winston, 114.

7. Hilda Scott, *Sweden's "Right to be Human" Sex-Role Equality: The Goal and the Reality* (Armonk, N.Y.: M. E. Sharpe, 1982): 69.

8. Adams and Winston, 114–115.

9. Adams and Winston, 116.

10. Schiff, 363–368.

11. Adams and Winston, 176. See also Helen Ginsburg, *Full Employment and Public Policy: The United States and Sweden* (Lexington, Mass.: D. C. Health, 1983).

12. Adams and Winston, 26.

13. See Birgitta Linner, "Society and Sex in Sweden," rev. ed. (Stockholm: Swedish Institute, 1971).

14. For a discussion of contraception and sex education, Adams and Winston, 37–38; Scott, 81–98.

15. Adams and Winston, 149–155.

16. See Scott; Ginsburg; Birgitta Wistrand, *Swedish Women on the Move*, trans. Jeanne Rosen (Stockholm: Swedish Institute, 1981): 29–38; Birgitta Wistrand, "Parental Insurance in Sweden—Some Data" (Stockholm: Ministry of Health and Social Affairs, International Secretariat, 1977).

17. Adams and Winston, 76–77.

18. Adams and Winston, 90.

19. Adams and Winston, 91.

20. Wistrand, 1981, 22.

21. Adams and Winston, 224; Scott, 1982, 3–6; Rita Liljestrom, "The Swedish Model," in G. H. Seward and R. C. Williamson, eds., *Sex Roles in Changing Society* (New York: Random House, 1970): 200–205.

22. Ginsburg, 161.

23. Scott, 7, 72–73; Wistrand, 1981, 37–38.

24. Liljestrom, Mellstrom, and Svensson; Scott, 25–30.

25. Scott, 24.

26. Scott, 33–34; Inga-Britt Tornell, "The Equal Opportunities Ombudsman at Work," Swedish Information Service, *Social Change in Sweden* 28 (April 1983).

27. Schiff, 370.

28. Wistrand, 1981, 27.

29. Murray Gendell, "Sweden Faces Zero Population Growth," *Population Bulletin* 35, no. 2 (June 1980): 16.

30. Steiner, 278–285.

31. Ann-Mari Sellerberg, "The Life of Young Working-Class Mothers in Sweden." *Journal of Marriage and the Family* 37 no. 2 (May 1975), 420.

32. Scott, 65–66.

33. Scott, 69.

34. Linner, 1971, 37–40; Scott, 1982, 83.

35. Scott, 88–89.

36. Reiss, 1980, 200; Gendell, 1980, 16.

37. Reiss, 1980, 205–206.

38. Reiss, 206–207.

39. Scott, 96.

40. Linner, 47.

41. Scott, 93.

42. Schiff, 367.

43. Wistrand, 1981, 80.

44. Wistrand, 1981, 80; Scott, 1982, 96–97.

45. Wistrand, 1981, 82.

46. Schiff, 363.

47. Wistrand, 1981, 73–75.

48. Trost, 1978, 159.

49. Trost, 159.

50. Trost, 167–168.

51. Gendell, 1980, 17.

52. Gendell, 1980, 14.

53. Jan Trost, "Children and Divorce in Sweden," *Journal of Comparative Family Studies* 12, no. 1 (Winter 1981): 131.

54. Scott, 81.

55. Liljestrom, Mellstrom, and Svensson, 64–65.

56. Liljestrom, Mellstrom, and Svensson, 94.

57. Liljestrom, Mellstrom, and Svensson, 52.

58. Liljestrom, Mellstrom, and Svensson, 52.

59. Liljestrom, Mellstrom, and Svensson, 69.

60. Liljestrom, Mellstrom, and Svensson, 94.

61. Jan Trost, "Parental Benefits—A Study of Men's Behavior and Views," Swedish Information Service, *Social Change in Sweden* no. 28 (October 1983).

62. Orjan E. Hultaker, "Attitudes toward Maternal Employment in Sweden," *Journal of Comparative Family Studies* 12, no. 1 (Winter 1981): 95–111.

63. Scott, 1982, 110.

64. Anne-Sofie Rosen, "Sex-Role Stereotypes and Personal Attributes within a Developmental Framework," in Anne Hoiberg, ed., *Women and the World of Work* (New York: Plenun Press, 1982): 92.

65. Maureen McConaghy, "Sex Role Contravention and Sex Education Directed toward Young Children in Sweden," *Journal of Marriage and the Family* 41, no. 4 (November 1979): 893–904.

66. Rosen.

67. Linda Haas, "Wives Commitment to Breadwinning in Sweden," Paper presented at the Tenth World Congress of Sociology, Mexico City, August 1982.

68. Wistrand, 1981, 39–49; Scott, 118–134.

69. Scott, 124.

70. Scott, 125.

71. Ginsburg, 162.

72. Ginsburg, 163.

73. Ginsburg, 164.

74. Scott, 130–131.

75. Wistrand, 1981, 64.

76. Wistrand, 1981, 65.

77. Ginsburg, 164; see also Karin Ahrland, " 'The Obligatory Women' in Committee Life," *International Journal of Sociology* 8, no. 3 (Fall 1978): 86–95.

78. Ginsburg, 171; Wistrand, 1981, 84–89; Scott, 1982, 151–153.

79. Wistrand, 1981, 89.

80. Ginsburg, 171.

81. Wistrand, 1981, 90–95.

82. See the many articles in the *Kodansha Encyclopedia of Japan* (Tokyo: Kodansha, 1983); Mikiso Hane, *Japan: A Historical Survey* (New York: Charles Scribner's, 1972).

83. H. Byron Earhart, "Religion," *Kodansha Encyclopedia of Japan* 6 (1983): 290.

84. Haruko Wakita, "Marriage and Property in Premodern Japan from the Perspective of Women's History," *Journal of Japanese Studies* 10, no. 1 (Winter 1984): 76–99; see also William H. McCullough, "Japanese Marriage Institutions in the Heian Period," *Harvard Journal of Asiatic Studies* 27 (1967): 103–167; Joyce Ackroyd, "Women in Feudal Japan," *Transactions of the Asiatic Society of Japan* 7, no. 3 (November 1959): 31–68; L. Crnmer Byng and S. A. Kapadia, eds., *Women and Wisdom of Japan* (London: Murray, 1905); Joy Hendry, *Mar-*

riage in Changing Japan: Community and Society (New York: St. Martin's Press, 1981): 14–36; Chiye Sano, *Changing Values of the Japanese Family* (Westport, Conn.: Greenwood Press, 1973; orig., 1958): 27–29; Dorothy Robins-Mowry, *The Hidden Sun: Women of Modern Japan* (Boulder, Col.: Westview Press, 1983): 1–30.

85. "The Confucian Ideal of Womanhood," *Journal of China Society* 13 (1976): 67–73.

86. Sharon L. Sievers, "Feminist Criticism in Japanese Politics in the 1880s: The Experience of Kishida Toshiko," *Signs* 6, no. 4 (Summer 1981): 602–616; Robins-Mowry, 1983, 31–114; Sievers, *Flowers in Salt: The Beginnings of Feminist Consciousness in Modern Japan* (Stanford, Calif.: Stanford University Press, 1983); Maude Whitmore Madden, *Women of the Meiji Era* (New York: Fleming H. Revell, 1919); Robert J. Smith, "Making Village Women into 'Good Wives and Wise Mothers' in Prewar Japan," *Journal of Family History* 18, no. 1 (Spring 1983): 70–84; Robert J. Smith and Ella Lury Wiswell, *The Women of Suye Mura* (Chicago: University of Chicago Press, 1982).

87. Haru Fujii, "Education for Women: The Personal and Social Damage of Anachronistic Policy," *Japan Quarterly* 29, no. 3 (July–September 1982): 301–304.

88. Masu Okamura, *Women's Status* (Tokyo: International Society for Educational Information, 1973); Sano, 1958; Margaret Geddes, "The Status of Women in Post-War Japan: A Critical Examination of the Contribution of the Occupation Authorities towards Raising the Status of Women in Japan," *Australian Outlook* 31, no. 3 (1977): 439–452.

89. Alice H. Cook and Hiroko Hayashi, *Working Women in Japan: Discrimination, Resistance and Reform* (Ithaca: New York State School of Industrial and Labor Relations, Cornell University, 1980); Hiroko Hayashi, "Japanese Women and Labor Market Policy," Paper presented at the Labor Market Policy Conference in Honor of Alice H. Cook, New York State School of Industrial and Labor Relations, Cornell University, Ithaca, October 5, 1983; Robins-Mowry, 1983, 181–189.

90. See Cook and Hayashi, 1980; Hayashi, 1983.

91. Rose Carter and Lois Dilatush, " 'Office Ladies,' " in Joyce Lebra, Joy Paulson, and Elizabeth Powers, eds., *Women in Changing Japan* (Boulder, Colo.: Westview Press, 1977): 75–88.

92. Linda Perry, *Mothers, Wives, and Daughters in Osaka: Autonomy, Alliance and Professionalism*, Ph.D. dissertation, University of Pittsburgh, 1976: 191–195; Robins-Mowry, 1983, 184–187.

93. "Women Graduates Need Not Apply," *Japan Quarterly* 28, no. 1 (1981): 18–22; Hiroshi Takeuchi, "Working Women in Business Corporations: The Management Viewpoint," *Japan Quarterly* 29, 3 (July–September 1982).

94. Yoko Kawashima, *Wage Differentials between Women and Men in Japan*, Ph.D. dissertation, Stanford University, 1983.

95. Hayashi, 1983; "Feminist News from Japan," *Asian Women's Liberation* no. 4 (August 1981): 31.

96. Sonya Blank Salamon, *In the Intimate Arena: Japanese Women and Their Families*, Ph.D. dissertation, University of Illinois at Urbana-Champaign, 1974: 55.

97. *Journal of Japanese Trade & Industry* (Jan., 1985): 49.

98. Perry, 200; Hayashi, 1983.

99. Perry, 203–204.

100. Kawashima, 138–159; Hayashi, 1983.

101. Kawashima, 138–159; Takeuchi, 1982.

102. Fujii, 304–305; Lebra, 1984, 50–58.

103. Perry, 95–97.

104. Perry, 97–102.

105. For discussions of professional and managerial careers, see Taki Sugiyama Lebra, "Japanese Women in Male Dominant Careers: Cultural Barriers and Accomodations for Sex-Role Transcendence," *Ethnology* 20, no. 4 (1981): 291–306; Elizabeth Knipe Mouer, "Women in Teaching," in Lebra, Paulson, and Powers, 1977, 157–190; Lois Dilatush, "Women in the Professions," in Lebra, Paulson, and Powers, 1977, 191–208; Joy Paulson, "Women in Media," in Lebra, Paulson, and Powers, 1977, 209–232.

106. Masako Murakami Osako, "Dilemmas of Japanese Professional Women," *Social Problems* 26, no. 1 (1978): 15–25.

107. Michiko Kanda et al., "Career Advancement of Women in Japan: Managers in Large Companies," 1983 Tokyo Symposium on Women, Workshop II.

108. Robins-Mowry, 319; Eileen Carlberg, "Women in the Political System," in Lebra, Paulson, and Powers, 1977, 233–254; Susan Pharr, *Political Women in Japan* (Berkeley: University of California Press, 1981).

109. Robins-Mowry, 190–285; Susan Pharr, "The Japanese Woman: Evolving Views of Life and Role," in Lewis Austin, ed., *Japan: The Paradox of Progress* (New Haven, Conn.: Yale University Press, 1976): 301–327; Pharr, 1981; Matsui Yayori, "Protest and the Japanese Woman," *Japan Quarterly* 22, no. 1 (1975): 32–39.

110. Cook and Hayashi, 1980, 83.

111. Economic Planning Agency, Japanese Government, *Annual Report on the National Life for Fiscal 1983: In Search of Greater Latitude in the Household Economy and a New Image of the Family* (Tokyo: Ministry of Finance, 1983): 222.

112. Perry, 154–157.

113. Sumiko Furuya Iwao, "The Feminine Perspective in Japan Today," in Kenneth Grossberg, ed., *Japan Today* (Philadelphia: Institute for the Study of Human Issues, 1981): 21–24; Perry, 111–150; Suzanne H. Vogel,

"Professional Housewife: The Career of Urban Middle Class Japanese Women," *The Japan Interpreter* 12, no. 1 (Winter 1978): 16–43.

114. Salamon, 1974, 96–100; Vogel, 1978, 22.

115. Salamon, 1974, 101–112; Vogel, 1978, 23–24.

116. Economic Planning Agency, 1983, 121–126.

117. Economic Planning Agency, 126.

118. Akiko Fuse, "Role Structure of Dual Career Families," *Journal of Comparative Family Studies* 12, no. 3 (Summer 1981): 329–338.

119. Economic Planning Agency, 130.

120. Economic Planning Agency, 113; Hendry, 1981, 116–132; Takie Sugiyama Lebra, *Japanese Women* (Honolulu: University of Hawaii Press, 1984): 77–98, 121–138.

121. Perry, 106–110; Hendry, 1981, 133–138.

122. Perry, 108–110; George DeVos and Hiroshi Wagatsuma, "Status and Role Behavior in Changing Japan," in Seward and Williamson, 1970, 355–356.

123. Economic Planning Agency, 147.

124. Economic Planning Agency, 148–149.

125. Economic Planning Agency, 144–146.

126. Economic Planning Agency, 143–144.

127. Perry, 197–198.

128. Fujii, 306.

129. Economic Planning Agency, 153.

130. Ibid., 152.

131. DeVos and Wagatsuma, 1970, 360–361.

132. Hiroshi Wagatsuma and George A. DeVos, *Heritage of Endurance: Family Patterns and Delinquency Formation in Urban Japan* (Berkeley: University of California Press, 1984), 174.

133. Economic Planning Agency, 250.

134. Perry, 178–190; Iwao, 24–27; Ezra F. Vogel, *Japan's New Middle Class* (Berkeley: University of California Press, 1963); William A. Caudill and Helen Weinstein, "Mother Care and Infant Behavior in Japan and America," *Psychiatry* 32 (1969): 12–43; William A. Caudill and Carmi Schooler, "Child Behavior and Child Rearing in Japan and the United States: An Interim Report," *Journal of Nervous and Mental Disorders* 157 (1973): 323–338; Robert Jay Lifton, "Women as Knower: Some Psychological Perspectives," in Robert Jay Lifton, ed., *The Woman in America* (Boston: Beacon Press, 1964): 27–51; DeVos and Wagatsuma, 1970: 358–360; Wagatsuma and DeVos, 1984, 24–26, 230–232; Karen C. Smith and Carmi Schooler, "Women as Mothers in Japan: The Effects of Social Structure and Culture on Values and Behavior," *Journal of Marriage and the Family* 40, no. 3 (August 1978): 613–62; Lebra, 1984, 32–49, 158–216.

135. Salamon, 1974, 113–131.

136. Perry, 1976, 200.

137. Keiko Fujiwara et al., "Learning in the Life Course of Japanese Women," 1983 Tokyo Symposium on Women, Workshop III; Lebra, 1984, 233–234.

138. Perry, 1976, 205–211; Salamon, 1974, 165–166; Vogel, 1978, 29.

139. Samuel Coleman, *Family Planning in Japanese Society: Traditional Birth Control in a Modern Urban Culture* (Princeton, N.J.: Princeton University Press, 1983), 60.

140. Perry, 1976, 162–163.

141. Coleman, 1983, 57–82.

142. Perry, 1976, 164.

143. Coleman, 1983, 1232; Samuel Coleman, "The Cultural Context of Condom Use in Japan," *Studies in Family Planning* 12, no. 1 (January 1981): 28–39.

144. Coleman, 1983, 3–6.

145. Coleman, 1983, 38; Perry, 1976, 172.

146. See, for example, Yuki Okuda, "A Move to Outlaw All Abortions: Revisions of the Eugenic Protection Act," *Asian Women's Liberation* no. 5 (August 1982): 4.

147. DeVos and Wagatsuma, 1970, 356–358; Perry Garfinkel, "The Best 'Jewish Mother' in the World," *Psychology Today* (September 1983): 56–60; Vogel, 1978, 25–28; Lebra, 1984, 192–208.

148. Economic Planning Agency, 172.

149. Economic Planning Agency, 125.

150. Economic Planning Agency, 125.

151. Perry, 119–121.

152. Salamon, 1970, 108.

153. Perry, 211.

154. Economic Planning Agency, 217; Vogel, 1978, 35–36.

155. Kazuyoshi Kobayashi, "Japan's Sex Industry as Number One," *Japan Quarterly* 33, no. 3 (July–September 1984): 278–279.

156. *Asian Women's Liberation*, Special Issue on "Prostitution Tourism," no. 3 (July 1980).

157. Julie A. Matthaei, "Consequences of the Rise of the Two-Earner Family: The Breakdown of the Sexual Division of Labor," *American Economic Review* 70, no. 2 (May, 1980): 198–202, 202.

CHAPTER 8

Capitalist Societies of the Third World

Most of the women and men alive today do not live under the conditions of advanced capitalism, but rather within societies that have been only partially and unevenly transformed by capitalist forms of economic production and organization and in which the masses of people continue to subsist at low or impoverished standards of living.[1] In the next chapter, we will look at some examples of societies that have responded to these conditions through the establishment of socialist political regimes. In this chapter we will concentrate upon poor or newly industrializing societies that continue to develop along the capitalist path, while at the same time retaining many social and economic features that derive from their horticultural or agrarian past.

The developing societies, both in their capitalist and socialist versions, are often identified as making up the "Third World." The "First" and "Second" worlds are made up of the advanced capitalist and advanced socialist industrial societies, respectively. In this chapter we will follow a common usage and refer to the capitalist societies of the Third World as *peripheral capitalist societies*. It should be kept in mind, however, that whether capitalist or socialist, Third-World societies are all decisively influenced and shaped by the fact that they exist in a world

system of market relations and international division of labor, which is dominated by capitalist relations of production and exchange. More specifically, they are vitally determined in their development by economic and by political decisions, interests, and institutional arrangements that find their primary location within the advanced capitalist societies. The lives of women and men in all societies are increasingly being transformed by social and economic forces that can only be understood in an international context.

Capitalist Economies of the Third World

Research and theoretical writing on the economic development of peripheral capitalist societies is vast and marked by considerable controversy. To provide background for our subsequent description and analysis of the changing relations between women and men in these societies, we will briefly outline three patterns or processes by which they have been caught up or "incorporated" into worldwide patterns of capitalist development. These patterns should not be thought of as mutually exclusive (in fact, we may find elements of each pattern occurring simultaneously in the same society) or as necessarily representing sequential stages of historical development. They are but simplified descriptions of some of the more important relationships and their effects that have linked peripheral economies to the capitalist world system.

The Development of Primary Export Economies

Many of today's peripheral societies look back on a long past and at an immediate present in which their economies have been characterized by the presence of an important mining or plantation sector producing raw materials and food products primarily for export to more developed areas. Historically, these export enterprises were often established with foreign capital. Whether foreign or domestically owned, however, these enterprises have generally been associated with "enclave" patterns of development. Economic growth is "skewed to the outside." Towns and cities have often been established or have expanded, not as productive centers oriented to the consumer demands or needs of the native populace, but as centers of distribution of goods and services to and from the capitalist centers abroad ("mother countries" in the case of formal colonies).

Small sectors of the native populace may prosper—especially those associated with the entrepreneurial or managerial aspects of trade and the expanding bureaucracies of the state. But the bulk of the populace realizes little gain; and significant strata may actually experience a deterioration in many aspects of their life conditions. This is so, not only because many are excluded from direct participation in the export economy, but also because: (1) Export economies of this type typically inject new dependencies on monetary income into a society, without creating

the corresponding required volume of adequately paid productive employment; (2) Export economies initiate or accelerate the sale of land as private property and impose the pressure of commercial competition on land previously available for subsistence agriculture or horticulture. (3) Export economies produce new forms of coercion (especially in the organization of labor), class relations, and exploitation, which transform but do not necessarily destroy older forms of social hierarchy and control. The instabilities and cycles of boom and bust of world trade in primary commodities, the fluctuating capacities of peripheral nations to import goods and capital from the outside, and the differences in power potentials of discrete nation states and their agents become the determining international environment for this type of development.

Import Substitution Industrialization

Often as a response to the limitations, contradictions, and state (governmental) interventions associated with overreliance on primary export trade, the elites of many peripheral societies as well as foreign capital investors have initiated and expanded industrial productive facilities for domestic markets. These industries substitute domestically produced goods for previously imported products. Characteristically, these types of industries (1) have relied on various protectionist strategies by the state; (2) have failed to achieve levels of efficiency that would make them competitive with their counterparts in the advanced capitalist societies; (3) have depended on large and often widening inequalities of income within the native populace to maintain profitability; (4) have been heavily reliant on costly imported technologies, equipment, and industrial inputs; (5) have had real but self-limiting effects in expanding industrial employment; and (6) have stimulated the development of capitalist relations in agriculture, but in a highly uneven fashion.

Consequently, import substitution industrialization has advanced and deepened capitalist relations of production and the money-based exchange economy in peripheral societies. At the same time it has excluded vast sectors of their populaces from most of the fruits of industrialization while making these same sectors more and more dependent for survival on the "modern" economy. This pattern of development also creates new forms of dependency on the advanced capitalist societies and heightens vulnerability to the fluctuations of international markets, especially when combined with persistent features of the export economy.

Export-Oriented Industrialization and the New International Division of Labor

Without abandoning import substitution as a goal and practice, many peripheral capitalistic societies began in the mid-1960s to place increasing emphasis on industrial production for export and the promotion of various forms of agrobusiness, also primarily for export. This strategy was particularly aimed at dealing with the chronic problems of debt, negative trade balances, and limitations on the import of capital associated with the export of primary products and import substitution industrialization.

A major aspect of this strategy was to create within these societies a more hospitable environment—through "favorable" tax, profit remittance, subsidy, credit, and (of paramount importance) labor policies—for foreign investment. Native capitalists also would be given greater economic incentives, subsidies, guarantees, and more reliable state-enforced control over the labor force.

At the same time, and intertwined with these initiatives by the governments and ruling groups within peripheral societies, large industrial corporations from the advanced capitalist societies were becoming more and more "internationalized" in their operations. This latter development continued a trend already in progress of setting up (or buying up) productive facilities abroad as branches or subsidiaries of home operations located in the advanced capitalist societies. But increasingly, it also involves closing down facilities in one area of the home country and moving them to greener pastures in another area (at home but also abroad). This is the so-called runaway-shop phenomenon. Perhaps more importantly, it also involves the breaking up of formerly integrated industrial productive processes into segments of activities or phases of production that can be distributed to more and more distant locales, not only within countries, but also among countries. The speed and flexibility of technological innovations, the increasing sophistication of worldwide communications systems, and the advances made in combining high-technology production processes with low-skill labor have created a true revolution in the ability to move capital resources around the world.

Among the most important effects of this development have been (1) the breakdown of the political and workplace balance of forces between organized labor and the owners and managers of corporate capital in the advanced capitalist countries and (2) the rapid incorporation of weakly organized, and often politically repressed, low-wage labor in peripheral societies into a *new internationally based system of production for global markets.*

The worker losing her job because of a footwear plant closing down in New England, the steelworker losing his job for a similar reason in Pennsylvania, the illegal Colombian immigrant working clandestinely in a new "sweatshop" apparel factory in metropolitan New York, the Vietnamese worker in a high-tech factory in northern California, the assembler of new low-priced VCRs in South Korea, and the young Haitian woman sorting manufacturers' coupons sent to her from the supermarkets of the United States all represent the reality of the new transnational integrated system of capitalist production.

Uneven and Combined Development

The patterns of economic development described above focus upon the incorporation of peripheral societies in an expanding and changing world capitalist system. The groups and individuals who make up these societies are not, of course, mere passive agents responding to international arrangements whose content has been irresistibly fixed by others. Neither have these societies been uniformly and predictably transformed by the spread of the world capitalist system. In almost all of them, we are faced with clear evidence that precapitalist social institutions and cultural values do not simply disappear with capitalist penetration. Various forms of capitalist relations (reminiscent of different historical stages of capitalist development in the advanced capitalist societies) mingle with one another and with precapitalist social relations in complex structures of what is sometimes called "uneven" or "combined" patterns of development.

The ox, the wooden plow, the digging stick, nonmonetary forms of extrafamilial economic exchange, kin-based forms of labor organization and economic redistribution, "penny-capitalist" forms of small trading enterprise may exist side by side with the chemical fertilizer factory, the automated packing plant, the modern steel mill, the posh advertising firm, the American-style supermarket, and even the potential to manufacture nuclear weapons. Startling forms of modern, sophisticated affluence can also exist side by side with appalling forms of mass poverty, which is just as modern in its origins, but whose victims may appear to use very unmodern forms of social defense against its more severe encroachments.

Recognition of the unevenness of the spread and deepening of capitalist relations in the peripheral societies and the articulation into a complex whole of what appear to be very different and often contradictory forms of economic and social organization becomes a major key to understanding the contexts in which Third-World women and men currently struggle to establish new relations with one another.

In this chapter we will analyze some of the important structures and dynamics of gender relations in peripheral capitalist societies on the bases of selected case studies within the major regions of Africa, Asia, the Near East, and Latin America. We will conclude with some general observations based on these cases and on wider research on peripheral capitalist development.

Africa: Ghana

The evolutionary drama of contemporary Africa is scripted by the volatile and contradictory processes by which traditional kin-based units of production and social organization have been progressively incorporated into the world capitalist system. Colonialism, new forms of economic dependency, migration, the spread of towns and cities without an adequate productive base, migration, apartheid,* families divided by permanent or near-permanent geographical dislocation, and the persistence of traditional forms of subsistence and other kin-based forms of social and economic defense

---

*The legally and militarily enforced system of racial segregation in South Africa.

in the face of capitalist expansion—all these are part of the protagonist forces in the drama. In this section we focus on the West African nation of Ghana as one historical act in that drama.

The area now making up the country of Ghana was officially colonized by the British in 1902, but its contacts with Europe extended back many centuries before that.[2] Portuguese forts were established on its coast in the late fifteenth century. The involvement of the peoples of this region with the capitalist world economy has been both long and gradual. Political independence from Great Britain was obtained in 1957, but the intensity of this involvement has deepened and extended Ghana's dependency and vulnerability in the postindependence period.

Ghana's traditional ethnic and sociopolitical groupings are the Akan, the Ewe, the Ga, and the Northern peoples. A significant feature of precolonial gender relations among these groups was the considerable independence and economic power enjoyed by women. This tended to be true whether the group was organized matrilineally or patrilineally and whatever the prevailing ideologies of women's place. While one need not subscribe to the view that precolonial Ghana was a paradise of gender equality, the following observation by Audrey Chapman Smock would, nevertheless, seem to be substantially valid:

Regardless of whether the woman's place was considered to be substantially equal to that of the male members as among the Akan, or subordinate as among the Ewe or Northern groups, men rarely interfered with or attempted to regulate directly women's conduct. In all these societies men and women had separate spheres of activities with their rights and duties deriving from them. Sex separation did not give rise to limitations on women's freedom; quite the contrary, it accorded them considerable independence. Among many of the groups women lived apart from men, further increasing their chances to develop a corporate sense of identity and social networks. The Ewe, Ga, and Akan all had institutionalized women's corporate sense of identity.[3]

Marriage was a characteristically loose arrangement, the partners resembling as much coequal business associates as they did a conjugal pair. The utilitarian aspects of sexual exchange were frankly acknowledged at the level of cultural practice, female premarital sex was widely accepted, and female adultery was only lightly punished. (The object of the punishment was usually the male offender and not the wife.)

Women's activities as cultivators and traders were as vital to the maintenance of traditional economies as was their domestic household work. Polygyny was commonly practiced (but always confined to a small minority of wealthier men). Polygyny was significant, not only in terms of its economic implications (more workers for the husband or father), but also as a culturally favored means to display male wealth and prestige. Within the corporate kinship system of common landholding, women had ready access to land use on an autonomous basis, along with the men.

The development of cash cropping, primarily cocoa, in Ghana and the transformations brought about by colonial rule enhanced and consolidated Ghanaian men's supremacy over women in many respects. Ghana was not a major settler colony. The British trained and educated African men to fill colonial clerical and middle-level administrative offices. Viewing Ghana, as it did all of Africa, through patriarchal eyes, they also biased the distribution of technical resources and training toward male rather than female cultivators.

Although it was the case that women had available to them earlier and wider educational opportunities in Ghana than in most other colonial African areas, men far out-stripped them in this respect, and do today. This fact is of special significance in present-day Ghana where careers linked to educational credentials are the major avenues for limited social mobility in a society that is still primarily a primary export economy with a very narrow (primarily import sub-stitution) industrial base. Women workers have been incorporated into industry, but under conditions of discrimination and sub-ordination, largely confined to small-scale, low-paying, more "informal" or cottage types of industries.[4]

Ghanaian women are still noted for their independence, both in spirit and in terms of their economic self-assertion. But as we will attempt to show in the following case anal-yses, this independence has been increas-ingly compromised and rendered vulnerable by the spread and deeper penetration of cap-italist relations in Ghanaian society. In these analyses we will pay particular attention to the survival and mobility strategies of Ghanaian men and women as they utilize the cultural, organizational, and material re-sources made available to them through the transformation of traditional institutions by colonialism and the penetration of capital-ism.

In the Countryside

The complexity of the effects of the pen-etration of capitalist relations and the re-sponses of women and men striving to adapt to and take advantage of this penetration by using the resources of traditional institutions is well illustrated by Gwendolyn Mikell's his-torical analysis of male and female cocoa farming among the Brong, one of the Akan peoples of south-central Ghana.[5]

Akan societies have been traditionally or-ganized along matrilineal lines. Sisters and brothers share rights and obligations based on descent from a common mother, and among their obligations is the expectation that they will contribute to the common re-sources or "estate" of the matrilineage. Land in recent times has been included within this estate—it was commonly administered by males within the matrilineage and passed on to nephews (sisters' sons) when they came of age. Administration, however, did not imply ownership during the period be-fore cash cropping and colonial rule turned land into a commodity for exchange on the market. Both males and females had *usufruct* rights to the use of the land. The matrilin-eage was overarching, subordinating and dominating of the relations among hus-bands, wives, and children and gave priority to relations among brothers, sisters, neph-ews, and nieces. Preference for cross-cousin marriage further solidified the system. Within the overall system of matrilineality, however, patricentric (male-centered) mech-anisms also existed. The most important of these was the structural principle of the *nturo*, which centered on the father and his offspring and which ideologically empha-sized the ties of wives and children to the husband and father. Within matrilineality, then, latent principles of male privilege fo-cused on patrilineal kin ties have long been available.

With the stimulation of cash cropping (co-coa) by the colonial powers from the late nineteenth century onward, various strate-gems were initiated among the Brong and other peoples to gradually turn *usufruct* rights over lands belonging to the matrilin-eage into private holdings owned by indi-viduals. These initiatives were mainly ad-vanced by men, but women were by no means totally excluded. Between 1900 and 1920, however, landholding and the working of land by women on their own account was on the decline. As males established more and more cocoa farms, female and child labor to work the farms was in ever-greater demand. There was a marked increase in polygynous unions, even to the point of men bargaining with women for marital rights to unborn daughters. Concurrently, as men began to appropriate more and more land for private use and to mobilize kin-based labor to work their farms, they progressively abandoned the practice of cooperative labor on matrilineage lands. After 1920 hired labor was needed as a supplement to inadequate supplies of kin-based labor—which increasingly had become nuclear family labor emphasizing latent patricentric ties of wives and children to husbands and fathers. Hired labor, of course, represented a substitution for customary exchanges of cooperative labor.

During the decades of the 1920s and 1930s, women's own-account cocoa farming experienced a resurgence. The reasons for this were rather different for each decade: (1) During the 1920s there was a cocoa boom. Land was also still widely available. Opportunity lessened the impact of male competition on women for land and production. (2) The 1930s was a period of worldwide economic pressure and falling cocoa prices. Men migrated to cities in search of urban jobs, increasing the burden on women to maintain the family and matrilineage-based rural economies. In this period some women gravitated to cocoa farming on their own account, despite depressed world prices, as one of the few rural opportunities for earning cash income available to them.

The present period is most striking because of the virtual absence, among the farmers studied by Mikell, of female cocoa farmers who have entered into own-account production in recent years. Female cash plots have always been smaller on average than those of males and the average income derived from these plots significantly less than the male averages. Political and economic instability has also aggravated the problems

of cash cropping for both males and females, particularly from 1967 onward. The supply of new land has also markedly dwindled. Added to these circumstances, however, is another major factor, which Mikell sees as having had a special negative impact on female access to own-account cash plots: increasing restrictions within the workings of the matrilineage on the ability of females to inherit land from their mothers and sisters.

The pattern had already been established for males, generally, to pass on privately appropriated land primarily to their sons (through their wives) and other male relatives. Females who own cash plots, on the other hand, have almost uniformly expressed the desire to pass on their lands to daughters and sisters. This intention is very much in line with the traditional practice, inherited from the precolonial past, of transmitting *all* female property through the female line. Ownership of cash-producing female property is especially critical to women at present, because women know that their husbands are faced with the divided responsibilities, under present conditions, of supporting their own nuclear families (most particularly their sons) as well as economically assisting their sisters' sons (especially for purposes of education). What has apparently happened, however, is that men, through manipulating structures of male solidarity *within* the matrilineage, have become increasingly successful in having female property revert to the matrilineage on the death of its owners, concentrating it in the hands of those who share the male *nturo* bond and eventually passing it on to younger males along patrilineal lines of inheritance.

Mikell gives due acknowledgment to the importance of the male bias of colonial administrators in facilitating the concentration of cash plots and producer's technology in the hands of males rather than females throughout the colonial period. At the same time, however, her analysis attempts to document the fact that Brong and other male Ghanaian cultivators reacted to the penetration of the cash-crop capitalist economy by manipulating the latent patricentric kin institutions within the matrilineage to monopolize productive resources along gender lines and to marginalize women from the ownership and control of cash-earning productive property. Coupled with the even more severe exclusion of women than men from both rural and urban alternative sources of viable income, women's overall position has deteriorated over time. In the last analysis, Mikell argues, matrilineality offered no more protection for women than patrilineality against the effects of women's participation in cash-crop production for world markets.

In Town: The Poor

Clare Robertson examined the changed economic status and gender relations of over two hundred, mostly poor Ga women of Ussher Town, a district in Central Accra, a congeries of quarters in the capital city of Accra.[6] The Ga historically have been a patrilineal people in respect to descent, cognatic in respect to inheritance (individuals inherit from both parents), and bilateral in respect to residence (individuals usually live in the compound of the parent of the same gender). Ussher Town, then, was characterized by male and female compounds, husbands living with their patrilateral relatives, women with their matrilateral relatives, female children remaining with their mothers, and male children leaving their mothers to live with their fathers between the ages of six to ten. A wife sleeps with her husband when called for and usually prepares food for him and sends it to him by her children. The husband has by custom been expected to provide his wife with money to pay for food and clothing for the entire conjugal family.

Although the Ga have long experience in urban living, most of the males were fishermen and farmers. Women have been involved in trading since the earliest times. In recent times they have been most prominent in the trading of manufactured cloth, fish, meat, vegetables, prepared foods, and hardware, as well as imported goods. Ga women customarily processed and traded their husbands' fish and food produce in a cooperative venture. Women handled the cash transactions and shared the income with their husbands according to negotiated agreement. Since both partners maintained a high degree of independence in their respective productive and marketing activities, the enterprise approximated much more the Western concept of a joint venture than that of a family business, while still resting on traditional kin ties.

Increasing involvement of the husbands in wage labor and the deepening of capitalist relations in the area of trade have, according to Robertson, brought about important changes in the status of Central Accra's Ga women and their relationships with their husbands. A major change has been in the degree of economic cooperation between husbands and wives. There are fewer farmers and fishermen and less self-employment among men. The men married to the women in Robertson's sample were also, on the average, involved in low-income occupations, and in many cases found it difficult or impossible to provide adequate financial support for wives and children. At the same time, their increasing access to independent sources of wage income made it easier for them to conceal the amount of their income from their (often illiterate or semiliterate) wives. This possibility of concealment facilitated the practice of keeping another woman "on the side" (a common West African male urban practice), without the wife's knowledge or capacity to interfere.

Wives, for their part, were showing an increased tendency not to cooperate economically with their husbands even when the opportunity existed. They too seemed to view possible economic relations with their husbands in increasingly market-oriented terms as opposed to relations of custom.* Robertson also reports that women engaged in trade were themselves displaying a tendency to conceal information concerning income and business finances from husbands, largely because of the suspicion—apparently not unjustified—that husbands with knowledge of wives' incomes might cease making support payments.

Both Ga husbands and wives in Central Accra, formerly highly interdependent within the complementary bonds of traditional kin relationships, are, then, becoming increasingly economically "independent" in a more modern sense. Wives as well as husbands tend to welcome this new independence, saying "Let him do his work and I will do mine."[7] A few of them were actually prospering under these circumstances. For most of them, however, Robertson argues that their independence is increasingly becoming an economic trap.

In Ghana as in almost all of black Africa, education has become the major source of economic and social mobility in an environment of extremely limited job opportunities. Children of these urban Ga mothers demand that they assume the costly burdens of educating them. Mothers accede to these demands and generally see it as in their long-range interests to do so. The mothers, however, receive less and less in the way of con-

tributions to children's education from increasingly independent husbands, not to speak of adequate contributions for general support. The situation is exacerbated by high rates of divorce and separation and persistent demands on urban Ga women to provide loans and other means of support to a variety of kin (especially matrilateral and most especially mothers). Men also continue to show a tendency to give greater priority to transferring income to their lineages than to their wives and children, restricting the joint economic role even further.

Finally, most female traders confront a situation of deepening capitalist relations in the area of trade. They find it more and more difficult to raise the capital to qualify for the credit accounts necessary to contract with large capitalist firms to purchase cloth and imported goods to sell. The modernization and mechanization of the fishing industry beginning in the 1950s and the etablishment by the government of the State Fishing Corporation in the 1960s have also created monopoly conditions in the supply of fish for trade, which have worked to the disadvantage of independent female traders. These women enjoy less and less autonomy within the framework of Ghana's present incorporation in the world economy. As women, and as generally poorly educated or uneducated persons, alternative sources of adequately remunerative employment are even scarcer for them than they are for their husbands. Of the hopes of these women for the future, Robertson makes the following observation: "They . . . have high expectations of economic betterment through the agency of their children. However, with a bad employment problem in Accra, their hopes are likely to be dashed as they watch their sons go unemployed and their daughters become prostitutes. They then must accept gratefully whatever the daughters can earn."[9]

---

*For example, some wives reported that they did not engage in joint ventures with their fishermen husbands because the latter did not catch the kind of fish that the wives specialized in selling.[8]

In Town: The Affluent and the Mobile

Carmel Dinan's field study of young, unmarried, female white-collar workers in Accra illustrates some of the sexual dynamics and social and cultural contexts of class formation and class competition in urban Ghana.[10] She carried out intensive interviews with and observations of twenty-five women drawn from a larger sample of single women in Accra in the mid-1970s.

Most of these women were between the ages of twenty-one and twenty-five, mainly immigrants from small towns, ethnically Akan or Ewe from polygynous family backgrounds, and had had vocational, technical, or secondary educations beyond the middle-school level. They worked, or aspired to work, as clerical workers, receptionists, saleswomen, or in similar white-collar occupations. Only two had been (but were no longer) married. But all had full and varied sexual careers, involving liaisons with a number of men, often from their early teens onward. Among them they had produced nine children out of wedlock (mainly cared for by matrilineal kin) and had undergone a total of thirty-two induced abortions.

In a Ghanaian society that is overwhelming in its pronatalist social pressure for women to marry at a very young age, almost all of these women expressed their ultimate intention to marry, but not in the immediate future. In the meantime all were vigorously and quite calculatingly exploiting the sexual marketplace of urban Accra to establish a more secure future for themselves and for their children when the time to marry did finally arrive. Dinan's data and analysis indicate that this marketplace has to be understood in terms of the transformations of traditional marriage and kinship institutions within the city; the cultural penetration of Western ideals of romantic love and consumerism; and class-specific survival strategies in an economic environment of general scarcity for most but relative privilege for the educated elite.

Dinan's informants were committed to the Western ideal of "companionate" marriage, based on love, mutual responsibility and caring, and the mutual sharing of life's valued experiences and resources. Yet, in their perception, contracting such a marriage in Ghana was for all intents and purposes impossible. In their view, urban Ghanaian men were not interested in romantic ties with wives and were committed to the pursuit of macho prestige. Through the constant pursuit and conquest of a variety of women, men in urban Ghana, as they saw it, married mainly to have children, to exploit the income of wives, and to have a housekeeper, "not only to cook, but somebody just to keep up the prestige of the man."[11]

The futility of expecting potential husbands to remain faithful not only violated the ideals of the myth of romantic love but also had very direct economic implications: Husbands would quite predictably divert economic resources to "outside women" or girlfriends. This was particularly the case since the essentially instrumental view of sexual services inherited from rural and village Ghana is based on expectations of reciprocity, in which sex is exchanged for (at least partial) economic support. Dinan and other commentators have also pointed out that the male maintenance of outside girlfriends in Ghana can be at least partially interpreted as an informal extension of the village practice and male prestige ideal of polygyny into urban environments.* In a

---

*Technically, this urban practice can be labeled as *polycoity*.

similar manner, these young women (again quite reasonably) anticipated that other portions of husbands' income would be continuously on call for the benefit of members of his lineage. The obligations here extend not only from the persistence of custom but are also rooted in the material functions of reciprocity within kin networks that continue to operate in modern Ghana and elsewhere in Africa to facilitate the survival and mobility of individual and lineal kin segments. One of Dinan's informants described the essential structural context of expectations as follows:

The extent of family relations in Ghana is also a problem—so many relatives. The man must still look backwards—grandmothers, mothers, uncles—so many. Because the mother or the uncle will say: "well we have contributed in looking after you whilst you were going to school so now that you are finished you can look after my son or whoever as well." So the man has to spend his money in that way as well. So it's entirely left to the woman to be giving out money for her own children.[12]

Most of these women were not only strongly committed to the education of the children they would eventually bear in marriage but also had long-range ambitions to establish profitable private businesses of their own, for which they were currently accumulating capital. With these aspirations linked to their equally strong commitment to live the good life—defined by the more spectacular aspects of Western middle-class consumption—now and in the future, these young women traded in a sexual marketplace that afforded them ample opportunity to supplement handsomely their wage income, to live well at present, and to save for the future. It should be emphasized that this mobility strategy was explicitly informed by the desire to bring *security* and *autonomy* to what was thought to be an inevitable (because of societal and cultural demands) mar-

riage relationship that in itself was anticipated to provide very little of either.

Dinan described three major ways in which these women manipulated their "sexual or sociosexual roles" to enhance their mobility strategies: (1) the cultivation of male "patrons" or sponsors in securing and maintaining employment; (2) the maintaining of more or less regular relationships with bachelor boyfriends with comfortable incomes (no marriage contemplated), involving the steady receipt of monetary and other "gifts";* and (3) maintaining "sugar-daddy"/ "gold-digger" relations—that is, liaisons with older, affluent married men (the most lucrative types of relationships from the standpoint of maintaining a luxurious life-style). Different sexual relationships, especially of the latter type, were frequently maintained simultaneously.

Dinan's informants were quite candid about the utilitarian nature of these affairs, from both their and their partners' points of view. They realized sizable amounts of discretionary income, life maintenance, and savings. Their partners obtained the prestige of being able to display publicly their conquest of young, well-dressed, attractive, and appropriately educated and Westernized objects and symbols of sexual and class prestige and mobility—what one informant called "an English-speaking vagina."[13]

Quite obviously, these young women were successfully exploiting the social, cultural, and gender relations that were in themselves the structural basis of the inaccessibility of their own romantic aspirations. Their success in this strategy reflects at the same time the transformation and encapsulation of tradition by modernity when the

---

*Failure of males to maintain "support" in these relationships would occasion the breaking off of the relationships by the women.

spread of capitalist relations generates new forms of class formation and class competition into a society of scarcity.

Christine Oppong in her admirable study of Akan civil servants, many of whom inherited the privilege, prestige, and affluence of their predecessors—the upper-level British colonial administrators, also focuses on the dilemmas presented by the effort to realize the Western ideal of conjugality in an environment in which the material obligations toward and demands from extended kin are still culturally and structurally compelling.[14] Already in the 1960s, she observed a few conjugal pairs and their children who were affluent enough and secure enough to achieve effective "closure" from intrusion by kindred and in great measure realize much of the behavioral substance and apparently many of the affective rewards of the Western middle-class ideal. Whatever the relative merits of this ideal, it is clearly sustained by material and social resources that are well beyond the reach of the vast majority of Ghanaians.

India: Hindu Women and Men

Historical Background

Settled agriculture in India grew out of a nomadic past.[15] Centuries of warfare led eventually to social and political centralization and the development of an agrarian civilization with marked class inequality in the form of the rigid caste system. As in other agrarian societies, women lost power and status as agricultural life replaced horticultural and pastoral patterns. Hindu law in particular became more restrictive of women.[16] Hindu law was first codified by Manu in the second century B.C. Under his reforms women lost much of their freedom and personal autonomy. Child marriage be-

came the ideal. Virginity and chastity were strictly required of females but not of males. Females were placed under the perpetual guardianship of males, first the father or elder brother, then the husband. They lost property rights, inheritance rights, divorce rights, rights over their children, and rights to participate in public life. They were forbidden to read the sacred scriptures and deprived of access to the more prestigious aspects of religious life and salvation. Widow remarriage was forbidden and some areas adopted the practice of *suttee*, which required widows to commit suicide by throwing themselves into the flames of their husband's funeral pyres. With Moslem domination in the twelfth century, *purdah*, or the rigid seclusion and veiling of women, was introduced into Hindu society. Ideologically, females came to be regarded as inferior, insignificant, and unclean. The role of women was to bear children and serve men.

The British came to dominate India in the nineteenth century. They opposed many of the Hindu and Moslem customs related to women, but they were cautious in their attempts to reform Indian society. The British did not want to disrupt Indian society and thereby threaten their own domination or profits. The few laws the British did enact (to abolish child marriage, for example) went largely unenforced. They did provide some facilities for education for girls but few people took advantage of them.

Independence from Britain in 1947 brought a wave of enthusiasm for both modernization and preservation of Indian tradition. Women had been encouraged by Mahatma Gandhi to come out of seclusion and participate openly in the independence movement. Many women did protest and many were jailed. The new Indian government recognized the female participants by granting women legal rights, heretofore unimaginable under Hindu tradition.

Twentieth-Century Rights for Women

India has done a great deal toward eliminating gender discrimination in the law. But such progressive social legislation relating to gender roles and women's position in society are virtually unenforceable. The vast numbers of poor, illiterate rural and urban women do not even realize what their rights are: If they do, they do not have the resources necessary to demand their recognition. Furthermore, even educated women who know the laws do not necessarily accept them or desire their implementation. For example, laws pertaining to inheritance now give daughters equal rights with sons, and another statute outlaws the dowry system. Traditionally, only sons inherit property, because in India's patrilineal family system only sons continue to belong to the joint family after marriage. Daughters therefore receive as large a dowry as possible at marriage, most of which goes to the groom's family. But they have no claims on the rest of the family estate. Most families ignore the laws that attempt to change this system. Daughters do not actively oppose the dowry system for fear they will not be able to marry, and they do not claim inheritance rights out of respect for tradition and to protect the economic interests and viability of their natal families.

The dowry system has, in fact, gotten worse and has made raising a daughter more financially taxing. An educated higher-caste male can often demand as much as $10,000 in dowry from a prospective bride's family. His family views his wife's dowry as a means of recovering the cost of his education. The bride's family sees it as important to marry her well, but the economic sacrifice can be severe.

Divorce is also now legal. But such a terrible social stigma is attached to divorce that relatively few people are willing to avail themselves of this legal right. The law also provides for the granting of alimony. However, the recipient of alimony must remain chaste or forego the alimony. This applies to males who receive alimony as well as to females, but, of course, females are more likely to be recipients and have to obey the law. Fathers have automatic custody over the children when divorce occurs.

Many laws still remain that discriminate against women by protecting them, especially in employment. Women are not allowed to work in certain dangerous occupations nor are they allowed to work at night. This limits the range of occupational choices available to women. Yet the "protection" is often questionable. Women, for example, do some of the hardest work in the construction industry. They are the rock breakers and haulers of heavy loads such as rocks and earth. As low-paid workers who are often recent migrants from impoverished rural areas, they cannot afford to rent rooms. Therefore, they camp at the edge of the construction sites and their children play nearby as they work.

Technically, the law requires that employers provide maternity benefits and child-care facilities for female employees. Employers who do not want to hire women use this law as an excuse: They say it makes women more expensive than male workers. However, employers such as construction firms who desire to use the lower-paid female work force often do so without bothering to provide the benefits required by law.

Indian women have the right to vote and equal rights with men to hold political office. India has even had a female prime minister. However, few women actually participate in politics. Women are not as likely to vote as men, and many who do vote follow their husbands' instructions as to whom to support. Immediately after independence there was a flurry of political activity by women who had participated in the independence movement. Several women have gained high-ranking political office. These women do not, however, always support women's issues or women's rights. Many see themselves as representatives of other social groups rather than as women's representatives. Furthermore, the percentage of female officeholders has declined in recent decades rather than increased.

Politics is still believed to be too rough or too dirty for women, and the example of Prime Minister Indira Gandhi did not affect the wide acceptance of this belief. Gandhi herself was not an active supporter of women's liberation. She argued that because Indian conditions are different from those in the West, many feminist ideas are inappropriate there. Furthermore, the harshness of her early authoritarian rule led many to maintain that she was proof that women should be kept out of politics. Women supposedly cannot be trusted to act honorably.

All women in India have basicaly the same political and legal rights, although the law does recognize differences in religious practice; for example, Muslim males are allowed multiple wives, but not Hindu males. The actual positions of men and women vary considerably according to their social and economic positions, however. Many religions are practiced in India: Hindu, Moslem, Sikh, Christian, Jain, Parsi, and Jewish. Since the majority of Indians are Hindu and since Hindu culture has had the greatest impact on India, only Hindu males and females are considered here.

The Caste System

India is characterized by a rigid *caste system*. Caste regulations and observances used to be enforced by law. The castes are no longer legally recognized, and government policy aims at eliminating discrimination against lower-caste individuals. However, as with the laws aimed at equality for women, laws supporting caste equality have had negligible effects.

There are thousands of castes in India, but these can be subsumed under five major divisions. The highest caste (in ritual status and prestige, but not necessarily in actual wealth and power) is the Brahmans or priests. The next highest is the Kshatriya caste of kings and warriors, followed by the Vaisya or traders, and then the commoners, the Sudra, or artisans and workers. The lowest in the hierarchy are the Harijan, or untouchables, who perform ritually polluting work such as butchers, launderers, and sweepers. In addition to the castes, there are other low-prestige poor peoples known as tribal peoples.

Traditionally, Hindus married and associated only with members of their own caste. Intercaste marriages and relationships are now legal, but they are such a violation of Hindu tradition that they invariably cause a scandal for the families involved and therefore are rare. The positions of women and men vary somewhat according to caste membership.

Another major division within Indian society is between the vast rural sector and the relatively small urban population. Life in the cities differs from life in the rural villages and among these differences are differences in gender roles and gender stratification. There is also an important dichotomy between the educated, modernized, Westernized elite and the more traditional urban and rural non-Westernized Indians. Important regional variations also affect women's and men's positions. Because it is impossible to describe fully the tremendous diversity that characterizes so large a country as India (one-sixth of the world's women live in India), this discussion is limited to the major social divisions of socioeconomic status, rural versus urban, and modernized versus traditional sectors.

The traditional norms are more closely adhered to by the upper-strata rural families and the more conservative middle-class and upper-class urban families. Poorer families are more likely to deviate, both out of economic necessity and because they have little ritual honor or status to lose by violating these customs. Members of the educated, liberal urban elite also often reject many of the traditional patterns in favor of Western practices. But Maria Mies in her study of middle-class and upper-class working women and students documents the fact that even the most decisive drift toward effective empowerment of women in the family is almost always covert in nature. It does not rise to the level of challenging the dominant cultural commitment to the norms and mores of male supremacy.[17]

Rural Indians

The vast majority of Indians still live in rural agricultural villages. Villagers on the whole tend to be more traditional than city dwellers, but this depends heavily on caste status. Higher-caste, richer villagers are far stricter in their adherence to Hindu customs than are poorer, lower-caste villagers. Among the tribal and lower-caste families in both rural and urban areas, it is usually economically impossible to isolate females in the home or to maintain a rigid gender division of labor. Women from these groups must work outside the home. Both genders contribute to the economic support of the family. The man's contribution is likely to be greater, however, because of wage discrimination against women. Women in agricul-

tural labor earn from 10 to 60 percent of what men earn for the same work. But even meager earnings give women a degree of economic independence they would not otherwise have. These working women still have responsibility for household upkeep and child care. Men do not help with domestic duties except in emergencies.

The man has the legitimate authority, but wives often resist it in poorer families. They may even talk back or strike back in a dispute or beating. Wives of these groups are also more likely to abandon abusive husbands and return to their parental households. There is little consideration of prestige loss among these already degraded peoples to keep them from breaking rules against marital separation. For the same reasons, these groups permit their females greater sexual freedom than is common in higher-caste groups.

The more prosperous, but not necessarily wealthy, Indian villagers continue to practice Hindu tradition. They have a patriarchal, patrilineal, patrilocal family structure. Authority and inheritance pass from father to sons. Men control the chief resource, the land, through the patrilineal family and inheritance system. Daughters are only temporary members of the household and will be transferred to their husbands' lineages at an early age. Daughters therefore do not inherit family holdings, but they receive a dowry of jewelry, cash, household goods, and clothing, which represents an important share of the family's resources. Families therefore prefer to have sons who will serve the family all their lives and will carry on the family line. Moreover, sons bring wealth into the family through their wives' dowries. The birth of a son is therefore a joyous occasion. A daughter is not so celebrated and may be an occasion for sorrow and grief. The midwife is paid more for the delivery of a boy than for a girl, and female infanticide was practiced among some of the warrior castes until about fifty years ago.

Child-Rearing Practices. Despite the difference in initial response to the gender of newborns, infants are usually treated equally. Boys are favored as they grow older, however. Girls are differentiated from boys at a very young age by distinctive clothing and the use of cosmetics. Hindu child-rearing practices clearly differentiate between the genders, socializing girls toward modesty and domesticity and the boys toward public work and authority. Daughters, for example, are encouraged to care for their younger siblings when they are about six years old.

Gender segregation is imposed on children during early adolescence. Boys and girls have different games and toys. It is unacceptable for girls to participate in boys' games and usually vice versa. Girls who attend school at all are often removed at adolescence to ensure their virginity and reputations. Girls are carefully trained to develop a modest demeanor. They must not act like boys. They must speak in a controlled low voice and walk with short steps, keeping their arms at their side and their heads bowed. Boys are not punished for hitting a girl, but a girl is severely punished for striking a boy. However, children of neither gender are encouraged to be independent or individualistic. From infancy onward Hindu socialization aims to build commitment and subservience to the interests of the familial group. The emphasis is on self-control and effacement of the individual will.

Marriage Customs. Child marriage is still the norm among traditional rural families. Indians believe early marriage works best because it allows the husband and his family to mold the young wife to best fit into their household. Her youth makes her vulnerable and compliant. By the time the girl is fourteen or fifteen years old, her parents will have arranged a marriage for her with a somewhat older boy from another village. The couple rarely meet before their wedding day, although members of the groom's family visit the girl to determine her suitability as a wife. She should be of similar caste rank, modest (virginity is essential), submissive, fair skinned, and have a dowry commensurate with her family's position and wealth. However, in some areas of India it is traditional for the bride's family to have lower rank than the husband's. Thus the bride and her kin must be deferential to the groom's kin. This places the young bride in an even more disadvantaged position in her new household than is usual in areas where brides and grooms come from families of similar rank.

After her marriage the young bride leaves her natal family and village and goes to reside with her husband in his extended family. The move is a fearful and painful event for the girl. Her introduction into the physical relationship of marriage makes the early stage of married life even more difficult. Sex is considered too embarrassing to discuss even between mother and daughter, so girls are given little or no information about it. Thus the sexual consummation of the marriage is often a traumatic experience, especially since the husband is a virtual stranger.

The young bride's position as daughter-in-law in her husband's household is not an enviable one. She is under the strict authority of a domineering and demanding mother-in-law. The mother-in-law directs the work of her daughters-in-law. The youngest daughter-in-law is given the most time-consuming, arduous, and menial work of the household. She is also kept under close surveillance by the mother-in-law. Her freedom of movement and personal autonomy are severely restricted. She has to show respect and strict obedience to her mother-in-law and her new male kinspeople. If she violates any of the appropriate standards of behavior, she brings shame to her natal family.

In the rural areas women born in a particular village do not have to veil their faces. However, women from outside must be veiled. This means that daughters-in-law must remain veiled and cannot move freely in the village. The daughter-in-law must remain veiled even within the household, especially in the presence of her father-in-law or her husband's elder brothers. She should even veil herself in the presence of her husband and not speak to him or hand him anything if other people are present. As she grows older and has several children, she becomes a more accepted member of the community and suffers fewer restrictions.

Doranne Jacobson argues that veiling and purdah observances of women help maintain harmony in the joint family, albeit at the cost of female status, independence, and freedom:

It emphasizes the subordinate relationship of the woman to those in authority in the family and deemphasizes her tie to her husband. Veiling and seclusion in her conjugal home constantly remind a woman of her position as a *bahu* [daughter-in-law] who must quietly subjugate her individual wishes to those of the group.[18]

The young bride usually receives little emotional support from her new husband. Husbands and wives are not expected to provide each other with companionship. Companionship comes from participation in the single gender work groups of the family. In traditional families recently married couples are not allowed to see each other during the day. They get to know each other only at night in bed.

Ideally, a woman should treat her husband as a god. She should never speak his name or speak to him in public. Indian women should never openly disagree with any man or offer a man information or advice. This shames a man even if he is the woman's husband. The male ego is thought to be easily injured: females are not supposed to have strong egos. Female subservience is also shown by the wife walking several paces behind her husband. A woman should also eat after her husband has eaten. She can eat his leftovers, but her leftovers would defile him.

The purpose of the marriage relationship is to produce children, sons in particular, to perpetuate the family line and to provide economic security for the couple in their old age. Children are a mark of wealth and prestige in rural areas. Marriage and children are necessary for full social adulthood for both men and women. In addition, women must have children to improve their position in the husband's family. The childless woman is in a pitiable situation. Her husband may even decide to take another wife. Therefore, the young daughter-in-law and her husband's kin anxiously await signs of her first pregnancy. When she does become pregnant, she becomes the center of attention. She thereby proves her usefulness to the household, especially if she has a son.

Despite the importance attached to childbirth, the new mother and her child are considered unclean and ritually polluting and therefore are kept away from other people for forty days. Similarly, a menstruating woman is subject to taboos because she is considered to be polluting to others. For example, she may not cook or enter the kitchen and she must eat separately from other members of the household. She is prohibited from touching other people and must sleep apart from her husband. Women are believed to be especially prone to pollution and difficult to purify, whereas men are relatively resistant to pollution and easy to purify. Men are strong, women are weak. Therefore, men are allowed much greater freedom of action and movement within Hindu society. Women do not oppose these taboos. They may even welcome the rest the taboos provide from some of their usual household duties.

Gender Division of Labor. A strict gender division of labor in traditional Indian society is part of the wider system of gender segregation. Males are to do the outside work, to provide for the support of the women and children, and to control and discipline them. Women are in charge of domestic and childcare tasks. But because it robs a man of status for him to undertake women's work, women have a fair degree of autonomy within the domestic confines. The rigidity of the division of labor and the domestic/public dichotomy is made clear in the task of burden carrying. It often shocks Westerners to see a man walking empty handed while his wife carries a heavy load of wood, clay pots, or cow dung. Men do not carry items intended for household use because that is the woman's domain.

Women work very hard within the household. For example, Indian food processing and cooking are time consuming. Meals are supposed to be as elaborate as family income allows. As Jacobson describes it:

In villages women clean grain, grind flour and spices, pare vegetables, pickle mangoes, and cook over smokey fires in dark kitchens. They sweep, fetch water from distant wells, mix straw and mud with their feet, and mud-plaster and whitewash their houses. They clean the barns and shape cow dung cakes for cooking fuel. They collect firewood, scrub dishes with mud and ash, and wash clothes, all the while caring for demanding children and waiting upon their husbands. In cities, women spend many hours in the kitchen each day, producing elaborate meals, in addition to scrubbing and ironing clothing for family members who must look neat at school and office. Many village women also work at agricultural tasks, while women of artisan and service castes have their traditional tasks to perform.[19]

Many women work in the fields, but no agricultural tasks are consistently assigned to females. Males do all of the heavy work associated with plowing. Very poor women are often forced to hire themselves out as day laborers. Wealthier village women may do little or no agricultural work except during harvest time. Indian women who bring income into the household are usually more independent than the higher-status women who confine their work to non-income-producing domestic production. But despite the hard work of women, both women and men perceive women's work as less important than men's, and women see themselves as dependents of men. However, in the wet rice culture areas, women have an important role in primary economic production, and they have greater freedom and a higher status in these areas.

Ursula Sharma in her study of two villages in northern India addresses the issue of the cultural and material bases of female exclusion and male power.[20] Her research focused on two village communities, pseudonymously called "Harbassi" and "Chaili." Harbassi is located in the fertile plain of the Punjab and is relatively prosperous: It has experienced considerable advance in respect to rising incomes, mechanization of agriculture, and class differentiation since the introduction of the "Green Revolution" in 1966.* Chaili is a community of small landholders in the soil-poor foothills of the Sivalik range in Himachal Pradesh.

Daughters in both communities are effectively excluded from the inheritance of land, despite the existence of national legislation

---

*The Green Revolution refers to the introduction of high-yield hybrid seeds and the agrochemical forms of cultivation associated with their use.

to protect their inheritance rights. If there is no male heir, daughters often "give" their property to a male cousin. More typically, they usually waive their rights to partible inheritance to brothers. The material basis of this general practice of women to forsake their rights of inheritance is, according to Sharma, economic dependency on males. Land is of litle value if women do not have access to the cultural and material resources to make it productive—which they do not. The practice of purdah is crucial here since it effectively excludes women from all public activities, including the most elementary economic transactions outside of the household. The male-administered concern for "female purity" also prevents women from traveling any distance from home to seek extradomestic employment.

Sharma also takes issue with prevailing theories of the Indian dowry. She argues persuasively on the basis of her observations that even the dowry does not accrue to the women as a source of personal security. Rather, the dowry is essentially a family hoard and is treated as such in the face of economic necessity or emergency facing family members. Murders or forced suicides—"bride burnings"— of young women because of familial dissatisfaction with the value of dowries or because of what amounts to familial speculation in dowries are tragic representations of this fact.

In Harbassi prosperity has allowed upper-caste males to begin to withdraw their women from family agricultural labor, reinforcing their seclusion. In Chaili poverty has transformed husbands into almost permanent migrants who must work elsewhere, while their women have had to assume almost total responsibility for agricultural production at home. But in neither case has the penetration of the capitalist economy enhanced the autonomy of women in relation to their men. In both cases women are effectively deprived of access to wage income,

more and more a necessity for survival in the shifting agricultural economy of northern India. In these communities, neither withdrawal from the fields through class ascendency nor the augmentation of the burdens of producer's labor has broken the bounds of dependency.

Rural Woman in the World Market: A Historical Case. The negative impact of women's participation in production for world markets is clear in Maria Mies's research on lacemakers around Narsapur in the West Godavari district of Andhra Pradesh.[21] Lacemaking was first introduced in 1860 by missionary women to the female Christian converts of the untouchable outcastes. To help them earn money, the missionary ladies contacted women's church groups in England and Scotland who sold the lace products. None of the women in this distribution network made a profit except the lacemakers themselves. This allowed these untouchable women to improve their class status by removing themselves from the degrading outside work in the fields and allowing them to become domesticated housewives and capitalist wage laborers simultaneously.

The organization and composition of the lace industry changed, however, when two of the local men decided to establish a lace-exporting business. As lace "manufacturers," they did not engage in manufacturing; instead they relied on the "putting-out system" and a more rigid division of labor. Before, the women made entire lace articles; now each one made only certain parts, which were put together into finished tablecloths and doilies under male supervision. Female agents supplied the lacemakers, collected the piecework products, and did the finishing work. Piecework rates were very low and the males were the real profiters from this arrangement.

The industry underwent further change between 1970 and 1978 when the demand for lace products in Europe and America expanded dramatically. This came at the time the profits from the Green Revolution—which had increased agricultural production in the area—were on the decline. Peasants who had prospered now had a surplus to invest, but agriculture was no longer a viable investment. They sought to enter the lace industry, which required almost no capital and only a few contacts. Thus the peasant caste, the Kapus, came to dominate the lace industry. Kapu males preferred to use their own wives or poorer Kapu women for this work, pushing the Christian untouchables out of lacemaking.

The domination of lacemaking by Kapu men as the businessmen and Kapu women as producers created a new dynamic that eliminated the female "middle-woman jobs." Kapus were originally a feudal warrior caste of high social standing, which was symbolized by the seclusion of their women. Therefore, Kapu women could not participate in agricultural labor or any other work outside the home. If women cannot leave the home, then they cannot be agents or finishers. All of the nonproductive roles in the lace industry were redefined as male roles justified by the ideology of female seclusion, which was just as acceptable to the females as to the males. Women clung to their seclusion as proof of their higher status and denigrated the untouchable women who worked in the fields even though the female agricultural workers earned substantially more than the lacemakers who averaged a paltry fifty cents per week working every day from early in the morning until late at night, taking breaks only for necessary domestic labor and to serve their husbands.

The ideology of seclusion and the domestic role for women provided the ideological justification for husbands to exploit their wives also. The Green Revolution had made some Kapu peasants wealthy, but it left many others landless and unemployed. Yet be-

cause of their caste standing, they would not accept any other kind of work; it would be "demeaning." Their wives were transformed into the breadwinners for the family without the men having to acknowledge the change or having to change their own behavior at all. Lacemaking had long been defined as "nonwork," just a leisure-time pursuit that allowed women to earn a little extra money while they sat at home all day doing nothing. Work done in seclusion is invisible. People in the local community often did not realize that the women were lacemakers, they thought the "manufacturers" made the lace. Husbands could also ignore the work and economic support of their wives because the wives were "just sitting home all day."

Some of these husbands, however, recognized the opportunity to take on the capitalist role in relation to their producer wives. They invested money in thread and put their wives to work for them. In this way the husband gained control over the wife's product, and she felt dependent on him because he took the lace to market and sold it. Women who worked without their husbands' involvement typically refused to give their husbands their earnings. They spent it directly on family consumption needs instead. But the other wives no longer had control over their wages. The husband had control over what were now his hard-earned profits.

The interaction of traditional gender relations and ideologies with new opportunities for production for the world market allowed a few high-status males to profit handsomely from the low wage labor of the female lacemakers. It allowed some pauperized male peasants to raise their status to that of lace hawker.

For the women, however, it only allowed them the back-breaking, eyesight-ruining labor necessary to keep their families from starvation as the traditional peasant economy failed their subsistence needs. Mies also found that when survival depended on it, the women would violate the rules of seclusion and perhaps sell their lace themselves in public, but they would never attack seclusion directly. The women's acceptance of the ideal of purdah and caste status kept them from being able to organize for a better wage and kept them seeking alternative and better-paying occupations and from leaving the area for job opportunities elsewhere.

Urban Indians

The conservative, traditional upper-strata urban families follow much the same customs and practices as described for the wealthier rural families. In urban areas, however, women do no agricultural work and therefore are even more permanently restricted to the home. Some girls are allowed to attend school. Primary school is usually considered to be sufficient. Secondary school is sometimes acceptable, but college is out of the question. Not only does it allow the female too much freedom from the household, but it is feared that attending college will interfere with the development of an appropriately submissive personality. Furthermore, a college education is a liability in the marriage market. Husbands must have a higher educational and occupational status than their wives to uphold the gender stratification system. A woman with a college degree has a limited field of prospective mates.

Poorer urban families and the small Westernized elite deviate from these traditional patterns. Poorer families do not have the means necessary to observe traditional customs. Their women must work outside the home, often in domestic service or the construction industry. The modern elite, however, favors what are to them the more prestigious Western customs.

According to Dube, the domestic and public spheres are not as firmly separated on the basis of gender in the modernized families.[22] Men have the responsibility to work to support the family, but women may work if they desire to and can find employment. Women of this group are also more likely to participate in voluntary social work outside the home. Women have greater autonomy and a greater share in family decision making and authority. Indian women active in the professions, politics, and the arts come from this group. But these women continue to shoulder the responsibility for household and child care unless the family can afford servants. Men do not share these tasks.

Even among the Westernized groups, arranged marriages are still the norm. The boy and girl are more likely to have veto rights over the parents' choice than they did in the past. Love marriages sometimes occur, but they are still uncommon.

Increasingly, urban middle- and upper-class women are taking jobs outside the home. Employment appears to have a liberating effect on women. Marjorie Wood found, for example, that "women who seek employment are more likely to make love marriages, have small families, and relate to members of their households in an egalitarian manner than are their unemployed counterparts.[23]

Educated urban women have more career opportunities now than in the past. But these are still largely in gender-segregated, low-prestige, low-paid occupations such as teaching in primary or girls' schools and clerical work. Women have great difficulty obtaining and retaining positions that require them to assert authority over men, especially if the men are of similar caste rank. The range of jobs is expanding, but there is still a high unemployment rate among educated women. Many Indians feel women should not be allowed to compete equally with men for scarce jobs.

It is still unacceptable for a woman to go out alone at night, and single women are a particular anomaly in Hindu society. It is expected that everyone will marry. Yet highly educated career women often find that no suitable mate is available. They cannot date or even develop friendships with men. If their work requires attendance at social gatherings, they cannot go alone or with a date. They usually rely on a brother or other close kinsman to escort them. Work at night severely damages a woman's reputation.

The traditional patterns are also still evident in the treatment of college women, even among the Westernized elite. College women are carefully protected from men to retain their reputations. Female colleges have high walls, night watchmen, and strict rules about male visitors. Even in coeducational colleges, male and female students are not allowed to speak or associate with each other. Friendships between males and females are impossible. The assumption is that contact between men and women always leads to sexual relations.

But education, like employment, seems to weaken the woman's commitment to some traditions. J. Murickan's study of middle-class women's attitudes found that the educated younger generation of women is less accepting of the traditional submissive role for women than is the older generation.[24] The younger generation is also more supportive of free choice in marriage and the sharing of child care and household work with husbands. They were more likely to believe that education is desirable for girls as well as boys and that the curriculum should be the same for the genders. They feel that women should be allowed to work but should not allow it to interfere with their duties as wife and mother. The young women also felt that women should be allowed to participate in activities outside the home such as politics, hobbies, or volunteer work.

Like other peripheral capitalist societies, India has a chronically high unemployment rate. This has affected women more than it has men. Despite attempts at modernization, women's participation in the labor market has declined in both rural and urban sectors, despite advances for college-educated elite women. Between 1911 and 1971 women's share of the Indian labor market fell from 34.4 percent to 17.3 percent.[25] Paradoxically, industrialization is hailed as the road to progress, but women's participation in industrial employment has declined markedly over the last few decades. This is true despite important gains by women in education.

Jacobson sums up the situation:

It is clear that the negative effects of automation and new technology in industry fall mainly on women, who being untrained are replaced by men and machines. Management and unions tend to train men in newly necessary skills, while women lose their jobs. Men tend also to have better access to employment information and job training since they are more educated and physically mobile than women. Thus, women's illiteracy and low social status work to their disadvantage in modernizing industry.[26]

The Near East: An Iraqi Village and Revolution in Iran

Historical Perspectives

Agrarian-based societies have existed in the Near East as far back as the beginning of recorded history. Agriculture was probably first invented in the area of the Tigris and Euphrates river valleys. As one would expect on the basis of theories of women's and men's positions in society, women have had an equally long history of subordination in this area. Ilse Siebert presents evidence indicating that as in India the earliest records show freer and more independent positions for women than are found under the later agrarian empires.[27]

According to Siebert, as early as the seventeenth century B.C. Hammurabi's code of laws clearly embodied the firm subordination of women. The code prescribed the patriarchal family structure, allowing men multiple wives, concubines, and easy divorce. Women, however, were denied divorce rights and required by law to remain chaste on pain of death. Women did have influential roles as priestesses and as queens, queen mothers, and princesses, if they had the intelligence, skill, and motivation to develop the power potential of these positions. Other than the queen, queen mother, and princesses, the women of the royal harems throughout the history of the Near East were the pampered prisoners of the king. They devoted their lives to beauty, singing, and play to be pleasing to the king who owned them either as wives or as slaves. They were strictly secluded in a separate building from the palace and carefully guarded by eunuchs.

Women were important as sexual property in these societies. The more powerful the male was, the larger his harem would be: Women served as objects of conspicuous consumption for men. Some particularly powerful kings are reported to have had as many as 12,000 young girls and women. Lesser kings and the lesser nobility had much smaller harems. Controlling the sexuality of large numbers of women was an important badge of male honor and status. Stealing another man's women inflicted the greatest humiliation on him. For this reason, women were often the objects of capture during warfare. It was especially prestigious for the victor and humiliating for the vanquished to have the royal harem captured by the conqueror.

Moslem Traditions

The Moslem religion, when it was first introduced into the Near East by the prophet Mohammed in the seventh century, constituted a move toward improving the status of women. Women were important supporters of Mohammed and his new religion. Mohammed preached the equality of all persons, including women. He laid out rules to protect women's rights of inheritance property, marriage choice, and divorce. These rights were not, however, equal to men's rights. As Islam spread throughout these patriarchal, war-torn, agrarian societies, it was reinterpreted and applied in such a way as to justify the almost total isolation of women in the domestic sphere, away from the public spheres of power. Women did not always accept these subordinate roles, and Elise Boulding documents the active underlife in which some women participated, which allowed a few women to become influential in the world of men.[28] These were, however, always positions of influence or power behind the throne. Power through the underlife rarely allows women to exercise legitimate, publicly recognized authority.

An Iraqi Village

With thousands of years of tradition weighing upon them, women in the Near East today still find themselves subordinated to men. In modernizing, heavily Western-influenced urban areas, women have been freed from some of the more repressive aspects of the traditional Moslem agrarian civilization. Among the rural peasantry tradition remains strong however.

In the late 1950s, Elizabeth Fernea and her husband, Robert, lived in an Iraqi peasant village and studied the women's lives in detail.[29] Fernea adhered to the accepted customs of the village. In particular, she obeyed the rules of *purdah*. The village women adhered strongly to the tradition of domestic seclusion and veiling. They never left the women's quarters without wearing the *abayah*, the heavy black cloaklike garment that completely covers the woman from head to toe.

Young girls are allowed to run almost as freely as boys in the village. However, at the age of about eleven years the girl dons the veil and begins her lifetime observance of purdah. She is strictly isolated in the women's quarters and may never associate openly with nonkinsmen again. She must remain above the slightest suspicion. Her reputation is ruined if men even speak about her in the coffee shops.

One of Fernea's experiences dramatically illustrates the seriousness of these requirements. Fernea was invited by a close female friend to go for a ride in a male cousin's car. This, of course, was of no danger to Fernea because her husband did not require her observance of purdah. She was practicing it only for research purposes. However, she made the mistake of inviting another of her friends, Laila, to go along. Even though Laila understood the seriousness of riding in a car with a nonkinsman, she accepted. They went for the ride covered in their *abayahs* and without speaking at all to the males.

The children of the community reported back to other adults that they had seen Laila enter the car. (Children and other close associates of the women are able to recognize them when they are veiled. They come to discern the slightest variations in dress and demeanor.) Upon realizing Laila's dangerous position, Fernea and the other woman denied she had been in the car. They covered her by saying that another female cousin, not Laila, had accompanied them. These lies protected Laila's reputation and kept her father from having to kill her to save the honor of the other women of the family and the reputation of the family as a whole. Had there been any more definite evidence against her, Laila would have paid for this brief outing with her life.

The segregation of the genders was almost total in the village. Wives typically saw their husbands only at mealtimes and in the bedroom. At meals they did not usually eat together. The men were served first and the women and children ate the leftovers from the men's dishes. Men lived in the public world of the village, the women in the domestic world. A woman could not speak to her own husband in public. As a result husbands and wives did not provide each other with emotional support or companionship. Close friendships were formed between members of the same gender. The women were allowed to visit one another in the women's quarters and to move about in the obscure alleys between the high-walled houses. They avoided visits, however, which brought them, even though heavily veiled, into the public eye. They would take a circuitous back route to avoid going near the public marketplace. (Men in this society took care of all purchases from the market.) It was considered shameful for a family's women to be discussed in any way—even if the mention were so mild as to say the women were seen visiting other women.

Women formed close ties with one another and produced an active underlife culture and support system. The segregation in the women's quarters provided some basis for the development of female solidarity. Such female solidarity was, however, more likely to be used for emotional support for a woman in distress than for any important or active opposition to male dominance or to specific men.

Most women of the village accepted their seclusion as right and proper. They did not chafe against it or attempt to rebel. Although they knew that some city women had abandoned the *abayah*, they had no desire to do so. Fernea points out that for the Iraqi village women to leave the women's quarters without her *abayah* would induce the same sort of shame and humiliation as it would for most Western women to go out in public naked. Most women firmly accepted the customs and traditions.

The gossip of the women formed an important part of the social control system over women in general. The women themselves were intolerant of violations of the feminine role by other women. They denounced the modern unveiled women who associated freely with men as strongly as the men did. Fernea notes, however, that they were not idle in their gossip. They tried to avoid false accusations of any sort because they knew how terrible the consequences of loss of reputation would be to a woman.

It was, of course, essential that a girl maintain her virginity. Marriages were arranged by the parents and the prospective bride and groom's mothers had an important say in the matchmaking. The couple could not meet before their wedding day without violating custom. However, the bride and groom were likely to be cousins because of the preference for marrying within one's patrilineage, and therefore they were likely to have known each other before the girl entered purdah.

On the wedding day the marriage had to be consummated while the mothers and other friends and relatives waited outside the bedroom. Afterward the mothers had to inspect the sheets for blood from the broken hymen and publicly announce the proof of the bride's virginity. If it was discovered that the bride was not a virgin, her family suffered severe humiliation and she would probably be put to death as a ruined woman.

Virginity, chastity and monogamy were not required of males. However, for the poorer males there was little opportunity for extramarital sexual liaisons. Only the wealthy could pay the brideprices for multiple wives or buy the sexual favors of concubines and prostitutes. In the village Fernea studied, the local sheik had four wives, but the other men rarely took even a second wife. The women themselves actively opposed being a cowife. First wives whose husbands were considering a second wife often made their husbands' lives so miserable that they relented and ceased negotiations for the second wife. New wives were often subjected to abusive treatment by first wives. Sometimes, however, the first wife welcomed a second wife to help run the household or to supply children if the first wife were barren.

Childlessness in this culture was always blamed on the woman. Barrenness or bearing only daughters resulted in shame, humiliation, and loss of status for the woman and for the husband, who had the right to divorce such a wife. A woman's and man's highest honor came from producing many sons to carry on the patrilineal, patriarchal family. Daughters were not as highly valued, despite the valuable labor they provided for the household.

Marriage was the only respected adult role for the village women. Yet lack of a dowry or an appropriate candidate for husband kept many of them in perpetual dependence in their fathers' or brothers' homes. Poor clan members often could not raise the necessary brideprice for marriage. Families resisted the idea of marrying their daughters to nonkinsmen even if it meant the women would never marry. The lack of brideprice could sometimes be solved if the prospective groom could arrange to marry his sister to the brother of his prospective bride. In this way the brideprice payments by the two families would be canceled out. It was not an enviable fate for either a man or a woman to remain unmarried.

Women had no real basis for economic independence in the Iraqi village. Even if they worked at income-producing tasks such as weaving or sewing, the money belonged to their husbands or fathers. A woman's only insurance against economic disaster was whatever gold jewelry her husband could or would give her. The women of the village were amazed by the paltry amount of gold worn by Fernea. Since her husband appeared both to love her and be a man of means, they could not understand why he had not given her the heavy gold bracelets, necklaces, and earrings they coveted so much.

The jewelry also served as a source of wealth the woman could draw on to help her children if the father either could not or would not support them. For example, one well-to-do father opposed his son's intention to attend college in the city. The mother sold her gold to support her son in opposition to her husband. This was within her rights even though it angered her husband. Thus women were not entirely submissive to their husbands' wishes.

Mothers often developed close and enduring ties with their children. Sons exhibited a familiarity with and love for the mother that was forbidden in their relationships with their father. In the presence of the father, the son was not allowed to speak without being spoken to. Fathers were to be treated with great awe and respect by their wives and children at all times. Mothers, therefore, supplied the parental warmth that was taboo from the fathers. The mother-daughter relationship was considered so important and enduring that only harsh circumstances would induce a family to marry a daughter to a man in another community. It was felt that daughters should be allowed to remain near their mothers' households all their lives. Again, the village women were chagrined that Fernea's husband had not brought her mother with them to Iraq to comfort Fernea and keep her company.

The women of the village worked hard in their domestic compounds. Household maintenance and meal preparation had to be done without any help from advanced technology. In addition, there were long hours to be devoted to needlework, laundry at the nearby canal, bread baking, food preservation, and water carrying. Tedious hours were spent by the women of each household cleaning rice by hand. The work was usually done in the presence of other females, however, and this added an element of enjoyment to the boring tasks.

The forces of change were evident in this village in the late 1950s. The modernization of gender roles that had affected significant segments of the urban population in Iraq had begun to filter into the village. Some young people were accepting of the new ideas.

The trend toward providing education for girls as well as boys has had a modernizing effect on many of the educated young women's and men's ideas concerning the feminine role and the proper relations between the genders. The older villagers live in fear that such ideas as breaking purdah will infect their youth. Change in gender roles and gender stratification is under way but is not likely to be rapid. The forces of tradition are sufficiently strong to keep most of the younger generation committed to the old ways. And the effects of industrialization are so slight among the poor peasant villages that industrialization has not as yet undermined the agrarian-based social structure.

Therefore, the social organization that gave rise to their patterns of gender roles and gender stratification is still largely intact.

Revolution in Iran

Recent events in Iran provide us with an example of a developing society with a long dependent relationship with the advanced industrial countries: Iran underwent a nationalist revolution overthrowing a government that had encouraged the penetration of Iran by the core industrialized societies.[30] But anti-imperialist nationalist movements are not necessarily progressive. They may emphasize nativism and the total rejection of outside cultural, as well as economic and political, domination. This can lead to a revitalization of past, often agrarian-based, practices, which is extremely disadvantageous for women. The Iranian Revolution may have in a limited way liberated the country from the hated West, but it did not liberate women.

Historical Background.   The high degree of female subordination and seclusion found in Islamic societies is not so much a result of Islam as the product of the socioeconomic-political conditions of the Middle Eastern setting in which Islam spread. The teachings of the Prophet Mohammed improved the position of women, clarifying their legal status and according them rights they had not clearly possessed under pre-Islamic conditions. But the improvements were lost over the centuries after the Prophet's death as Islam was reshaped and reinterpreted under the impact of a highly centralized agrarian empire.

Preimperial and pre-Islamic nomadic, tribal societies accorded women the freedom typical of nomadic pastoralists. Seclusion and domestic isolation were unknown. In the seventh century the Sasanian Empire conquered many of the local chieftains. This agrarian empire introduced the strict seclusion of women, the legal requirement of obedience and subservience of women to their husbands, the cultural belief of women's innate inferiority to men, a devaluation of women's work in the domestic sphere, and a stronger image of women as sex objects and reproducers of male lineages. The control of women by men enshrined in the moral code reflected the actual economic and political control by men in the wider society.

When the Sasanians fell from power, the gender stratification system they had constructed over five centuries did not fall with them. Islamic views of women did not undermine the gender stratification system so much as Islam came to be reconciled with this highly subordinated social position for women. Islamic religious leaders began to incorporate these views into Islamic teachings and gradually many of the ideas came to be attributed incorrectly to the Prophet.

As cities grew and prospered, the heterogeneity and density of urban life encouraged even tighter control over women to demonstrate male and lineage honor through the control of female sexuality. Seclusion became even more rigid. Women had no legitimate place except as wives and mothers. Girls married very early, between nine and twelve years of age. But their positions as wives was rendered insecure by the practices of polygyny and easy divorce for men. Seclusion, the veil, and female subordination spread from the cities to the rural areas until they came to characterize almost the entire Islamic world from Morocco to China.

Iran as a separate nation state arose out of this context in the sixteenth and seventeenth centuries. The Shiite sect of Islam was declared the state religion (despite the commitment of most of the population to the Sunni sect). It provided a strong religious and ideological basis for creating a national identity among the diverse peoples of the region.

Shiite teachings are particularly emphatic on the subservient role of women in society, and this was written into religion and law in the new Iranian state. Veiling was more complete and stricter in Iran than in the Ottoman or Arab states. Tribal traditions according women greater freedom and a higher status were not completely destroyed, however. During the nineteenth century Western influence also served to undermine some of the commitment to the strict subordination of women, especially among the educated, traveled, urban upper middleclass. A large harem declined as a symbol of high status for elite men.

Some men of this class argued for modern education for their sons and daughters as a means of improving Iranian society. A few women were able to travel to the West themselves and aided the process of diffusing the less highly stratified gender relations to Iran. Furthermore, the Iranian economy was gradually linked to the wider world capitalist market, which brought with it some of the social relations of industrial capitalism.

At the beginning of the twentieth century, Iran underwent a revolution and instituted parliamentary constitutional government. Women activists participated in the revolution but were not rewarded by the new government. Instead, these activists were insulted with epithets such as "wanton" and "whore" by all but the few intellectuals and writers who espoused the cause of women's rights. Women activists turned their attention to trying to educate and enlighten the masses of illiterate, backward Iranian women. Female education was condemned as immoral at first. But a few schools re-

mained open despite the harassment of their personnel and students. After World War I public girls' schools were provided by the state. Women's societies and a women's press supported a more modern role for women, and the very brave dared to shed their veils in public.

In 1925 Parliament declared Riza Khan as king. The new Shah created a centralized government on the European model and supported the women's movement. In 1936 he dared even to outlaw the veil as Attaturk had done in Turkey. The veil was the foremost symbol of women's subordination and backwardness. But most women as well as men opposed this measure. Police were ordered to forcibly pull veils from women in public. The women felt protected by this "symbolic shelter" and many stayed home rather than emerge without it. The law was repealed in 1941 after the Shah's abdication. His policies produced a strong backlash led by religious leaders and supported by most women against a more public role for women. Schools were closed and many other gains lost as the religious leaders regained powers lost to the first Shah.

But the following decades were a period of rapid economic development that provided a strong modernizing influence on women and society in general. Women's rights continued to be a subject for debate. There was strong support for women's suffrage, but the opposition of religious leaders killed the petition.

In 1953 the United States helped engineer a coup d'etat, which brought the second Shah to power. Political freedoms were curtailed, but this silenced the religious leaders who opposed women's rights as much as it did the women's political organizations. Women continued to establish groups to pressure for the vote and other rights. They eventually succeeded. Women gained the vote in 1963, and the Family Protection Law of 1967 and 1973 improved women's rights in polygyny, divorce, and child custody matters.

The oil boom increased employment opportunities for women as well as men. Women moved out of the domestic sphere in larger and larger numbers. Important changes were under way in the social structure and culture. The legal marriage age for women was raised to eighteen. Well-to-do urban women received university educations in Iran and abroad. Many became doctors, lawyers, university professors, administrators, and members of Parliament. Even less well-off women had more schooling and could find jobs. Labor needs far outstripped the numbers of the male labor force, and women were drawn into the labor force from the top to the bottom. They were also incorporated into high-ranking political positions.

Fundamentalist Religious Rule. These improvements in women's status were abruptly halted and the clock turned back by the Iranian Revolution, the overthrow of the Shah, and the new leadership of the Ayatollah Khomeini in 1979. Many women, especially radical young women, participated in this revolution. In fact, the presence of women and children on the battle lines had an important restraining effect on the Shah's troops.

But the coalition of forces against the repressive, authoritarian regime of the Shah was very diverse. The left opposed him for his dependence on the powerful advanced capitalist societies and for the lack of political freedom under his regime. The right opposed him for his ties to the infidel West and his support for modernization, which they saw as undermining the morals of the people. These otherwise ideologically opposed groups joined together under the symbolic umbrella of Islamic nationalism to protest the penetration of their country by the forces of imperialism, especially the United States. They disagreed dramatically on the type of revolutionary society they desired to build after deposing the Shah. The women participants opposed the Shah but had no ideological vision of women's role in the new society. They had simply expected things to be better for them. They did not expect to experience new forms and even greater repression after they fought so hard to rid themselves of a repressive regime.

The religious leaders quickly used the American hostage situation and the emotion-laden confrontation with the United States to solidify their control of the government. Khomeini had long been a symbol of opposition to the Shah, but with his long exile in France, the more liberal elements of the revolution were unacquainted with his fundamentalist religious views. Khomeini and his followers used their power to turn against their previous allies on the left. Their ideals included a reinstitution of theocracy and the patriarchal family with women secluded in the domestic sphere. The veil again became the symbol the appropriate role for women.

During the revolution women had donned the veil for as diverse a range of reasons as their reasons for opposing the Shah. Some truly believed the veil was right and proper, that women belong in the domestic sphere and should venture into public only when necessary. Others merely regarded the veil as a symbol of their national and cultural identity. The veil was a temporary device to set them apart from the West and from the supporters of the Shah. They, however, did not intend it to go beyond this type of identity-solidifying function. They did not want women removed from the public world of work, politics, and education. They were themselves students and workers and political activists.

But the nationalist fervor they helped to unleash was turned against them when they attempted to continue their public activities instead of devoting themselves to the wife and mother roles. These young, politically active women had participated in the revolution without obtaining any guarantees for the future protection of their rights. They did not realize how rapidly things could change. They supported Khomeini. They heard his messages from France assuring them that women would gain from the revolution. They did not realize that his idea of a higher place for women was the traditional domestic, subservient role. They had assumed that the past gains for women were permanent and that the new government would be anti-West and pronationalist without being anti-women's rights.

It could have been, but under the extremely conservative control of the fundamentalist Shiite religious leaders, Islamic nationalism was defined as a return to gender stratification, a strict division on the basis of gender between the public and domestic spheres, and a reaffirmation of the belief in the innate basis for gender differentiation. Allah has ordained men as superior in intellect and power, and women are pleasing to men, emotional, and weak. Furthermore, to be a good mother, raising her children according to divine principle, a woman must be uncorrupted by the public sphere. The Ayatollah Khomeini argues that this elevates women, but many women and men can see this is far from the truth.

The idealization of the pure, secluded, and veiled woman belies a contradictory Shiite view of women. Women are a very dangerous and destructive force in society if they are uncontrolled by men. Islamic culture has an image of sexuality quite distinct from that of Northern Europe and most of North America, although it shares important similarities to Mediterranean and Latin American cultures.[31] In northern countries, the belief is that sexuality can be seen as something to be controlled internally by the individual through the exercise of will or self-restraint, through the inculcation of an appropriate character structure. Both males and females can be socialized to keep sexual impulses under control. Therefore, men and women can associate freely in the public world with only limited fears about illicit sexual encounters. The Islamic world, however, has historically given strong emphasis to the idea that sexual drives can be controlled only through external constraints, through keeping males and female separate. The assumption is that if a man is in close contact with a woman, his sexual needs and perhaps hers too will always result in illicit sexual intercourse. To protect against such violation of the moral order, female sexuality must be strictly controlled by men. Women must be segregated. They need the real shelter of the home and the symbolic shelter of the veil to avoid causing chaos by enticing men to violate God's laws.[32]

This justified marrying girls at a young age to put them under the control of a watchful husband. It justifies polygyny, as a man must have access to a legitimate sex object at all times, even during his wife's menstrual period when she is believed to be unclean and unsuitable for intercourse, even during late pregnancy and after childbirth. He must always be producing children too. So when his wife reaches menopause, he needs a younger one who can continue to reproduce his lineage. The current regime has therefore reinstituted polygyny, lowered the age of marriage, and repealed the Family Protection Law. Women now have little protection when their husbands divorce them, and the children are now the sole property of the husband and his lineage. Women who commit adultery are now guilty of a capital offense and several have been executed for this "crime." The regime has also reinstituted the old practice of "temporary marriage," which allows a man to contract with an unmarried woman for sexual relations over a specified period of time, one day or months or years. Women who are left without the protection of family often turn to these legal "temporary marriages" for support and for sexual satisfaction. It differs little from prostitution, except that prostitution is illegal. Again the view is that a man needs to be able to provide for his sexual needs in a way that does not violate religious precepts.

The birthrate has gone up significantly since the revolution. The leaders have not condemned contraception, although they now forbid abortion, but contraceptives are more difficult to find in the disrupted economy.

Khomeini began very early to demand more modest dress and demeanor for women. His first order to return to the veil met such opposition from women that he retreated temporarily and turned to encouraging government departments and businesses to establish dress codes requiring the veil of women on pain of being fired. By April 1983 his power was sufficient that he could order all women to wear at least the lighter form of veil if not the full *chadur.* Women who went unveiled even before the law was passed faced heavy verbal and physical harassment; and now those without the full *chadur* may be unsafe. It has indeed become a form of shelter for women.

The use of the female body as a sex object by Western advertisers and mass media serves to justify the sweeping condemnation of all aspects of Western life and culture and particularly practices related to gender equality. To this end, female professionals have lost their positions, women judges have been removed because the "inferior intellect" of females renders them unsuitable, and women can no longer hold administrative posts. For women to have authority over men in the public sphere upsets the social order as defined by the current regime. Attendance at school by females is down and job opportunities have dwindled. Economic problems associated with the disruption caused by the revolution, the war with Iraq, and the drop in oil prices have increased unemployment. Women are not needed in the labor force in large numbers. Economic factors therefore do not impede the reimposition of the domestic sphere on women.

The government is also considering rescinding the vote for women. Women are considered as intellectually inferior; therefore all the problems faced by the West today are the result of allowing women to participate in the political process.

It is clear that women of the educated, urban, upper middle-class, especially professional or career women, have lost a great deal under the new regime. But also the more traditional village women who had continued many of the old practices even under the forced modernization of the Shah find these new restrictions excessive and do not believe they are required by Islam.[33] These still-illiterate peasant women cannot conceive of publicly protesting against religious and political leaders, but they have begun to refuse to observe the religious rituals as a personal, albeit largely ineffective, symbol of their discontent.

Whether the current regime can continue with these policies and maintain a viable economy and political power remains to be seen. The war with Iraq helps to focus people's energies on the immediate problems of warfare and to deflect some of their discontent onto the enemy. But this is a temporary solution to the political discontent that remains.

Latin America: Mexico

Prior to the conquest by the Spanish and the Portuguese in the fifteenth and sixteenth centuries, the native peoples had not adopted agriculture. The area was dominated by advanced horticultural societies such as the Aztec, Incan, and Mayan civilizations; some areas were simple horticultural and some contained hunting and gathering peoples. Mexico was controlled primarily by the advanced horticultural empires of the Aztecs and Mayans. Women's positions in these societies were subordinate to men's but women of the upper classes had important powers and privileges.

The Spanish conquest of Mexico in 1525 introduced agrarian technology and civilization. This included much more subordinate and oppressive roles for women. The Spaniards brought their ideology of female inferiority and restriction with them. Their positions as conquerors added a further exploitative element to the roles they assigned to native women.[34] The racist beliefs of the Spaniards concerning non-Europeans led them to treat native males as inferior. Native females were ranked below native males, as European females were ranked below European males.

The Spaniards also imposed the Catholic religion on the defeated Indians. Spanish Catholicism embodied negative views of women and supported male dominance. The church supported the division of women into the good, asexual, devoted mother figure of the Virgin Mary and the bad, seductive Eve figure. The church has continued to maintain up to the present such gender role images and the ideology of woman's place as in the home. In spite of its role in the subordination of women, Mexican women continue to be very religious and support the church in much larger numbers than men do.

Machismo *and* Marianismo

One important cultural tradition the *conquistadores* and the Catholic church introduced into Mexico is the *machismo* and *marianismo* ideals for men and women. *Machismo* has been described as a "cult of virility." It is an "exaggerated aggressiveness and intransigence in male-to-male interpersonal relationships and arrogance and sexual aggression in male-to-female relationships."[35] Males are overly concerned with maintaining their honor and showing no weakness with men or women. The other face of *machismo*, according to Evelyn Stevens, is *marianismo*, or the "cult of spiritual superiority for women . . . women are semidivine, morally superior to and spiritually stronger than men."[36] The Virgin Mary is the ideal for this cult. Women are supposed to be self-sacrificing, submissive, self-abnegating, and long suffering. They suffer whatever their men force upon them. Their children, especially their sons, are expected to revere their mothers as the embodiment of ideal womanhood. However, this leaves the sons free to abuse and degrade other women. Any woman who insists on enjoying herself or being assertive violates the cult of *marianismo* and is therefore a "bad woman." Stevens notes that *marianismo* does not have to be forced on women. They not only accept it and support it themselves, but they also help perpetuate it into future generations through the socialization of their children. Women who complain of the poor treatment they receive from their husbands still encourage their sons to develop the same behavior patterns and often take pride in their sons' manifestations of *machismo*.

Nora Scott Kinzer argues that North American writers have exaggerated the importance of *machismo* and *marianismo* in Latin American cultures.[37] She points instead to women's active resistance to their husbands, to their hostility to men, and to their participation in extramarital affairs. However, it is possible for conflicting behavior patterns to exist side by side. *Marianismo* and *machismo* may be cultural norms without all or even most of the society's members upholding those norms. Stevens argues that many women devote their lives to living up to the ideal of humility and submissiveness while others deviate from it to a lesser or greater degree.[38] Despite strong pressures to conform, many women reject *marianismo*. This does not mean, however, that the *machismo-marianismo* pattern does not exist or that it is unimportant. It remains a part of the colonial legacy. It seems, however, to have affected the *mestizo* or *ladino* (Europeanized) populations more than the indigenous communities, which remain closer to precolonial traditions.

Twentieth-Century Mexico

Mexico gained independence from Spain in 1810. But between 1810 and 1910 little changed in the racial, class, or gender stratification systems. The Mexican Revolution overthrew the quasi-enlightenment dictatorship of Porfirio Diaz in 1910 and its leaders attempted to set up a more equalitarian society. Women had been important participants in the revolution. Many had served as soldiers and a few were officers and led battles. The new revolutionary government rewarded them with important legal and civil rights. (Women did not receive the vote until 1953. It was feared that most women

were so conservative that they would oppose the progressive measures of the new government.) Tradition remained strong, however, and the changes were more apparent than real.

The positions of women and men in Mexico today vary among the different sectors of Mexican society. Rural peasant women and men are in a different position from urban and town women and men. Indians differ from *mestizos*. Lower-class women and men differ from those of the middle classes and upper classes. Regional variations also occur. Drawing on various case studies, the next sections glimpse the lives of Mexican women and men in several of these social and economic circumstances.

Rural Peasants.   Oscar Lewis described in detail the lives of Indian peasants living in a highland village near Cuernavaca, Mexico.[39] His research on the Martinez family was conducted between 1943 and 1948 and again in 1960.

The daily life of Mexico's peasants is hard. Men rise at 4 or 5 A.M. and often walk for one or two hours to their fields. The labor is extremely taxing and the workday is long. Peasant women arise at 3 A.M. to grind corn for the breakfast tortillas. Preparing and grinding corn is tedious and arduous work that requires several hours bent over a grinding stone. The domestic tasks of water carrying, laundry, sewing, and caring for farmyard animals and gardens are also demanding and neverending.

Although agricultural techniques are widely used by better-off peasants and large landowners in Mexico, the poorest peasants with the smallest plots on rugged terrain still rely on horticultural methods of production. Hoe agriculture requires much labor but little capital. The tools are simple and easy to make or acquire. Tractors, chemical fertilizers, and pesticides, which are beyond the economic reach of such poor peasants, are unnecessary. Productivity per acre is furthermore often more predictable and higher than in the one-crop field method using plow agriculture.

But these small plots usually do not produce enough to sustain the family throughout the year. To maintain themselves at a subsistence level such peasants often have to supplement their farm production. Men work for wages as day laborers in richer people's fields or in village shops. Some migrate temporarily or permanently to the city looking for work in order to send their earnings home. Lucky men get positions as *braceros* (temporary immigrant laborers) during the harvest season in the United States. Women add to their already burdensome domestic and gardening tasks such income-producing work as sewing, embroidery, laundry, fruit and vegetable peddling, and day labor in the fields. Some migrate to the cities as domestics. Few have the skills to find other employment.

The gender division of labor in the Martinez family and in their village clearly embodied the domestic/public dichotomy. Men worked in the fields and women in the household except for emergency situations. Some of the women's work brought income into the household. But in general, women's work was primarily for use value while men dominated production for exchange value. Women were often in charge of expenditures for household consumption and managed that part of the budget. But the man could withhold the money for food and other necessities whenever he chose.

Rural indigenous families such as the Martinez' are patrilineal and patrilocal. The father is an authoritarian power figure. The mother and children must obey him and show him respect or face sometimes harsh physical punishments. The father remains aloof from his wife and children. He shows affection by working hard to provide for their material necessities. Emotional displays would weaken his image of strength and power.

The father's image of complete control over the family is belied, however, by the often greater psychological control exercised by the mother. Mothers encourage emotional attachment and dependence from the children. The mother-child bond is extremely strong and children, particularly sons, often idealize their mothers. Children are given little freedom by either parent as long as they remain in the parental home, even if they marry.

Parents try hard to restrict their daughters' freedom and in particular to keep them from meeting men. Virginity is prized in unmarried women as chastity is for married women. Even young girls are not allowed to leave the household compound unescorted. Dating is still rare in the villages. It is assumed that females cannot control themselves sexually. If a girl has been alone with a male, it is assumed that she had sex with him and her reputation is ruined.

Despite the attempted close surveillance of their behavior, daughters do often manage to have affairs. Pedro Martinez' daughter Conchita had an affair with a married teacher while she was away at school. Her parents were angry and humiliated. But even a wayward daughter is usually taken back into her family home. Pedro and his wife raised Conchita's illegitimate son and continued to help her complete her education so she could support herself as a teacher. Many parents oppose education for their daughters precisely because they fear the consequences of allowing girls that much freedom.

Although virginity is preferred, women with children by other men often find husbands or are able to establish fairly stable free consensual unions. Conchita eventually married a local peasant and became a typical peasant wife despite her training and experience as a teacher and her sexual involvements.

Unlike daughters, sons are expected to involve themselves in sexual experiences early. Village sons are not given much freedom of movement, but parents do not feel it necessary to keep them away from sexual experimentation. If a woman agrees to have sex with a man, it is her fault and not his. Men are expected to pursue sex whenever the opportunity arises. Not to do so would threaten a man's sense of virility. Sexual exploits, both real and imaginary, are the subject of boasting among these males. If a man impregnates a woman, he may or may not recognize the child as his own. He supports it only to the degree that he chooses.

Men prefer that their wives be frigid and sometimes avoid sexually satisfying them. Frigidity on the part of the wife helps convince the husband that she would not be interested in sexual relations with any other man. Lovemaking techniques are therefore used primarily to seduce and maintain the interest of women other than one's wife. Pedro Martinez described several of his sexual affairs to Lewis. His wife was jealous and angry about his affairs, but she could not complain too openly without risking a scolding and a beating. However, her responses to her sexual use by her husband vividly portray the dilemmas for women of both the economics of fertility and female subordination in the peasant/capitalist economy of Mexico:

It didn't matter to us whether the child was a boy or a girl. Pedro said that it was all the same to him. Whatever the ladle brings, all children mean money, because when they begin to work, they earn. . . . I didn't want any more children. I have always had a horror of having children. The thought of being pregnant would frighten me and sometimes it would make me angry because I was the one who was going to suffer. I cried and cried every time I thought I was pregnant. . . . At night when my husband took me, I became angry because of the danger he put me in. But when I didn't want Pedro to come near me he scolded, saying, "You didn't want me because you have some other man." So I had to let him and then I would be pregnant again. I know that what happens is God's will, so I say, if children come, good, if not, so much the better.[40]

Women are expected to stay in the home except when it is absolutely necessary to go out. Wives should not even have close friendships with other women, because such friends could be used to arrange meetings with lovers.

Females are expected to act modestly at all times. In public they should walk with downcast eyes and pull their shawls over their heads. A woman who held her head high or smiled at people would be considered flirtatious and a "bad woman."

Families are large. Husbands see children as proof of their virility, and they feel more secure about their wives' sexual fidelity if they are pregnant or have an infant to care for.

Women are supposed to be ambitious for their men but not for themselves. However, even these traditional peasant women sometimes violate this norm. Conchita Martinez, for example, actively pursued her education and her career as a teacher, sometimes arguing vigorously with her father to be allowed to continue in school.

Despite their belief in male superiority, the village males fear witchcraft from their wives and other women. However, females do not fear witchcraft from males. Fear of sorcery is therefore probably in part a manifestation of underlying male fears that their power over women is not complete and that women may seek revenge on them.

Women's attitudes about men were often contradictory among Lewis's villagers.

Women admired the tough, domineering man and agreed that males were superior to them. But they expressed a desire for husbands who were more passive. The women also said that the truly submissive wife was a fool even if that was the ideal for women. In violation of the publicly acknowledged ideal of female subordination, the women of the village told Lewis they were proud of their efforts at self-assertion.

Conflicts between the genders are common. Lewis notes that the women openly expressed hostility toward the men but often reacted to their subordination and abusive treatment with self-pity and resignation. For example, wife beating was a legal offense in the village, but wives did not avail themselves of the law's protection. The women were martyrs instead. (Younger women, however, seemed to be taking a more independent attitude by 1960.)

Wives were expected to tolerate mistreatment by their husbands, but many did not. A favorite alternative was to return to the natal family. In the Martinez family both Conchita and Macrina married men who beat them and barely supported them. In addition, Macrina's husband spent their already scarce income on his mistress. Macrina returned to her father's house and did not remarry for many years for fear that a second husband would not treat her or her children well either. She did have an affair, however, which resulted in another child and further angered her family. Eventually, she remarried and left her father's house for another part of the village.

In another Mexican Indian village, Doren Slade found that remaining single could increase a woman's public power if she also owned land.[41] The important public office of *mayordomo* was open only to heads of households with sufficient cash and corn to support religious ceremonies and fiestas. For a man to be a head of household, he had to

be married and to carry out the tasks of *mayordomo* he needed the support of his wife. A married woman could never be a head of household in this patriarchal family structure, but a single woman with land could be a head of household. And through the use of hired labor she could farm her land and might accumulate sufficient cash and corn for the fiestas. Because of patrilineal inheritance of land, most females never receive land. However, daughters without brothers did inherit. Although rare, it did sometimes occur that a female could assume this public office.

Slade also points out that the concept of submissive wife and dominant husband is the ideal, not the reality. The wife loses her legal status as a full adult on marriage, but she does not lose her ability to exert influence on her community. The division of labor—males in the fields and females in the kitchen—produces an interdependence between the genders that prevents husbands from ignoring their wives' advice. Publicly, wives are deferential to husbands, but privately they participate in making family decisions about such matters as whether to invest in land or livestock and whether the husband should attempt to assume the *mayordomo* office: "Male dominance . . . does not extend to the point where men engage in important activities independent of the approval and cooperation of women."[42]

Despite the harshness of village life, it does not give rise to the rootlessness and alienation of the urban milieu. The villages are often ancient, with the same families residing within them for untold generations. Men and women and boys and girls have a strong feeling of belonging to a stable community. But the villages are subject to outside influences, especially now that radios have become common. Better highways and transportation systems have also allowed villagers to venture into the outside world and for outsiders to enter the villages. Educational facilities that have expanded into Mexico's rural areas have introduced new ideas and practices. Lewis noted some of the effects of outside penetration when he returned to his village in 1960. The village appeared to be moving away from patrilocality to neolocality, which seemed to undermine the control of husbands over wives. The new wife could not be watched over and dominated by her mother-in-law while her husband was away at work. Girls had more freedom of movement about the village and could associate more freely with both girls and boys. Parents were more affectionate with their children: Lewis noted that village child-rearing methods had become child oriented. The villagers depended less on agriculture and more on nonagricultural jobs. More women held jobs outside the home. But the lower economic group had become poorer as a result of inflation and a curtailment of some agricultural activities. Modernity had its costs.

Urban Mexicans.   The urban environment offers a greater variety of lifestyles and job opportunities to women and men than does the traditional village. But life in the city is not necessarily more satisfying. In Mexico there is a constant flow to the cities from the countryside. Rapid population growth means that the rural areas cannot support the younger generations. Sometimes individuals migrate, such as the thousands of young girls who go to the cities as domestic workers each year. Sometimes entire families, especially the landless, migrate in search of a better life.

Lewis studied several poor urban families in Mexico City in the 1950s.[43] Economic insecurity was ever present. Although it violates the *machismo* ideal, wives and daughters as well as widows and divorced women were often forced to work. Those with little education worked outside the home in such low-paying jobs as street vendor, waitress, and factory operative. Others worked at home as laundresses, seamstresses, and embroiderers. Educated women might find jobs as secretaries or teachers. Poverty often forced families to take their children out of school, however, and put them to work at an early age.

In this crowded urban milieu, females could not be guarded as closely as they were in the country. Girls and women often spent a great deal of time out of the household at school, shopping, or working. More opportunities were therefore available to violate female gender role norms of modesty and sexual purity. Although they were disapproved, premarital sex and early illegitimate pregnancy were common. If the male refused to marry or live in free union with the female, she usually had to depend on her irate family for support. Even if the couple did set up a household together, the chances were high that it would not last long. Lewis's studies of five families in Mexico City are filled with descriptions of abandoned wives, husbands, and children. Husbands who deserted their families might not continue to help in their support. The economic circumstances of such deserted women and their children were often severe. If they were lucky they had kin to turn to. If not, the mother might be forced into dance-hall work or prostitution.

In addition to desertion, husbands often established families with other women and thereby spread what little income they had even more thinly. First wives resented this and often complained vociferously. Jealousy was a constant fact of life for both men and women. But if a woman pushed her husband too far, she might lose what little of his attention and money she still received.

The women tended to take the view that "that's the way men are—a woman has to put up with whatever her man gives her." The women and children were also frequently abused by their men. Beatings were common. The patriarchal family was the ideal and men tried to demand the respect due their position. Any sign of disrespect from any family member might send the father into a rage. A woman with a stable income of her own would be less likely to tolerate severe beatings and humiliations than one who was more dependent economically on her man. Girls were, however, socialized by their mothers to accept even abusive treatment by their husbands. As one woman put it, "He had a right to hit me. He was my man."[44] In fact, women often respected these violent, "macho" men more than the husbands who were gentle and generous with their families.

In families studied by Lewis, men appeared to use their economic resources consciously to control their women. Wives would be forced to beg for money for household expenses. Men preferred that their wives not work so their economic dependence could be maintained. As one man with a working wife complained, "If I hadn't let her go out selling I would still be giving orders. But now, well she doesn't pay attention to me."[45] In addition to being the economic backbone of the family, this particular woman also lived close to a network of kin who could be counted on for support in disputes with her husband. More economically dependent and isolated women were much more vulnerable to domination and abuse.

Wives accepted it as "bad luck" if their husbands did not support them. One of Lewis's respondents complained that her man wasted his money on other women and only rarely stayed with her and their children, but she accepted his behavior and continued to love him and need him. She did, however, refuse to marry this man legally for fear that he would then use his legal position to take her children away if he wanted to hurt her.

Lower-class urban women are exploited both at home and in the workplace. Their domestic tasks are burdensome. A woman who does not engage in paid labor still works very hard all day cooking and cleaning under adverse, overcrowded, and unsanitary conditions. Those who work as maids are given living quarters in the employer's home. Their hours are long and employers often disturb their sleep for a midnight snack or some errand. Maids are paid low wages and treated with little dignity or respect. The little time off they get is sometimes closely supervised by the employer, who thinks she should act as the guardian of the maid's virtue in place of the girl's parents or brothers. Young female domestics, especially those fresh from the country, do often get pregnant, sometimes by their employer or his sons, other times by their boyfriends. This often costs them their jobs. If they do not return to their families in shame, they often end up in prostitution.

Virve Piho described the plight of the female factory worker in Mexico City.[46] These women also work long hours for low pay. Many of them were the major economic supports of their families and often of nonkinspeople as well. Husbands had either disappeared or suffered chronic unemployment or underemployment. In addition to the demanding nature of their factory work and their domestic tasks, some of these women moonlighted. Piho found that in line with the *marianismo* ideal, the women tended to accept their situations with passivity, resignation, and self-abnegation. At work the woman worker did not protest the company's demands for fear of losing her job; at home she "never protested the demands of the persons she loved, but saw helping them as a sacred duty even if she had to do additional work that taxed her to the limits of her physical and psychological endurance.''[47]

Industrialization in Mexico has not greatly altered the gender division of labor. Occupations are highly gender segregated, and women who work are still responsible for the home. Furthermore, the jobs available to women are often extensions of their domestic roles: maid, waitress, cook, textile worker, teacher, and nurse.[48] Lower-class men also suffer exploitation in the labor force. However, a man's position in the gender stratification system allows him to vent his frustration on his wife and children and to demand respect, obedience, and service for them.

In the urban middle classes, women are less likely to work.[49] The husband's income, although often inadequate to maintain an acceptable middle-class life-style, is usually sufficient to support the family. It is a matter of male honor and *machismo* that the wife not work: She is to devote herself fully to her husband and children. Large families are preferred and the birthrate is high. The wife's domestic burdens are lightened by domestic help, but usually she is still firmly tied to the domestic sphere. Husbands prefer that their wives go out as little as possible to guard against possible sexual encounters with other men and against gossip.

Virginity and chastity are more firmly enforced on middle-class than on lower-class women. Families can afford to be restrictive of the female's freedom of movement, since they are not dependent on female incomes. Extramarital affairs are viewed as signs of virility for men, however. Middle- and upper-class wives complain but put up with male infidelity just as lower-class women do.

The upper-class women have more freedom from domestic tasks than middle-class women. They are more likely to receive university educations and to enter professional careers. However, their roles as wife and mother are supposed to take precedence over career goals and therefore career advancement is likely to be more difficult for them than for men. In addition, the professional woman usually must have a supportive husband who does not hold strongly to the traditional ideal of the woman's place being in the home. This does not mean, however, that the husband will share domestic chores. The wealth and class position of the upper-class woman allows her to free herself from the domestic sphere by passing the burden on to lower-class domestics.

Women continue to be discriminated against in Mexican society, even in its more modernized sectors. Politics, for example, is considered a male sphere. Women who venture into this arena usually emphasize their adherence to female roles in other spheres. They must prove they are exemplary wives and mothers and that their political concerns are merely extensions of these typical feminine humanitarian interests. They take a *supermadre* role in politics, which does not threaten the male-dominated gender stratification system or gender role ideology.

Women and the International Division of Labor. The increasing involvement of women in work outside the domestic sphere and work linked to the world market does not necessarily produce much improvement or long-term change in the gender stratification system. Lourdes Arizpe and Josefina Aranda's case study of strawberry packing-plant workers in the state of Michoacan, Mexico, demonstrates how international business interests can take advantage of women's subordinate position in the patriarchal peasant family and culture to pay below-market wages and increase their competitive edge in the world market.[50]

The Green Revolution programs in the 1960s increased the yields and efficiency of Mexican strawberry production, but they also encouraged the concentration of land under the ownership of multinational agro-businesses, undermining the peasant family economy and turning many of the men into day laborers or sending them as migrants to fields in the United States. Business interests have often used the slogans of women's liberation as a public relations program to justify the transfer of jobs from high-wage developed economies to low-wage peripheral economies. In fact, as in the case described by Arizpe and Aranda, low wages (65 cents per hour or similar piecework rates), insecure work (plants are closed four to six months a year and some days no strawberries are picked so the women are sent home with no pay), and no fringe benefits indicate, at most, a very ambiguous form of "liberation."

Packing-plant managers and accountants are all male. The secretaries are young females from the town. The plant production workers are young single females from the middle-level peasant families of the surrounding rural villages. Older women and poorer peasant women remain in the backbreaking field work. Thus the class and gender structure of the region is reproduced in the opportunity structure of the packing plant and the strawberry export business.

The packing-plant workers still live with their families and contribute most of their earnings to the family economy, keeping small amounts for small luxuries such as romantic comics and cosmetics. They are as the local culture dictates, under the strict control of their fathers who decide whether they will work and where they will work. Young men of the region can migrate to the United States and earn much higher wages, but the women cannot leave their fathers' homes without ruining their good names and rendering themselves unmarriageable. This makes them a captive labor force for the plants. There are few other employment opportunities in the area except domestic work and agricultural field labor, both of which are less desirable than the packing plants. Most of these women would not work outside the domestic sphere at all were it not for the jobs in the plants. Local female recruiters promise the young women's fathers that they will be carefully chaperoned and protected from any untoward male advances.

The women are not motivated to organize to demand better wages or working conditions because they and their families view the work as a temporary stage in their lives between elementary school and marriage. (The women who had wanted to continue in school were not allowed to because their fathers considered it a waste to educate a daughter.) Their only aspiration in life is to marry, quit working in the public sphere, and return full time to the domestic sphere as a housewife.

But if they did try to demand higher wages, the jobs would quickly disappear. The plants require very little capital investment; they can be disassembled quickly and shipped to a more compliant country. A slump in the world market for Mexican strawberries could also ruin the industry overnight, leaving these women in exactly the same position they were in before the plants opened, doing domestic chores and sewing and knitting for sale while waiting for marriage at age seventeen or twenty. Traditional gender roles have not been "modernized" and the traditional gender stratification system has not been undermined. Men still control the better-paying employment opportunities and husbands and fathers keep "their women" under strict control and surveillance. The young women report that they like the freedom of being away from their homes and villages for work, but this is a very limited form of freedom and does not constitute any real advance in personal independence or individualism for them.

Maria Fernandez-Kelly has described another case of the incorporation of young female workers into the new international division of labor.[51] The object of her study was the export manufacturing plants or *maquiladoras* along the northern Mexican border. These factories came into being as a result of the Border Industrialization Program (BIP) established by the Mexican government in 1965. Most of them produce electrical/electronic or textile/garment products and are subsidiaries of—or subcontractors to—U.S. multinational corporations. The BIP was designed expressly to create "enclave" conditions along the Mexican border that would be attractive to foreign investment. Over half of the *maquiladoras* are concentrated in the three cities of Ciudad Juarez, Tijuana, and Mexicali. Eighty-five percent of the workers in these factories are female. They are generally between the ages of seventeen and twenty-five. Seventy percent are single and on average they contribute more than half of their earnings for support of their families.

Fernandez-Kelly focused on the situation of the female workers in Ciudad Juarez. The majority of these workers are immigrants from small towns and other urban areas not far from Ciudad Juarez, but most have spent the greater part of their lives in that city with their families. Most of them are well above the average educational level of the majority of Mexicans, whether female or male. Typically, they have completed the six years of elementary schooling, and many have gone on to study in secondary, technical, or vocational institutions. The younger, better-educated, childless workers, however, are concentrated in the electrical/electronic plants; the somewhat older, less-educated, and especially female-heads-of-household are concentrated in the textile/garment factories. Working conditions and fringe benefits are on average better in the former type of establishment than in the latter.

These relatively well-educated or vocationally qualified young women eagerly seek semiskilled manual labor in the *maquiladoras* because most white-collar service jobs in Ciudad Juarez are generally unstable and even less well paid than factory work. Only the possession of bilingual skills qualifies women with intermediate educational credentials for the choicer service occupations. The irony of this situation is that the *maquiladora* jobs are the most attractive in the region for women of this category, although paying an average wage (at the time of the study) of fifty-eight cents per hour for a forty-eight hour work week. Fringe benefits, such as qualification for social security, medical services, and eating in the company cafeteria, also place these jobs in great demand.

Even with these advantages, however, average income derived from these jobs is not sufficient for the adequate support of a family. These women opted for *maquiladora* work as members of *households* (usually quite large) for whose economic survival their earnings are indispensable but in which they usually are not the sole source of income. Even so, one-half of the women working in the more disadvantaged textile/garment factories were the sole breadwinners in their families.

The earnings contributions to households of these women takes on added significance within the context of the widespread unemployment and underemployment of Mexican males. The *majority* of the men belonging to the households in which female *maquiladora* operators lived in Ciudad Juarez were unemployed or underemployed. More than half of the operators interviewed by Fernandez-Kelly reported having one or more immediate male relatives living in the United States as illegal aliens. The majority of these were brothers and fathers. Other female workers were coping with the crises provoked by the desertion of husbands, usually for economic reasons.

Why do the *maquiladoras* seek out mainly single young women for employment rather than selecting from the ample pool of unemployed young men? The views communicated to Fernandez-Kelly by *maquiladora* managers and promotors are revealing:

[According to them] . . . women are hired because of their putative higher levels of skill and performance; because of the quality of their . handiwork, because of their willingness to comply with monotonous, repetitive and highly exhausting work assignments, and because of their docility which discourages organizing efforts by union leaders. Men, on the other hand, are invariably described as being more restless and rebellious than women, less patient, more willing to unionize; and perhaps, more importantly, less resigned to tolerate rigorous work paces and inadequate working conditions for a low wage.[52]

Through this litany of cultural stereotypes interwoven with pragmatic perceptions of *maquiladora* administrators, Fernandez-Kelly perceives a line of interpretation of the incorporation of these women into international capitalist productive relations, which coincides with Arizpe's and Aranda's analysis of Michoacan strawberry packers: *Internationalized capitalist firms, under specific circumstances, take advantage of the gender divisions as well as the gender dependencies of Third-World labor forces to maximize profits and to enhance control of labor.* These gender divisions and dependencies involve not only the preexisting material conditions that differentiate men from women but also the prevailing ideological norms and expectations that define female and male identities and "proper" or "natural" gender roles in society. The ideology of *el hombre para el trabajo y la mujer para la casa* (man is for work; woman for the household) has complex implications for exploitation—even and especially in those situations where capitalism denies "work" to the man, provides it for the woman, and renders life in the household precarious for both.[53]

Conclusion

Since the publication of the classic study by Ester Boserup, *Women's Role in Economic Development* in 1970,[54] much of the social scientific literature on gender relations in Third-World societies has focused on the question of whether the general condition of women deteriorates as these societies "modernize" or, more specifically, as they undergo the process of capitalist development. More recently, this concern has been broadened through a series of studies that center the analysis of Third-World development within the framework of an understanding of the expanding and changing capitalist world system.

The negative consequences for women's life situations resulting from the spread of international capitalist relations in the Third World has been, and continues to be, amply documented and widely deplored. Even here, however, ambiguity remains: As Linda Y. C. Linn—commenting on the operation of "offshore" multinational capitalist firms—points out, the uneven development of world capitalism is contradictory at many levels:

The almost exclusive employment of female labor in many relocated industries is based on women's inferior position in the wage labor market, resulting from patriarchal social relations. Although women workers in these multinational factories are exploited relative to their output, relative to male workers in the same country, and to female workers in developed countries, their position is often better than in indigenous factories and in traditional forms of employment for women. The limited economic and social liberation that women workers derived from their employment in multinational factories is predicated on their subjection to capitalist, imperialist, and patriarchal exploitation in the labor market and the labor process. This presents a dilemma for feminist policy towards such employment: because exploitation and liberation go hand in hand, it cannot be readily condemned or extolled.[55]

Research has, moreover, increasingly clarified the fact that the volatility of international capital movements, the quest for cheaper and more controllable forms of labor, and the increasing integration of world markets have preserved, reproduced, or created varying forms of "Third-World" conditions in the advanced capitalist societies. One of the most perceptive students of this process, Alejandro Portes, comments in respect to the United States:

> Arriving by the hundreds of thousands, illegal immigrants during the last two decades have . . . reproduced in the United States the backward capitalist relations described as "informal" in less developed countries. As in the latter, the unprotected condition of informal workers benefits firms that subcontract production to this sector and individuals who purchase its services.[56]

In the advanced capitalist societies also, women have been major victims as well as the ambiguous emancipees of the process of labor "informalization" and the widening and deepening of the capitalist world system.

Students of peripheral capitalist development have also underscored and dissected the dynamics of class formation in Third-World societies. Nathan Keyfetz writes of the spread of a "worldwide middle class culture,"[57] a process that we would see both as a consequence and a means of penetration of worldwide capitalist relations.

For the wealthier sectors of developing countries, increased prosperity and experience with modernization can have two quite different effects on the positions of women and men. For some groups, especially the middle classes rather than the elite, prosperity allows them to follow traditional gender roles more closely: Having idle, isolated wives and daughters becomes a mark of prestige. Hence women in these groups often find themselves more firmly tied to the domestic sphere and segregated from the public world. This may bring them prestige in their cultural setting, but such prestige comes at the price of personal autonomy and prevents women from gaining equality with men or exercising overt power and authority in the society.

More modernized segments of the elite, however, are likely to take as their role models men and women of the developed countries. They are likely to be open to fuller female participation in the public world. However, this does not mean that males participate more fully in the domestic sphere. Whatever household duties women of this class may abandon are taken over by an ample supply of domestic servants drawn from the impoverished masses. Modernized elite women are likely to pursue higher education. They may be sent abroad to study. After completing their educations they may be free to practice their professions and even to enter political life. Traditional gender role ideologies limit their activities somewhat, but their high-class status allows them to break with many traditions with little or no prestige loss. The men of these classes are so wealthy and powerful that the achievements of their wives and daughters in the public sphere do not threaten their masculine identities. Male dominance is not challenged by the greater public participation of these few elite women.

The middle-class model of family life and consumption and the market relations that underlie them also exercise a strong influence over the aspirations of the poor and repressed classes of Third-World societies. For most, these aspirations are beyond any hope of realization. While the dreams remain, the practical imperatives of survival lead to innovative and pragmatically flexible strategies of rearranging and manipulating the ties of kin and family, especially on the part of women, as a means of social defense.[58] The spread of "matrifocality" in many areas of the Third World provides an illustration.

The incidence of matrifocal family structures, in which the mother and her kin form the permanent core of the household while husbands or lovers may come and go, is increased by the spread of capitalist relations in many areas of the Third World. The instability of male-female relationships characteristic of many Third-World areas is often an adaptive response to the poverty and insecurity of life among the poorest groups.

Susan Brown's analysis of mating patterns among landless peasants and those with insufficient land in the Dominican Republic indicates that the females in the multiple-mate pattern were better off than those in the more desirable single-mate pattern.[59] The multiple-mate pattern was characterized by free consensual unions, male marginality in the household, and a matrifocal family structure. The ideal single-mate pattern included legal marriage and male-headed nuclear family households. Women in the multiple-mate pattern had more flexibility to make the best use of whatever resources might be available. They did not have to defer to a man's wishes. If the man wasted money on drinking, gambling, or other women, the women could throw him out. Married, single-mate women, however, had to tolerate whatever their husbands did. The multiple-mate woman could take a job locally or migrate to look for work. The single-mate woman was usually forbidden to take outside employment even if the family desperately needed the money: It reflected badly on the husband to have an employed wife. The wife had to make do on the husband's earnings no matter how inadequate they might be.

The multiple-mate women could maintain close reciprocal ties with her mother and other relatives and share domestic tasks, child care, and economic resources. She could also place her children temporarily in other people's homes to earn their own keep. These practices were unacceptable to the single-mate couples. Thus the women in the multiple-mate pattern suffered a loss of prestige for not establishing a permanent household with a man. But they gained in economic viability in a situation where a man would not typically be able to provide for a family's needs.

Patricia Fernandez-Kelly describes the informal patterns of economic exchange and reciprocity at the household and neighborhood levels in the Mexican border town of Ciudad Juarez. She points out the dual functions of such survival strategies: (1) to cheapen the subsistence and reproductive costs of workers from the standpoint of the national and international capitalist economy and (2) to extend workers' purchasing power beyond the immediate capacities of the inadequate individual and family wage, a collective survival strategy. Hence the exploitative features of capitalist relations and the active, resilient efforts of workers to innovate for social defense appear as a "package," a compounded structure of bondage and freedom.

The ironies of these adaptations to uneven capitalist development—and the difficulty of distinguishing traditional and modern components within them—is exemplified by Fernandez-Kelly's description of the incorporation of the local, informal sale and distribution of Avon products in the working-class neighborhoods of Ciudad Juarez.

Women purchased a jar of facial cream, a bottle of cologne or a lipstick not only because they were interested in the products but also because in buying they felt they were doing the seller a personal favor. They knew the favor would be returned when the opportunity

arose. . . . These exchanges operated as a re-
distributive mechanism by means of which the
limited earnings of neighbors were widely and
legitimately shared. The secret was to maintain
a steady flow of money among the participants. . . . Avon representatives received a
commission proportional to the sales achieved.
This too enhanced the flow of money. Redistri-
butive mechanisms exist in all societies . . .
what made it unique, as an example of present
living in Ciudad Juarez, was the intervention of
a highly impersonal modern commercial firm in
the process of neighborhood living. Avon, an
enterprise whose primary purpose is to peddle
superfluous luxuries, was one of the links by
means of which poverty could be evened out in
the barrio.[60]

Not incidentally, the example described by
Fernandez-Kelly focuses on the activities of
women. All over the Third World, both
women and men with inadequate resources
struggle, often desperately, often ingen-
iously, to survive within, adapt to, and take
advantage of the changing world of capitalist
relations in which they live. In given situations, as we see in Chapter 9, many have
joined together collectively to attempt to create a socialist alternative to these relations
at the level of the national society. But
throughout these struggles, women have
borne the greater burden of economic and
political exclusion, marginality, and exploitation. They have also borne the weight of
the essential contradictions of the imperatives for the social defense of the individual,
the family, and the community.

Notes

1. Among the many sources that could be cited for
the general interpretive framework of this chapter, the
following are of special interest: Immanuel Wallerstein,
The Capitalist World Economy (New York: Cambridge University Press, 1979); June Nash and Maria Patricia Fernandez-Kelly, eds., *Women, Men and the International Division of Labor* (Albany: State University of New York
Press, 1983); Maria Patricia Fernandez-Kelly, *For We Are

Sold, I and My People: Women and Industry in Mexico's
Frontier* (Albany: State University of New York Press,
1983); Lourdes Beneria, ed., *Women and Development: The
Sexual Division of Labor in Rural Societies* (New York:
Praeger, 1982); *Signs* 7, no. 2 (Winter 1981), Special Issue
on "Development and the Sexual Division of Labor";
Kathryn B. Ward, *Women in the World System: Its Impact
on Status and Fertility* (New York: Praeger, 1984); Fer-
nando Henrique Cardoso and Enzo Faletto, *Dependency
and Development* (Berkeley: University of California
Press, 1979); Folker Fröbel, Jurgen Heinrichs, and Otto
Kreye, *The New International Division of Labor: Structural
Unemployment in Industrialized Countries and Industrialization in Developing Countries* (London: Cambridge University Press, 1980); Barry Bluestone and Bennett Har-
rison, *The Deindustrialization of America: Plant Closings,
Community Abandonment and the Dismantling of Basic Industry* (New York: Basic Books, 1982).

2. This section is based mainly on Audrey Chapman
Smock, "Ghana: From Autonomy to Subordination," in
Janet Zollinger Giele and Audrey Chapman Smock,
eds., *Women: Roles and Status in Eight Countries* (New
York: John Wiley, 1977): 173–216. For added historical
perspective, see Claire C. Robertson, *Sharing the Same
Bowl: A Socioeconomic History of Women and Class in Accra,
Ghana* (Bloomington: Indiana University Press, 1984).

3. Smock, 178.

4. William F. Steel, "Female and Small-Scale Employment Under Modernization in Ghana," *Economic
Development and Cultural Change* 30, No. 1 (October 1981):
153–167; Eugenia Date-Bah, "Female and Male Factory
Workers in Accra," in Christine Oppong, ed., *Female
and Male in West Africa* (Boston: George Allen & Unwin,
1983): 266–274.

5. Gwendolyn Mikell, "Filiation, Economic Crisis,
and the Status of Women in Rural Ghana," *Canadian
Journal of African Studies* 18, no. 1 (1984): 195–218.

6. Clare Robertson, "Ga Women and Socio-economic Change in Accra, Ghana," in Nancy J. Hafkin
and Edna G. Bay, *Women in Africa: Studies in Social and
Economic Change* (Stanford, Calif.: Stanford University
Press, 1976): 111–133. Robertson presents a more am-
plified description and theoretical interpretation of this
case in Robertson, 1984.

7. Robertson, 1976, 122–123.

8. Robertson, 1976, 119.

9. Robertson, 1976, 133.

10. Carmel Dinan, "Sugar Daddies and Gold-Dig-
gers: The White Collar Single Women in Accra," in
Oppong, 344–366.

11. Dinan, 350.

12. Dinan, 352.

13. Dinan, 358.

14. Christine Oppong, *Middle Class African Marriage* (London: George Allen & Unwin, 1981).

15. This section is based largely on the following works: Margaret Cormack, *The Hindu Woman* (Westport, Conn.: Greenwood Press, 1975; orig. 1953): S. C. Dube, "Men's and Women's Roles in India: A Sociological Review," in Barbara Ward, ed., *Women in the New Asia* (Paris: UNESCO, 1963): 174–203; Vatsala Narain, "India" in Raphael Patai, ed., *Women in the Modern World* (New York: Free Press, 1967): 21–41; Doranne Jacobson, "The Women of North and Central India: Goddesses and Wives," in Carolyn Matthiasson, ed., *Many Sisters* (New York: Free Press, 1974): 99–176; Doranne Jacobson, "Indian Women in Processes of Development," *Journal of International Affairs* 30, no. 2 (Fall–Winter, 1976–77): 211–242; Doranne Jacobson, "Purdah in India: Life behind the Veil," *National Geographic*, 152, no. 2 (August 1977): 270–286; Marcus Franda, "India," *Common Ground* 2, no. 1 (January 1976): 17–28.

16. See A. S. Altekar, *The Position of Women in Hindu Civilization: From Prehistoric Times to the Present Day* (1938; Delhi Motilal Banarsidas, 1973); Narain; and Dube.

17. Maria Mies, *Indian Women and Patriarchy: Conflicts and Dilemmas of Students and Working Women* (New Dehli: Concept Publishing, 1980).

18. Jacobson, 1974, 142.

19. Jacobson, 1976–77, 223.

20. Ursula Sharma, *Women, Work and Property in North-West India* (New York: Tavistock, 1980).

21. Maria Mies, "The Dynamics of the Sexual Division of Labor and Integration of Rural Women into the World Market," in Beneria, 1–28.

22. Dube, 200–202.

23. Marjorie Wood, "Employment and Family Change: A Study of Middle-Class Women in Urban Gujarat," in Alfred de Souza, ed., *Women in Contemporary India* (New Delhi: Manohar Book Service, 1975): 51.

24. J. Murickan, "Women in Kerala: Changing Socio-Economic Status and Self-Image," in de Souza, 73–95.

25. Murickan, 77.

26. Jacobson, 1976–77, 230.

27. Ilse Siebert, *Women in the Ancient Near East* (New York: Abner Schram, 1974).

28. Elise Boulding, *The Underside of History* (Boulder, Colo.: Westview Press, 1976): 384–391.

29. Elizabeth Fernea, *Guests of the Sheik* (Garden City, N.Y.: Doubleday, 1965).

30. For this section we have relied on Guity Nashat, "Women in the Islamic Republic of Iran," *Iranian Studies* 13, nos. 1–4 (1980): 165–194; Guity Nashat, ed., *Women and Revolution in Iran* (Boulder, Colo.: Westview Press, 1983); Adele K. Ferdows, "Women and the Islamic Rev-

olution," *International Journal of Middle East Studies* 15, no. 2 (1983): 283–298; Hassan N. Gardezi, "The Resurgence of Islam: Islamic Ideology and Encounters with Imperialism," *Journal of Contemporary Asia* 12, no. 4 (1982): 451–463; Farah Azari, ed., *Women of Iran: The Conflict with Fundamentalist Islam* (London: Ithaca Press, 1983); Eliz Sanasarian, *The Women's Rights Movement in Iran: Mutiny, Appeasement and Repression from 1900 to Khomeini* (New York: Praeger, 1982); R. M. Burrell, "Iran: Revolution, Illusion—and Reality?" *Middle Eastern Studies* 19, no. 1 (1983): 17–27; Mary Elaine Hegland, "Traditional Iranian Women: How They Cope," *Middle East Journal* 36, no. 4 (Autumn 1982): 483–501; Kate Millet, *Going to Iran* (New York: Coward, McGann & Goeghegan, 1982); Janet Bauer, "New Models and Traditional Networks: Migrant Women in Tehran," in James T. Fawcett, Siew-Ean Khoo, and Peter C. Smith, eds., *Women in the Cities of Asia: Migration and Urban Adaptation* (Boulder, Colo.: Westview Press, 1984); Shahla Haeri, "The Institution of Mutca Marriage in Iran: Formal and Historical Perspective," in Nashat, 231–252.

31. Hannah Papanek, "Purdah: Separate Worlds and Symbolic Shelter," in Hannah Papanek and Gail Minault, eds., *Separate Worlds: Studies of Purdah in South Asia* (Columbia, Mo.: South Asia Books, 1982): 3–52.

32. Erika Friedl, "State Ideology and Village Women" in Nashat, 217–230.

33. Fatima Mernissi, *Beyond the Veil: Male-Female Dynamics in a Modern Muslim Society* (New York: John Wiley, 1975): 1–41.

34. Thomas G. Sanders, "Mexico," *Common Ground* 2, no. 1 (January 1976): 45–55.

35. Evelyn P. Stevens, "*Marianismo:* The Other Face of *Machismo,*" in Ann Pescatello, ed., *Female and Male in Latin America* (Pittsurgh: University of Pittsburgh Press, 1973): 90.

36. Stevens, 91.

37. Nora Scott Kinzer, "Priests, Machos and Babies: Or, Latin American Women and the Manichaean Heresy," *Journal of Marriage and the Family* 35 (May 1973): 300–312.

38. Stevens, 315.

39. Oscar Lewis, *Pedro Martinez: A Mexican Peasant and His Family* (New York: Vintage Books, 1964).

40. Lewis, 1964, 116.

41. Doren Slade, "Marital Status and Sexual Identity: The Position of Women in a Mexican Peasant Society," in Ruby Rohrlich-Leavitt, ed., *Women Cross-Culturally* (The Hague: Mouton, 1975): 129–148.

42. Slade, 147.

43. Oscar Lewis, *Five Families* (New York: John Wiley, 1959); Oscar Lewis, *The Children of Sanchez* (Baltimore: Penguin Books, 1961).

44. Lewis, 259.

45. Lewis, 1959, 172.

46. Virve Piho, "Life and Labor of the Woman Textile Workers in Mexico City," in Rohrlich-Leavitt, 199–245.

47. Piho, 241.

48. Mary Elmendorf, "Mexico: The Many Worlds of Women," in Giele and Smock, 147.

49. Sanders, 49.

50. Lourdes Arizpe and Josefina Aranda, "The Comparative Advantages of Women's Disadvantages: Women Workers in the Strawberry Export Agribusiness in Mexico," Signs (Winter 1981): 453–473.

51. Fernandez-Kelly, 1983 and Maria Fernandez-Kelly, "Mexican Border Industrialization, Female Labor Force Participation and Migration" in Nash and Fernandez-Kelly, 1983, 205–223.

52. Fernandez-Kelly, in Nash and Fernandez-Kelly, 219.

53. Fernandez-Kelly, in Nash and Fernandez-Kelly, 213.

54. Ester Boserup, Women's Role in Economic Development (New York: St. Martin's Press, 1970).

55. Linda Y. C. Linn, "Capitalism, Imperialism, and Patriarchy: The Dilemma of Third-World Women Workers in Multinational Factories" in Nash and Fernandez-Kelly, 70–91, 85.

56. Alejandro Portes, "The Informal Sector: Definition, Controversy, and Relation to National Development," Review 7, no. 1 (Summer 1983): 151–174, 170.

57. Nathan Keyfetz, "Development and the Elimination of Poverty," Economic Development and Cultural Change 30, no. 3 (April 1982): 649–670, 651.

58. The literature on adaptive and survival strategies is very extensive. Among the most useful treatments in the present context are Norman E. Whitten, Jr., "Network Analysis," in John J. Honigman, ed., The Handbook of Social and Cultural Anthropology (Chicago: Rand-McNally, 1973); Norman E. Whitten, Jr., Black Frontiersmen: A South American Case (New York: Schenkman, 1974); Carol Stack, All Our Kin (New York: Harper & Row, 1974); Lydia Morris, "Women in Poverty: Domestic Organization Among the Poor of Mexico City," Anthropological Quarterly 54, no. 3 (July 1981): 117–124; Larissa Lomnitz, Networks and Marginality (New York: Academic Press, 1977); Tony L. Whitehead, "Residence, Kinship and Mating as Survival Strategies: A West Indian Example," Journal of Marriage and the Family 40 (November 1978): 817–828; Caroline Moser, "Surviving in the Surburbio," Bulletin of the Institute of Development Studies (Sussex, England) 12, no. 3 (1981): 19–29; William Rowe, "Caste, Kinship and Association in Urban India," in A. Southall, ed., Urban Anthropology (London: Oxford Univrsity Press, 1973): 211–250; and David Jacobson, Itinerant Townsmen (Menlo Park, Calif: Benjamin/Cummings 1973).

59. Susan E. Brown, "Lower Economic Sector Mating Patterns in the Dominican Republic: A Comparative Analysis," in Rohrlich-Leavitt, 149–162.

60. Fernandez-Kelly, 1983, 159.

CHAPTER 9

Socialist Societies

The Soviet Union, the Israeli Kibbutz, China, and Cuba

Beginning with the work of Frederick Engels and August Bebel, socialist theorists have argued that the ultimate cause of gender stratification is capitalism and that the only solution is a socialist form of social organization.[1] The revival of the feminist movement in the 1960s and 1970s resulted in a renewed interest in socialist feminism as well as the liberal feminism of the mainstream women's movements.

The early socialists often argued that problems associated with gender stratification would simply disappear under socialism. The leadership in socialist countries today still gives ideological lip service to the ideal of gender equality and includes it among its long-term goals. Socialist feminists today continue to argue that socialism is at least a necessary first step towards women's liberation and human liberation.[2] Although socialism may encourage some alleviation of women's "double burden" at work and at home, the examples provided by existing socialist countries make it difficult to argue convincingly that socialism will automatically liberate women.[3]

Ideological support and official rhetoric are certainly not sufficient to achieve gender equality or women's liberation. To overcome the legacy gender stratification inherited from the social structures of the past requires a high degree of commitment, a willingness to allocate important and often scarce resources to this end, and programs designed to change men's attitudes and behavior. Contemporary socialist societies have not been willing to undertake such commitment. The following examination of the history of the "woman question" in the Soviet Union, the Israeli kibbutz, the People's Republic of China, and Cuba under Castro indicates the problems and pitfalls that befell these societies' limited attempts to institute gender equality.

The Soviet Union

Prerevolutionary Russia

In prerevolutionary Russia the majority of women and men were still rural peasants living in rigidly patriarchal family structures with gender roles typical of agrarian societies.[4] Males as well as females were exploited by the landlord class, but women suffered further exploitation on the basis of gender. Females were subordinated to the will of their fathers and then to their husbands and mothers-in-law. They had few legal or property rights. They were not believed to be fully human, but were viewed as a subhuman category inferior to males. Furthermore, much of Asian Russia was under the domination of the Moslem religion and practiced even more extreme forms of female subordination, veiling, and seclusion. Feminist consciousness and movements for social change do not arise and flourish under such oppressive conditions.

In sixteenth- and seventeenth-century Russia, even Russian women of the urban elite were in positions inferior to that of women in other parts of Europe. They had fewer rights and were more firmly secluded. Peter the Great in the early eighteenth century, however, attempted to introduce Western ideas and practices into Russian social life. He instituted reforms that gave women more property and legal rights and supported marriage by choice instead of arranged marriages. He also introduced mixed-gender social gatherings The reforms were aimed only at the elite few and did not reach many of them. Russia remained among the most backward of European societies.

Russia was not, however, immune to the changes taking place in the rest of Europe and the United States. By the mid-nineteenth century industrialization was underway in the cities of Russia and the serfs were freed from their legal if not their economic bondage in the countryside. As in the West, both idealized femininity and feminist movements accompanied these wider social changes toward modernization.

Radical Feminism in Nineteenth-Century Russia. Women's movements arose a few decades later than in the West, but by the 1860s they were an important phenomenon among a small group of well-to-do, educated urban women.[5] An important and influential feminist novel, *What Is to Be Done?* was published in 1863 by Nikolay Chernyshevski. He at-

tributed female subordination to the general backwardness of Russian society and called for revolutionary change in the social order, including woman's place. The novel also provided a model for young women of the time to adopt in their search for personal liberation and their struggle for social change.

Many young women answered this call and left their homes for the cities in search of education and employment. They entered study groups and lived in communes with like-minded men and women. Some of them contracted fictitious marriages to gain freedom from their fathers' authority and the necessary passport to live on their own. These fictitious marriages were legal but the men agreed in advance not to exercise the rights of husbands, and most of them honored their agreements. The communes were not places of sexual license, although every attempt was made by the public and the authorities to portray feminists as immoral and depraved. The women, however, rejected all aspects of the sex-object role for females. They refused feminine clothes and grooming and preferred a more mannish look, although they were not so daring as to wear trousers. The males of the communes were expected to support gender equality and respect for women and to practice sexual self-denial. Sex was considered frivolous, a diversion from more important work.

These first steps toward feminism soon led women into broader radical movements that subordinated the woman's question to the wider problems of freeing all oppressed and exploited peoples. Unlike their Western counterparts, the men and women in these movements interacted fairly equally. Gail Lapidus suggests that the backwardness of Russian society contributed to the solidarity between male and female radicals.[6] The radicals constituted such a small, isolated minority that the men needed the female participants. Neither gender held important political or civil rights, so the males were as concerned about these issues as the females. The males could also see the analogies between woman's oppressed position in Russian society and the oppressed positions of the peasantry and the proletariat (working class). Yet, as Lapidus explains, the women came from a similar class background and were educated sufficiently to speak the same language and share the same world view as the male radicals.

Liberal Feminist Groups. Numerous radical fractions were active in the 1870s, but the Marxists did not appear in Russia until the mid-1880s. Alongside the radical groups also developed an important liberal feminist social movement. Both the radicals and the liberals came from urban, educated, privileged backgrounds, but the liberal feminists concerned themselves primarily with the problems of privileged women. They sought greater educational and professional employment opportunities and greater political rights. They worked through philanthropy and education and did not seek revolutionary change in the political, social, and economic structures of Russian society. They demanded only that women be given greater opportunities, not disrupting of class privilege to any significant extent. After the 1905 revolution (which resulted in the establishment of the Russian parliament, or Duma, with male suffrage), the liberal feminists pressed hard for woman's suffrage. The fact that suffrage had finally been given to males, but withheld from females, increased women's feelings of relative deprivation. This was true for many poorer women as well as for the urban privileged groups that composed the feminist organizations.

Marxist Attitudes toward Feminism. The Marxist groups, including the Bolsheviks,

supported women's liberation in theory. Drawing on Engels's and August Bebel's works, they saw women's oppression as part of the overall oppressiveness of class societies.[7] Yet at the practical level they were suspicious of and often hostile to feminism, feminist movements, and feminist issues. They viewed the woman question as diversionary, as a bourgeois concern that drew energy and attention away from the more important issue of class oppression. Therefore, the Marxists undertook few organizing activities among women. This was true even for women industrial workers, despite the Marxist emphasis on the vanguard role of the industrial proletariat. According to Rose Glickman, "in real situations as opposed to paper ones, the workers called to action were envisaged as exclusively male."[8]

This neglect of the female factory worker occurred despite the fact that women were drawn into the industrial labor force in large numbers in the late nineteenth and early twentieth centuries. By 1887 females constituted 38 percent of the textile workers, 27 percent of the chemical workers, and 11 percent of those working in the manufacture of lime, brick, and glass.[9] Females constituted 15 percent of the industrial labor force as a whole in 1887, and they continued to move into industrial employment whenever occupational categories opened to them. By 1900 women were 26 percent of the industrial labor force; they were up to 32 percent by 1914.[10] World War I greatly increased female employment opportunities as millions of men were mobilized for the war effort while industry continued to expand.

Industrial work was highly gender segregated, and males received much better wages than females. But this followed traditional patterns of the agricultural sector. Women had been engaged in hard physical labor in the rural areas for centuries and generally received about 25 percent of what male workers received for similar work. Their low wages made them desirable to factory owners and helped to increase female representation in industrial labor, especially as the even cheaper child labor was made illegal or difficult to obtain. Employers also believed women workers would be more obedient, less troublesome, and less likely to drink.

The Marxist myopia concerning the women workers was not shared by the movement's few feminist members such a Aleksandra Kollontai and Inessa Armand, who encouraged organizing and educational efforts among working-class women. They pointed out the successes that liberal feminists were achieving among working women in gaining support for woman's suffrage. Kollontai and Armand were largely responsible for the Bolshevik party's development of a stand on the woman question at all. They attempted to unite feminism and socialism, but most of the other female as well as male leaders accepted this only as a tactical expedient and remained hostile to any separate concern for feminist issues.

Like the rest of the Bolsheviks, Kollontai and Armand were adamantly opposed to the liberal feminists. This was especially apparent during World War I when the Russian liberal feminists, like their counterparts in Western Europe and the United States, actively supported the war in the hopes of being rewarded with the vote after it ended. According to Lapidus, the war served to increase both women's economic and political activity. Women were involved in strikes and demonstrations, and it was women workers who started the massive strike that ended in the February 1917 revolution and the Provisional Government which did finally grant women the vote. This activity furthermore convinced the Bolsheviks that they should establish a department for party

work among women if they were to hope for this important source of support in their own bid for power.[11]

The Bolshevik Revolution

The Bolshevik faction of the Marxist groups seized power on November 7, 1917. Under the leadership of Lenin they attempted to establish in practice the visions they supported. Part of their vision included gender equality, but they had no firm blueprint for its achievement. Instead, most of the new leadership held a vague belief that once the country had been modernized and industrialized with a socialist political structure, the woman question would be solved. This, of course, meant that nothing specific needed to be done for women: it was sufficient to dismantle the structures of Czarist Russia and build in their stead a socialist republic.

The Bolsheviks' formal commitment to gender equality and opposition to the old society were expressed in early legislation related to gender roles and the family. Full political and legal rights were extended to women. Legal restrictions on women's freedom of movement, legal supports for female subordination to males, and unequal property and inheritance rights were abolished. Females were given rights to individual rather than household pay and equal pay for equal work was written into law. Abortion and birth control were legalized. De facto marriages were recognized as legal. Divorce was made easily available on the request of either partner. The distinction between legitimate and illegitimate children was abolished. In addition to this support for equal rights, the new laws also supported the protection of motherhood. Aleksandra Kollontai, as new Minister of Social Welfare, promulgated the view that the state was responsible for the welfare of mothers and children and for state supported child care services.

But however important these laws were as symbols, they did little to change or improve the actual position of women in the new Soviet society. Enacting legislation was easy, but putting these laws into effect would prove to be too costly for the new regime. In the midst of the chaos and civil war that followed the Bolshevik seizure of power, matters relating to the creation of egalitarian socialism were subordinated to the political and military requirements of consolidating power. Social engineering was postponed.

The Zhenotdel. In the interests of consolidating power and building a strong constituency for the new government, some programs aimed at increasing women's participation in the new regime were undertaken. To mobilize women for political participation, a woman's bureau, the Zhenotdel, was established and the party's female activists were placed in charge.

The Zhenotdel met with opposition among both the highly traditional Russian people and the increasingly antifeminist Communist party membership and hierarchy. Despite the controversy, the Zhenotdel achieved important successes. It mobilized women for party membership, created a communications network for dealing with women's problems and raising women's consciousness about gender equality and their new rights, and spread literacy to facilitate propagandizing among women and women's political participation. It also gave women the opportunity to participate in a network of female delegates within the party. This allowed women to gain the necessary skills, experience, and self-confidence to compete with men in the political arena.

The Zhenotdel also worked to increase women's economic participation to give women the economic independence necessary for equality. To this end they encouraged the party to undertake educational and training programs to upgrade women's skills and to establish communal dining and childcare facilities to free women from their domestic burdens.

The Moslem areas of the Soviet Union provided a special target for the Zhenotdel. The members worked particularly hard to mobilize the Moslem women to undermine the traditional repressive social structures in these areas. Tactics included encouraging the women to exercise their new rights and to file for divorce against abusive husbands. They also encouraged the women to join in throwing off their veils as an important symbolic rejection of their past subordinate roles. The males reacted to these actions with rage. In 1927, for example, 250 women were killed in Uzbekistan for unveiling their faces.[12] To undermine male resistance, the party showed particular interest in appointing women to high posts in the Moslem areas and in incorporating these women into all areas of the political and economic structure, thereby forcing the men to take orders from and to work with women.

Consequences of Reformist Action. The policies pursued by the Zhenotdel and the party were not entirely beneficial to women, whatever their intent. The new freedom of divorce, for example, left many women abandoned by their husbands without the necessary skills or experience to support themselves or their children. Furthermore, the high unemployment that characterized the years following the revolution meant that real economic gains for women were minimal. What the party preached for women often could not be put into practice. The impact of reform was more limited in the rural areas than in the cities. Peasants remained committed to traditional values, family structures, and gender roles. Self-assertion for women was difficult to bring about here.

The Zhenotdel itself represented a contradiction in the Communist party position on the woman question. On the one hand, strong women ran the department in the interest of women's greater integration into the new political, economic, and social structure. On the other hand, the department served to segregate these strong female leaders from the rest of the party hierarchy. It also served to perpetuate traditional gender role divisions by assigning these women to "social housekeeping" functions (social, health, and cultural issues) and women's issues. The problem of gender segregation was further exacerbated by the fact that the Zhenotdel staff was not treated equally with staff of other departments. Women were often excluded from general policy meetings and called upon to participate only when women's issues were directly involved.

The problem of the second-class status of the Zhenotdel was further increased as the Communist party widened its base among the male population. As the revolutionary vanguard was joined by new male recruits, the new recruits brought with them a much stronger commitment to traditional gender roles. This increased the party's general hostility toward feminism. Ardent feminists such as Kollontai were subject to attacks and smear campaigns. Hostility toward Kollontai focused special attention on her advocacy of sexual freedom. This was used to turn women as well as men against her and her policies. The end result was the abolition of the Zhenotdel in 1930.

Lenin had at least given ideological support to feminist issues. He recognized the limiting effects of the domestic/public dichotomy on women's full social participation and advocated the industrialization of housework to free women from its stultifying effects. Lenin was, however, unable to put these ideas into practice because of the military problems of consolidating power and because of the extremely limited resources of the early days of Communist rule. Priority was given to the development of heavy industry and capital investment in productive resources rather than to the expansion of the service sector necessary to free women from their domestic burdens.

The Stalin Era

When Stalin came to power in the mid-1920s, the emphasis on heavy industry continued, but the earlier recognition of women's unique needs as an especially oppressed segment of the population was lost. The five-year plans, designed to promote rapid industrialization, brought women into the industrial labor force in vastly increased numbers. But this did not stem from a commitment to feminist ideals: It was expedient to draw on the widest labor supply possible and to allow no resource to go untapped. Stalin himself held particularly negative views of women, seeing them as ignorant, backward, and having a responsibility to society to overcome these limitations. He emphasized the need for solidarity between women and men and condemned feminism as "bourgeois deviationism."

Stalin reversed the party's earlier stand on the need to free people from the repressive traditionalism of the family. Earlier policy had aimed at removing the functions of the family to the wider social order and at freeing people by making marriage and family ties dependent only on love and mutual attraction. These family policies were used as the scapegoat for the disruption and social disorganization that occurred in the aftermath of the revolution and the civil war. The declining birthrate was of particular concern to party officials who wanted population growth to strengthen the new country. Stalin reaffirmed the family as a cornerstone of the new socialist society and introduced legislation to promote its stability. Abortions were banned again in 1936. The law did not appreciably affect the number of abortions performed, but it served to drive women to unsafe illegal abortionists as in prerevolutionary Russia. Large families were also encouraged by material incentives such as state allowances. Sexual deviance was attacked as a crime and campaigns against prostitution and homosexuality were undertaken.

The Soviet Union entered a period of idealized family life and femininity and sexual repression. Housework was redefined as socially useful rather than stultifying. Women were praised for feminine graces such as exhibiting an interest in beautifying the home. Motherhood and child rearing were proclaimed woman's highest calling. However, these redefinitions of woman's role did not preclude paid employment for women. Women were to work full time in the wider economy while simultaneously devoting themselves to their homes and families, and the dual burden was not eased by any increase in the service sector. Stalin's policy was to discourage production in services and consumer goods in favor of heavy industry. The household was forced to provide for itself and suffered a standard of living much lower than that found in other industrialized societies of the period.

In 1944 Stalin issued a Family Edict aimed at further strengthening the family. Divorce was restricted. Unregistered marriages were denied legal recognition. Unmarried mothers were prohibited from filing paternity

suits or support suits against the fathers of their children. The state would, however, provide an allowance for the illegitimate child's maintenance. Legitimacy and illegitimacy were written back into law and illegitimate children were marked for life by their birth certificates. The law absolved men of all responsibility toward their lovers and children and encouraged a frivolous attitude toward women. The purpose of these laws was most likely to encourage a higher birthrate among unmarried women by removing the fear of economic responsibility from men and simultaneously to shore up the family by making legitimacy important. This was a period of severe demographic imbalance between the genders. Massive numbers of men had died in the civil war, World War II, and in Stalin's purges. Millions of women of childbearing age could not marry for lack of men and Stalin did not want these women to remain childless. Women were to be childbearing machines in the service of the state.

As in the United States during the forties, in the thirties and forties in the U.S.S.R. the demands of the economy drew women into the labor force in ever-increasing numbers and in a wide range of jobs. But this occurred in the absence of a feminist consciousness or an organized woman's movement and therefore could be combined with a Russian version of the "cult of domesticity" and very limited female participation in the political structure or the more powerful sectors of the economy. Women were made to suffer a double exploitation in the public and domestic sectors in the service of the state, and the appropriate "convenient social virtues" were upheld to convince women they wanted to sacrifice themselves. Cultural images of women emphasized submissive heroines who devoted themselves to motherhood and domestic work while shouldering a job. The independent, politically active heroines of the past who refused to let family responsibilities compete with political duties largely disappeared.

An organized woman's movement no longer existed under Stalin, both because of Stalin's and the party's opposition to independent feminism and because the Soviet Union was affected by the worldwide decline of feminism in the thirties and forties. No international movement existed to prod Soviet women or the Soviet government to recognize women's needs and interests.

The Contemporary USSR

After Stalin's death in 1953, the USSR underwent a change of direction. It repudiated many of his policies, including many of those directed at women and the family. There was, for example, a stepped-up recruitment of women into party membership, which is a prerequisite for political power in the Soviet Union. Increased attention was also given to lightening women's domestic burdens by improving housing and the service sector. The sacrifice of consumer needs to industrial needs had chiefly burdened women by making households responsible for their own services. The 1944 Family code came under attack and was finally revised to make divorce and abortion more readily available. Despite impressive achievments, however, women's position in contemporary Soviet society is still subordinate to men's.

Class Structure. Although communist ideology denies the existence of a class structure under communism, it is clear that the Soviet Union has failed to abolish class stratification. On top is a tiny elite of top Communist party leaders and government officials who wield tremendous power and enjoy economic rewards commensurate with high status. A second level consists of managers, bureaucrats, technicians, and intellectuals—those with advanced educations. Their positions give them some power and a more comfortable life than most Soviet citizens enjoy. A third class consists of white-collar and skilled blue-collar workers. These people are urban dwellers and usually have a high school education. The majority of the population fall into the lowest class of unskilled urban workers and rural agricultural laborers. The unskilled usually have less than seven years of education and are quite poor.[13]

The Economic Sphere. Women's representation in the economic sphere is far higher than in the non-Communist world. Women constitute 51 percent of the civilian labor force and women are found in large numbers in occupational categories such as professional employment (for example, medical doctors and technicians), which are dominated by males in the West.[14] Women's work is facilitated by a widespread, though still inadequate, network of nurseries, day-care centers, boarding schools, and after-school programs for older children. Women receive generous maternity leaves, maternity benefits, and pension plans. There is also a large body of protective legislation limiting the type of work women can do and barring women from many of the more strenuous jobs. Legislation forbids discrimination against women workers and requires equal pay for equal work.

But the work world in the Soviet Union is as gender segregated as it is in the West, and the gender segregation produces similar consequences. There are women's jobs and women's industries and men's jobs and men's industries. The distribution of men and women in the labor force has not changed significantly since 1939. Also, just as in the West, the women's sector of this dual labor market is paid substantially less than the men's sector. The average female worker earns 65 percent of the average male worker's salary.[15] The Soviet emphasis on heavy industry includes the policy of better pay for workers in this area to attract more personnel to these occupations. These are the occupations in which men predominate and from which women are often barred by protective legislation.

Even in occupations in which men and women both participate, fewer and fewer women are found as one moves up the scale of power, pay, and prestige. For example, it is a much publicized fact that women constitute 69 percent of the physicians in the Soviet Union. Yet the more prestigious positions and the administrative positions are disproportionately male. Over 90 percent of the pediatricians are female, yet the more prestigious field of surgery has only 6 percent females. The gender stratification within medicine is further evidenced by the fact that almost all nurses are female. Moreover, current policies are aimed at reducing the overrepresentation of females among medical doctors and the percentage of females in the field is dropping. Male applicants to medical schools are being given preferential treatment over female applicants. Thus this avenue of professional advancement for women may be closing somewhat while other avenues are not opening at a comparable rate.[16]

It is also true that Soviet policies have forced women into paid employment. Wages of both males and females have been kept low enough that most families cannot live on one income. To meet their basic subsistence needs, Soviet couples must rely on the wife's income. Furthermore, until recently extra money could not be earned through part-time work for wives. Political leaders had purposely not allowed the creation of part-time employment to force wives and mothers into full-time jobs.

The Political Sphere. Soviet women may have made important strides in the economic sphere compared with women in other countries, but their representation in the political sphere is as low as in the West. Women hold some lower-level political offices, but the higher one goes the fewer women one finds. Women have been virtually absent at the apex of the Soviet power structure—the Central Committee of the Communist party and the Politburo. Only 3.3 percent of the Central Committee were female in 1976 and only one woman has ever served on the Politburo.[17] Women who are appointed to high political office are usually there for symbolic purposes. They do not achieve important political positions because they have built up political power in their own right: They are tokens. Furthermore, as with the Zhenotdel in the early years of the Soviet Union, female politicians are still primarily found in areas of "social housekeeping": They tend to participate in issues related to health, cultural affairs, public welfare, education, and marriage and family law. They do not take part in issues related to planning, the budget, or foreign policy. Females participate primarily at the local, not the national, level.

Women are also underrepresented in the membership of the Communist party. They constituted only 24.7 percent of the membership in 1977.[18] Party membership is an essential prerequisite to political advancement and for many high-level economic positions as well. The party has increased recruitment efforts among women in the last decade and membership did increase a few percentage points, but there have been no corresponding attempts to increase women's representation in the party leadership.

Women's marginal position in the political power structure is of primary importance in explaining the lack of attention given to women's needs by the Soviet leadership. Since the early feminist sector of the Communist party either was silenced or died out, there has been no powerful voice within the political elite to support women's interests. Thus policies have been aimed at using women as a resource but not at serving women or promoting women's causes.

The Domestic Sphere.   The absence or underrepresentation of women in the higher reaches of the economic and political spheres can be partially attributed to the continued existence of the domestic/public dichotomy. Women are not isolated in the domestic sphere and cut off from participation in the public sphere, but they still retain the burdens of the household and child care. The domestic sphere is still women's responsibility. Soviet men do not share domestic tasks with their wives on anything approaching an equal basis. Women provide the necessary backup services to allow their husbands to pursue education or training to improve their occupational status or participate in political work to improve their position in the party or government bureaucracy. Husbands do not take care of domestic tasks to free women for this type of after-work economic and political advancement. Women often prefer the less demanding, less responsible jobs with lower prestige, power, and pay because such jobs are less likely to interfere with family responsibilities. Sufficient services have been provided to allow women to work full time in the interests of the economy, but not enough services are provided to allow them the time to compete equally with men.

Outright discrimination continues to exist as well. Employers, politicians, and educators prefer not to hire or admit women. They believe women to be less reliable because of their domestic duties, especially pregnancy and child care. Because of this discrimination, women perceive the limits on their opportunities and invest less time, energy, and commitment to their jobs and educations and to politics. Since men have a better chance for advancement, women are willing to support their husbands' careers rather than their own. This in turn reinforces administrators' prejudices against women.

Women have been integrated into middle and lower levels of the economic sphere and into the lower levels of the political spheres, but at no time in Soviet history have men been integrated into the domestic sphere of housework and child care. This has been particularly burdensome because of the inadequate service sector. Shopping, for example, is a much more frustrating and time-consuming process in the Soviet Union than in the West. Shortages, long lines, discourteous clerks, and the necessity of going to several specialty shops instead of supermarkets have characterized Soviet shopping for decades.

Housing is also crowded and often substandard by Western standards. This makes upkeep more difficult. Few labor-saving devices have been available until recently and now that appliances are available the better off and better educated are the people who purchase them. Among poorer, less-educated couples, the husband usually judges it more important to spend the family's savings on a television than on a refrigerator or washing machine.

These problems exist on rural agricultural collectives as well as in urban areas. Even where collectivization has been extensive, peasant women still carry the primary responsibility for household tasks, and these tasks are still very time consuming. Household chores have not been shifted to the collective or shared by men to a significant degree. Furthermore, there is no ideological commitment to the ideal of shared roles in the household. Peasant women, like their urban counterparts, ease their burdens by having fewer children. They also work out informal sharing arrangements with other women for cooking and child care.[19]

Sex Ratios and Pronatalism. The Soviet Union has suffered a drastic shortage of men, beginning with the exceptionally high numbers of young men killed during World War II and continuing today with a significantly higher mortality rate for adult males than females.[20] This sex-ratio imbalance may have, as Guttentag and Secord suggest, exerted pressure toward more sexual permissiveness and economic independence for women. The divorce rate is very high, men take a somewhat exploitative attitude toward their sexual relationships with women, and the illegitimacy rate is high. Many women cannot marry. Marriage is a scarce resource coveted by women. This is seen in the importance Soviet women, unlike women in more gender-balanced communist societies, place on the status of being married, even though they often complain of brutish alcoholic husbands and a heavy work load in both the public and domestic spheres.[21]

In our country, official or civil marriage is considered a big step for a woman—perhaps the most important achievement in a woman's life, no matter how educated or independent she is and no matter how successful she has been in her profession. The stamp *married* in a passport confers innumerable social benefits, and, perhaps more important, Soviet women need this stamp for their own psychological sense of well-being, for their self-affirmation.[22]

The authorities have reacted to the demographic problems by trying to impose a marital and procreative imperative. Birth control is difficult to obtain and often ineffective. Abortions are available, but involve humiliating procedures, insensitive practitioners, and often inadequate medical facilities.[23] The intent seems to be to discourage women from seeking an abortion by making the experience as difficult as possible without creating the life-threatening situations that usually surround illegal abortions.

Women in European Russia, despite official policies, continue to limit their fertility. There is little the women can do to alleviate the burden of the household upkeep, but they can limit the amount of child care and the increased housework that comes from having many children. Abortions outnumber live births in some areas. Most women indicate that they would prefer to have two or three children but do not because of the money and time necessary to care for them. Birthrates remain high, however, among the heavily Moslem peoples of Soviet Asia. This is increasingly a source of anxiety for the Soviet leadership, who see it as a threat to the continued dominance of the Russian and other European ethnic groups.

The political leadership's concern over persistent labor shortages and the continued low birthrate has led to the adoption of an official pronatalist policy to reward women materially for motherhood. Policies aimed at supporting the "convenient social virtue" of motherhood, such as awarding medals to mothers of large families, did not work well. Allowances are now paid at the birth of each child and the payments are larger for second and third births than for first. No extra payments are given to mothers for fourth or more births. This is to avoid encouraging the traditional family practices and very high birthrates in Central Asian Moslem areas. Maternity leave is now partially paid for one year and small maintenance allowances are given to single mothers. There is also more political concern with upgrading the service sector, child-care facilities, and housing and arranging for both parents to have time off together for family vacations.[24]

Part-time work is also allowed now to some mothers.[25] Since productivity is higher, the loss of female labor seems preferable to the loss of potential citizens. Although it may fail to induce Soviet women to have more children, part-time work may help ease some of women's "double burden." But the experiences of women in the United States, Japan, and Sweden suggest that it might hinder the implementation of gender equality. If fathers stay in the labor force full time and mothers go to part-time work, this will provide adequate justification to fathers to resist any attempts to press them into service in the domestic sphere.

Child Rearing.   Children are very important to the Soviet people. Adults love their own and other peoples' children. They will give their seat on a crowded bus or subway to a child or pregnant woman and go out of their way to make sure a child alone on a street or in a park is not lost or in trouble. They may also stop to chastise the mother for not keeping a close watch on her child. Despite shortages in most consumer items, children's items are usually available.[26]

Parents have very long days of work, commuting, shopping, and political meetings, but they try to devote uninterrupted time to their children every evening if at all possible. The fact that almost all mothers work full time and fathers participate only minimally in child care and housework creates a heavy burden for women. The difficulties are compounded by such seemingly small matters as the lack of an adequate telephone system. For example, a working mother cannot check on her child by phone when he or she gets home from school; she cannot relay mes-

sages to the father or children if she is going to be late.[27]

Women take little time out of the labor force for childbirth, even though they do not lose seniority or all their pay. Time out hurts their chances for promotion and career advancement just as in the United States. Poorer couples often cannot afford any loss of the wife's income.

The government has had a strong ideological emphasis on collectivized care for infants and has made many infant nurseries available. But parents are very reluctant to use them before the child is three years old. Parents feel certain that it is not good for the child's health. Only 10 percent of the children under three were in nurseries in 1971.[28] Soviet people continue to feel strongly that a child belongs in a home environment during its first years.

Until recently, the problem was solved primarily through reliance on *babushkas*, which can be translated as either "grandmothers" or "elderly women." With the heavy loss of men in the wars, there has been an adequate supply of widows or unmarried older women willing to care for their grandchildren or the children of other relatives, friends or neighbors.[29] Retirement age is fifty-five for women and sixty for men. Women in low-level jobs will often retire at fifty-five and then turn to baby-sitting to supplement their pensions. Since Soviet people are not allowed to move about freely, the generations of a family may still live close by, so child care can be shared. Although it is not the desirable pattern, young couples may continue to live with their parents and turn domestic responsibilities, including care of young children, over to the grandmother.

But the supply of willing *babushkas* is dwindling.[30] The women of the better-educated classes particularly are unwilling to retire from their careers completely at fifty-five and take over responsibility for their grandchildren full time while their daughters work. Furthermore, by age fifty-five their grandchildren may no longer be preschoolers, and these women are certainly unwilling to give up their careers earlier. Given the distaste for early group child care, the increasing difficulty of finding *babushka* care may exert more pressure on women to stay out of the labor force for two or three years for the sake of the child.

Single parents have a particularly difficult time earning enough money and having sufficient time and energy to run a household and take care of a child. Some of these parents opt for the weekly boarding schools, seeing their children only on Saturday afternoons and Sundays.[31]

Education. Soviet parents have a great respect for education and place a great deal of importance on upward mobility through education for their children. This is true for girls as well as boys. Parents realize that girls will work all their adult lives and they desire good positions for their children of both genders. (They do still expect their daughters to have a child and to provide most of the care for it herself.) Females have even higher levels of educational attainment than males, but they are channeled away from the types of vocational training that would qualify them for the better jobs.[32]

Educational encouragement is true for the lower classes as well as the higher classes. But the higher classes have an unequal advantage in obtaining advanced education for their children. A university education is difficult to obtain and usually guarantees its possessor a good job and better life. (Also, it costs very little. Anyone who can gain entrance can afford the university.) But the children of the already well educated, the intelligentsia, have an advantage from the education they receive at home, from the tutors that better-paid parents hire, from the

political connections parents might have, and sometimes from the bribes their parents pay. Rural children are the most disadvantaged. The schools are substandard in rural areas. There are few well-educated people on the agricultural collectives. There are no university students to hire as tutors even if you have the money. And few rural people have political connections. The chances of rural children or the children of the urban poor to compete successfully on entrance exams or through the illegal entry network are much lower than for the children of the intelligentsia.[33]

Even after children have become adults, married, and have children of their own, parents continue to help with their support. They provide domestic help and often money as well. With the predominance of the one-child family, it is possible for even poorer people to spare something extra for their adult children—helping them buy an apartment, furniture, or even food.

Gender Role Stereotypes. Child rearing and children's education still embody traditional conceptions of gender roles. Girls are socialized toward "feminine" interests and occupations and boys toward "masculine" activities. In Soviet schools, girls but not boys are given home economics training. Traditional gender roles predominate in Soviet children's literature.[34] The effects of this gender role socialization show up very early in the occupational aspirations of boys and girls, and there is little reason to expect change in the near future. Soviet authorities and the public continue to believe that anatomy is destiny and that gender roles are embedded in the different biological natures of women and men. They see no reason to attempt to socialize girls and boys away from gender roles and traditional femininity and masculinity.

Lapidus concludes:

The central thrust of Soviet policy has been to superimpose new obligations of work and citizenship on more traditional definitions of femininity and to reshape to some extent the boundaries between public and family responsibilities—in short, to facilitate women's performance of both their roles—rather than to radically redefine both male and female roles.[35]

In fact, with increased affluence has come renewed emphasis on femininity for females. This is expressed through concern for feminine and stylish clothing available only through the black market, for cosmetics, and for work assignments and domestic appliances that preserve a woman's hands and complexion.

There is little or no support for feminism among most Soviet women today. One young divorced mother in love with a married man told a researcher that there was no women's movement. "We don't need a women's movement. Here we're all convinced that everything is the way it ought to be. But I think when women were emancipated, it actually amounted to man's liberation from the family."[36]

The Feminist Movement.   Women and men are not allowed free participation in feminist social movements in the USSR today. In 1979 a group of women attempted to build a woman's movement again. They began an illegal underground publication, *Women and Russia: An Almanac to Women About Women*, which discussed women's issues, rejected militarism, and supported peace. To their surprise most of the male dissidents, with the exception of Andrei Sakharov, rejected their positions on gender equality. The secret service harassed and finally arrested the editor, Tatyana Mamonova. She and three others were eventually exiled; others remain underground still trying to organize a women's movement.[37]

The status of women has improved significantly in comparison to their lot in the traditional agrarian society of prerevolutionary Russia. But the Soviet Union has not achieved gender equality or liberation for women. Furthermore, trends do not indicate that this is likely to change in the near future. There may be in fact a tendency to differentiate male and female roles further with an increasing emphasis on family life, motherhood, domesticity, and femininity for women, an increased gender segregation in the labor force as the service sector expands and absorbs more women workers, no real increase in political power or economic control for women, and only limited signs of feminist activity or ideology.

The Israeli Kibbutz

An alternative to the patterns of social organization and development in most modern industrial societies can be found in the planned communities of the Israeli kibbutzim.[38] The founders of the kibbutzim consciously rejected the class and gender stratification systems as they knew them in their home countries. Although Israel as a whole has never been a socialist society, the local kibbutz communities represent one of the most important and enduring attempts to put the collective ownership and communitarian institutions idealized in socialist theory into practice.

Aims and Development of the Kibbutzim

The first kibbutz was founded in 1909, but most kibbutzim were established in the twenties or later. They experienced an important surge of growth in the forties as

Jewish people fled the horrors of Europe before and after World War II. The first generation of settlers came primarily from Eastern Europe where anti-Semitism and pogroms (attacks on the Jewish communities) were common. They were radical young men and a few radical young women who refused to follow their parents' traditional life-style. They were no longer willing to submit to the tyranny of the Christian majority group. They rejected the culture and life of the urban ghetto and the *shtetl* (small Jewish town or village). They were imbued with the vision of a classless society based on socialist principles. Many of them were ardent admirers of the Russian Bolsheviks until it became clear that the Soviet revolution had failed to achieve many of its ideals. Although these young radicals were dedicated to founding a Jewish homeland, they were not religious. They saw Judaism as an ethnic identity and for the most part rejected it as a religion, and they did not want to found their new society on the hierarchical mode of organization embodied in the sacred Jewish writings. The founding generation spurned in particular the traditional patriarchal Jewish family structure. They accepted the principle of equality between the genders, even if this meant abolishing the family altogether.

These young socialist radicals were also devotees of the German youth movement, which idealized nature, and of Tolstoy's reverence for agricultural labor. They repudiated the urban life of European Jewry and the urban occupations of their fathers. Agricultural work was considered ennobling; it was believed that the rural life would bring out the best in human nature. Imbued with these principles, the pioneer generation settled in the inhospitable swamps and mountains of Palestine to found egalitarian communal societies, the kibbutzim.

To avoid the development of social classes, the settlers abolished private property. All property would be owned communally, and each person would contribute according to his or her skills and abilities and would receive according to his or her needs and the community's ability to provide. For the early pioneers the austerity of the life meant that everyone lived simply and worked very hard. The communities were too poor and the life was too harsh to support the very young, the elderly, or the physically unfit.

But the communities took hold and prospered. The farmlands and more recently the industries began to produce abundantly. The kibbutzim now have pleasant living quarters, good meals, better clothing, recreational facilities, medical centers, and educational facilities. They can afford to provide members with vacations and spending money for personal luxuries. They also send some of the young people to the universities for advanced training. But with this prosperity they have remained committed to their socialist ideals. Property and income are still owned by the kibbutz as a collective. Members who work outside the kibbutz contribute their salaries to the kibbutz treasury. Decisions concerning allocations are made through town-meeting-style deliberations and through elected committees. Each person's remuneration is unconnected to his or her work role, political office, or social status. No one is economically dependent on any other person. The kibbutz as a whole provides for the needs of the unproductive members such as the children, the elderly, and the infirm. Thus children are not dependent on their parents and wives are not dependent on their husbands. This principle was important both in avoiding the development of inherited wealth and privilege and breaking the power of the patriarchal father over his family.

In addition to economic equality, the kibbutz has continued to pursue political equality. Every kibbutz member has an equal right to participate in the decision-making process. Most decisions are made in the "town meeting" through group discussion, debate, and voting. Limited powers are vested in certain elected managerial offices, but to avoid the development of an entrenched bureaucracy that may accumulate power through its experience in organizing and overseeing activities, managerial positions are rotated. No one can serve a long term in office and leaders, although temporarily vested with more power than other members have, do not benefit materially from their positions. No special privileges and no deference practices are associated with office holding. The leader serves the community just as the agricultural laborer or the teacher serves it. However, agricultural work and leadership roles are more prestigious than other work.

The Socialization of Housework and the Kibbutz

The example of the Soviet Union has shown us that socialism by itself is insufficient for establishing gender equality. Margaret Benston has argued that "industrializing" housework is a necessary first step toward abolishing gender stratification.[39] According to Benston, women's domestic labor in the modern industrial world remains preindustrial, that is, it is small-scale, reduplicative, and kin-based production of use values. Work outside the household has, however, been industrialized. It is large-scale and nonreduplicative. (One large factory produces masses of clothes rather than large numbers of separate households each producing its own clothing.) Industrialized work is not organized on the basis of kinship ties and it is performed for a salary or profit rather than for simple use value.

In a society organized around market relationships as advanced industrial society is, especially capitalist societies, work is evaluated on the basis of its exchange value. A doctor is seen as being "worth more" than a garbage collector because he or she earns much more. Work that does not earn exchange value is therefore "worthless" under this system of valuation. Benston points out that women's domestic labor falls into this category of nonpaid and therefore worthless work. Thus when the full-time housewife is asked "Do you work?" she replies, "No, I'm just a housewife." This indicates that she does not see her work as real work.

Benston proposes that modern society industrialize housework as a step toward ending gender stratification. This would include a tremendous expansion of twenty-four-hour child-care facilities and a change in domestic architecture and organization to facilitate professionalized food processing, household maintenance, and laundry. In short, she argues that it is necessary to remove the bulk of household work and child care from the family or household setting just as we have removed most of our food, clothing, furniture, and tool production, educational and religious instruction, and recreation from the household. She believes, however, that this is not likely to occur in capitalist societies because it is more profitable to keep women doing these tasks in the household without direct compensation. Women's ties to domestic work also make them an easily exploitable reserve labor force for the business community to call out in times of labor shortage and return to the home without cost in times of labor surplus. Benston argues that a socialist setting would be more conducive to creating the institutional change she describes. But she does not believe that socialism will automatically result in these changes.

Benston's model has been introduced on a limited scale in Sweden with all its backup supports for child care and housekeeping. In conjunction with their full-employment policy and their policy of encouraging men into "feminine" roles, the Swedes have reduced the level of gender inequality somewhat. But the most progressive of the Israeli kibbutzim, out of ideological commitment as well as practical necessity, developed communitarian equivalents to Benston's "industrialized" housework that socialized child rearing and domestic labor to an extent as yet unknown in the rest of the modern world.

They aimed at impeding development of the patriarchal nuclear family, freeing women from the limitations of child rearing, freeing children from dependence on their families, and socializing children into the socialist or communal way of life. The communal child-rearing practices involved placing the infant, only a few days after its birth in an infants' house to be cared for by a professional staff. Mothers were encouraged to spend a great deal of time with the newborn and to breast-feed them. They were therefore given time off from their jobs for the first few weeks of the infant's life. But until recently, infants did not live with their parents. They slept in the infants' house at night, although parents were called if there were any problems. After a feeding schedule had been established, the mother returned to her usual job with time off to breast-feed. Fathers were expected to take a great interest in their children, but they were not given time off during the day to spend with them.

As children grow older they were moved from the infants' house to other age-graded houses where they lived with other children under the care of trained nurses. The work of child care, such as cleaning, feeding, and disciplining, was carried out by professionals. Parents, however, developed close emotional and affectional ties with their children. They spent several hours each evening in uninterrupted play with the children, and

mothers often visited the children's residences during the day as well. Parents were a source of constant love and indulgence.

The other domestic chores of the kibbutz were executed communally. Communal kitchens, dining halls, laundries, sewing and mending centers, and maintenance services took care of the usual housekeeping chores. These jobs were filled either by trained permanent workers or by rotation for jobs considered onerous or boring. The family was not important as a consumption or production unit or even as a private child-care unit. These usual family functions were removed from the household to the community.

Despite the undeniable achievements of the unprecedented historical experiment of the kibbutz in the socialization of child rearing and domestic labor, the experiment itself has in recent years experienced significant modifications of many of its more celebrated features. What appear to be reversions to more conventional forms of familism and gender roles have been noted and documented by a number of researchers. Moreover, it is quite clear that even during the period when the collectivist approach to child rearing and domestic labor was most fully implemented, it did not create full gender equality either structurally or ideologically. Why has the experiment turned out this way? In the following sections we will discuss contrasting approaches to answering this question.

The Woman Problem: Sociobiological and Precultural Explanations

The kibbutz movement has been successful in fulfilling its ideals of abolishing class inequality and competition; it successfully established communal housekeeping and a child-care system that produced healthy, well-adjusted children and adults; it has been successful in its rural life-style. It has not, however, been successful in establishing gender equality or in abolishing gender differentiation in social roles and social participation. The kibbutzim have instead been plagued for years by what they call the "woman problem." Men are more satisfied as kibbutz members than women are, and women are more likely than men to want to leave the kibbutz. When couples do leave, it is usually at the insistence of the wife. Women are also more likely than men to oppose kibbutz principles regarding the family structure. In recent years women have agitated for more "feminine prerogatives," in particular for the right to keep their children in their apartments overnight. In all but the most radical federation of kibbutzim, women have been successful in their demand to reinstate the nuclear family. Children live with their parents and go to the children's houses only during the day. Apartments are larger and more housework is done in the nuclear family setting.

When it has succeeded in solving other difficult problems related to establishing an egalitarian society, why has the kibbutz movement failed to implement its ideology in the area of gender equality?

Sociobiologists, who argue on the basis of Darwinian theories of natural selection and evolution that gender roles and gender stratification are biologically determined, have viewed the lack of true gender equality on the kibbutz as support of the biological basis of traditional gender roles and gender stratification. Tiger and Fox have argued that male dominance and strong maternal/child bonds are part of our genetic heritage because they supposedly contributed to the survival of the species under primitive prehistoric conditions.[40] They argue that human beings possess a "biogrammar" that predisposes them toward traditional gender roles. Shepher's research on the kibbutz seemed

to support this perspective.[41] He and Tiger have further developed this view.[42]

They maintain that the reemergence of the gender division of labor, women's exclusion from the productive sphere and leadership positions, women's exclusive participation in child care and early education and kitchen and laundry work, and women's demands for more familistic living and child-rearing practices are the result of biological propensities. Drawing on more recent sociobiological work based on research on birds, they now argue that the key factor is the assymmetry of the parental investment in children.[43] Women invest much more in the reproductive process and in child rearing than men do. This frees men to do more in the political and productive spheres and focuses women's attention on domestic tasks, which can be undertaken near the children.

It is possible to delegate the burdens of child care to someone other than the biological mother; they call this *allomothering*. But this goes against the usual biological predisposition of mothers. They have already invested nine months in the child. They do not want to endanger that investment by trusting someone else to care for the child. Under the extreme conditions of the early kibbutz—the economic hardships, defense problems, and the ideological fervor of the founding generation—the motivation was strong enough to invest parental responsibility in the collective. But this situation is inherently unstable, it goes against biology, and the predispositions soon reemerge as these social pressures lessened. Shepher and Tiger state that it was the women who insisted on the *reindividuation of the parental investment*. Men, with a naturally weak bond with children, resisted, retaining their commitment to the communal ideology. The men relented, however, and allowed their wives to tie them more closely to the nuclear family. The wives took over the new household and child-care tasks and kept their jobs in the world of work. This overburdened them to such a degree that their husbands began sharing some of the tasks. In such a way women create bonds of solidarity with men and commit men to protecting and providing for the women and children. Economic dependency is removed in the communal setting, but women are still predisposed to forging bonds with men. This "biogrammar" supposedly evolved with the species and became a part of our genetic inheritance.

Melford Spiro has developed a similar explanation of gender differentiation on the kibbutz, but he avoids identifying directly with the controversial sociobiologists.[44] He prefers to refer to his theory as *psychobiological* and to use the term *precultural motives* instead of *biological predisposition*. According to Spiro, the maternal nurturing role and the male disposition to act in the public sphere are precultural; that is, they do not depend on socialization or culture. Human beings will usually establish these patterns even if they are not socialized into them.

Spiro views the second-generation kibbutzniks, the sabras, as exemplifying these precultural patterns of gender behavior. The sabras were not exposed to any of the traditional gender role socialization; in fact, they were overtly discouraged from these patterns. Yet they have embraced these roles of their own accord and demanded changes in the kibbutz practices to allow for the female domestic and service roles and the male production and leadership roles. The first generation was able to repress this "precultural motive" temporarily because of special circumstances. But the repression could not be sustained in the second generation. Spiro argues, however, that this does not constitute real gender inequality. He takes a "separate-but-equal" stance and argues that the feminine role has a "status equivalence" with the masculine role even though women

and men operate within and control very different spheres of kibbutz life. The equivalence argument is especially hard to accept in view of the fact that the kibbutz has never given work in the domestic sphere or the service industry the respect it accords agricultural, planning, or defense work. People are not paid differently for their different contributions, but the types of work retain a very male-oriented ranking system with the "feminine" domain clearly devalued.

The Woman Problem: Historical and Socio-cultural Perspectives

Both the sociobiological and precultural explanations miss important features of the historical development of the kibbutz. They have uncritically accepted the ideological postures of the kibbutz without investigating the reality behind these public images of kibbutz life.

These authors assume that the kibbutz began with as strong a commitment to gender equality as they did to the other tenents of their ideology, that they worked as hard to establish gender equality as they did to abolish private property and competition and failed only in this one area because they were fighting nature, not culture. This is not the case.[45] Early kibbutzniks talked a lot about gender equality but showed little commitment to putting it into practice. Problems associated with establishing gender equality were not subjected to the same intense public debate as were other problems; organization and structural changes requiring the integration of men and women in the different areas were never voted on or put into practice.

Gender Roles in the Pioneer Stage. For the pioneers life was hard. Having grown up in urban environments, they knew little about farming. But they persevered, living in tents and eating the most meager of food. Most were males and many resisted allowing females to join them. A few women insisted and were admitted, but even with the undeveloped domestic sphere of these rugged camps, women were usually assigned cooking and laundry tasks. A few worked alongside the men in heavy physical labor, but the men felt it was unseemly and made them look bad as "men." With the constant threat of attack from their hostile Arab neighbors, women helped with defense too. There was little distinction between domestic and public or between front and rear military lines. Women shared guard duty and shouldered rifles in defense of their new homes along with the men. But when the men went out on attacks, they usually insisted that the women remain behind.

The Second Stage of Institutionalization. Rae Lesser Blumberg suggests that the kibbutzim lost much of their revolutionary zeal as they succeeded in taming the land and establishing themselves as viable communities and economic enterprises.[46] They became dedicated to goals of efficiency. The ideal of efficiency added further support to discrimination against women in the agricultural sphere, because although women could do the same work as men, they could not always do it as quickly or combine it easily with pregnancy and lactation.

It was at this stage that the kibbutz could afford a second generation. Despite their communal ideology, the early kibbutzniks initially had no theoretical design to deal with the problems of child rearing and child care on a gender egalitarian basis. The first mothers were left to solve the problems of combining work and child care on their own. Men never entertained the notion that they would have to change their lives. Women were, sometimes reluctantly, allowed to adopt some of the masculine roles, but men were not expected to take on the feminine

roles. Male kibbutzniks had brought very traditional ideas of the gender division of labor with them to the new societies. Egalitarian ideals as well as material necessity eventually led to the development of communal child-rearing practices and the industrialization of domestic tasks but the traditional ideas continued to exercise an important influence.

Freudian psychoanalytic theory had also made an important impact on kibbutz child-rearing ideology. In particular, psychoanalysis led to an emphasis on breast-feeding. New mothers were expected to breast-feed and to devote several hours a day to their infants. The paternal-child bond did not receive attention analogous to the maternal-child bond. This interfered even further with women's agricultural contribution relative to men's. The fields are usually located some distance from the residential community, thus requiring mothers to walk many miles through the hot sun to attend to both their children and to agricultural work. Most mothers responded to these difficulties of combining field labor with child care by transferring into occupations located closer to the children's houses.[47]

The demand for labor continued to be high in the kibbutz. The need for their labor kept women in the fields during the pioneer stage. But in the second stage an important new source of labor was available through immigration. The immigrants were predominantly young childless males who were attracted to the kibbutz ideology and the ideal of an agricultural commune. They did not come to the kibbutz to care for children or to cook, clean, or to do dishes; they came to labor in the fields. Blumberg argues that it was so important to attract and maintain the commitment of these young men that kibbutz seniority rules were violated to place them in the "glamour sector" of agriculture.[48] The dedication of the pioneer mothers was strong enough that they could be assigned the domestic chores with little fear of their defection.

This was also the period of rapid expansion in the service industries. Children's houses were established, residences were built and enlarged, and kitchens and laundries were built. All of this required a staff that was drawn almost exclusively from females. Thus the gender-segregated division of labor between the domestic sphere and the public sphere was never broken. As soon as domestic tasks were necessary on a large scale, they were assigned to women.

Even though the service sector expanded in importance in the life of the community, its importance was not recognized in the ideology or the prestige system. Agricultural work continued to be idealized. The kibbutz bookkeeping methods reflected this ideology and reinforced the prestige and importance of agricultural work. Blumberg points out that the kibbutz members, as subscribers to Marx's labor theory of value, considered labor hours as the only valid measure of productivity and efficiency. The only cost they considered in computing the relative efficiency of different sectors was the number of labor hours expended versus the return. They did not include the cost of capital investment or land in their calculations. This made agricultural production appear much more productive than other areas of production, because the large costs of capital investment and land were not considered. By contrast, the more labor-intensive horticultural gardens worked by the women near the settlements looked inefficient. They required a great many labor hours but little capital or land. On the basis of their labor theory of value bookkeeping, the kibbutz decided to abandon the horticultural mode of farming.

The service sector, the dairy, and the poultry sectors staffed primarily by women were also judged to be less important than agriculture. The dairy and chicken farms used up more work hours relative to profit than field cultivation. The service sector, of course, produced no profit at all. Workers in these areas were judged less important and the kibbutz was less willing to allocate money for improvements in these areas. Capital was channeled into advanced technology for agriculture while the women labored under primitive conditions in the kitchens and laundries. The lack of prestige combined with poor working conditions further decreased women's satisfaction with and commitment to the kibbutz. The men reaped most of the benefits of kibbutz life.

The prestige differential between the male-dominated agricultural sector and the female-dominated service sector also served to undermine political equality. The kibbutz still accords equal rights to all members, and each member has an equal right to take part in political discussion and debate. But the general feeling is that those who actively participate in and have expertise in a particular area are the appropriate discussants. Thus matters concerning new investments in agriculture are debated almost exclusively among the male agricultural workers. Policy regarding the children's houses or kitchens is debated by women. Yet the most serious decisions, especially about economic allocations, are likely to involve agriculture rather than services. Thus these norms effectively exclude women from political participation in the most important decisions. Furthermore, a great deal of decision-making authority is vested in the economic committees that organize and run each sector. Again, the most important committee is the one for the agricultural sector and women rarely hold office in it. The prestige of this committee and of agriculture in general gives it workers an edge in running for other kibbutz offices. The general management of the kibbutz is predominantly male.

A further factor contributing to the failure of gender egalitarianism in the kibbutz is the wider social, political, and cultural environment in Israel and the international setting. As noted above, Freudian psychoanalysis with its traditional subordinate role for women influenced the kibbutz for several decades. The decline and almost total disappearance of feminism around the world from the twenties through the sixties undermined kibbutz support for feminist goals. The founding of the state of Israel in 1948 brought a great many traditional, conservative Jews to the area. Middle Eastern Jews and Orthodox Jews from Eastern Europe brought with them patriarchal family structures and a firm commitment to male dominance and female subordination.

These groups had an impact on the Israeli nation. The state was based on the Jewish religion and rabbinical law, which the kibbutz movement had rejected. The kibbutz members now found themselves bound to a legal structure that often incorporated rabbinical law into secular law. For example, Israel recognizes only religious marriage ceremonies and restricts the legal rights of illegitimate children. The kibbutz had rejected religious marriage and divorce in favor of free consensual unions entered into whenever a couple decided to move into shared quarters and dissolved when they decided to separate. Traditional marriage was believed to demean women and to embody female subordination. Under Israeli law, however, kibbutzniks must undergo the religious marriage ceremony to protect the rights of their children. This serves to emphasize the couple and the family as a unit instead of the individual and the community. Such practices have at least a subtle effect on the gender roles of the kibbutz.

The Threat of War. Another factor in the wider environment of the kibbutz that has negatively affected the position of women has been the impact of war and the constant threat of war. In the years of struggle preceding the founding of the Israeli state, females often participated in combat duties. Several female soldiers are national heroines. Today females continue to serve in the Israeli army and are subject to the draft just as males are but they are not given combat training; they do not serve as long as men do; and there are many more exceptions for females such as marriage, pregnancy, or orthodox religious beliefs.[49] Females are given clerical jobs and other noncombatant tasks which free men for combat. Female soldiers are also given lessons in beauty "to improve the morale of the men," emphasizing their role as sex objects.[50]

These practices apply to kibbutz members as well as to other Israeli citizens. Thus kibbutzniks are placed at the age of eighteen into the highly gender-segregated military setting and are introduced to the male dominant values that underly it. A great deal of prestige accrues to the brave fighting man who defends his country. Women are not so honored for their contributions to the war effort. Kibbutz males have been especially prominent in the elite corps and among the lists of war heroes and war casualties. This has increased their prestige within the kibbutz as well as outside it and given males a further advantage over females.

The constant threat of war has also led to an increased emphasis on the maternal role for women. Throughout Israel, including on the kibbutz, mothers of sons in combat are expected to play important supportive roles for their sons. They are to keep in close touch with their soldier sons and provide emotional support in their letters and telephone calls. They should send food packages and other homemade luxuries to comfort the soldiers. They should also follow the war-related news closely as a demonstration of their concern for their sons' welfare. Again, this serves to emphasize male importance in society and females as supporters of the more important males.

Fear of being "outreproduced" by the Arabs increases the pressures on Israeli women to marry early and to have many children. A pregnant woman may be congratulated for producing another "little soldier" for the nation.[51] One second generation kibbutz woman expressed her discontent with this aspect of woman's place:

Women are so helpless and frustrated here that they can hardly see their situation with the proper perspective anymore. The situation is explained by the fact that everyone wants to have many children here. . . . Women breed babies and then, of course, they have to take care of them: it's a cycle that traps them all. . . . I simply couldn't stand it.[52]

The war threat increased the emphasis on the maternal role and the family in another way as well. It led many parents, especially mothers, to insist on keeping their children in their own quarters at night.[53] In response to the tensions engendered by terrorist raids, parents often felt more secure with their children nearby when in fact taking the children from the children's houses made their collective protection more difficult. The wartime situation exacerbated the trend for second- and third-generation kibbutz women to demand greater maternal involvement. But this increased the emphasis on the family unit at the expense of collectivity and contributed to an increased emphasis on women's familial roles at the expense of public roles.

The Experiment That Never Took Place. From the beginning women were assumed to be "naturals" in the laundries and kitchens, and after the children arrived, in the nurseries and schools as well. With the increased birthrate, this work eventually required half the labor of the kibbutz, and as men would not enter such work, women were drawn from what few agricultural and productive work assignments they had. A rigid gender division of labor was the result of men never relinquishing the traditional male role.

"Precultural motives" and "biogrammars" did not force them to abandon gender equality; the kibbutz had never rejected traditional gender roles, nor had they ever really established gender equality. A popular image of the kibbutz as gender egalitarian developed and that image blinded people to the realities of kibbutz life.[54] Kibbutz life does not constitute an experiment in gender equality and dedifferentiation that failed so much as an experiment that never took place.

Furthermore, kibbutz children were not socialized in a unisex or gender-role-free environment as these theorists assume. A moderate acceptance of traditional gender roles always remained even at the ideological level. But more important from the standpoint of both social learning theory,[55] which emphasizes the importance of role models and imitation in gender role acquisition, and of cognitive development theory,[56] which focuses on the child perceiving patterns around him or her and using these patterns to construct a coherent view of the world and the child's place in that world, the children are raised in the domestic sphere by women. The men are away at work in the public sphere and spend very little time with children. This is a crucial part of the socialization process of kibbutz children and has been from the births of the first kibbutz babies.[57] Sabras do not therefore serve as a test case of children raised without gender roles who turn to gender roles naturally without the direction of cultural forces.

The extent of the socialization of children into traditional roles is also clear in the practice of giving high school boys work assignments only in the productive spheres and girls assignments only in the children's houses. Educators who have attempted to reverse this pattern and mix up the assignments were prevented from doing so by the work foremen who refused to accept girls.[58] These early work assignments are very important for adult occupations. The training received during the work assignments is a primary consideration for career patterns after the young men and women return from their compulsory military service. Women's prior compulsory experience in the children's houses keeps them assigned to domestic and service tasks while males' previous experience in the productive sphere is the ostensible reason for giving them full-time adult assignments in the same area.[59] Occupational choice and training opportunities are actually lower for kibbutz women than for other Israeli women or for Western women. The degree of gender segregation in the labor force is one of the highest in the world. One woman complained, "I didn't want to be a child-care worker, but I am one . . . the people here are very narrow minded. When you are younger, you are working with children, and then in the kitchen, and when you are older—in the clothes' care, laundry, and sewing . . ."[60]

Shepher and Tiger's assertion that women forced traditional gender roles on reluctant males who eagerly supported gender role equality and the dedifferentiation of the genders is incorrect. The men had never been committed to abolishing traditional gender roles; they only resisted the women's turning away from the system of female-run cooperative child-care arrangements which had become an accepted principle of kibbutz life, which as Blasi points out, is hardly a sufficient basis for female liberation.

Dead-end Jobs.   As Rosabeth Moss Kanter has found, women and men in low-mobility, routine, dead-end jobs, "the stuck," react in

typical ways.[61] They cease to be ambitious and striving. They turn their interests to family, friends, hobbies, or relationships with coworkers. The social aspects of the job come to be preeminent. Although Kanter was describing reactions to being "stuck" in a large, competitive, profit-oriented corporation, her analysis may apply equally to kibbutz women.

These women are blocked by the structural barriers of gender-based training and work assignments from advancement to the prestigious leadership and productive sectors of the kibbutz. Young kibbutz women are described as reacting to their lack of opportunity with resignation and withdrawal and with more symptoms of emotional and personal problems than nonkibbutz girls.[62] It is not surprising that they seek to make as comfortable an environment as possible in the service and domestic sector. This includes an emphasis on the emotional benefits of closer attachments to children and the social relationships of private family life.

Since the men are not as likely to be stuck, they are less likely to resist the kibbutz communal child-care and minimalized family practices. But little research has been conducted on kibbutz men. Men who are stuck may be making similar accommodations to their situation. In the corporation men and women responded similarly to dead-end career lines.

Sex Ratios, Industrialization, and Gender Equality.   Numbers or demographics can be an important force in human life. Kanter also points out that members of the minority group in skewed or imbalanced mixed groups have a difficult time being recognized as competent full-fledged members of the group. If they try to take active or leadership roles, they are likely to be seen as "uppity" and threatening; if they use low-key strategies, they are likely to be ignored altogether. On the kibbutz women have always been in the distinct minority. In the early days there were very few women and even fewer participated in the male work groups. This may also account for women's lack of success in and withdrawal from these male-dominated spheres.[63]

In addition, according to Guttentag and Secord's theory, such a shortage of women would have created a strong force in support of traditional gender roles. The description of the emergence of gender role differentiation in the kibbutz as life became more settled and children were born in larger numbers sounds exactly like Guttentag and Secord's description of a high-sex-ratio society. Shepher and Tiger note that the following appeared—"the romantic love complex, early dating and early sex life of the young females, early marriage, great formal ceremonialism of the wedding, stability of the marriage, descending divorce rates, ascending marriage rates, almost unbearable social status of singles, especially of females in the age of fertility, institutionalized and informal matching for singles, and rising fertility rates reaching a new modal average of four children per couple" and a much stronger commitment of males to women and the family.[64]

Without resorting to a biogrammar, Guttentag and Secord have argued in the case of other societies that the scarcity of females combined with male control of structural power leads men to compete for females—the scarce resource—and to protect their successful "catch" by emphasizing romantic love and the domestic rather than public roles of women. Women are viewed as more vulnerable and in need of male protection. The kibbutz has avoided the Victorian extremes of such a position, but within the context of its radical ideology, it has accepted the view that women are much weaker than men and more fit for the more routine, less-demanding tasks of the domestic and service sectors. Simultaneously with devaluing such work in other ways, the kibbutz idealizes the work in the children's house as "sacred."[65] It may not be exactly the same as the cult of true motherhood, but it is a form of idealized communal motherhood and not fatherhood.

The exceptionally high birthrate in the contemporary kibbutz keeps women involved with pregnancy, lactation, and the demands of early child care (even though greatly reduced by communal facilities) for relatively long periods of their lives compared with women in other developed societies. But this high birthrate is stabilizing the kibbutz population. Kibbutzim do not have to rely so heavily on the predominantly male immigrants. Consequently, the sex ratios are becoming more balanced. This may bode well for future advances in establishing gender equality. The kibbutz ideology lends itself to supporting gender equality, and the social structure is probably more adaptable than that of most societies to such change. If the pressures created by high sex ratios and the need for a high birthrate lessen, perhaps the discontent of women with their double burdens will become a more viable political force for social change in the direction of greater equality instead of the current move toward greater privatization for a four-child family.

The kibbutz has also entered a third stage of development. Recent increased involvement in industrial production may help bring women back into the productive sector. Industrialization and automation have been more fully implemented in the service sector, freeing many women from these jobs. Automation has also eliminated some of the work in the kitchens and laundries which women found particularly oppressive. Industrialization has also created more opportunities for women to engage in profitable labor. Blumberg notes that kibbutz industry is more profitable than agriculture and that profitability lends the work and workers prestige in the kibbutz.[66] According to Blumberg, if the kibbutz can keep industry gender integrated and avoid developing a pattern of male managers and higher-level technical staff and female factory operatives, there may be a rise in gender egalitarianism.

Another factor promoting greater gender equality is the rebirth of the international feminist movement. The new wave of feminism affects the kibbutz just as the demise of feminism hampered gender egalitarianism on the kibbutz in the twenties. The feminist movement in Israel is still small, but it does provide women with an explanation for their frustration and an ideological basis for resisting male dominance. But this may be offset by the increased numbers of more conservative oriental Jews and the power of the religious parties they support. Orthodox Jewish law is being applied to ever more areas of Israeli life, constricting the lives of nonobservant Jewish women on the kibbutz as well as in the rest of the country.[67]

The People's Republic of China

The development of socialism in China has followed a very different path from that in the Soviet Union or the kibbutz.[68] Both the USSR and the kibbutzim faced difficult if not desperate settings for putting their ideals into practice. But when the Chinese Communist Party (CCP) came to power in 1949 it faced what was perhaps an even bleaker situation. Centuries of agrarian depotism, followed by colonial domination by Western powers and the Japanese, the destruction of World War II, and the ravages of the civil war left a massive population; backward, crippled agriculture and industry; and mammoth social problems, not the least of which

was widespread famine. Despite the limitations of the authoritarian society the CCP has constructed, the gains in economic well-being and personal security are vivid to the majority of the population, particularly to those who lived under preliberation conditions.

Historical Background

Before about the eighth century, China was a feudalistic agrarian society. Powerful warlords were able to bring the regional lords under their control and centralize the government under a series of dynastic imperial lineages, which ruled through an elaborate bureaucracy of literati. The literati were scholars of classical Confucian thought who had passed through a rigidly hierarchical and demanding education and examination system. Only the well-to-do could afford a classical education for their sons, but the positions were not hereditary so some possibility existed for upward mobility into the ruling elite. The literati also gained access to land, the important economic resource in an agrarian economy, and as scholar-gentry forged strong links with the local landed gentry classes.

The bulk of the population were peasants who worked fragmented plots of land as owners, renters, or day laborers, or in some combination of the three. Depending on the amount of land they controlled, peasants could be quite comfortable or desperately poor. But in an agrarian society they held a higher social status than the merchants. The merchant class was disdained for its occupation; but those who became wealthy could gain entrance to the landed gentry through land purchases and intermarriage and could sometimes educate a son into the official bureaucracy. At the bottom of this extremely hierarchical and oppressive social structure were the slaves and degraded or pariah classes, who worked in unclean occupations including entertainment and prostitution.

Confucianism. Confucian religious principles provided the ideological basis for the political, economic, and kinship structure of China. It permeated the fabric of social life prescribing strict obedience to the emperor and his official representatives, to one's lord, to one's father, and for women to their husbands and later their sons. The duty of *filial piety* encompassed all these relationships and constituted the backbone of Confucian morality. The head of the patrilineage ruled over his sons, wives, concubines, daughters-in-law, unmarried daughters, and servants just as the emperor ruled over his subjects. There was no room for a concept of individuality under such a system. In fact, the Chinese language had no words for individual, individualism, or freedom until Western penetration. The individual was embedded in the lineage or clan.[69]

Women occupied a very subordinate position in the Confucian world view and in the patriarchal kinship system it enshrined. Daughters were merely a drain on their natal families. They had to be fed, cared for, and provided with a dowry in keeping with the family's social standing. Families so disdained their daughters that they often gave them insulting names such as "Little Useless One."

The Position of Women

Female infanticide produced a shortage of marriageable girls. The shortage was compounded by well-off men conspicuously consuming women through polygyny and concubinage and enjoying the services of prostitutes, who were then too degraded for marriage. Marriage was highly valued under such a sex-ratio imbalance. The poorest males were dishonored by not being able to marry at all. Marriage constituted an exchange of women between lineages, an economic bargain entered into by the two families, with no consideration to romantic love or the views of the individuals to be married. Girls were married at a young age often to much older men. Wives were secluded to whatever extent the family could afford. The domestic sphere was ideally the innermost compartments of the house. The emperors' women were never to come in contact with males, and their guards were eunuchs.

Families considered the daughter's dowry a loss to the family, but the elaborate weddings and brideprices paid for their sons' brides were considered the high point of the father's life. Peasants would sometimes ruin themselves with debt to marry an eldest son. The marriage of an eldest son and the sons that marriage would provide meant the lineage would continue. A peaceful afterlife depended on the maintenance of ancestor veneration rituals by one's descendants. Filial piety required that nothing be spared in ensuring the continuation of the lineage. (The other occasion for ruinous debt in the service of conspicuous consumption was funeral ceremonies for one's father and sometimes one's mother, especially if she had demonstrated fidelity as a chaste widow.)

The new daughter-in-law was in a very difficult position. She almost always came from a family of lower social standing (in periods of female shortage females marry up socially), increasing her inferiority to her in-laws. She had been carefully segregated from contact with males since childhood, so her knowledge of sexuality was very limited. The wedding night was often traumatic for these young girls. Her natal family relinquished all rights over her, so she could not turn to them to protect her when she was mistreated. Mistreatment was very common and even expected, especially before she bore a healthy son and demonstrated that she was worth her brideprice. Suicide rates were higher for women than for men in all age groups, but young daughters-in-law had the highest rates of all. It was often the only means of escape from an intolerable situation.

The young married woman was under the total domination of her often cruel mother-in-law and was often in a strained relationship with her sisters-in-law too. No affection was expected between husbands and wives, particularly during the first years of marriage. The husband's duty was to his parents, not his wife. It was considered very poor taste for husband and wife to interact any more than absolutely necessary in front of the other members of the household. The only persons a wife could be truly affectionate with were her children, and mothers tied their children, especially their sons, as closely to them as possible. Obedient and loyal sons were a woman's primary source of protection.

The patriarch of the family had the right of life and death over the members of his household. He could even legitimately rape his daughters-in-law. The joint family with the father presiding over all his sons and their wives and children was the ideal, although the poorer people could not afford it and sent excess sons to find work elsewhere if this was at all possible. The daughter-in-law was an outsider in this strong fraternal interest group. She had no bargaining resources except her beauty and personal wits. Some women used their personal resources to become very influential in their families and, if their families were politically powerful, in the public arena as well. But they had no legitimate right to participate in decision making in the family or in society.

The constrained position of women in traditional China is probably best symbolized by the debilitating, painful, and life-threatening cosmetic practice of *footbinding*. Beginning in childhood, the girl's feet would be tightly bound with the toes turned under, preventing the feet from growing and forcing them into what were considered appealing shapes. These hideously deformed feet would be clad in elaborately embroidered slippers. Bound feet began among the ruling class in the tenth century, but the practice quickly spread to almost all sectors of Chinese society. Since girls could expect to be married into a higher-status lineage, parents were concerned with making the best deal possible. Mothers wanted their daughter to have as good a life as possible, and much depended on her beauty. When bound feet increased her value in the marriage, parents eagerly adopted the practice.

An adult woman would hobble along on torturously shaped feet three inches long. But this walk was seen as very attractive to men. Women worked in the fields and households despite this severe handicap. Footbinding was outlawed in 1902 after contact with the more technologically advanced West brought it into disfavor among some of the elite. During the early decades of the twentieth century, it came under attack by antifootbinding movements which met with success in the cities. But the practice was not halted among the bulk of the population until the Communists launched a major campaign against it in the early fifties when they came to power.

Decline of Imperial China. Each of the various dynasties that ruled China eventually experienced decline and was overthrown and replaced by a new, more vigorous clan. But the decline experienced in the nineteenth century did not result in a new clan coming to power. Imperialistic domination by foreigners combined with crushing internal problems led to an end of the imperial system. The British victory in the Opium War in the mid-nineteenth century and the Japanese victory over China in 1895 shattered imperial faith in the classical Confucian-scholar bureaucracy.

Rapid modernization was undertaken in an attempt to catch up with these powerful barbarians. The examination system was abolished, modern education was introduced, the Confucian basis of the social order was challenged. This was all very disrupting to the society and did not result in China catching up with the West or Japan. Instead, the decline and disorder deepened. By 1911 the ruling Manchu dynasty fell to the Republican revolution, but the Republicans failed to establish a strong central government to take its place. Local warlords of various political persuasions competed for local and regional power.

Modernization, including feminist movements, was underway in the cities, but the rural areas simply suffered internal warfare and massive poverty and disruption. Women and men participated in the political and social movements of the postimperial period. Consistent with their rejection of the traditional political order was a rejection of the Confucian family and gender system that underlay it. Abolishing age and gender stratification was part of the ideology of abolishing traditional patriarchal rule.

Out of this political chaos the National Party (Kuomintang) or KMT, and the Chinese Communist Party of CCP emerged as power centers in the cities. They formed an alliance between 1923 and 1927, but when the KMT felt strong enough in its urban base it purged its allies, dispersing the CCP to the distant rural hinterland. Feminists, easily identified by their bobbed hair, came under particular attack. Many were raped, murdered, or mutilated. The terror against modern women was a severe blow to the women's movement. Relatively few survived to accompany the men on the retreat to the countryside.

The Communist Revolution

After their purge by the KMT, the communists were forced to abandon their Marxist-Leninist focus on the urban working classes. They turned their attention to the peasantry and reworked their program to fit the requirements of a peasant revolution. This required that they tolerate many aspects of the traditional patriarchal peasant social structure and culture. The communist respect for local norms led the men to act in terms of male dominance and to cast their women into subordinate roles. When the women protested, they were told it was necessary for the cause. Problems of gender stratification were considered secondary to those of class struggle, and that continues to be true today.

In winning the peasantry over to the revolutionary cause, the Communists had to demonstrate that their vision of a new social order would benefit the peasants. What the peasant male wanted most was land, which would provide him the opportunity to found and maintain a lineage. If the Communists supported a drastic restructuring of the family and kinship to undermine the patriarchal lineage system, the peasants would not have supported them. So the CCP embraced the patriarchal family but cut it off from much of its Confucian base, ridding it, for example, of its requirement of obedience to landlords.

Land reform was the cornerstone of the Communist program, which they handled masterfully. They encouraged the peasants to turn against the parasitic landlords, but did not take the land from small holders. The peasants for the most part responded enthusiastically to land reform and the Mutual Aid Teams that were established as a forerunner to the later collectivized agriculture.

With land the peasant male could marry. The poverty and desperation of the previous decades of disruption had severely undermined the peasant family. Family rituals had been abandoned. Children were sold as concubines, prostitutes, and slaves. There were some cases of cannibalism among starving families. The policies of the CCP allowed families to return to the patriarchal structure they desired. As Judith Stacey has analyzed so well, what the CCP did was to democratize the patriarchal family.[70] They made it available to almost all men instead of to the privileged few. They did not liberate women from its domination, for that would have earned them the enmity of the fiercely patriarchal males and meant disaster for the CCP. The women did not gain equality, but their lives were so much improved by the economic and political security provided by the party that they did not argue for more. Peasant women had no involvement with feminism; they had no vision of gender equality to influence their demands. The rural base of the CCP, then, hindered the development of any strong policy of gender equality.

The Red Army was very disciplined and respectful of the peasantry on whom it depended. The soldiers tried to produce their own food without relying excessively on peasant labor or products. Significantly, they did not violate peasant women. The KMT soldiers, by contrast, were themselves recruited forcibly and brutalized in the army. One of their rewards for service was the looting and raping of the local populations. They were feared and hated by the people, while the Communists were welcome saviors. The Red Army gained further support by defending the peasantry against the Japanese and eventually defeating them. In 1949 the CCP was strong enough to militarily defeat the KMT and to return to the cities from its rural base.

The People's Republic of China

The Peasantry. The CCP immediately undertook land reform programs nationwide, encouraging the peasants to turn on their landlords. The family economy was restored as the basis of the rural economy. Family production and consumption units with the traditional gender division of labor were an accepted part of the Communist program. Women were accorded a much higher legal status, and a great deal of ideological lip service was paid to the liberating effects of the new society on women. But gender stratification was not undermined. Land was distributed to the head of the family on the basis of the number of dependents in the family he ruled. Individual members earned work points that were credited to the family unit. Women were given much lower work points than men for a day's work, and work done primarily by women was rated lower in work points than work done primarily by men. Women retained full responsibility for the domestic sphere. Families continued to have their own gardens, tools, and small livestock, further strengthening the family economy.

Arranged marriages were banned as were brideprices and dowries and child betrothal. But all these laws continued to be violated as the father retained the control over the family economy and the family members. Young women continued blindly to enter patrilocal, patrilineal marriages as outsiders from different clans and usually from different villages as well. They remained dependent and vulnerable in this setting.

Urban Classes. In the urban areas the patriarchal lineage had been in decline for a long time. The nuclear family was already widespread. It was much easier for the Communist state to intervene directly in the lives of urban residents without having to respect and work through family patriarchs. Stacey characterizes the urban situation as one of domination by public patriarchs, the government, rather than the private patriarchs of the peasant family.

Economic and Domestic Spheres. Almost all working-age women in the cities are employed outside the home, but as with the rural women, the work is highly gender segregated and women earn considerably less than men. Despite a strong ideological emphasis on socializing the domestic sphere, housework and child care remain quite private. Communal dining arrangements proved to be unpopular and they are rather limited today. Subsidized child care is available to many but it is insufficient to meet the needs. Couples rely heavily on the services of the elderly. Since adult children are required by law to support their aging parents, many multigeneration households continue even in crowded urban households. The grandparents will also help with the housework, but the main responsibility lies with the wife. There have been some educational campaigns to encourage men to share the domestic burdens, but they have been largely ineffective. Women therefore suffer the same limitations in terms of competing for promotions and better jobs and for advancing through party work as the women of the Soviet Union. Chinese women have entered many previously male-dominated occupational categories, but they are still concentrated in the lowest-paying, low-prestige jobs, primarily in the service sector or marginal industries and often in jobs seen as extensions of the domestic role.

Economic production in China is still uneven and of variable quality. Shortages and shoddy goods hurt men and women both but they make the housewife's burden even heavier. China cannot, of course, afford the household appliances and labor-saving devices common in the West. But inadequate housing, lack of running water, and time-consuming shopping bedevil the urban housewife as well as her rural cousins. Women's concerns are focused on practical improvements within the immediate situations in which they live. Interest in feminism is limited. As one woman told a reporter,

You must also remember China's level of economic development. Chinese women can't afford to be interested in feminist issues. They focus on the things that are important to them—getting a decent apartment with a toilet of its own, buying groceries, figuring out who will take care of the children while they work. They don't yet identify with their jobs or careers. Fulfillment for them comes at home with the family.[71]

The public sphere still depends on the services provided by women in the domestic sphere, but women get little reward or recognition for their contributions. There are no work points and no salaries for domestic labor.

Divorce and Sex Ratios. An interesting contrast with the Soviet Union, however, is the marital stability that has followed the Chinese but not the Soviet revolution. Although both societies condemned traditional arranged marriages in favor of free-choice marriage, China never emphasized free love as a communist ideal. The CCP has generally reinforced conventional conservative views on sexuality. Perhaps more important, however, is the contrast in the sex imbalance experienced by the two nations. The USSR with its oversupply of women does not place as high a value on marriage, has a high divorce rate, and a pattern of gender exploitation of women in and outside of marriage. China, however, probably has a shortage of women and idealizes marriage, values wives highly, makes divorce very difficult, and has very low rates of premarital and extramarital sexual relationships. The government has recently liberalized the divorce laws to allow a couple to divorce if there is no mutual affection and all efforts at mediation fail. But the government's definition of mutual affection is much narrower than in the West. Couples are supposed to help each other when they need it, but they are still not expected to have a strong romantic attachment or to fulfill themselves through the marital relationship.

Marriage. Chinese adults are ideally more committed to their work unit than to their marriage. They should be willing to accept work assignments that will keep them separated for months if not years, willing to work late night after night to meet production goals, and willing to devote leisure time to study or political work. Whether individuals agree with this ideology or not, they will be strongly controlled by their work unit. It is through this unit that they receive not only their salary, but also their ration coupons and their housing assignment and, perhaps the clearest expression of public patriarchy, is that it is in the work unit that they receive permission to marry and permission to have a child.

Marriage choices are often made on the basis of the desirability of the prospective spouse's work assignment and the housing assignment or other privileges that come with it. A man with one of the coveted state industry positions (who receives much better benefits than nonstate workers) will have a wider selection of potential brides than a man with a less desirable work unit. Marriage is the primary means people have of

changing their residence from the country to the city or to a more desirable city.

Even in the city marriages are still arranged, but it is not a matter of the patriarchal father looking for the best match from his point of view as it is young people having little opportunity to find a mate and friends and relatives helping out with introductions. Courtships still tend to be formal and short. There does seem to be some loosening of the public condemnation of courtship, and visitors to China now report young couples openly showing affection in the public parks.

Population Control In the post-Mao Zedong era, the Chinese leadership has used Western demographic techniques to chart its population growth and now realizes it will be impossible to sustain economic growth without a drastic reduction in the birthrate. Mao's anti-Malthusian position kept the country vacillating in its support for population control in the past, but the situation is so severe now that the state has embarked on an all-out "one child per couple" policy.* This includes a massive education campaign enjoining people to marry late and have only one child. Propaganda is backed up with

---

*Thomas Malthus, an early nineteenth-century English economist and cleric, argued that human populations would always expand beyond the food supply necessary to support them, unless growth was checked by factors such as disease, famine, and war. Some twentieth-century development experts and politicians have also argued that the poverty of the Third World today is caused or perpetuated primarily by population pressure. Socialist leaders and scientists, however, often reject this "neo-Malthusian" approach on the basis that it obscures the problem of the inequitable distribution of the world's resources in favor of the developed world and underestimates the degree to which promotion of equitable economic growth itself releases social and economic forces which lead men and women to make the decision on their own to limit their fertility.

material incentives to those who accept the policy. They receive bonuses, extra maternity leave, free medical care and other privileges for their child, and free education and preferred entrance to the university. Those who disobey will be denied these benefits and are required to repay all they received for the first child. They may also lose salary and suffer demotion or less desirable work assignments.

Strong normative pressure is exerted by the work group and neighborhood. Stacey suggests this is an example of the public patriarch controlling women's sexuality.[72] Each woman worker's menstrual cycle is monitored by special family-planning representatives in the woman's work unit and in her neighborhood. The "granny police," neighborhood elderly women elected to family-planning work, visit regularly to check on contraceptive usage and to watch out for any unauthorized pregnancies. Each work unit is given a quota of births per year and allocates them on the basis of such factors as the age of the waiting couples. If anyone in the unit has an unauthorized baby, then the entire unit loses certain bonuses. This keeps everyone in the group concerned that each member obeys the rules. A woman with an unauthorized pregnancy is expected to obtain an abortion and will come under very strong pressure from her coworkers, neighborhood, and the family-planning workers to get the abortion.

This policy is very effective with urban couples whose first child is a boy, but it meets strong resistance among parents of girls and is not enforced as stringently in the countryside where children continue to be economically useful and are the only support available for elderly people. Female infanticide appears to be on the rise. Parents destroy the female babies in the hope that the next pregnancy will produce a son. Women will sometimes arrange with medical personnel to induce labor near the end of their pregnancy but before full term, knowing the child will likely be viable. If it is a son it will be declared a premature birth; if it is a girl, it will be registered as an abortion and the infant killed. Mothers still bear the blame for producing daughters, and the suicide and murder rate of mothers of daughters may be increasing in the countryside.

Although the law allows the couple to enter either the bride's or the groom's family, women still usually marry out of their natal family and contribute their labor and offspring to the husband's lineage. The law now requires daughters as well as sons to support their aging parents, but it is often impossible for both sets of parents to reside with the couple. The one-child policy may undermine patrilineality and raise the status of daughters as parents are forced to rely on whatever gender child they have. If patrilocal marriage patterns persist, however, a new form of inequality may emerge with parents of daughters disadvantaged compared with parents of sons. The shortage of wives produced by female infanticide could be used by parents of daughters to encourage their daughters to insist that prospective husbands agree to live matrilocally as a condition of marriage.

The Political Sphere. The decision to implement a one-child policy is a symbol of the marginality of women's role in the political sphere in China. There are almost no women in the higher reaches of the political structure and state bureaucracy. The important decisions are made by men with little or no input from women. No powerful independent women's organizations exist to act as advisers or as watchdogs over government policy as it affects women. In the CCP women are underrepresented (much more so than in the communist parties of Eastern

Europe and the Soviet Union) at all levels and are concentrated at the bottom of the party hierarchy. The party assigns very few high-level managerial positions to women. Perhaps because almost all women in China marry, unlike the Soviet Union which has the opposite sex-ratio imbalance, there are few dedicated single career women who can devote full-time energy to high-level political and managerial careers and demonstrate the requisite party loyalty through overtime party work and study. But women are assigned the jobs directly associated with implementing policies affecting women. They are, for example, the family-planning representatives and "granny police" who enforce the one-child policy.

Many of the problems of integrating women more fully into the higher economic and political spheres are due to China's continuing battle with economic underdevelopment. The government cannot afford to provide the social welfare services to free women from the burdens of the domestic sphere that a nation like Sweden can provide. But it is also clear that gender stratification has never been viewed as one of the major problems to be tackled by the CCP except when it interferes with other state interests. There is no doubt that women's and men's lives have improved greatly under CCP rule, but inequality and stratification have not been eradicated. Class inequality still exists, with elites having much more power and privilege than the masses, with some categories of worker profiting much more than other categories, and with males still having more power, pay, and prestige than females.

In the mid-1980s China was experiencing a new revolutionary turnabout. Head of state Deng Xiaoping and his associates were pressing forward with efforts to modernize the Chinese economy through the introduction of market incentives, privatization of certain forms of production and commerce, and an "opening to the West" to encourage the inflow of technology and capital. The effects of these innovations—if indeed they are sustained—on gender relations in this vast socialist society remain to be seen. Insofar as they may strengthen the male-dominated nuclear family as a competitive productive and consumption unit, the prospects are at the very least ambiguous.[73]

Debate on the issue of gender equality was silenced in the aftermath of Jiang Quing's (Mao's widow) attempt to seize power after her husband's death.[74] As part of the ideological campaign to prepare for Jiang Quing's assumption of leadership, the now discredited "Gang of Four" initiated a mass campaign to study women's history and the ideological roots of women's oppression. But since their fall from power, criticism of gender inequality and suggestions that women are not biologically inferior to men are politically suspect and mark a person as espousing the principles of the Gang of Four. A feminist critique of Chinese society and interest in women's studies have, once again, fallen victim to the sweep of male-oriented concerns of political reform and economic development in the People's Republic of China.

Cuba

Historical Background

Fidel Castro led his 26th of July Movement to victory over the Batista dictatorship in Cuba on January 1, 1959.[75] Cuba's history had been one of centuries of colonial domination by Spain, which included a plantation economy with African slavery. The Spanish-American War brought Spanish rule to an end at the turn of the century. Cuba entered the twentieth century ostensibly a republic, but in reality a backward, underdeveloped peripheral society under the political domination of a series of dictator's and under the economic domination of primarily U.S. business interests. Havana was a center for organized crime and gambling. The night life was world renowned as was the Cuban reputation for prostitution and the production of pornography.

A wealthy white elite following the traditions of the Spanish aristocracy occupied the apex of the social structure. This class practiced Iberian familial and gender relations. The father was the absolute head of the family; his word was law. The mother was the emotional center of the family, overprotecting her sons and her daughters. Wives and daughters were kept in semiseclusion. They could go out, of course (it was important for them to demonstrate the status of the husband through their beauty, clothing, and ability to consume luxuriously), but only to respectable places and with a chaperone. Virginity for unmarried girls and chastity for wives were important for male honor. But males were expected to have varied sex lives from an early age, beginning perhaps with the young maids of the household and eventually graduating, along with marriage to a respectable girl of his class, to one or more mistresses—a "casa chica" in addition to his "casa grande." Wives had no right to complain about such behavior in their husbands and no right to divorce for adultery unless the husband's behavior resulted in a scandal. Husbands could, of course, divorce even a discreetly adulterous wife.

Below the aristocratic Spanish-oriented class was the white middle-class of well-to-do professionals and businessmen. These people drew upon Spanish traditions in their family and gender relations, but they were also strongly influenced by the United States and were more modern in many respects.

Their daughters as well as their sons might be given a university education in Cuba or abroad. Some of the wives of this class were well-educated professionals also. But the father was still the patriarchal head of the family and he was still dishonored if he could not control the sexuality of "his women."

The urban white and black lower classes could not afford such family structures. They were also influenced by African as well as Spanish cultures. The women of this class had to work. Poverty took its toll through high rates of family disruption, leaving many females as heads of households. Employment opportunities for women were limited. The cigar industry employed women in some numbers, but the majority of these women had little opportunity except in domestic service and prostitution. Many employers would not accept maids with small children, so these mothers had to place their children in someone else's home or turn to prostitution or other crime to support themselves and their families.

The gap between the urban and rural populations was extreme in prerevolutionary Cuba. The wage-earning agricultural labor force—concentrated in the sugar-export economy—and the small landowning peasantry were very backward and poor. They had little or no access to the trappings of modernity.

Yet Cuba was often viewed as one of the more modern Latin American countries of the time. The birthrate was one of the lowest in Latin America, and the urban population was clearly oriented to the consumer economy and to emulating what they saw in the movies and in the tourist industry as the "American Dream." But poverty was widespread; 40 percent of the population was hungry. Disease and parasites were rampant. Infant mortality and maternal morbidity were high. Life expectancy was high for an underdeveloped country at sixty years, but low compared with the United States. Only one-sixth of the population was literate. Extremes of wealth and poverty existed side by side.

Castro's Cuba

Castro and his revolutionaries fought a long and difficult guerrilla war to restructure Cuba along more equalitarian lines. Many women as well as men fought in the revolution, and Castro began his leadership announcing his support for dismantling gender stratification as well as class and racial stratification and rural/urban differentials.

The New Patriarchal Family. But somewhat similar to China, Cuba began a program of land reform and nationalization that actually served to strengthen the patriarchal family rather than to destroy it. The redistribution of resources so improved the lives of the poorest classes that they could now afford to marry and have children and thereby create the families that had been denied to them under crushing poverty. In fact, Cuba had a significant baby boom in the 1960s as people hopeful about their futures responded by having children they had previously felt they could not afford. (Some of the increase in births may also have been the result of the United States economic blockade, which drastically reduced the supply of contraceptives.)

The postrevolutionary situation was clearly an improvement for the impoverished classes, but the middle and upper classes experienced it as a loss. They emigrated from Cuba, primarily to the United States, in the hundreds of thousands. This "brain drain" of the best-educated classes was a difficult blow to economic development, but it opened up a great deal of housing and land for the poorer people. Currently, however, one of the most important hindrances

to marriage is the continuing housing shortage. The Mariel sealift in the early 1980s allowed more Cubans to emigrate to the United States and again temporarily relieved housing problems for many.

Reorganization of agriculture and an increase in industrialization for import substitution, coupled with large-scale emigration, created labor shortages instead of unemployment. The government attempted to draw women into the labor force but with limited success. Women participated in voluntary work groups to help at peak labor periods such as during the sugar cane harvest, but married women were reluctant to remain in the labor force. The commitment to traditional gender relations was strong, and both men and women continued to feel that a woman's place was in the home. With the baby boom, many women were likely to have infants and young children to care for.

The new communist government openly expressed its support for the family and encouraged people to legitimate their consensual unions (widespread among the poor who could not afford the fees charged by church and state for legal marriages) with mass ceremonies and registrations. The government even made some of the luxurious buildings of the aristocracy available for weddings and receptions. This offered an alternative to marriage by the church, which the communists preferred to discourage, and also served as a symbol of the new equality for everyone to share what had before been reserved for an elite few.

Population Policy. The government has not taken an openly pronatalist or antinatalist stand. Cuba suffered neither the drastic population shortages of the Soviets nor the overpopulation of the Chinese. It rejects neo-Malthusian explanations of underdevelopment as a result of overpopulation and lack of fertility control (it argues instead that imperialism is at the root of the problem) and prefers to leave family size as the choice of individuals. To that end, contraception and family-planning services are widespread and free. Abortion is available as a backup measure, but it is seen as a health hazard to be avoided if possible. Illegal abortion was widespread in prerevolutionary Cuba, and the current regime does not want to encourage its reemergence by restricting legal abortion too rigidly.

The support the government provides to children, education, and child-care centers could be viewed as pronatalist, but China provides similar support as part of its fiercely antinatalist policy. The necessities of life such as adequate food, housing, health care, and education are considered basic rights, and the Cuban government has gone to great lengths to provide these to everyone. This relieves much of the burden of supporting children, but that is a secondary rather than the primary goal of such policies.

One immediate blow to the traditional family and gender system was delivered by the literacy campaign. To reduce illiteracy as rapidly as possible, Castro encouraged all those who could read and write to go to the countryside in literacy brigades to teach those who had had no education. Thousands of teachers accompanied by even more adolescent and teenage boys and girls took up the challenge. For most of the girls and many of the boys, this was their first experience of freedom from parental supervision. The campaign was accorded such ideological and moral importance that most parents felt they could not refuse permission even to their daughters.

Femininity. Cuban culture has also retained its emphasis on beauty and femininity for females. Despite the economic blockade and shortages, Cuban industry has shown ingenuity in keeping cosmetics available to women. Women serve in the military, but they can opt for skirts as well as pants.* Beauty contests are still important events, but they have been stripped of their aristocratic elements. The "Carnival Queens" of old are now "Carnival Stars," and in addition to their beauty, their political credentials are examined. Black and mulatto women can compete successfully with white women. And as a reaction to what is viewed as the sexual exploitation of Cuban women by foreigners in the old tourist industry, the stars do not appear in bathing suits. (The famous Cuban nightclub dancers are now modestly clad, whereas they used to be nude or seminude.)

Training and education programs for women embody traditional gender roles and often include lessons in makeup and good personal grooming. This was true even for the adult education classes offered in the early years of the new regime to prostitutes and maids to retain them for work more suitable to revolutionary goals. Peasant girls were brought to Havana for sewing lessons (and a few beauty lessons) and given sewing machines to improve the quality of clothing available to the peasantry. In this way traditional family relations serve to produce goods for the revolution and help the government ease the current costs of economic development. Women's unpaid labor in the domestic sphere have proved costly to replace in the public sphere.

Structural Hindrances to Gender Equality. Material conditions in Cuba have prevented the Castro regime from achieving its ideal of equal rights for women. Castro has given strong ideological support to women's

---

*When visiting Cuba in the late 1970s, we saw women soldiers in mini-skirts, heavy make-up, and long, carefully manicured nails.

equal participation in the political and economic spheres and men's equal participation in the domestic sphere. In 1975 Cuba enacted a new Family Code that explicitly requires that husbands must share the responsibilities for housework and child care equally with their wives. Passage of the Code was preceded by months of public debate and discussion of the Code and of women's position in the family and society. The government wanted feedback from the people and changed some aspects of the law as a result of this input. More important, however, the debate was a powerful tool for consciousness raising in the population. But despite all this attention to the problem a decade after its enactment it is clear that the law has not decisively affected the behavior of Cuban husbands.

The government recognized at a very early stage that to undermine gender stratification along with class stratification, it would be necessary to socialize many aspects of housework and child care. Muriel Nazzari points out that the crucial factor in gender stratification in Cuba and elsewhere as well is probably the burdens of child care and not housework.[76] Housework can almost always be postponed, but child care cannot. The more children a person has to care for, the less time the person will have for other activities.

Castro began with a strong commitment to providing free child care to all who needed it. But the problems of economic development facing a nation trying to pull itself up from the poverty typical of peripheral societies proved to be more difficult to solve than the new government had anticipated. The economic growth required to absorb the costs of taking women's domestic services out of the private sphere to the public sphere has not been achieved. Free child care is no longer available. Women are not paid for their housework in any way, but their duties

in the home are recognized by law in the requirement that all men must work outside the home, while for women this is a choice.

Few married women choose to work; instead they prefer to live on their husbands' wages. One informant described herself as "Like *mama*, I live exclusively for my family. I try above all to be a good wife and good mother."[77] Such women are content that the revolution has provided them with the economic security to devote themselves to the housewife and mother role.

Divorced women who have children and heavy domestic responsibilities do work, however. It is the availability of the husband's wage combined with a heavy domestic load that explains why married women constituted only 18 percent of the female labor force in 1972, while divorced women represented 43 percent, single women 30 percent, and widows 9 percent.[78] Because married women stay out of the labor force, women compose only 30 percent of the Cuban labor force. This is true even though women have access to the higher-ranking jobs and even though the pay gap between male and female workers is probably narrower than in many other societies where women participate in much larger ratios. Women workers also receive generous maternity leave benefits, and some absenteeism for family responsibilities is a legal right. Gender segregation does exist, however, with females dominating in the lower-paid service-sector jobs and males filling the better-paid industrial jobs.

Nazzari argues that it is the material conditions in Cuban society that hinder female participation in the public sphere, although the persistence of *machismo* and male-dominated cultural traditions and attitudes may play some role. The Cuban government has as an ideal the communist maxim "From each according to his ability, but to each according to his needs," and it has made impressive progress in providing food, housing, education, medical care, and other important services for free or at very low cost. The government found, however, that if it wanted to increase productivity substantially, moral exhortations to work hard were insufficient to motivate workers who had their basic needs taken care of for little money and for whom extra money was meaningless because of the lack of a significant market in consumer goods. The state responded by raising prices, charging for many previously free services such as telephones, and increasing the importance of one's wage-earning ability. Increasing the importance of wages in a society where husbands are still likely to earn substantially more than wives is a strong structural hindrance to shared roles within the family and a strong support for the maintenance of gender stratification. It emphasizes the husband's importance as the chief breadwinner for the family; and it makes it much more likely that his wife will defer to his needs and take up the slack for a better job, or pursue political work to enhance his position. As one woman put it, "When a husband gives his wife an order, his wife should never answer 'No I won't.' Not unless she wants to find herself out in the street."[79]

Another economic policy enacted to enhance growth and productivity is the new requirement that industries should show a profit; that is, they should produce more than it costs to run the industry. This gives managers a powerful disincentive for hiring women, especially married women with children. Maternity leave, absenteeism for domestic problems, and other special benefits for female workers add to the cost of the plant and may decrease productivity as well.

Women's Organizations. Unlike other socialist governments, Cuba has not chosen to suppress feminism, but it does direct the course that feminism can take. The Federation of Cuban Women was established to recruit women more fully into the productive sphere. It has sufficient autonomy to research women's special problems and to make recommendations, but it never openly opposes the government. The first appointed head of the FCW was a revolutionary war heroine and sister-in-law of Castro. The FCW also serves as a bureaucratic means for involving women in the government and for approving women's political credentials. It is difficult for a woman to get a good job or other government-supplied scarce resources without a federation card.

The Political Sphere. As an example of the federation's work in support of gender equality, when the first experiments with local elections produced very few female officeholders or delegates, the federation was empowered to study the problem. It ascertained, not unlike the situation in other socialist and capitalist societies, that women's domestic burdens deprived them of the free time necessary for politics. It had reached similar conclusions in its studies of married women's failure to participate in the labor force outside the home. The federation has repeatedly recommended that the government undertake policies to ease what Cuban's call women's "second shift." But this interferes with policies designed to increase economic growth, which is seen as vital to Cuba's long-term development. In the short term, gender stratification is allowed to remain largely unchallenged.

Lack of progress in eliminating gender segregation is not solely a matter of economic scarcity. The government has shown little enthusiasm for integrating women into the political structure or for appointing women to high-ranking administrative or policy-making positions. The few women who do hold important government positions are concentrated in the Federation of Cuban Woman and in general confined to the "social housekeeping sphere." Even the war heroines receive less mention and fewer banners at public rallies than the war heroes. Women politicians and women in general would have little basis for protecting women's interests if the next leader should reject Castro's position favoring gender equality. The situation may be similar to that of the early decades of the Soviet Zhenotdel.

Conclusion

When compared with their presocialist past, most socialist societies have made remarkable advances in breaking down certain aspects of gender stratification and in improving the general position of women. Most socialist societies also compare very favorably with the major capitalist countries in both these areas. Moreover, the socialist societies have achieved these advances within a very brief historical time span.[80] Nevertheless, the real achievements in the area of gender equality have, as yet, noticeably fallen short of the ideals of socialist ideology. How is this to be explained?

Evaluating relative progress toward gender equality in socialist societies is difficult not only because of the various biases that both ideological defenders and opponents of socialism bring to this task, but also because of the complex historical, cultural, and political *international* realities which have informed the development of socialism in each society where it has been established. The Soviet, Chinese, Cuban, and other socialist regimes have existed in extremely hostile international environments since their inception. However much weight one is to give to the actions of these regimes themselves in stimulating such hostility, the antisocialist

ideologies and activities of the capitalist powers have had decisive effects in shaping the social, economic, and political institutions of these societies. They have been societies on the defensive, distorting whatever genuine goals of socialist egalitarianism they may have pursued (or may have wished to pursue) into conformity with what their political leaders have perceived as necessary programs for political, economic, and military survival in the face of threats from both internal and external enemies. After all the morally compelling condemnations and criticisms of the cruelties, repressions, and despotisms perpetuated by certain of these regimes have been made, the seige-environment in which twentieth-century socialism has developed still stands as one of the principal factors that must be taken into account in evaluating both its successes and failures.

Even without the international threats and constraints faced by developing socialist societies, the challenges of internal economic and social transformation would have been formidable. Socialism, as yet, has not developed within any advanced industrial society.* Rather, modern socialism has by and large been perceived as a political organizational *means* to *achieve* advanced industrialism. As such, socialism has not resisted what seem to be the "rational" imperatives of first consolidating centralized political rule in order to control and mobilize a population, and then exercising that control and capacity for mobilization to achieve rapid

---

*Socialism was of course, militarily imposed by the Soviets on industrially advanced East Germany at the end of World War II. The peculiar relationship of dependency which existed between the German Democratic Republic and the Soviet Union would seem to make it inappropriate to consider this as a case of genuine socialist transition taking place within a capitalist society.

economic growth. The alternative goals of achieving human liberties, democratic participation, and egalitarianism have not only typically been given secondary consideration in these efforts, but have often been perceived as contradictory to the prospects of advancing economic development itself. Clearly, the movement toward full gender equality has been hindered by this order of priorities in socialist societies.

The achievement of gender equality in socialist societies, as in any other modern societies, would require not only a frontal ideological attack on patriarchal attitudes and theories, but also the alternative use of costly economic and social resources whose investment in the direction of creating a society which is more egalitarian from the standpoint of gender is often not obviously economically "rational" or "efficient," especially in its more immediate consequences. One of the most astute observers of gender stratification among socialist societies, Elizabeth Croll, has posed the essential dilemma and unanswered question for gender relations in these societies.*

In the development programs of each of these nations, the emphasis on attracting women into the collective waged labor force has outweighed the concern for redefining women's reproductive and domestic roles. The limited development of the service sector, the existence of a large private subsistence sector of the economy, and the persistence of a traditional sexual division of labor within the household have meant that the burden of subsistence and domestic responsibilities continues to devolve upon peasant women, who in effect subsidize the rural development programs with their intensified labor. In order to reduce this burden, each society must provide a new material base for subsis-

tence and domestic services, and must allocate resources and investments at both national and local levels. Yet in the absence of well-defined long-term policies concerning the reproductive sphere, the demands of production and economic development take priority. The question is, Are the present inequalities in the sexual division of labor, which may be justified by the scarcity of social funds, caused by the inadequate implementation of socialist policies themselves? We must begin to search for an answer as we examine the important achievements and the very considerable problems in socialist development experiences.[81]

Given the current structure of military and political confrontation between the major capitalist and socialist powers and the competitive dictates of a world economy dominated by the institutions of capitalism, the choices of new as well as older socialist societies to respond creatively to the dilemma described by Croll would appear to be exceedingly narrow in scope. To the degree this continues to be the case, it represents perhaps not only an inevitable "failure" for socialism, but for humankind as a whole.†

Notes

1. Frederick Engels, *The Origin of the Family, Private Property and the State* (New York: International Publishers, 1972; orig. 1884); August Bebel, *Woman Under Socialism* (New York: Schocken Books, 1971; orig. 1904); V. I. Lenin, "International Working Women's Day," in *Lenin on the Emancipation of Women* (Moscow: Progress Publishers, 1921, 1972): 83–85); V. I. Lenin, *Women and Society* (New York: International Publishers, 1938).

2. See for example, Shulamith Firestone, *The Dialectic of Sex* (New York: Bantam Books, 1971); Charnie Buettel, *Marxism and Feminism* (Toronto: The Women's Press, 1974): Linda Jenness, ed., *Feminism and Socialism* (New York: Pathfinder, 1972); Evelyn Reed, *Problems of Women's Liberation* (New York: Pathfinder Press, 1971).

---

*Croll's comments specifically refer to the rural sectors of these societies, but similar implications exist for the quest of gender equality throughout their social structures.

---

† Immanuel Wallerstein has argued that in a world economy dominated by capitalist institutions, true socialism does not and indeed, cannot exist.[82]

3. See, for example, Hilda Scott, *Does Socialism Liberate Women?* (Boston: Beacon Press, 1974); Marilyn Rueschemeyer, "The Demands of Work and the Human Quality of Marriage: An Exploratory Study of Professionals in Two Socialist Societies," in George Kurian and Ratna Ghosh, eds., *Women in the Family and the Economy: An International Comparative Survey* (Westport, Conn.: Greenwood Press, 1981): 331–344; Marilyn Rueschemeyer, *Professional Work and Marriage: An East-West Comparison* (New York: St. Martin's Press, 1981); Barbara Jancar, *Women Under Communism* (Baltimore: Johns Hopkins University Press, 1978); Barbara Jancar, "Women in Communist Countries: Comparative Public Policy," in Naomi Black and Ann Baker Cottrell, eds., *Women and World Change: Equity Issues in Development* (Beverly Hills: Sage, 1981); Shirley A. Nuss, "The Position of Women in Socialist and Capitalist Countries: A Comparative Study," *International Journal of the Sociology of the Family* 10, no. 1 (1980): 1–13; Shirley A. Nuss, "The Commitment of Fathers to Equality in the Performance of Family Maintenance Activities: A Comparison of Developed Market-Oriented and Centrally-Planned Countries," *International Journal of the Sociology of the Family* 11, no. 1 (1981): 11–14; Shirley A. Nuss, "Family Maintenance Activities: Husband's Participation in Centrally-Planned and Market-Oriented Countries," *Insurgent Sociologist* 12, nos. 1–2 (Winter/Spring, 1984): 13–24; Alexander Szalai, ed., *The Use of Time: Daily Activities of Urban and Suburban Populations in Twelve Countries* (The Hague: Mouton, 1972); Elina Haavio-Mannila, "Convergences between East and West: Tradition and Modernity in Sex Roles in Sweden, Finland and the Soviet Union," *Acta Sociologica* 14, nos. 1–2 (1971): 114–125; Veronica Stolte-Heiskanen and Elina Haavio-Mannila, "The Position of Women in Society: Formal Ideology vs. Everyday Ethic," *Social Sciences Information* 6 (1967): 169–188; Elizabeth J. Croll, "Women in Rural Production and Reproduction in the Soviet Union, China, Cuba, and Tanzania: Socialist Development Experiences," *Signs* 7, no. 2 (1981): 361–374; Erwin Marquit, *The Socialist Countries* (Garden City, N.Y.: Anchor Press, 1975); Elaine Mensh and Harry Mensh, *Behind the Scenes in Two Worlds* (New York: International Publishers, 1978); Ivan Volgyes and Nancy Volgyes, *The Liberated Female: Life, Work, and Sex in Socialist Hungary* (Boulder, Colo.: Westview Press, 1977); Margery Wolf and Roxane Witke, *Women in Chinese Society* (Stanford, Calif,: Stanford University Press, 1975); Paul Chao, *Women Under Communism: Family in Russia and China* (New York: General Hall, 1977); Alena Heitlinger, *Women and State Socialism: Sex Inequality in the Soviet Union and Czechoslovakia* (Montreal: McGill-Queens University Press, 1979); Tova Yedlin, ed., *Women in Eastern Europe and the Soviet Union* (New York: Praeger, 1980).

4. In addition to the sources mentioned above, the discussion of the U.S.S.R. relies on Alastair McAuley, *Women's Work and Wages in the Soviet Union* (London: George Allen & Unwin, 1981); Murray Feshbach, "The Soviet Union: Population Trends and Dilemmas," *Population Reference Bureau* 37, no. 3 (August 1982); Gail Lapidus, *Women in Soviet Society: Equality, Development, and Social Change* (Berkeley: University of California Press, 1978); Gail Lapidus, ed., *Women, Work, and Family in the Soviet Union* (Armonk, N.Y.: M. E. Sharpe, 1982); Dorothy Atkinson, Alexander Dallin, and Gail Lapidus, eds., *Women in Russia* (Stanford, Calif.: Stanford University Press, 1977); Michael Paul Sacks, *Women's Work in Soviet Russia: Continuity in the Midst of Change* (New York: Praeger, 1976); Jerry G. Pankhurst and Michael Paul Sacks, eds., *Contemporary Soviet Society: Sociological Perspectives* (New York: Praeger, 1980); Jenny Brine, Maureen Petrie, and Andrew Sutton, eds., *Home, School, and Leisure in the Soviet Union* (London: George Allen & Unwin, 1980); Feiga Blekher, *The Soviet Woman in the Family and in Society: A Sociological Study* (New York: John Wiley, 1979); Wesley Andrew Fisher, *The Soviet Marriage Market: Mate-Selection in Russia and the USSR* (New York: Praeger, 1980); A. M. Belyakova, et al., compilers, *Soviet Legislation on Women's Rights: Collection of Normative Acts* (Moscow: Progress Publishers, 1978); Susan Jacoby, *Inside Soviet Schools* (New York: Hill & Wang, 1974).

5. Barbara Alpert Engel, *Mothers and Daughters: Women of the Intelligentsia in Nineteenth-Century Russia* (Cambridge: Cambridge University Press, 1983); Richard Stites, *The Women's Liberation Movement in Russia: Feminisim, Nihilism, and Bolshevism, 1860–1930* (Princeton, N.J.: Princeton University Press, 1978).

6. Lapidus, 1978, 37.

7. Engels, Bebel.

8. Rose Glickman, "The Russian Factory Woman, 1880–1914," in Atkinson, Dallin, and Lapidus, 81.

9. Sacks, 15.

10. Sacks, 7, 23.

11. Lapidus, 1978, 49; Beatrice Farnsworth, "Bolshevism, the Woman Question and Aleksandra Kollontai," in Marilyn J. Boxer and Jean H. Quataert, eds., *Socialist Women: European Socialist Feminism in the Nineteenth and Early Twentieth Centuries* (New York: Elsevier, 1978): 182–214.

12. Marlis Allendorf, *Woman in Socialist Society* (New York: International Publishers, 1975): 59.

13. Jacoby, 1974, 137.

14. Michael Swafford, "Sex Differences in Soviet Earnings," *American Sociological Review,* 43 (October 1978), 657; Sacks, 1982, 20; McAuley, 48–97.

15. McAuley, 206; William Mandel, *Soviet Women* (Garden City, N.Y.: Anchor Books, 1975) argues it is 75 percent.

16. Lapidus, 1978, 188.

17. Lapidus, 1978, 216.

18. Lapidus, 1978, 210.

19. Croll, 1981, 367–368.

20. Feshbach.

21. Tatyana Mamonova, ed., *Women and Russia: Feminist Writings from the Soviet Union* (Boston: Beacon Press, 1984).

22. Ekaterina Alexandrova, "Why Soviet Women Want to Get Married," in Mamonova, 1984, 31.

23. Mamonova, 1984.

24. Barbara Jancar, "Women in Communist Countries: Comparative Public Policy," in Naomi Black and Ann Baker Cottrell, eds., *Women and World Change: Equity Issues in Development* (Beverly Hills: Sage, 1981): 139–158.

25. Jancar; Carola Hansson and Karin Liden, *Moscow Women: Thirteen Interviews* (New York: Pantheon Books, 1983).

26. Jacoby, 26–27.

27. Jacoby, 40.

28. Jacoby, 40.

29. Jacoby, 33.

30. Jacoby, 45.

31. Hansson and Liden.

32. Jacoby, 103.

33. Jacoby, 24–25, 143–155.

34. Mollie Schwartz Rosenhan, "Images of Male and Female in Children's Readers," in Atkinson, Dallin, and Lapidus, 1977, 293–305.

35. Lapidus, 1978, 344.

36. Hansson and Liden, 25.

37. Tatyana Mamonova, "The Feminist Movement in the Soviet Union" in Mamonova, xiii–xxiii.

38. This discussion of the Israeli kibbutzim relies on Rae Lesser Blumberg, "Kibbutz Women: From the Fields of Revolution to the Laundries of Discontent," in Lynne B. Iglitzin and Ruth Ross, eds., *Women in the World: A Comparative Study* (Santa Barbara, Calif.: Clio Books, 1976): 319–344; Rae Lesser Blumberg, *Stratification: Socioeconomic and Sexual Inequality* (Dubuque, Iowa: Wm. C. Brown, 1978): 112–116; Rae Lesser Blumberg, "The Women of the Israeli Kibbutz," *The Center Magazine,* 7 (May–June 1974): 70–72; Elaine Soloway, "Kibbutz Women: In Transition," *Communities,* 23 (November–December 1976): 8–9; Hyman Mariampolski, "The Decline of Sexual Egalitarianism on the Kibbutz," East Lafayette, Ind.: Purdue University, Institute for the Study of Social Change, Working Paper No. 89, April 1975; Yehuda Don, "Industrialization in Advanced Rural Communities: The Israeli Kibbutz," Madison, Wis.: University of Wisconsin, Land Tenure Center, Paper No. 112, January 1977; A. I. Rabin, "The Sexes: Ideology and Reality in the Israeli Kibbutz," in Georgene H.

Seward and Robert C. Williamson, eds., *Sex Roles in Changing Society* (New York: Random House, 1970): 285–307; Melford E. Spiro, *Kibbutz: Venture in Utopia,* 3d ed. (New York: Schocken Books, 1970); Menachem Rosner, ed., *Democracy, Equality, and Change: The Kibbutz and Social Theory* (Darby, Pa.: Norwood Editions, 1982); A. I. Rabin and Benjamin Beit-Hallahmi, *Twenty Years Later: Kibbutz Children Grow Up* (New York: Springer, 1982); Menachem Gerson, *Family, Women, and Socialization in the Kibbutz* (Lexington, Mass.: Lexington Books, 1978); Michal Palgi and Menachem Rosner, eds., *Sexual Equality: The Israeli Kibbutz Tests the Theories* (Norwood, Pa.: Norwood Editions, 1982).

39. Margaret Benston, "The Political Economy of Women's Liberation," *Monthly Review* 21 (September 1969): 3–27.

40. Lionel Tiger, *Men in Groups* (New York: Random House, 1969); Lionel Tiger and Robin Fox, *The Imperial Animal* (New York: Holt, Rinehart & Winston, 1971).

41. Joseph Shepher, "Reflections on the Origin of the Human Pair Bond," *Journal of Social and Biological Structures* 1, no. 3 (1978).

42. Lionel Tiger and Joseph Shepher, *Women in the Kibbutz* (New York: Harcourt, Brace, Jovanovich, 1975); Lionel Tiger and Joseph Shepher, "Kibbutz and Parental Investment: *Women in the Kibbutz Reconsidered*" in Palgi et al., 1983, 45–56.

43. E. O. Wilson, *Sociobiology: A New Synthesis* (Cambridge, Mass.: Harvard/Belknap Press, 1975); R. L. Trivers, "Parental Investment and Sexual Selection." in B. Campbell, ed., *Sexual Selection and the Descent of Man, 1871–1971* (Chicago: Aldine-Atherton, 1972).

44. Melford Spiro, *Gender and Culture: Kibbutz Women Revisited* (New York: Schocken Books, 1980).

45. Joseph R. Blasi, "A Critique of *Gender and Culture: Kibbutz Women Revisited*" in Palgi et al., 1983, 91–99; Marilyn Safir, "The Kibbutz: An Experiment in Social and Sexual Equality? An Historical Perspective," in Palgi et al., 1983, 100–129; Marilyn Safir, "Sex Role Socialization: Education in the Kibbutz," in Palgi et al., 1983, 216–220; Rosanna Hertz and Wayne Baker, "Women and Men's Work in an Israeli Kibbutz: Gender and Allocation of Labor," in Palgi et al., 1983, 154–173; Dorit Padan-Eisenstark, "Girl's Education in the Kibbutz," in Palgi et al., 1983, 210–215; Michael Nathan, "Counterrevolution without Revolution?" in Palgi et al., eds., 1983, 221–226; Suzanne Keller, "The Family in the Kibbutz: What Lessons for Us?" in Palgi et al., 1983, 227–251; Michal Palgi and Menachem Rosner, "Equality between the Sexes in the Kibbutz: Regression or Changed Meaning?" in Palgi et al., 1983, 255–296; Nira Yuval Davis, *Israeli Women and Men: Divisions Behind the Unity* (London: Change International Reports, n.d.); Blumberg, 1974, 1976, 1978; Martha Mednick, "Social

Change and Sex-Role Inertia: The Case of the Kibbutz," in Martha Mednick, Sandra Tangri, and Lois W. Hoffman, eds., *Women and Achievement* (New York: John Wiley, 1975): 85–103; Yaffa Schlesinger, "Sex Roles and Social Change in the Kibbutz," *Journal of Marriage and the Family* 39, no. 4 (November 1977): 771–779.

46. Blumberg, 1974, 70.

47. Blumberg, 1976, 329.

48. Blumberg, 1974, 71.

49. Davis, n.d., 10–13; Lesley Hazelton, *Israeli Women: The Reality Behind the Myths* (New York: Simon & Schuster, 1977): 38–62; Nancy Datan, Aaron Antonovsky, and Benjamin Maoz, *A Time to Reap: The Middle Age of Women in Five Israeli Subcultures* (Baltimore: Johns Hopkins University Press, 1981).

50. Davis, 13–18.

51. Davis, 17.

52. Davis, 18; Hazelton, 1977, 63–90; 162–184.

53. Shimon S. Camiel, "Some Observations about the Effect of War on Kibbutz Family Structure," *Family Coordinator* 27 (January 1978): 43–46.

54. Hazelton, 15–37.

55. Albert Bandura, "Social-Learning Theory of Identificatory Processes," in David A. Goslin, ed., *Handbook of Socialization Theory and Research* (Chicago: Rand McNally, 1969): 213–262; David B. Lynn, "The Process of Learning Parental and Sex-Role Identification," *Journal of Marriage and the Family* 28 (1966): 466–470; Walter Mischel, "A Social-Learning View of Sex Differences in Behavior" in Eleanor E. Maccoby, ed., *The Development of Sex Differences* (Stanford, Calif.: Stanford University Press, 1966): 56–81.

56. Lawrence Kohlberg, "A Cognitive-Developmental Analysis of Children's Sex-Role Concepts and Attitudes," in Maccoby, 1966, 82–173.

57. By age eight to ten kibbutz children identify "correctly" the appropriate sex of each work role. See Uri Leviatan, "Why Is Work Less Central for Women? Initial Explorations with Kibbutz Samples and Future Research Directions," in Palgi et al., 1983, 202; see also Safir.

58. Padan-Eisenstark, 210–215; Hertz and Baker, 154–173.

59. Quoted in Amia Lieblich, *Kibbutz Makom: Report from an Israeli Kibbutz* (New York: Pantheon Books, 1981): 260.

60. Quoted in Hertz and Baker, 165.

61. Rosabeth Moss Kanter, *Men and Women of the Corporation* (New York: Basic Books, 1977): 136–139, 155–159. See also Hertz and Baker, 166; Seymour Parker and Hilda Parker, "Women and the Emerging Family on the Israeli Kibbutz," *American Ethnologist* 8 (1981): 758–773; Dorit Padan-Eisenstark, "Are Israeli Women Really Equal? Trends and Patterns of Israeli Women's Labor

Force Participation: A Comparative Analysis," *Journal of Marriage and the Family* 35, no. 3 (August 1973); 538–545.

62. Padan-Eisenstark, 214.

63. Kanter.

64. Tiger and Shepher, 1983, 53.

65. Hertz and Baker, 168.

66. Blumberg, 1976, 335.

67. Davis; Hazelton, 185–205.

68. This discussion of China relies on Judith Stacey, *Patriarchy and Socialist Revolution in China* (Berkeley: University of California Press, 1983); Elizabeth Croll, *Chinese Women Since Mao* (Armonk, New York: M. E. Sharpe 1983); Elizabeth Croll, "The Sexual Division of Labor in Rural China," in Lourdes Beneria, ed., *Women in Development: The Sexual Division of Labor in Rural Societies* (New York: Praeger, 1982): 223–247; Elizabeth Croll, "Women in Rural Production and Reproduction in the Soviet Union, China, Cuba, and Tanzania: Socialist Development Experiences," *Signs* 7, no. 2 (Winter 1981): 361–374; Elizabeth Croll, ed., *The Women's Movement in China: A Selection of Readings* (Peking: Anglo-Chinese Educational Institute, 1974); Carolyn Teich Adams and Kathryn Teich Winston, *Mothers at Work: Public Policies in the United States, Sweden, and China* (New York: Longmans, 1980); Margery Wolf and Roxanne Witke, eds., *Women in Chinese Society* (Stanford, Calif.: Stanford University Press, 1975); Delia Davin, *Woman-Work: Women and the Party in Revolutionary China* (Oxford: Clarendon Press, 1976); H. Yuan Tien, "China: Demographic Billionaire," *Population Bulletin* 38, no. 2 (April 1983); H. Yuan Tien, "Wan, Xi, Shao: How China Meets Its Population Problem," *International Family Planning Perspectives* 6, no. 2 (June 1980): 65–73; Judith Banister, "An Analysis of Recent Data on the Population of China," *Population and Development Review* 10, no. 2 (June 1984): 241–271; Emily Honig, "Private Issues, Public Discourse: The Life and Times of Yu Luojin," *Pacific Affairs* 57, no. 2 (Summer 1984): 252–269; Marilyn B. Young, "Introduction," *Pacific Affairs* 57, no. 2 (Summer 1984): 209–212; Gail Hershatter, "Making a Friend: Changing Patterns of Courtship in Urban China," *Pacific Affairs* 57, no. 2 (Summer 1984): 237–251; Chen Muhua, "Birth Planning in China," *International Family Planning Perspectives* 5, no. 3 (September 1979): 92–100; Fox Butterfield, *China: Alive in the Bitter Sea* (New York: Bantam Books, 1982); Katie Curtin, *Women in China* (New York: Pathfinder Press, 1975); William L. Parish and Martin King Whyte, *Village and Family in Contemporary China* (Chicago: University of Chicago Press, 1978); Hugh D. R. Baker, *Chinese Family and Kinship* (New York: Columbia University Press, 1979); Ruth Sidel, *Families of Fengsheng: Urban Life in China* (Baltimore: Penguin Books, 1974); *Women and Child Care in China: A Firsthand Report*

(Baltimore: Penguin Books, 1973); Maxine Molyneux, "Socialist Societies Old and New: Progress toward Women's Emancipation?" *Monthly Review* 34, no. 3 (July–August 1982): 56–100; Agnes Smedley, *Portraits of Chinese Women in Revolution* (Old Westbury, N.Y.: Feminist Press, 1976); Kay Ann Johnson, *Women, the Family and Peasant Revolution in China* (Chicago: University of Chicago Press, 1983); Margery Wolf, *Revolution Postponed: Women in Contemporary China* (Stanford, Calif.: Stanford University Press, 1985).

69. Stacey, 33.

70. Stacey, 108–157.

71. Butterfield, 1982, 177.

72. Stacey, 230–231.

73. Wolf, 260–273.

74. Emily Honig, "Women's Liberation in China," *Journal of Asian Studies* 44, no. 2 (February 1985): 335–336.

75. This discussion of Cuba relies on Muriel Nazzari, "The 'Woman Question' in Cuba: An Analysis of Material Constraints on Its Solution," *Signs* 9, no. 2 (Winter 1983): 246–263; Elizabeth Croll, 1981; Sergio Diaz-Briquets and Lisandro Perez, "Cuba: The Demography of Revolution," *Population Bulletin* 36, no. 1 (April 1981); Marjorie King, "Cuba's Attack on Women's Second Shift: 1974–1976," in Eleanor Leacock et al., eds., *Women in Latin America: An Anthology from Latin American Perspectives* (Riverside, Calif.: Latin American Perspectives, 1979): 118–131; Margaret Randall, *Women in Cuba: Twenty Years Later* (Brooklyn, N.Y.: Smyrna Press, 1981); Margaret Randall, "Development of the Family in Cuba," *Two Thirds* 1, no. 3 (1978–79): 25–37; Margaret Randall, " 'We Need a Government of Men and Women . . .': Notes on the Second National Congress of the Federacion de Mujeres Cubanos, November 25–29, 1974," in Leacock et al., 1979, 132–138; Margaret Randall, *Cuban Women Now: Interviews with Cuban Women* (Toronto: Women's Press, 1974); Oscar Lewis, Ruth M. Lewis, and Susan M. Rigdon, *Four Women: Living the Revolution, An Oral History of Contemporary Cuba* (Urbana: University of Illinois Press, 1977); Jose Gutierrez Muniz, Jose Camaros Fabian, and Jose Cobas Manriquez, "The Recent Worldwide Economic Crisis and the Welfare of

Children: The Case of Cuba," *World Development* 12, no. 3 (1984): 247–260; *Family Planning Perspectives*, "Cuba: Family Planning Spur to Maternal, Child Health," *Family Planning Perspectives* 8, no. 1 (January–February 1976): 32; Paula E. Hollerbach, "Recent Trends in Fertility, Abortion and Contraception in Cuba," *International Family Planning Perspectives* 6, no. 3 (September 1980): 97–106; Eugenia Meyer, "The Double Battle of Cuban Women: Eight Life Stories Before and After the Revolution," Paper presented at the Tenth World Congress of Sociology, International Sociological Society, Mexico, 1982; Virginia Olesen, "Context and Posture: Notes on Socio-Cultural Aspects of Women's Roles and Family Policy in Contemporary Cuba," *Journal of Marriage and the Family* 33, no. 2 (August 1971); Lisandro Perez, "The Family in Cuba," in Man Singh Das and Clinton J. Jesser, eds., *The Family in Latin America* (New Dehli: Vikas, 1980): 235–269.

76. Nazzari, 247–248.

77. Quoted in Lewis, Lewis, and Rigdon, xiv.

78. Nazzari, 257.

79. Quoted in Lewis, Lewis, and Rigdon, xiv.

80. On all these points, see Nuss, 1980, 1981, 1984; Joan Ecklein, "Obstacles to Understanding the Changing Role of Women in Socialist Countries," *Insurgent Sociologist* 12, nos. 1–2 (Winter/Spring 1984): 7–12; Joan Ecklein, "Women in the German Democratic Republic: Impact of Culture and Social Policy" in Janet Zollinger Giele, ed., *Women in the Middle Years: Current Knowledge and Directions for Research and Policy* (New York: John Wiley, 1982):151–198.

81. Croll, "Women in Rural Production and Reproduction in the Soviet Union, China, Cuba, and Tanzania: Case Studies," *Signs* 7, no. 2 (1981): 375–399.

82. This argument is fundamental to the "world systems theory" which informs the many publications by Wallerstein on problems of development. For a succinct summary, see Immanuel Wallerstein, "Dependence in an Interdependent World: The Limited Possibilities of Transformation Within the Capitalist World-Economy," in Immanuel Wallerstein, *The Capitalist World-Economy* (New York: Cambridge University Press, 1979): 66–94.

CHAPTER 10

Conclusion

Now that the positions of women and men in different types of societies and at different points in history have been examined, what implications are there for the future of gender roles and gender stratification systems? One conclusion that can be drawn from this analysis of cross-cultural and historical data is that no specific types of gender roles or gender stratification are universal or inevitable. Diversity and change are hallmarks of the social positions of the genders.

But it is nonetheless impossible to select the type of gender roles we would like from the many possible ones. Gender roles cannot be borrowed from one context and adopted into a quite different context. For example, the communal egalitarianism of foragers may be appealing. But a society cannot implement these gender roles without simultaneously adopting their system of economic production and distribution and the social and cultural systems associated with their mode of production. This would not, of course, be feasible for the large-scale, densely populated nation states that characterize most of the world today.

Gender roles are part of the wider evolutionary changes in society and therefore are constrained by environmental imperatives. Gender roles change with the environment. What we have found in the past and present does not necessarily tell us what we can or shall have in the future. The social, cultural, economic, political, and ecological conditions of the future will undoubtedly differ from those of the past. Yet for those interested in directing social change—in particular for those interested in working for liberation from the constraints of gender roles and the inequities of gender stratification—knowledge of the factors giving rise to, supporting, and destroying past systems can help in attempts to discover what must be done to dismantle such systems and to prevent their reemergence. Human beings can affect the direction of social change, but they do so only within the limits imposed by the conditions of their time and place. Individuals and organized groups can change the course of history, but they do not always achieve the results they desire. Some changes are impossible in specific social settings. Understanding the influence of wide social forces can help us understand what aspects of gender roles and stratification may be altered and under what circumstances such changes may be achieved.

For example, it is true in various societies that a sharp division between the domestic and public spheres isolates one gender in the domestic sphere and contributes substantially to the subordination of that gender.

Not all societies have isolated women into the domestic sphere, and in the modern context it is probably unnecessary to continue to do so. Functional alternatives to the full-time housewife now exist. Many of the burdens of the domestic sphere have been taken over by other institutions such as the school system and the food-processing industry. Bottle-feeding has freed many women from the necessity of breast-feeding and made possible a much greater participation in early child care by fathers. But this technological advance has not resulted in much change in women's roles because women have continued to be assigned the tasks associated with bottle-feeding. Therefore women are no less limited than they were with breast-feeding.

Thus far, the gender subordinated within the domestic context has always been the female, and females have consequently exercised less power in society than have males. However, if males were systematically isolated in the domestic sphere and cut off from participation in political, economic, and social institutions, we could expect males to be less powerful than females. To avoid gender stratification based on the isolating effects of child care, both men and women must participate in this sphere as well as in public spheres.

The domestic/public dichotomy as we know it today will probably continue to be altered. With the current problems of population growth and limited global resources, the full-time housewife and full-time breadwinner roles are in many respects dysfunctional.[1] Full-time housewifery seems to encourage women to have more children, further increasing population problems. It also encourages consumerism, exacerbating the problem of scarce resources. One of the housewife's main tasks in modern society is directing family consumption. Freeing large numbers of women to pursue this task full-time has been one of the effects of indus-

trialization and has greatly increased the amounts of goods and services consumed by residents of the developed countries. Similarly, the full-time breadwinner role for males cuts men off from the satisfactions of child rearing and encourages men to fulfill themselves through wasteful materialistic consumption. It also encourages men to value mastery of the environment over a more ecologically adaptive or conservationist approach. These consumption and production practices have in turn created disastrous problems of pollution and the depletion of finite resources. The excessive consumption habits of the developed world have also increased the problem of the worldwide maldistribution of resources and have thereby contributed to the problems of international inequality and the resulting international tensions. This way of life cannot continue unchanged.

Changes in the domestic/public dichotomy may also be related to future problems of population pressure. Population pressure has been an important variable affecting gender roles in technologically less advanced societies. It may reemerge as a relevant factor in the future. By tremendously expanding productivity, industrialization rendered population pressure relatively unimportant in the developed world. It is becoming apparent, however, that there are limits to such expanding productivity, again because of pollution and scarce resources. For example, overcrowding may in the long run make the isolated nuclear family dwelling unit impossible. The small-scale, reduplicative, kin-based production and consumption units for domestic tasks may be too wasteful of space and other resources to be maintained for the masses in the future. The domestic role for women associated with the single-family house or apartment may not be able to survive. But the 1980s idealization of the super-consuming "yuppie" two-career couple does not constitute a solution to the conspicuous consumption problem, even if it is an example of women moving into the public sphere.

We must understand also that what we perceive as "domestic" and "public" and their associations with concrete activities of women and men are not the *causes*, but more the consequences, of structured patterns of inequality between gender groups in society. These patterns of inequality in turn are linked to larger forms of struggle by which classes, castes, ethnic groups, kin groups, nations, states, and religions and ideological movements struggle for privilege, opportunity, dominance, and survival in human societies. All social relations are not marked by strife and conflict, to be sure; but little that is harmonious, rewarding and liberating in life does not at some point intersect and intertwine with the distribution and consequences of inequality and dominance in society.

The late Michelle Zimbalist Rosaldo, more responsible than anyone for the introduction of the "domestic/public" dichotomy into the theoretical discussion of gender relations, advanced the following reconsideration in one of her last published statements:

By linking gender, and in particular female lives, to the existence of domestic spheres, we have inclined, I fear, to think we know the "core" of what different gender systems share, to think of sexual hierarchies in functional and psychological terms, and thus, to minimize such sociological considerations as inequality and power. . . . It now appears to me that woman's place in human society is not in any direct sense a product of the things she does (or even less a function of what, biologically she is) but the meaning her activities acquire through concrete social interactions. . . . Gender in all human groups must . . . be understood in political and social terms, with reference not to biological constraints but instead to local and specific forms of social relationship and, in particular, of social inequality.[2]

It is possible that, in the short run, the domestic role may again become the only respectable role for women. Periods of severe economic decline have in the past led to a backlash against women's fuller participation in the public sphere. Current problems with high unemployment and economic recession in the developed world as well as in underdeveloped countries may lead to attacks on feminism as the scapegoat and a return to the "cult of domesticity" among those who can manage to afford it.

Paradoxically, periods of high economic opportunity may also encourage a voluntary return to domesticity in young women. This would be the case if economic prosperity allowed more young people to marry earlier, to have children earlier, to have more children, and to afford the luxury of a non-working wife. This development could only take place, however, if both men and women, and especially women, still lived under the cultural dominance of more traditional images of gender roles. Of particular importance in this regard is the future course of fertility. Women even under the current double burden can manage careers, marriage, and children if they have only one child or if their children are spaced four or more years apart. But having several preschool children and a husband whose career prevents him from any real sharing of child-care responsibilities exerts strong pressure on these mothers to accept a full-time domestic role. While housework can be postponed indefinitely, small children's needs cannot. Each child requires several hours of parental attention every day. With more than one child, a full-time career becomes extremely difficult.

Thus we see that where women have few, widely spaced children, they can stay in the labor force (whether as foragers or as the "new corporate woman") and are generally supportive of gender egalitarianism or feminism. Where women have several closely spaced children, they are more likely to be full-time housewives for significant periods of their lives and to support an antifeminist ideology justifying the domestic role for women and condemning their public participation. It is possible therefore that the children of the 1970s, the generation produced by feminists, will by the turn of the twenty-first century reembrace domesticity and antifeminism. Will the rosy job prospects of the low-birthrate cohort again encourage early marriage, early childbearing, and closely spaced children cared for by a full-time mother? Easterlin's work indicates such a swing is possible,[3] but the present course of economic change and the structural effects of women's accumulated experience in the world of paid labor in the post-World War II period suggest strong counterpressures. Still, the type of swings predicted by Easterlin are not without historical precedent, and such predictions should not be taken lightly. We would emphasize that not only are economic and demographic developments crucial to the determination of the relationship between relative poverty or affluence in the rise and fall of familism but political choices ultimately have their bearing also.

The study of contemporary and past societies also points out the importance of warfare and competition in the subordination of women. Women have in general fared better in peaceful, noncompetitive environments. If the future is one of greater population pressure, competition over scarce resources, high crime rates, and other forms of internal feuding and endemic warfare, female subordination will probably increase. Controlling population, competition, fighting, and warfare may be of the utmost importance for women's liberation.

Economic roles and economic control are important variables for an understanding of variations in women's and men's positions in society. Economically dependent people tend to be subordinated people. To free women as well as other oppressed groups, it is necessary for them to gain some degree of economic independence or an equal measure of economic interdependence with others. Women and men, as well as slaves and masters and the lower class and the upper class, have traditionally been economically interdependent: Men as breadwinners have needed the services of their wives, slave owners have depended on the work of their slaves, and the upper class has depended on the labor of the lower class. However, the bargaining positions of the groups have been unequal. The two groups' control over resources must be roughly equal to avoid the inequities of a stratification system, whether gender-based, economic, or racial. One group cannot be allowed to monopolize important resources of wealth, education, jobs, political power, or the instruments of coercion.

The current feminist movement has attacked this type of gender inequality. But it is not sufficient merely to integrate a few women into the predominantly male elite that now control these important resources. Liberation from the inequalities of class and racial stratification is relevant to achieving liberation from the inequities of gender stratification. Having elite women share power with elite men does not liberate either the women or the men of nonelite groups, although it may benefit women of the elite relative to men of the elite. It will require a radical restructuring of most modern societies' social, economic, and political structures to equalize the bargaining positions of most of their members. It will also require a radical restructuring of the international situation to equalize the bargaining positions of individuals in poor countries relative to individuals in rich countries. All of this is probably necessary if we are to avoid the negative effects on women and on human freedom in general of resource scarcity, warfare, and competition.

To achieve this egalitarian future will probably require action among many different groups of subordinated peoples. Feminist movements, both reformist and radical, can contribute to this process. But the problems of women's liberation cannot be separated from wider issues of human liberation, which will require active, committed persons willing to work and sacrifice for these goals. The forces arrayed against such liberation are many and powerful. Revolutionary changes to advance human freedom cannot be brought about easily, but this difficulty is insufficient reason to accept defeat.

Notes

1. For a further discussion of this topic see Janet Zollinger Giele, *Women and the Future* (New York: Free Press, 1978); Elise Boulding, *Women in the Twentieth-Century World* (New York: Halstead Press, 1977); and Rosemary Radford Ruether, *New Woman; New Earth: Sexist Ideologies and Human Liberation* (New York: Seabury Press, 1975): 186–214.

2. Michelle Zimbalist Rosaldo, ''The Use and Abuse of Anthropology: Reflections on Feminism and Cross-Cultural Understanding,'' *Signs* 5, no. 3 (Spring 1980): 389–417, 400.

3. Richard Easterlin, *Population, Labor Force, and Long Swings in Economic Growth* (New York: Columbia University Press, 1968); Richard Easterlin, *Birth and Fortune: The Impact of Numbers on Personal Welfare* (New York: Basic Books, 1980). See also Landon Y. Jones, *Great Expectations: America and the Baby Boom Generation* (New York: Balantine Books, 1980) for a popular treatment of the same problem.

NAME INDEX

SUBJECT INDEX

Date

MAR 31 2003